ONLINE
RESEARCH
ESSENTIALS

ONLINE RESEARCH ESSENTIALS

Implementing and Designing Research Studies

BRENDA RUSSELL
JOHN PURCELL

JOSSEY-BASS
A Wiley Imprint
www.josseybass.com

Published by Jossey-Bass
A Wiley Imprint
989 Market Street, San Francisco, CA 94103-1741—www.josseybass.com

Readers should be aware that Internet Web sites offered as citations and/or sources for further information may have changed or disappeared between the time this was written and when it is read.

Limit of Liability/Disclaimer of Warranty: While the publisher and author have used their best efforts in preparing this book, they make no representations or warranties with respect to the accuracy or completeness of the contents of this book and specifically disclaim any implied warranties of merchantability or fitness for a particular purpose. No warranty may be created or extended by sales representatives or written sales materials. The advice and strategies contained herein may not be suitable for your situation. You should consult with a professional where appropriate. Neither the publisher nor author shall be liable for any loss of profit or any other commercial damages, including but not limited to special, incidental, consequential, or other damages.

Jossey-Bass books and products are available through most bookstores. To contact Jossey-Bass directly call our Customer Care Department within the U.S. at 800-956-7739, outside the U.S. at 317-572-3986, or fax 317-572-4002.

Jossey-Bass also publishes its books in a variety of electronic formats. Some content that appears in print may not be available in electronic books.

Library of Congress Cataloging-in-Publication Data

Russell, Brenda, 1962–
    Online research essentials : designing and implementing research studies / Brenda Russell, John Purcell.
        p.   cm.
    Includes bibliographical references and index.
    ISBN 978-0-470-18568-1 (pbk.)
        1. Research—Methodology.   2. Internet.   3. Web sites—Design.   4. Research—Data processing.   I. Purcell, John, 1951–   II. Title.
    Q180.55.M4R87   2009
    001.4'202854678—dc22

                                                                              2008055678

Printed in the United States of America
FIRST EDITION

PB Printing   10 9 8 7 6 5 4 3 2 1

To Kathryn—my love and my life.—JP

To my students and friends, and to my biggest fans of all—my parents, Carl and Janice Russell, my son, Dillon, and my family. Thank all of you for you all have touched my heart.—BR

CONTENTS

FIGURES AND TABLES

FIGURES

TABLES

PREFACE

This book is designed to assist people who have little or no experience with research design or Web page creation. This text will take you through the journey of proposing, creating, and implementing online research designs. It is important that you have a fair understanding of research before implementing surveys or experiments. Conducting research without proper guidance and instruction in design, procedure, and ethics can lead to inefficient, misleading findings and can be potentially harmful and downright unethical. That is why we have incorporated an overview of basic research methods into this book—from theory development and hypothesis testing to understanding ethics, and from sampling considerations to learning how to develop and implement proper surveys and experiments that can be administered online.

After reading this text, you should be able to successfully develop a survey or experiment, upload it to the Web, test it, and get results. We cover introductory research methods and address the technical aspects of publishing a survey or experiment on the Internet. You will find that the text provides an introduction to research from conception to developing practical research designs. We focus on social science, but the principles outlined here can be applied to any discipline that conducts research. This book differs from other Web-based research books in that it demonstrates how to conduct online rescarch without the hassle of having to write code.

Although writing code can be rewarding, it can also be difficult and time consuming to learn. That's why we've decided to use Microsoft Expression for Web development. Most users will find themselves already familiar with the interface and basic operations of Microsoft Expression. Survey forms that are linked to an online database can be created quickly and efficiently, with no outside programming; Expression takes care of it all. Finally, a simple procedure similar to a flowchart will be used to plan how a user will interact with the Web site and simple JavaScript procedures will be integrated to allow for more advanced functions. These will be fully explained in Chapter Eleven and the scripts will be provided to users of the text. Those who want to program a Web site might use Microsoft's Visual Studio, Dreamweaver, or, for the truly dedicated, there is Notepad, a very limited text processor bundled with all versions of Microsoft Windows. However, Microsoft Expression is an excellent tool for Web authoring. Its main advantage is that it does most of the coding for the user and offers an interface similar to that of Microsoft Word. This greatly reduces the learning curve. Microsoft Expression is a complete rewrite of a popular Web page creation program from Microsoft, FrontPage, which for nine years was Microsoft's entry-level

Web page creation tool. FrontPage had some notorious problems and the code that it created was not as error free as it could have been. Expression produces far cleaner code and follows the latest standards for Web page design. The results are superior to all previous versions. A trial version is available at the Microsoft Web site; a student purchasing price is available as well.

THE ORGANIZATION OF THIS TEXT

After years of teaching Web design and research methods, we realized that students and individuals interested in research for business or the social sciences would benefit from understanding what is involved in designing and implementing online research. Thus we set out to write a text that would arm its reader with the knowledge necessary to produce online research projects in a classroom or organizational setting. Each chapter provides essential tools to help you understand how to begin a research project, select a research method that will help answer your research question, and implement your study using the Web. The research methods portion of the book should help readers identify the strengths and weaknesses associated with each research design. The text begins by providing a general description of all research designs as well as the scientific method. We believe ethical considerations are of the utmost importance when planning a research project and so we introduce ethics early, in the second chapter.

The text is designed to introduce research topics and immediately implement these topics using Web design. For example, upon completion of the ethics chapter, we introduce Web design and immediately encourage readers to learn Microsoft Expression by creating a consent form. We then address some of the more essential elements that need to be considered when planning a research project, such as the basics of Web survey design. We follow up with a chapter highlighting survey methods and development in greater detail. The later Web design chapters capture the nuances of online surveys such as style and text formatting, allowing readers to create more complicated Internet surveys. Sampling techniques for online research are introduced and, finally, explanations of experimental design and Web programming in the later chapters explain how to implement more sophisticated techniques when conducting research online.

The goal of this text is to help individuals plan, create, and implement their online research study. The text provides sufficient information to assist readers in critically analyzing their research methods and understanding the limitations inherent in each method. Analyzing, interpreting, and communicating research findings are beyond the scope of this text. However, we believe that you will find in the last chapter the basic information needed to analyze and test your research hypotheses. Finally, we have included a Resources section at the end of the book where you can find other sources of information to guide you in your research activities.

INTRODUCTION TO THE INTERNET AND INTERNET RESEARCH

Before we begin, a short introduction to the Internet will be useful to help understand how online research works and where it started. Understanding the history of the Internet should help place things into perspective. All research has advantages and disadvantages, and online research shares many of these. However, you will see that online research has its own unique advantages and disadvantages.

THE HISTORY OF THE INTERNET: PAVING THE WAY TO THE FUTURE

The Internet is the product of over forty years of work. Using technology developed initially by the U.S. Department of Defense, a network of computers was created that shared a common language. In the 1970s, researchers used what eventually became the Internet to share scientific information around the world. With the advent of more powerful personal computers and the creation of the first browser software, Mosaic, developed in 1992 and released in 1993, access to the Internet was opened to others. Mosaic became Netscape in 1994 and public usage of the Internet began to soar. Microsoft introduced Internet Explorer in 1995 (*Microsoft*, 2002). The competition between Netscape and Microsoft was very intense and became known as the "Browser Wars." At the end of the 1990s, these wars subsided as Microsoft's Internet Explorer became the dominant browser. The Internet became an accepted tool for research, commerce, and entertainment.

As the Internet gained popularity for commerce and entertainment, it has also changed our economy. In 2007, one report predicted that online retail sales would increase 18 percent to over $259.1 billion (Ecommerce, 2008).

The Web has also broadened our access to information. The Internet is analogous to a world library, allowing us to sit at computers, information conveniently at our fingertips—but sometimes that information can be misleading.

Over the past ten years, Internet use has skyrocketed. In 2003, just over half of U.S. citizens had access to the Internet at home (U.S. Department of Commerce, 2005) and by 2006, this number almost doubled to over 74 percent (Nielsen/NetRatings, 2006). Research methods are changing in response to these technological advances. The natural progression toward conducting online research has changed research methodology and design in the twenty-first century. Psychologists, sociologists, and communications, business, and marketing firms are just some examples of those using the Internet to conduct research. Research techniques have moved far beyond simple paper-and-pencil surveys with various programs now allowing researchers to use elaborate experimental designs, video-based simulations, virtual reality, and adaptive testing.

Although there is little data telling us the true extent of how much online research is being used or published, an examination of various disciplines demonstrates that the use of online research is growing, particularly in such fields as business. Cho and Khang (2006) examined trends, patterns, and rigorousness in research studies about the Internet in fifteen major journals representing communications, marketing, and advertising between 1999 and 2003. Their results indicated that approximately 13 percent of research papers discussed online research. Furthermore, the study concluded that almost half (41 percent) of Internet-related studies used online samples, which were fairly divided between students and the general population. More important, over half of Internet-related studies used quantitative research methods when testing research-based hypotheses on diverse research topics.

Internet research is popular for a variety of reasons. Depending on the specialization, one might choose online research to conduct anything from marketing trends to customer satisfaction surveys to more in-depth experimental research studies. Business and market researchers have been paving the way in conducting online survey research. Their usage is extensive primarily because of the speed with which researchers can get results and the lower cost of deploying a survey online. Psychologists are quickly following suit, employing various psychological assessment tools (for example, personality inventories) designed to measure attitudes and mental illness. Even dating companies now use the Internet to match potential couples based on similar personality profiles (such as eHarmony). When applied effectively, the Internet can be a powerful research tool for any discipline.

One of the first examples of published research based on data gathered online was a within-subjects (testing the same people more than once) experimental design examining predictors of female attractiveness (Krantz, Ballard, & Scher, 1997). As online research became more popular, there were very few studies that examined the quality of research conducted online. In 2000, the American Psychological Association (APA) organized a task force to assess new technologies associated with psychological assessment, particularly computer-based assessments. The goal of the task force was to examine the practices of online research and consider the validity and ethical and legal implications of its use (Naglieri et al., 2004). The primary concern for most psychologists at the time included a host of "preconceptions about Internet data" (Gosling, Vazire, Srivastava, & John, 2004) such as diversity, composition, motivation, anonymity, and psychometric properties of Internet samples. Research by Gosling et al. (2004) and Riva, Teruzzi, and Anolli (2003) found that overall, research samples obtained via the Internet were more demographically diverse than college participant samples.

What limited information we have demonstrates that recent studies have consistently found that traditional methods of data collection (paper-and-pencil) do not differ from data obtained from the Internet, and that Internet findings replicate traditional methods of data collection (Ballard & Prine, 2002; Buchanan, 2000; Epstein, Klinkenberg, Wiley, & McKinley, 2001; Gosling et al., 2004; Potosky & Bobko, 2004; Riva et al., 2003; Sandler, 2007). Knapp and Kirk (2003) conducted a study to examine the effectiveness of collecting personally sensitive information (such as information regarding general honesty, academic honesty, prejudice, illegal behavior, alcohol use, substance use, violence, and sexual behavior) using the Internet, paper-and-pencil, and touch-tone phones. Their study found no differences between the three conditions.

Continually increasing use of the online administration of self-report psychological assessments has led to many new computerized versions of psychological inventories (Butcher, 2003). Both computer-based and written formats have been found to be equivalent in psychometric properties, reliability, and validity (Butcher, Perry, & Atlis, 2000; Finger & Ones, 1991).

Advantages of Using the Internet for Research

Many have argued that online research provides access to much larger and diverse populations, thus obtaining greater external validity and the possibility of obtaining more representative samples than the often used undergraduate student population (Sandler, 2007; Studebaker et al., 2002). For example, online research may be a suitable strategy for increasing ethnic minority representation in research samples and collecting sensitive information (Brown, 2003; Knapp & Kirk, 2003). Working with a sample of African-American college students, Brown (2003) found no differences between paper-and-pencil and Internet strategies and suggested that the Internet would be an effective strategy for obtaining ethnic minority samples. However, we must keep in mind that although household access to the Web continues to increase annually, a large number of people continue to be without Internet access. Online research can be less costly, more efficient, and accessible twenty-four hours a day (Riva et al., 2003). In addition, online samples allow for a standardized set of procedures that do not create an experimenter effect—that is, effects associated with the experiment that are not related to the actual study but to the experimenter's presence (Birnbaum, 2004). With regard to psychological assessments, online formats also allow for ease of scoring with less possibility of scoring errors (Allard, Butler, Shea, & Faust, 1995; Butcher, 2003).

Issues associated with anonymity and confidentiality can be considered advantages or disadvantages depending on the skill and professionalism of the researcher. Sensitive information can be collected online, where participants may feel more comfortable answering difficult and sensitive questions. In all research, researchers should painstakingly endeavor to maintain participant anonymity and confidentiality. Anonymity and confidentiality were previously thought to be the albatross associated with Internet research, but great strides have been made to overcome these issues; this will be discussed at length in the next section.

Disadvantages of Using the Internet for Research

Of course there are disadvantages of online research—including a lack of knowledge of who is taking the survey and lack of control over the environment. Furthermore, creating online research is not a simple process. Though the design of a simple survey can be easily navigated, conducting a randomized experiment can be more cumbersome and time-consuming. Decisions must be made with regard to what formats would be best to collect the data in the most appropriate way. For example, would a drop-down list, text box, or multiple choice format be the best choice? In addition, before developing your study, you must consider who will host your research. If you are from an academic institution, you must first obtain authorization from your ethics board, typically referred to as an institutional review board (IRB) or human subjects research board (HSRB). Once you obtain permission to conduct your study, you might host it from a server at your university or college. There are other options to consider, such as existing listservs and online recruitment companies that do the job for you. However, there are questions that all researchers, whether online or not, must consider when creating their study (Who will serve as my sample? is a basic question all researchers must ask). Buchanan (2002) reported that online research can be desirable, yet dangerous, if potential problems such as breaches of confidentiality and anonymity are not considered when using online research, as well as when important theoretical issues need to be resolved. For instance, some have argued that, due to "digital divide," the availability of technology will differ from country to country and group to group within each country (Advogato.org, 2002) and, therefore, true representation remains elusive.

The main challenge is to obtain greater control over experimental internal and statistical validity (Riva, 2001). When researchers are not present and lack control of the administration of the study or the environment in which the participant takes the study, they lack what researchers call "control" over their study. Lack of control in using Internet research can also include not knowing whether the people taking the survey are who they say they are, whether they are old enough to consent to the research, or, potentially, how many times one person participates. All of these issues decrease experimenter control and can jeopardize the internal and statistical validity of your study. We acknowledge that these are serious concerns to be addressed, and Chapters Four through Fifteen will provide you with knowledge and tools to address some of these challenges.

Due to technological advances, online researchers can now set up their surveys or experiments, ensuring participant anonymity and confidentiality, but there are other ethical issues to consider, particularly with regard to archival data collection. The Internet is a literal gold mine of archival research opportunities. For example, one can examine humor in blogs (otherwise referred to as a Web log—where individuals write about specific topics or discuss personal information in a kind of online diary), types of online interaction between couples, youth, and other special populations that are typically difficult to examine. A detailed discussion of these issues is beyond the scope of this book, but the ethical issues regarding this type of research should be considered. For instance, what would you do if you were conducting archival research and encountered disturbing, suicidal, threatening messages, such as those found by researchers examining online social networks (such as MySpace or Facebook) who came upon a Web page describing two boys' frustrations with peers who bullied them and their intentions to assault those peers. These two boys were ultimately responsible for the massacre at Columbine, Colorado. These issues are not unique to online researchers. We need to decide the extent to which researchers are responsible for disclosing the identity of their supposedly anonymous assessment of online Web pages. If researchers recognize that online participants are writing about harming themselves, to what extent are the researchers responsible for reporting possible self-destructive behaviors or homicidal behaviors?

Conducting online research can promote anonymity, greater access to sensitive information, more diverse samples, and general public access. However, we must ask ourselves to what extent are we, as researchers, responsible for reacting to private self-disclosures? When and under what situations should we consider disclosing information about otherwise anonymous people? Just what is our responsibility? These answers remain unknown, yet there are ethical consequences for researchers to ponder particularly when they use the Internet to research personal home pages or personal blogs.

Technological Advances That Make Online Research Easy to Use

While there are many ethical dilemmas that remain with regard to online research, recent technological advances have addressed some of the more pressing concerns. In response to the initial difficulty of creating online surveys, Buchanan (2002) points out that putting an online survey or experiment together takes time and effort (just as any good research project does). However, in the past few years, many new texts have been published to teach researchers how to conduct online studies. Most often, these texts have used difficult coding processes such as JavaScript to create html forms to demonstrate how to develop online surveys. However, recent software programs (such as Dreamweaver and Microsoft Frontpage and Expression) have made Internet research much easier to develop and administer and data easier to collect. We believe that these new software programs are much more user friendly and, therefore, we present our text in light of these new software programs.

Additionally, students or faculty from all disciplines may be able to host their online research from their own school's server, or associations can (with permission) utilize listservs to gather data from purposive samples. Some colleges (for example, Hanover College) have made it easier to access online surveys and recruit participants for psychological research by creating a Web site for students. In addition to these recruitment methods, some companies (such as StudyResponse Project and SurveyMonkey) have made it even easier for researchers to create and distribute their data. For instance, the

StudyResponse Project facilitates online research for behavioral, social, and organizational science researchers by distributing e-mail participation requests to adult research respondents who register to participate in psychological research (StudyResponse Project, 2004). All participants recruited from StudyResponse are sent an e-mail outlining the study (also covering purposive sampling issues) and requesting participation. In order to address the issues of confidentiality and the possibility of duplicate entries, StudyResponse Project participants are given a participant number which is entered online. Most respondents participate for the sake of some type of incentive (for example, a chance to win a $100 gift certificate for Amazon.com), and StudyResponse is responsible for keeping track of respondents, conducting the random drawing for the incentive, and distributing the award. As another precaution, each participant's Internet protocol (IP), a unique numeric address assigned to a specific system connected to a network, can be tracked to prevent duplicate submissions (Birnbaum, 2004). Finally, a combination of the aforementioned methods could also be used to collect data. One more important aspect of these online studies is that the data collected go directly into an assigned database, making data entry a thing of the past.

Although we advocate the use of multiple methods to obtain data, this book primarily focuses on providing information on survey or experimental research. All researchers should consider using multiple method approaches to gather data from multiple sources. We believe that Internet research, conducted smartly and ethically, can complement existing research and ultimately provide evidence that will lead toward stronger, more convincing arguments and theories.

Summary

While there are many challenges to consider, online research has clear advantages. Online research offers researchers the ability to transcend geographical, physical, and time barriers previously limited by regular research. For example, online research has enabled us to investigate families dealing with rare medical diseases and eating disorders, sexual minorities on campus (Leider, 1999), working-class gay men (Appleby, 2001), and suicidal individuals (King, 1995). The Internet offers us the ability to assess customer satisfaction, conduct surveys, experiments, psychological assessments, collect sensitive information, and generally obtain more representative samples.

In summary, online research offers the potential to include greater diversity in research, ensuring more representation and external validity. However, we cannot ignore its inherent limitations. We must weigh the costs and benefits of all research methods. Furthermore, technological advances have brought concerns regarding anonymity and confidentiality. However, we admit that problems remain with conducting online research. We are not saying online research is the "be-all and end-all" response to conducting research. What we are advocating is the use of online research to help supplement existing methodologies and to replicate existing experiments, helping demonstrate external validity. We recognize that the use of multiple methods should always be considered.

Because online research is a relatively new process, there is little information on legal liabilities encountered online. Perhaps we should also consider the possibility of research accreditation agencies. An American Psychological Association task force was initially created to investigate aspects of online research back in 2000; one of its primary motives was to explore online research with regard to online psychological assessment. APA accreditation is associated with clinical programs, and with the increased use of online research, it is no surprise that the validity of online research is a primary concern of the task force. We suggest that perhaps an APA task force or organization of accreditation be considered to assess the rigor of online research and accountability of companies that host sites used to recruit and obtain samples. Accreditation or standardization can limit the potential legal liabilities associated with online research.

As we progress into the twenty-first century and further into the age of technology, ways of gathering data and conducting research are shifting. Much of the research conducted just thirty years ago (including case studies, or studies lacking control groups, and so on) may not be considered or accepted as rigorous by contemporary standards. Research designs, statistics, and methods have improved drastically over the years, along with changes within our disciplines.

With online research, the possibilities of extending our research and creativity are enhanced. We should embrace this new paradigm and imagine the potential it might have to enhance our knowledge and our lives. Chapter One introduces the reader to the basics of research methods, addresses the importance of research in everyday life, and explains how the scientific method is necessary to conduct research.

SETTING UP FOR ONLINE RESEARCH

Before you get started, there are three things you must do before you read Chapter Three of this text. First, you must get a copy of Microsoft Expression. This is the Web editing and publishing tool that we will use for the exercises. New versions are available at various retail stores (such as Best Buy, Amazon.com, and BarnesandNoble.com) and you can find academic pricing at the Web sites mentioned for Expression as well. It is also available on a trial download from Microsoft. This software will run only on Windows XP Service Pack 2 and above. Make sure that your system meets the minimum requirements. The URL for the download is www.microsoft.com/expression. Follow all of the instructions to install the download. It is always a good idea to back your system up before performing a major install.

Second, you'll need to have a Web site. In Chapter Three, we'll discuss more about the requirements for a site. At this point, it is essential to have a site on a Microsoft Windows Server with unlimited use of Microsoft Access. The systems administrator will give you a site address, username, and password to access the site.

Since this book has gone to press, Microsoft has released an update to Expression Web titled Expression Web 2. The changes in Expression 2 are more for advanced functions (use of PHP for creating Web pages, and so on). For our purposes the only differences between Expression and Expression 2 are cosmetic. The menus and dialogs are the same and all of the functions that we will use exist in both versions. Screen shots in the book were taken from Expression Web.

Your final task is to download the exercise and setup files that accompany the book. You can find these at the Jossey-Bass Web site by searching for this title or by going directly to www.josseybass.com/go/onlineresearchessentials. When prompted save the downloaded files to your desktop.

EXERCISE 0.01. Extracting the Exercise Files

1. The files will be in a compressed folder titled *Setup.zip* located on the desktop (or wherever else you decided to save it). Your first task will be to extract the files from the compressed folder.

2. Right-click the compressed folder and, from the menu, select **Extract All. . . .** In the dialog box, make sure that the title **Show extracted files when complete** is checked and click **Extract**. The files will be extracted into a folder on the desktop titled *Setup*. The folder will open when the extraction is complete.

3. Inside the setup folder are two additional folders: *webs* and *exercise data*. Right-click and hold the *exercise data* folder and drag it outside of the setup folder. When you release the right mouse button, select **Move** from the menu. This will move the folder outside of the setup files.

4. Inside the *webs* folder are ten additional folders and a Web page titled *default.htm*. These ten folders and the files they contain will be placed on your site in Chapter Three (see Figure 0.01).

FIGURE 0.01 *Files in Folder List after Importing*

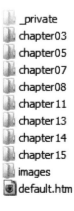

EXERCISE 0.02. Setting the File Extension Setting

1. Open Microsoft Word, create a new document, type something in that document and save the file on the desktop with a filename of your choice. Close Word. Examine the document that you created. If the filename shows a period and the three-letter extension *doc*, then file extensions are visible and you do not have to do this exercise. If, however, there is no period or extension, then extensions are not showing and you must change this setting.

2. Click the **Start** button and click the link to the **Control Panel**.

3. On the left side of the **Control Panel** window, click the link to display the control panel in **Classic View**.

4. Locate the link for **Folder Options** and click it.

5. In the **Folder Options** dialog click the **View** tab.

6. Scroll down through the advanced settings list and find the check box for **Hide extensions for known file types** as shown in Figure 0.02. Uncheck this setting.

FIGURE 0.02 *Uncheck Hide Extensions for Known File Types*

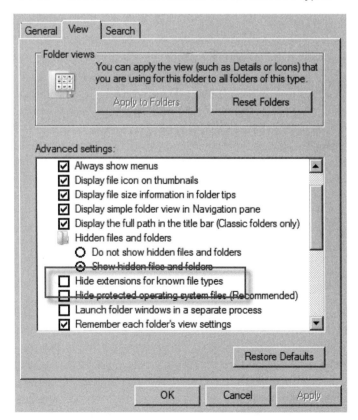

7. Click **OK** and then close the **Control Panel** window. The files in the *webs* folder should now have the extension showing.

In order for Windows to know to open a Web site in Microsoft Expression for editing, it must be set so that Expression will always be used as the default. The installation process for Expression should take care of this, but if it doesn't, it can be manually set. The following exercise will allow you to do this.

EXERCISE 0.03. Setting the Default HTML Editing Program

1. Start the Web browser Internet Explorer (IE). For this book it is *essential* to use Internet Explorer. You can preview Web pages in any browser (and you should), but you can open

FIGURE 0.03 *Set Microsoft Expression to Be Default Web Page Editor*

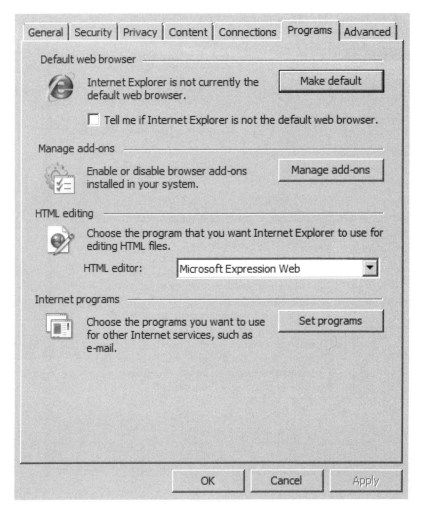

a site directly in Expression only with IE. Our first task is to determine if Expression is set as the default Web page editor.

2. In IE, click **Tools** > **Internet Options**. Click the **Programs** tab to see the dialog box shown in Figure 0.03. About halfway down the dialog box is a section for HTML editing. HTML is the computer language that creates Web pages. Click the down arrow in the box to the right of the **HTML editor** heading. You will see a list of all of the programs that are installed on the computer that *could* be used to edit Web pages. From that list select Microsoft Expression. Click **OK**. Expression is now the default program for creating and editing Web pages.

Congratulations—you are ready to go. The setup for the text is complete. You can now close Expression Web and any other open windows and move on to the text.

THE AUTHORS

Brenda Russell, PhD

Brenda Russell is associate professor of psychology at Penn State Berks in Reading, Pennsylvania. She completed her MA at Central Connecticut State University and earned her PhD at St. Louis University in 1999. She serves as a program evaluator for various educational and crime prevention projects. She has published research on a wide variety of topics but specializes in issues pertaining to psychology and the law. Her interests include issues pertaining to legal decision-making in cases of sexual harassment, rape, sexual coercion, domestic violence, duress, and crimes of passion. Russell taught undergraduate and graduate courses in research methodology for more than eight years. The majority of her recent research involves using the Internet to design, administer, and collect survey and experimental research data.

John Purcell, MBA

John Purcell is recently retired from Castleton State College, Castleton, Vermont. His interests include web design and programming, project management, and location analysis of markets, and he maintains an active consulting and corporate training practice. For more than sixteen years, Purcell taught undergraduate and graduate courses in web design, e-commerce, web programming, advertising, consumer behavior, and online survey research. Prior to entering the education field, Purcell worked in the aerospace and advertising industries.

ACKNOWLEDGMENTS

Thanks to Brenda Russell for her optimism and hard work bringing this to fruition under incredible personal circumstances. You're an inspiration! Thanks to all my students who pushed me to do this the first time and worked hard to master creating online surveys. Special thanks to Kristen Trigg who stopped in with a question one day and started the whole thing off. Thanks to Katie Boucher, Emily Purcell, and Richard Balian for the technical review of the Web manuscripts. Your feedback helped make this book better.

Thanks to all my family for their support and counsel throughout the process. A special thanks to Emily for her persistence and hard work at life. You are an inspiration to me and a source of great pride. Thanks to Evan for his spark and energy. Finally, thanks always to Kathryn for her support and solid presence in my life.

—JP

For assistance with resources and helpful ideas, I would like to thank some student assistants from Penn State Berks, Amro Fadel, and Abbey Hafer, as well as my partner in research, Shane Kraus. I would also like to thank my family and friends for all of their support during this process. Without their support and encouragement, this would not be possible. A huge heartfelt thank-you to Dillon Russell Kenniston and Richard Balian for their unwavering support and editing suggestions.

—BR

We would like to thank Cheri Dellelo for her excellent editing and feedback, as well as Kelsey McGee, Donna Cohn, Andy Pasternack, Seth Schwartz, and all the other hardworking editors and behind-the-scenes people at Jossey-Bass.

ONLINE RESEARCH ESSENTIALS

CHAPTER

UNDERSTANDING THE BASICS OF RESEARCH

LEARNING OBJECTIVES

- To be able to understand the many ways research affects our everyday lives
- To be able to identify the research process using the scientific method
- To be able to formulate a testable research hypothesis
- To be able to define variables and differentiate between independent and dependent variables
- To be able to recognize some of the research methods that can help answer your research questions
- To be able to define scales of measurement and understand their importance in research

Each day, we learn things from the news on the television, the Internet, the radio, and in the newspaper. Research is conducted on everything from a new diet suggesting different weight-loss methods, to ways to improve your love life, to new drugs that cure diseases, to how your personality attracts different types of people, among so many others. Gallup polls might show that the president is losing popularity or that people don't support the president's economic policies. Research findings change over time, though, and what was good for you yesterday may not be good for you today. How do we evaluate this information? Do we blindly accept these reports or do we question them? Learning about research methods will help you evaluate the validity of these claims.

Almost every occupation uses research in some way. For example, clinicians depend on research findings to diagnose a patient or prescribe drugs. Educators use research methods to create new and better curricula and teaching strategies. Business professionals use research to examine product and marketing strategies to increase customer satisfaction and sales. Legislators rely on research findings to create new laws. Seat belt laws were enacted based on findings that the use of seat belts significantly reduces the number of people injured or killed in car crashes. Research on eyewitness testimony has helped change federal legislation so that law enforcement officials use a uniform approach when questioning eyewitnesses. Research can also examine issues pertaining to media, aggression, and pornography, just to name a few.

Some question whether the Internet and other forms of media should be censored. How do we reconcile our First Amendment right of freedom of speech with allowing hate groups to publicize and entice others to join them? In essence, research can change the world. It can change the way we behave and how we perceive the world. If it weren't for social scientific research we might still live in a segregated world (*Brown v. Board of Education*, 1954). Research findings also lead to continuous amendments of existing laws and passage of new laws. Laws pertaining to law enforcement, business transactions, and new medical and social programs are continually changing as new research is done examining the effectiveness of the programs. Because research affects our lives in such fundamental ways, it is essential to understand the underlying aspects behind the findings.

When you think of research, what comes to mind? ***Basic research*** is conducted to address essential questions about human behavior. Questions might relate to thinking, learning, memory, biology, personality, and social behavior. The researcher gathers data on a variety of questions and tests theoretical assumptions. Researchers who conduct basic research publish results in scholarly journals after the research has been reviewed by fellow scholars. Research concerned with the practical application of research findings is called ***applied research***. For instance, an applied researcher might examine the effect of a new drug's effectiveness in treating AIDS or depression. A marketing researcher might look at the effectiveness of new product packaging. Clinicians might research a new theory of behavioral intervention and use the new behavioral treatment approach with a client.

One area of applied research is program evaluation. New federal and state programs are constantly being created or reformed within our educational, criminal justice, health care, and mental health systems. Program evaluators research the effectiveness of these programs. Basic and applied researchers work together to provide a systems approach (to bring together or combine) theory and research into real world settings. Basic research provides and perpetuates new research findings and theory. Applied researchers utilize these basic findings within their own research to discover whether the theory and research can be applied to the real world.

In our experience, students taking courses in social science research methods tend to have a natural inclination toward investigating human behavior. You might enjoy observing people in an attempt to explain their behavior. Perhaps people tend to come to you for information. Your observation skills are so acute that your friends might rely on you for insight to assess whether they are perceiving or reacting to an incident in an appropriate manner. Based on your experience and your own personal observations, you offer advice to your friend. How does the way you approach your friend's problem differ from scientific approaches toward solving problems?

An empirical approach would be more scientific. The word *empirical* means that we base our knowledge on observation. Non-scientific approaches—such as taking a wild guess, relying on intuition, basing decisions on vicarious experiences of others, or simply relying on an authority to tell you what to think—are not empirical. By itself, empiricism is not necessarily a systematic, scientific approach to research. We can describe behavior we observe, but these descriptions are not considered scientific because they are not conducted in a systematic way that limits error and bias.

MAKING DECISIONS: INTUITION VERSUS SCIENCE

When we add a systematic approach to observing behavior, our observations become more scientific. Using the scientific approach often leads us to conclusions that are not always what we expected them to be (that is, intuitive). One example of false intuition is that, when the home computer was first invented, many believed it would be a short-lived fad.

Some researchers conduct studies that conclude with what many would believe to be obvious findings. In some situations, scientific research does find what we believe to be the obvious answer, but often research findings are surprising and generally not intuitive. For example, a famous psychologist, Leon Festinger, examined how people rationalize their behaviors, particularly when their behaviors are not consistent with their own values or personality. Festinger set up a research study where students were offered either $1.00 or $20.00 to participate in a study. Once participants came to the laboratory, they were told to sit in the lab and simply turn a wooden peg in a peg board for one hour. Upon completion of the task, Festinger asked the participants how satisfied they were with the task and how happy they were to participate in the study. Which group do you think reported they were more satisfied and happy to participate? Think about it.

Most students believe the group receiving $20.00 would be more satisfied with the task. Surprisingly, Festinger found that participants who were given one dollar reported being happier and more satisfied with their experience. How do you think Festinger explained this? This study actually became a major theory called cognitive dissonance theory. Festinger believed that participants who received the dollar had to justify their behavior. They had practically wasted one hour of their lives, therefore they had to rationalize why they participated. When our behaviors are not consistent with our values and morals, we feel uncomfortable, experiencing disharmony or cognitive dissonance. In order to reduce this dissonance, we justify the behavior to ourselves. We tell ourselves what a great experience it was. By doing this, we reduce the dissonance we are experiencing. Perhaps you have done this. Have you purchased something one day and then found something better and cheaper the next day? If so, you may have justified your behavior by telling yourself how much better your original purchase was.

Festinger and his colleagues took this idea a little further (Festinger, Riecken, & Schacter, 1956). Festinger had a colleague infiltrate a cult that believed the world would end at the start of the new year. The cult was formed by a woman who began hearing voices that she believed were from aliens. Eventually others were attracted to the cult. Most of the individuals in the cult gave up all of their material belongings because they believed they would not need them when the spaceship came to pick them up before the total annihilation of the world. When the time for the world to end came and went, the group then rationalized their behavior by saying the world did not end because their group was so cohesive and had such a connection to the aliens that they themselves were the reason that the world did not end. When we do things that are contrary to our usual behavior, our human nature will provide justifications for our behavior so we don't feel so bad. The point here is that things are not always what they seem. In fact, more often than not, when we scientifically investigate things, researchers are likely to be surprised by something they have found in their data. Results are not always intuitive and science has helped us realize this.

USING THE SCIENTIFIC METHOD IN RESEARCH

Using empiricism in conjunction with the scientific method, you can be more confident that the outcome is based on a behavior you are measuring and not something else. The scientific method allows scientists to get rid of alternative explanations (confounds) and bias that lead to errors and erroneous judgments. With the scientific method you not only can describe behavior, but you can ultimately predict and explain it.

The scientific method has four goals: describing behavior, predicting behavior, explaining behavior, and understanding behavior.

Describing Behavior

Researchers conduct scientific observations of individuals, behaviors, and events. Dodd, Russell, and Jenkins (1999) examined the simple aspect of smiling. Previous research had found that boys and men smile significantly less than girls and women

(Hall, 1984). The study of gender differences in smiling can contribute to theory and research on the development of gender roles. According to both social learning theory (see Lott & Maluso, 1993) and gender schema theory (Bem, 1985), the socialization of gender occurs during childhood, but gender schemas change and evolve after childhood (Jacklin & Reynolds, 1993). Dodd et al. (1999) studied the onset of these gender differences. For instance, did females always smile more than males? Or was smiling a function of societal norms and expectations? After observing over sixteen thousand school yearbook pictures of individuals in kindergarten through adulthood, the researchers found that though females do tend to smile more than males overall, there were no differences in smiling between females and males until approximately age ten. Gender differences were found in fourth grade and reached a peak by ninth grade, at which point, there were significant differences between males and females in smiling.

It is amazing to note that simply by observing and describing behavior, researchers are able to find relationships between variables such as gender differences and smiling—ultimately leading us to make a prediction that if you are a female between the ages of nine and thirteen, you will most likely be smiling in your school picture, but males between the same ages will be less likely to be smiling. Researchers can also make inferences from these results that imply social smiling may be a function of societal expectations.

Predicting Behavior

Once a behavior has been observed and described, a researcher can make a prediction based on previous behavior. For example, if you look outside your window each morning at approximately 7:45 AM and see your little six-year-old neighbor Joey waiting for the bus, you would likely conclude that your neighbor will be waiting for the bus on the next day. You also notice that Joey is not there waiting for the bus on weekends (when there is no school). Hence, you conclude that little Joey will be outside waiting for the bus Mondays through Fridays. If today is Monday, you can make a pretty safe prediction that Joey will be at the bus stop at 7:45 AM. Similarly, researchers can predict that a female in a yearbook picture will be smiling before they see her picture. However, they cannot explain *why* females smile more than males.

Explaining Behavior

Descriptions and predictions of behavior can imply relationships between variables; however, they cannot imply explanations for the observed behavior. For instance, many people wonder whether the use of iPods and cell phones leads to more car accidents. Researchers can explore the relationship between the use of cell phones and iPods and their role in accidents to determine whether a relationship exists. However, researchers cannot say that using your cell phone or iPod in the car will lead to a car accident. Wouldn't it also have to be true that younger people tend to have more iPods and cell phones and are less experienced drivers, and this too might lead to car accidents? Another example might be that playing violent video games causes one to become aggressive and violent. We must also consider whether individuals who are already violent or aggressive might also be more attracted to violent video games.

In order to infer causation, researchers conduct experiments using the scientific method. In order to make causal inferences, three elements are required. The first element is ***temporal precedence***. This means that the cause must precede the event or outcome. For instance, according to this element, researchers must demonstrate that playing violent video games actually comes before violent and aggressive behaviors, or that using a cell phone comes before a car accident. Next, researchers must find a relationship between aggression and video games. The second element is that cause and event must *covary*. This means that when the cause is present the event must occur, and when the cause is not present the event does not occur. The third element needed to explain behavior is using experimental control to eliminate alternative explanations. ***Experimental control*** is a necessary element of the scientific method that uses manipulation, holding conditions constant, and balancing to isolate effects of various variables. For example, research has found a relationship between the use of hands-free cell phones and poor driving performance (Beede & Kass, 2006). We can take this a bit further and suggest that cell phone use is related to car accidents. However, research demonstrating relationships between variables can never conclude that one thing causes another or, in this case, that cell phones *alone* cause accidents. Similarly, if we cannot determine that playing violent video games and *only* violent video games causes aggressive and violent behavior, then we cannot say with certainty that playing violent video games causes violent and aggressive behavior. One would be hard-pressed to find that the use of iPods and cell phones alone are the cause of car accidents. Researchers would have to take into consideration other issues that might affect the outcome. In the case of cell phones, we would have to control for factors such as weather, number of people in the car, the age and experience level of drivers, road conditions, and the possibility of drug or alcohol use.

Understanding Behavior

The last goal of the scientific method is to understand how and why behaviors occur. When relationships are found, researchers need to explain why they exist. In our example of female students smiling in yearbook photos, we find a relationship between age and social smiling. Why would the gender differences in smiling—at least in school photographs—emerge during the ages of nine to thirteen years? In a general sense, it seems likely that younger children are not fully attuned to social expectations related to gender roles (Salkind, 1990) and have thus not yet incorporated the way they smile as part of their gender identities. According to gender schema theory (Bem, 1985), ideas about gender develop throughout childhood, but these schemas change and evolve to organize new information and influences (Jacklin & Reynolds, 1993). Preadolescent children (between the ages of nine and twelve) are particularly susceptible to gender roles as we see in the increased interest of opposite-sex relationships and interest in sexual information. They are also influenced by how men and women are portrayed in the media. There may be many explanations for such a finding. It is the job of researchers to find what might be the best explanation for their findings.

All of the four goals of the scientific method mentioned are related to one another. In order to make predictions one must first find, observe, and describe behavior. To find an explanation for behaviors, researchers must also observe, describe, and find relationships between variables. Researchers conduct experiments that demonstrate temporal precedence, that find covariation among cause and effect, and, finally, that address possible alternative explanations. Finally, when trying to understand the "how" and "why," researchers provide theories that provide explanations for the research findings.

> *Researchers attempt to describe, predict, explain, and understand behavior.*

FORMULATING A RESEARCH QUESTION

Great research theorists develop theories and research based on their interests and passions. You probably have some ideas or questions on topics about which you are particularly passionate. Ideas for research can come from a professor's lecture, something you heard in the media, or from personal experience. Let's say you are interested in psychology as it relates to law. You might study jurors or legislators and how they make their daily decisions that affect many lives. One important research question you might ask is, Does the way in which eyewitnesses are questioned affect the accuracy of their testimony? Scheck and Neufeld's pivotal work (1992) led to the Innocence Project, which has found that over the last ten years more than one hundred individuals on death row have been released following revelations of inaccurate eyewitness testimony. Or you might investigate the effectiveness of a new measure designed to assess competence to stand trial. From these ideas you create research questions and a corresponding design that will help you measure what you want to measure.

When you create a research question or idea, you are creating a hypothesis. A *hypothesis* is a tentative question that can be tested. Evidence may support or refute the hypothesis. As you formulate your own hypothesis, ask yourself a question about the topic and make a specific prediction as to the outcome of your research. Hypotheses are usually stated in a way that suggests the direction of relationships or cause and effect between variables. For example, one might investigate whether spending habits differ according to a person's gender. Before you can make a good testable hypothesis about this, there are two things you must do. First, as a researcher, your job is to examine the literature regarding your topic to see what has already been found. Perhaps someone already conducted a study examining the same question. As you read the research on the topic, you come across evidence that men are less likely to make purchases on a regular basis then women. However, men tend to spend more money on large ticket items than women do. Based on this finding, you can make a hypothesis that predicts men make fewer purchases than women, yet the amount of money spent for both men and women is approximately the same. Second, after reviewing the extant literature on the topic you will want to pay close attention to research theories that can provide an explanation for your research findings.

As you read the literature and formulate your hypothesis, you will also want to consider finding a research theory that can be used to explain why you think purchasing trends differ for men and women. A ***theory*** helps us organize and explain information. According to Myers (2008), a theory is "an integrated set of principles that explain and predict observed events" (p. 17). Theories are used to summarize explanations for research findings as well as to infer testable predictions. For instance, you would need to find a theory that explains why you believe females evaluate defendants differently than males. This new theory must be tested and evaluated, and, as this is done, new knowledge is gained.

As you create a hypothesis, you must also remember to try to identify potential relationships that can exist between variables. A ***variable*** is defined as "any event, situation, behavior, or individual characteristic that varies" (Cozby, 2004, p. 62). The weather is a variable, as it changes from day to day. Some examples of variables in the study about using hands-free cell phones and driving ability include the type of hands-free phone, average speed, changes in speed, reaction time, attention, and traffic violations.

Researchers must clearly identify which variables they will study. In the study examining the effect of hands-free cell phones on driving performance, driving ability would be considered the outcome (measured by speed, reaction time, traffic violations, and so on). In investigating gender differences in spending habits, spending habits would be considered the outcome variable. As you create your hypothesis, you can discuss variables within the context of a relationship—typically one of cause and effect. Researchers call these variables independent and dependent variables. An ***independent variable*** is the variable that is considered to be the cause of the results. A ***dependent variable*** is considered to be the effect (or outcome variable). For instance, you want to determine whether socioeconomic status (SES) of an individual (lower SES or higher SES) affects perceptions of academic achievement. In this situation, socioeconomic status is the independent variable and perception of academic achievement (as measured on a scale where 1 = "extremely low academic achievement" and 7 = "extremely high academic achievement") is the dependent variable. In experiments, the independent variable is the variable that is typically manipulated to "cause" the effect. For instance, if you wanted to determine whether socioeconomic status made a difference in ratings of academic achievement, you could manipulate the socioeconomic status of the individuals in the study. Half of the participants would receive a scenario depicting an individual with high SES and half of the participants would receive a scenario portraying the individual with low SES. You would then examine ratings of perceived academic achievement to determine whether these ratings change as a function of socioeconomic status.

Based on previous research and theory, your hypothesis might be that individuals with low socioeconomic status are perceived to have lower academic achievement.

In order to assess your hypothesis, you could then measure whether ratings of perceived academic achievement differed among individuals with low or high SES to determine whether your hypothesis is supported or refuted. If the research findings show that those with lower SES are perceived to have less academic achievement, then your hypothesis is supported. If the research does not find any differences among the ratings, then the hypothesis is refuted.

UNDERSTANDING RESEARCH TERMINOLOGY

Keep in mind that all research questions and hypotheses must be testable. Most research questions and hypotheses aim to explain why something happens. If a hypothesis cannot be tested, it is not useful to anyone. Terms must be clearly defined in a way that can be tested. For instance, Freud's theory of id, ego, and superego continues to be one of the most famous psychological theories but lacks the ability to be tested. One cannot test the existence of an id, ego, or superego. Therefore, most researchers do not consider this a "testable" theory. When developing a testable theory, questions must be clearly written and not circular in meaning. Therefore, as you create a research question, you cannot say a child has Attention Deficit Disorder (ADD) and therefore has more behavioral problems in the classroom. This rationale is circular as more behavioral problems in the classroom may be a result of the child's ADD. Furthermore, the topics you decide to study cannot be abstract—they must be measurable. For example, researchers cannot investigate topics such as "hell" or "the devil," because these topics are abstract concepts that cannot be measured. You must be able to test your hypothesis using a research methodology. Let's say you hypothesized that a new after-school program would lead to student success in the classroom. This is a great start. However, you must be very specific as to what you mean by "student success." How will student success be measured? Each variable in your study needs to be clearly defined.

Researchers use *operational definitions* to define the variables they decide to measure. An operational definition is the way we define our hypothetical construct so that the construct is now measurable. In the example above, you could define student success in many ways. If you considered academic achievement to be success, you might measure changes in student grades from year one to year two. Or student success might be measured by the number of social interactions with peers. However you decide to define student success, definitions must be very clear so you and your readers know exactly how the variables in your study will be measured before any research is conducted. This would also include the variable "after-school program." Because the after-school program is a variable of interest that is expected to lead to success, you would also need to define the after-school program in detail. What will the program include? How long will it be? Where will it take place? How do students participate? Are there eligibility criteria?

Defining your variables clearly is necessary for several reasons. Let's say that you created an after-school program. You or someone else conducted a study that found student success (as measured by better grades) increased once the after-school program was implemented. The results of the study were published and you and your after-school program became famous. Other schools around the country now want to implement your after-school program into their schools. How do they do this? Without a clear definition of what your program entailed, they cannot implement it properly. If you do not provide a clear definition to assess student success, others cannot replicate your research. If something such as your after-school program was successful, you might want to re-create similar programs around the world. Once these other programs were implemented, they could be evaluated to determine whether the program works with students in different areas. Researchers call this *reliability*. Research is reliable when it is replicated with other populations and samples. Researchers look for consistency among research findings. When findings are replicated across different groups and situations, this increases our ability to generalize to the greater population.

An important goal is to ensure your measures are valid and reliable. If you are studying student success, do student grade changes actually capture "student success"? Perhaps they do in one way or another, but certainly if we limit our definition of success to grade change, we neglect to look at other aspects that can be defined as success. Measures are ***valid*** when they measure what they are supposed to measure. Validity tries to capture the "truth and accurate representation of information" (Cozby, 2004, p. 79). Measures are ***reliable*** when they are consistent across time and populations. It is certainly not wrong to define student success as change in grades, but be sure to realize whether the method you are using to define your terms actually captures the definition of what you intend to measure. Later in the text, we will address many other types of reliability and validity that researchers consider when conducting research.

RESEARCH METHODS THAT CAN HELP ANSWER YOUR QUESTION

Always remember the phrase "Correlation is NOT causation."

Choosing a research method will depend upon your research question. In order to describe, predict, explain, and understand behavior, researchers collect data. They have many options for collecting data using qualitative and quantitative measurements. Some data collection methods include describing behavior in naturalistic observations, systematic or repeated observations, case studies, archival research based on previously obtained statistical records from the mass media or other communication records, interviews, or surveys. Keep in mind that when your goal is to describe or predict relationships between variables, you can establish only that the variables are related.

You cannot infer that one thing causes another thing. In order to explain or understand behavior, a researcher must conduct an experiment. This book will help you establish which of these methods will help you answer your research question.

Describing and Predicting Behavior	*Explaining and Understanding Behavior*
Naturalistic observations	Conduct experiment
Systematic observations	
Case studies	
Archival research	
Interviews	
Surveys	

Why Scales of Measurement Are Important in Survey Construction

Before researchers can conduct their studies, they have to consider how each of the variables in the study will be measured. They must operationalize all of the variables in their study. This clear definition of variables will help readers and other researchers understand exactly how the study was conducted. When discussing how a variable is measured, researchers must explain the exact way in which they measured. For example, as a researcher studying depression, you might be collecting data to determine whether depressed individuals differ from non-depressed individuals. One way to study the effects of depression would be to simply ask individuals whether they are depressed. This would be a categorical way of obtaining information. When you offer a participant categorical options such as "yes," "no," or "other," these are *discrete categories* (variables that are not continuous, but categorical). If a participant says "yes," he or she cannot be placed in any other category. An example can be seen in Figure 1.1.

Another option in investigating the construct of depression might be to use a scale that already exists and has been proven valid and reliable, such as the Beck Depression Scale (Beck & Steer, 1987). This scale measures depression on a Likert-type scale or a continuous scale. *Likert-type* or *continuous scales* are rating scales that provide greater options for your participants and more variability for your study. In a continuous rating scale, participants choose a numeric value, giving you quantitative information about the amount of depression that each of them experiences. For instance, you could ask participants to rate how depressed they felt in the last week on an 8-point scale where 0 = "not at all depressed" and 7 = "completely depressed." For example, see Figure 1.2.

FIGURE 1.1 *Question with Discrete Categories for Answers*

Please rate whether you have experienced depression in the last week (check one box)

☐ Yes   ☐ No   ☐ Not Sure

FIGURE 1.2 *Question with Likert-type or Continuous Scale for Answers*

Using the scale below please rate how depressed you have
felt in the last week.

| 0 | 1 | 2 | 3 | 4 | 5 | 6 | 7 |

Not at   Completely

all depressed   depressed

It is important to be aware of how you are measuring the variables you have chosen to study. The decision of whether to measure depression as a categorical variable
or a continuous variable will affect how variables will be defined and ultimately determine which statistics you can use to analyze your data. Understanding the scales of
measurement will help you understand your options in measuring variables.

The Scales of Measurement

A *nominal variable* has no numeric or quantitative properties. Researchers refer to these
measurements as categorical data. In this situation, participants' responses are placed into
categories. Their response to the question will render them in one category or another. For
instance, you might wonder what percentage of students in your class passed the last exam.
If an individual passed the exam, he or she cannot be in the "did not pass" category. Hence,
categories in nominal scales are always *mutually exclusive* (meaning that if you are in one
category, you cannot be in another). Gender is considered a nominal variable. A person is
male or female, pregnant or not pregnant, dead or not dead; and so forth.

    Ordinal variables are those variables that are measured by ordering or ranking.
With ordinal values, the categories can be ordered from first to last, from long to short,
or from top to bottom. Examples include college football standings, pop music charts,
or rating your favorite ice creams. Some questionnaires ask us to rate something from
least important to most important. This is evident with regard to measures of our general concern for environmental issues. For instance, you might be asked to rank the
order of importance of the environmental factors you believe to be the most significant
in affecting our air quality today.

    Figure 1.3 depicts a nominal scale used in a situation where someone might favor
one thing much more than they do another thing; the amount of difference between
rankings 1 and 2, or between 2 and 3, may be very different from each other.

Interval and Ratio Scales

The difference between the numbers on an *interval scale* is assumed to be equal and
meaningful. In other words, the difference (or distance) between 2 and 3 and between

FIGURE 1.3 *Question with Ordinal Ranking Scale for Answers*

Please rank the following problems by writing the number in the blank:
1 = most important to 3 = least important. Use each rank only once.

_____ Car emissions

_____ The diminishing rain forest

_____ Industrial waste pollution

3 and 4 are equal. You have probably seen interval scales when you have completed a short survey where a Likert-type scale or continuous scale was used to assess your thoughts on a given topic. An example of an interval scale was noted earlier, where $0 =$ "not at all depressed" and $7 =$ "completely depressed." An interval scale is differentiated from a ratio scale wherein an interval scale has no true zero value. For example, if you checked your own temperature (in degrees Fahrenheit), it would most likely be 98.6°. The difference in the temperature of 78.6° and 88.6° is equal to the difference between 98.6° and 108.6°, yet there is no true absolute zero on the scale that suggests temperature does not exist. In this case, the number 0 is only a random reference point. When there is no absolute zero reference point, you cannot form ratios with numbers. For example, you cannot say the person who scored 100 on the depression scale is twice as likely to be depressed than someone scoring 50 on the depression scale. You will find interval scales are particularly useful when measuring attitudes toward virtually any topic.

Ratio scales have an absolute zero point and are separated by equal intervals. The best examples of ratio scales are scales measuring physical attributes of objects (such as weight, width, or length). In this situation, ratios can be assumed. For instance, a table weighing one hundred pounds weighs twice as much as a table weighing fifty pounds. Ratio scales are most often used to study things such as time and duration. You will find that analysis of data using interval or ratio scales is virtually identical—both are considered continuous in nature.

Researchers need to choose carefully which scale of measurement is appropriate to obtain the most useful data. Computers techies coined the phrase "garbage in, garbage out" to describe the dangers of inputting bad data when creating a program. The same goes for doing research. Quantitative research is data-driven and the data you collect are an essential part of conducting a good study. Scales of measurement ultimately limit your ability to analyze data in the manner you choose. That is why it is important to carefully

Scales of measurement (nominal, ordinal, interval, and ratio) are important to consider when designing a research study.

consider two key things when designing your study. First, will the measurement you choose enable you to answer your research question or hypothesis in a valid manner? Second, because the measurement you choose will dictate which statistics you can use, will the scale of measurement you choose enable you to statistically examine the outcome of your study as you intended?

SUMMARY

In this chapter, we addressed the importance of research in everyday life and explained the scientific method that researchers use to conduct research. This chapter introduced many key terms to which we will refer in greater detail in later chapters. After reading this chapter, you should have a fundamental understanding of the difference between basic and applied research. You should also remember that researchers do not rely on intuition or anecdotal information to draw conclusions. Instead they establish testable research hypotheses using the scientific method. This empirical approach has four goals: to describe behavior, predict behavior, explain behavior, and understand behavior.

A careful review of the extant literature on your topic will help you formulate your research question and create a testable hypothesis. Be sure to include research theory to support your hypothesis. Your research question should also have clear independent and dependent variables; how you define these variables will be based on the definitions you choose. When deciding how to define your variables of interest, you must also consider how reliable and valid your study will be based on the operational definitions of your independent and dependent variables and your target sample. Clear definitions with an explanation of how each variable is measured are necessary to help you, your readers, and other researchers understand exactly how the research is conducted.

We discussed the importance of understanding the scales of measurement (nominal, ordinal, interval, and ratio) and their role in formulating an operational definition of your variables and ultimately in dictating the type of statistics you can use to evaluate your research results. Then the research method you choose (correlational or experimental) will be based on your research question and the operational definitions you choose.

By now, you should have an understanding of some basic concepts in research. At first the thought of conducting your own research can be quite overwhelming. Our text will walk you through the necessary steps needed to conduct a high-quality research project.

KEY TERMS

basic research
applied research
empirical
temporal precedence

experimental control
hypothesis
theory
independent variable

dependent variable
operational definition
valid
reliable
discrete categories
Likert-type or continuous scales

nominal variable
mutually exclusive
ordinal variable
interval scale
ratio scale

DISCUSSION QUESTIONS

1. Think of at least three examples of how research has affected your personal life.

2. What are some of the key differences between empirical and nonscientific approaches to research and what are the primary reasons researchers use the scientific method?

3. Name and distinguish between the four research designs that describe and predict behavior and experiments that explain behavior.

4. What is the importance of using an operational definition?

5. What are the four scales of measurement and why are they so important to conducting research?

CHAPTER

2

ETHICAL CONSIDERATIONS FOR USING THE INTERNET FOR RESEARCH

LEARNING OBJECTIVES

- To be able to define ethics and understand its crucial role in research
- To be able to identify risks in research and consider issues of physical, social, and psychological harm
- To be able to explain the important elements of an informed consent and its relation to issues of respect
- To be able to identify when deception in research is justified and the importance of maintaining participant privacy and anonymity
- To be able to understand what can be learned from debriefing statements
- To be able to recognize researcher responsibilities

All of the ethical issues noted in this chapter must be considered before conducting any research. Unethical research can be harmful to participants, wasteful, and damaging to general worldviews. Research helps define our values and, if our values are based on unethical research, this can be very damaging to society. There are many historical examples of unethical research that harmed participants and ultimately changed societal values and attitudes toward social science research. For instance, in the late nineteenth century eugenicists (those who wanted to improve the human race through selective breeding) advocated giving intelligence tests to immigrants as they entered the United States (Gray, 1999).

Online research now offers researchers a much broader opportunity to assess issues across the globe. Although there are no specific policies and procedures in place for online research, scientific organizations have come together to address how to protect human participants while at the same time promoting scientifically sound research on the Internet (Siang, 1999). Advisory groups have been created to assess ethical issues associated with conducting online research (see www.apa.org). In 1999, members from the American Association for the Advancement of Science's Program on Scientific Freedom, Responsibility, and Law and the U.S. Department of Health and Human Service's Office for Protection from Research Risks met to take on the task of creating guidelines and recommendations for all online research (see www.aaas.org for their report).

The policies and recommendations created by these organizations offer some assistance when identifying the advantages and disadvantages associated with online research and bring to the forefront how unclear the distinction still is between public and private domains. For example, what is considered private information online? If an individual is a member of an online incest survivor discussion group, at what point should the information that he or she discloses be considered private? If someone has a Facebook page or blog online and it is accessible for researchers to review, is that information in the public domain? Would tracing network connections to pornography sites from workplace or school computers be ethical? These questions and many others remain unclear. Because Internet research is a fairly new technology, behavioral scientists are learning as they go. Despite the uniqueness of online research, policies and recommendations continue to adhere to the basic ethical standards offered by social and behavioral scientists. It is the researcher's duty to consider the fine line that exists between the costs and benefits of the research. The foundation of all ethical standards results from evaluating what is morally right and legally binding.

DEFINING ETHICS AND ITS ROLE IN CONDUCTING RESEARCH

Whether you are conducting research as a class requirement for school or for a private organization, there are ethical concerns that must always be considered. The definition of ethics is somewhat elusive, but the general idea is that ethics refers to a set of guidelines that provide direction for solving moral problems and dictate how research should be conducted (Keith-Spiegel & Koocher, 1985). Ethical guidelines are essential in all aspects of research.

Ethics should be considered when planning, conducting, interpreting, and reporting the results of your research (Cozby, 2001). For example, let's say you were asked to assess the general well-being of employees and to recommend programs that could enhance employee health and potentially reduce employee health insurance costs. You would need to carefully consider all research questions, being careful not to harm potential participants of the study. For some research topics, questions referring to controversial topics such as abortion may be necessary to ask. For example, medical doctors may need to research the psychological and physical effects of abortion. However, some questions could be considered offensive or may induce unexpected emotional responses. Researchers must take extreme care to think through all questions so that ethical problems are eliminated or at least minimized. When questions are considered sensitive or controversial, it is essential that researchers obtain feedback from various authorities (such as church members, priests, doctors, and so on) to determine whether the questions would be considered offensive or potentially stressful.

Just as professional disciplines or organizations hold their members to ethical standards, so are all researchers held to ethical standards. The standards discussed in this chapter pertain specifically to research conducted with human participants and can be generalized to virtually any institution that conducts research. Certain precautions need to be met when doing research within an institution of higher learning, typically including an institutional review of the ethics of your study before you begin research.

Codes of ethics for research are relatively new. Providing a thorough analysis of the history underlying the need for ethics in research is beyond the scope of this chapter; however, we will provide a broad overview that offers a context for ethics pertaining to human participants.

Codes of ethics and institutional review boards should be consulted before conducting any research.

Protection of human participants originated with the Nuremberg Code, a policy designed in 1947 by the Nuremberg Military Tribunal to act as the internationally recognized code of ethics in response to the trials of Nazis who had committed atrocious acts while conducting human experimentation on Jews and other concentration camp inmates. This standard eventually led to the National Research Act (1974), developed by the Department of Health, Education, and Welfare (DHEW), which set guidelines for conducting research on a federal level. The regulations associated with the National Research Act led to the National Commission for the Protection of Human Subjects of Biomedical and Social Science Research (NCPHS). After numerous revisions, and consultation with the National Commission for Protection of Human Subjects **institutional review boards (IRB)** or **human subjects review boards (HSRB)** were established and became the standard used for all biomedical and social science research at local levels. Revisions that took place during the 1940s through the 1970s were extremely important. For example, in the 1940s, researchers studying the effects of syphilis did not inform poor black men of their condition and denied them treatment for the disease. Similarly, the drug thalidomide (a sleeping pill prescribed to many pregnant women to alleviate morning sickness) was found to cause birth defects in babies born to women taking the drug. The effects of thalidomide may have caused an ethical crisis, but this crisis also led future researchers to keep in mind potential harm to participants when conducting research. Many other misuses of research have been documented, leading to even more stringent ethical standards.

Similar to the U.S. Constitution, a code of ethics should be considered a living document. Ethics are needed in this ever-changing world to help maintain the integrity of a profession (Keith-Spiegel & Koocher, 1987). We strongly recommend that any and all researchers follow ethical standards and work with their local IRBs to ensure that all human participants are treated appropriately and that the scientific integrity of the research is preserved.

Another classic study conducted in the 1960s by psychologist Stanley Milgram will further demonstrate the importance of acting ethically when conducting research. Astounded and perplexed by the number of people killed during the Nazi Holocaust, Milgram performed a series of experiments to understand obedience toward authority. Milgram first recruited men from the local New Haven, Connecticut, area to become participants in an experiment designed to assess the effects of punishment on learning (1963). Male participants were instructed to come to Yale University where the study was being conducted. As a participant entered the laboratory, he found two other men in the room. One was the experimenter (Milgram or a staff assistant); the other was a person whom the participant believed was a fellow participant in the study, but this person was actually a *confederate* (someone who worked with Milgram and was a part of the study). Participants (the participant and confederate) were told they had been randomly assigned as either a "teacher" or a "learner." The assignment was not actually random, though; each new participant was assigned as the teacher and the confederate was the learner. Having received their assignments, they were sent to different rooms out of each other's sight. Teachers were instructed to shock the learner with increasingly higher voltage shocks every time the learner got a word association pair incorrect. Each time an incorrect word pair was given by the learner and a shock was dispensed, an audio recording playing in the teacher's room nearby indicated increasingly distressing noises with each shock. The confederate screamed more loudly and pled for the experiment to be stopped because of his "heart condition." If the teacher demonstrated reluctance to continue shocking the learner, the experimenter would insist that the teacher continue with the experiment.

The goal of Milgram's study was to measure levels of obedience to authority by determining how far the "teachers" would go in shocking the "learners" simply because an experimenter told them they must continue with the experiment. Surprisingly, over 60 percent of the teachers continued on to shock up to "severe" levels despite cries of pain and pleas to stop the experiment. Participants were debriefed (told about the actual intent of the study) at the close of the experiment and told that they had not actually hurt the learners. However, this study was dangerous because it could have caused undue stress on participants. Although all participants proclaimed the experiment to be a learning experience, it placed them in jeopardy. Many would argue that what we learned from this study outweighed the potential costs. However, this and other studies that followed led much of the public to believe that psychologists were deceivers, that if they told you they were researching one thing, they were most likely actually testing something else.

In the next twenty years, other ethically questionable research that used deception or placed individuals at risk of psychological or physical harm was conducted, such as the Stanford Prison experiment (Haney, Banks, & Zimbardo, 1973).

Assessing Benefits and Risks

The ethical guidelines to which we currently adhere can be attributed to the *Belmont Report: Ethical Principles and Guidelines for the Protection of Human Subjects of Research* (NCPHS, 1979). The Belmont Report was the result of the inquiry by the National Commission for the Protection of Human Subjects of Biomedical and Behavioral Research regarding ethics, the goal of which was to clarify ethical regulations in association with the American Psychological Association's ethics code as well as federal policy for the Protection of Human Subjects. This code provides standards to which researchers must adhere when assessing the degree of risk to participants. The doctrine emphasized "beneficence, respect for others, and justice." You may have heard the medical motto (also known as the Hippocratic oath) "First, do no harm." Otherwise known as **beneficence** and **non-malfeasance**, this simply means "be kind" and "do no harm." This ethical rule also extends to all research.

According to the Belmont Report, beneficence was an ideal intended to encourage all researchers to maximize the positive outcome of their research while minimizing potential harm to participants. Some researchers consider this a **risk-benefit analysis** (Cozby, 2001). One of the first questions you should ask yourself as a researcher is "What is the *risk* to participants?" When discussing risk, researchers should consider things such as psychological or physical harm and confidentiality. If a research project has any potential for harm, then researchers must undertake a risk-benefit analysis. If the research is not conducted, will the benefits to society be neglected at the cost of potential harm to participants?

Be sure to consider a risk-benefit analysis before conducting any research. Do the benefits outweigh the risks? Consider whether risks are minimal or greater than minimal. If you are not sure after reading the following section, please contact your IRB or the National Commission for the Protection of Human Subjects of Biomedical and Behavioral Research.

When considering benefits, take into account those that benefit society as well as participants. For instance, could your research demonstrate the success of a new educational reading program or a new medical treatment that might ultimately benefit society? Perhaps your research could teach participants a new skill that would benefit the individual. Additional outcomes might include tangible benefits such as monetary payment or intangible benefits such as the satisfaction a participant receives simply by being included in your research study. In any case, risks and benefits must be weighed before any research begins.

Defining Risks in Research

According to the Belmont Report, one of the first ideals to be considered when assessing risk in research is to "do no harm." Any research conducted on participants should not harm participants in any way—physical, psychological, or social. Some researchers will argue their research causes no harm to participants and, therefore, their participation carries no risk. We argue that all research has inherent risks.

Minimal Risk   There are variants of risk that should be considered when planning a research study. For example, *minimal risk* is risk that a participant would normally encounter in everyday life. People take surveys everyday. Participants may take part in a marketing survey, psychological survey, or observation. However, if the research does not induce stress, physical harm, or social risk (potential for embarrassment) and retains all aspects of confidentiality, such research would carry minimal risk.

Greater Than Minimal Risk   When there is the possibility of participants being hurt either physically or psychologically in your research study, the standard of risk may be considered *greater than minimal risk*. In additional, if prospective research participants are considered "protected" (for example, children, mentally challenged individuals, prisoners), then they are assumed to be at greater than minimal risk. Research that presumes greater than minimal risk will always require a full review from your institutional review board.

Physical Harm   Researchers in all disciplines must consider the issue of physical harm. This issue usually arises in medical research. For example, an experiment that employed a new drug could be risky because it might have unexpected side effects or there might be problems with the administration of it. Kinesiologists examine such things as exercise and stress on the body, where there is the potential for physical harm to the body. Experimental psychologists might examine sleep deprivation or caffeine withdrawal. Sociologists might conduct an experiment that elicits or exacerbates anger or aggression that could cause someone to be physically violent. Despite even the best of intentions and screening processes, some people could get hurt. When you consider the issue of physical harm, you must very carefully weigh the costs and benefits to decide whether such research should be conducted.

Psychological and Physiological Harm   A great deal of medical and social science research examines the role of psychological stress in everyday life. Without this research we would not know about such things as the link between high levels of cortisol (the hormone associated with stress) and heart disease. Studying the effects of psychological or physiological stress differs from causing undue stress. Researchers can easily study correlations between stress without necessarily causing stress to a participant. However, when researchers purposely induce stress, there is always the potential for harm. In addition, researchers can unknowingly induce participant stress. For instance, some research examines issues of violence and abuse (such as homicide, rape, abortion, and domestic violence). As researchers, it is our responsibility to realize these topics may cause high levels of anxiety in some participants. Responding to experiments or survey questions related to such sensitive topics might trigger traumatic memories in some participants. When ***psychological harm and stress*** might be a problem, you must ask yourself whether you've taken the proper precautions to deal with the potential adverse effects of your study. In some cases, this can simply be addressed when recruiting participants by providing information pertaining to the study's potential risks. But even if you do this, you must also offer self-help or hotline telephone numbers or referrals at the conclusion of the study.

Social Harm Social harm refers to protecting participants' privacy. When we evaluate social risk we must determine whether the information that participants provide will be anonymous. If maintaining anonymity is not possible, we must then evaluate whether (and how) confidentiality can be maintained. Each participant has a right to privacy, and if this right is violated, we place our participants at risk for social harm. Social harm can lead to public embarrassment if sensitive, confidential material is revealed. For instance, if participants' intelligence scores or previous criminal activity were revealed to others this would constitute a breach of confidentiality that could lead to public embarrassment. To minimize or eliminate the risk of social harm, safeguards must be established to maintain privacy at all times. Participants should be informed of how their confidentiality will be maintained so that they can determine whether they want to take part in the research.

Informed Consent and Issues of Respect

Another essential element discussed in the Belmont Report is that of ***respect***. In essence, the report states that researchers must value a participant's autonomy, meaning that participants must be treated as individuals capable of making their own conscious decisions about whether to participate in research. In order to make such a conscious decision, they need to be fully informed of the purpose of the research and exactly what they are getting themselves into. Participants need to be informed of all potential risks inherent in the research as well as their right to refuse participation or to terminate participation at any time.

According to the American Psychological Association's *Ethical Principles of Psychologists and Code of Conduct* (1992), there are eight essential elements that should always be included in all ***informed consents*** to ensure participant autonomy and respect.

First, all participants should be *informed about the primary purpose of the study.* What are your intentions? What issues will you study? Though you need to disclose the purpose of your study, you never want to reveal your hypotheses in your consent form; doing so could bias participants' responses. Researchers must therefore be cautious about how they word the purpose of the study. For instance, if your study examines how sexism affects attitudes toward women, then you probably do not want to inform participants they will be completing a survey designed to measure sexism and their attitudes toward women. Instead, the purpose of the study should be worded in a more general way, such as that you wish to examine general attitudes toward social relationships. If items or surveys of your study include attitudinal measures such as sexism, rape myth acceptance, or other attitudes about people, events, or groups, then you should also inform participants that the research will examine their perceptions of interpersonal relationships.

Second, *consent forms must provide information pertaining to the basic procedures* that will take place. This should include how long it will take to complete the study (expected duration) as well as the basic procedures that will be involved. What will happen? Where will the study take place? If your online research presents participants with a series of questionnaires, then simply state that upon agreeing to participate in the study they will be asked a series of questions that pertain to the purpose of the study. If respondents are provided with any experimental treatments (such as a new drug versus a placebo), this must also be stated in the consent form.

Third, all research *participants should be notified that they have the right to decline participation or choose not to answer* any particular question or questions, and that they can withdraw from participating at any time during the study. This element is a safety mechanism that ensures participants that their participation is completely voluntary and that, if at anytime they feel uncomfortable, they have the right to not continue with the study.

Fourth, *foreseeable consequences of declining or withdrawing from participation need to be addresse*d. Researchers should always consider the potential consequences of a participant's choice to refrain from parts of the study or to withdraw from the study altogether. For instance, if respondents choose to refrain from answering particular questions, what will be done with the incomplete data? Similarly, if participants will receive some type of incentive (such as extra credit, lottery) for participating in your study and should chose to withdraw before the study begins or ends, then they should be not be excluded from their entitled incentive.

Fifth, *all foreseeable risks and benefits should be disclosed to participants.* Risk factors and benefits generally influence an individual's willingness to participate. Therefore, you need to disclose any potential risks, discomfort, or adverse reactions as well as any possible benefits associated with the study.

Sixth, *incentives for participation* should also be included. Many researchers offer lotteries or compensation for participation. Students participating in research might also be awarded extra credit. These are all considered incentives. While some institutions consider incentives as the "norm," other institutions and organizations disagree with the use of incentives because students may be unduly influenced to participate in studies that offer incentives compared to those that do not. Incentives may be considered coercive when used to recruit underprivileged populations. We recommend that you follow the accepted procedures of your institution.

Limitations to participant confidentiality should be included in all consent forms. This seventh element informs individuals *what will happen with their responses.* Will names be used? Will identifying information be in some way tied to their responses? If so, will the data be held in a safe place? What are the *limits to confidentiality*? With online research, issues of confidentiality are still being hotly debated. We address this issue in more depth later in the chapter.

The eighth element should include *contact information of the researcher and institutional review board* in case participants would like to contact the researcher with questions about the study or their rights as participants. It is a participant's right to ask questions and receive answers. Ideally, contact information should be provided not only in the informed consent but also in debriefing statements.

Finally, it is important to note that an informed consent should be visual appealing with 11-point type as the minimum font size (Cozby, 2004). Most consent forms are written at an eighth-grade reading level or lower without technical jargon that could confuse the reader (for an example of informed consent, see Chapter Three).

Essential Elements That Should Be Included in All Informed Consents

- Participants should be informed about the primary purpose of the study
- Consent forms must include information pertaining to the basic procedures that will take place in the study
- Participants should be notified that they have the right to decline participation or choose not to answer any particular question or questions
- All foreseeable consequences of declining or withdrawing from research need to be addressed
- All foreseeable risks and benefits should be disclosed
- Incentives for participation should be included
- Limitations to participant confidentiality should be addressed
- Contact information of the researcher should be provided

The Use of Deception in Research

When we addressed issues pertaining to informed consent, the first principle discussed was divulging the purpose of your research study. However, there are many circumstances where divulging the true purpose of your study would invalidate your results. Let's use the Milgram experiment as an example. If Milgram had actually instructed participants that he was investigating obedience to authority, the results most likely would not have been the same. Furthermore, the Milgram studies were conducted before the APA ethics code was adopted and published in 1973. If Milgram had adhered to the APA ethics code we now use,[1] he would have had to instruct participants that they could withdraw from the study at anytime. If respondents had had this option, it is likely the number of participants giving what they believed to be severe electric shocks would have been much lower.

Deception is a research procedure that is used to hide the true nature of the research study (Graziano & Raulin, 2004). The use of *deception* in research is acceptable only if the benefits of the research outweigh the risks to participants. When deception is necessary in a study, it is up to the researcher to justify its use to the IRB and note that there is no effective alternative procedure that can be used. Researchers can never deceive participants about potential psychological or physical harm. If deception is used, participants must be informed of the true purpose of the study in a debriefing statement. During the debriefing, it is the respondents' right to have their data withdrawn from the study if they so choose. To Milgram's credit, he did conduct thorough debriefings with individuals, telling them the true purpose of the study. He also followed up with many of the respondents to determine how they felt about their role in the study.

When conducting online research, the role of deception is still hotly debated, primarily because research conducted with online chat groups or discussion board forums can be considered private or public domain depending on whom you ask. It is agreed, for the most part, that obtaining consent is not necessary for data collected in public domains. *Public domain* in this regard is typically associated with existing media sources, such as television, radio, government records, newspapers, magazines, books, or conferences, or locations where behavior can be observed in a natural setting with no interference or manipulation by the observer (Siang, 1999). Data collected from these resources do not require consent. However, conducting research on the Internet brings up a whole new series of questions regarding what constitutes private and public information. There is some information (such as existing records, media, and so on) that obviously falls into this category, but what of other online sites such as newsgroups, listservs, Facebook, blogs, personal Web pages, or chat rooms? Some scholars believe that this information should be considered public domain, but others argue informed consent is necessary in these situations because participants should be advised that their messages are a part of a research study (Siang, 1999). Exactly what constitutes private information remains unclear. Therefore, if you are unsure whether your study meets the requirement of informed consent, we recommend you review ethical guidelines (see www.apa.org) or contact your IRB (for further information also see Ess & Association of Internet Researchers, 2002).

What if you would like to study the long-term psychological effects of rape? One way to do this is to access victims of rape via online chat rooms that offer support groups for victims. In this situation, you have two options. First, you can choose to let everyone in the online chat room know you are a researcher and ask for informed consent from each individual to conduct your study. One of the main caveats of using this option is that respondents may act differently when they know they are being observed or recorded. In order to avoid this problem, your second option would be to disguise yourself as a victim and become part of the group. If you chose this route, it would be essential that participants in your study be debriefed at the completion of the study. However, one of the unfortunate aspects of conducting online research is the fact that some individuals who participated in the discussions may not be online when the debriefing takes place. Therefore individuals would not have known they participated in your research.

WHAT CAN WE LEARN FROM DEBRIEFING STATEMENTS?

We advocate that ***debriefing statements*** be used in all research. Debriefing is a procedure used at the end of a study to inform participants of the true nature of the research and to allow participants to voice their comments about the study (Graziano & Raulin, 2004). Researchers always debrief participants following a study; participants are usually more than happy to provide feedback on your study. Debriefing gives researchers the opportunity to discuss the study with participants and thus gain valuable information. A debriefing statement has three main functions. First, it can provide you with valuable information regarding your study. Second, when deception is used in any research study, debriefing participants is necessary to explain the true nature of your research study, and it also enables you to determine what participants believed was the focus of the study. Third, you can address any potential problems regarding participant stress during this time and offer additional information or help if needed.

DECEPTION AND ONLINE RESEARCH: PARTICIPANT PRIVACY, ANONYMITY, AND OTHER ISSUES

Ensuring ***participant privacy*** and anonymity is also considered a risk. It is the researcher's responsibility to maintain anonymity and confidentiality of data by keeping all data in a secure area, not accessible to others, and by ensuring that identifying information does not appear anywhere on the surveys. As a researcher, you must ask yourself whether your study will include information pertaining to the identity of a participant. The federal code of regulations [C.R. § 102(f)] is responsible for establishing IRB's state ethical reviews. These reviews are necessary if researchers interact with participants or collect "identifiable private information," whereas observations of public behavior, where participants are not directly identifiable, are exempt from federal regulations [C.R. § 101(b)] (Kraus et al., 2004). Researchers can eliminate risk associated with confidentiality by not asking for identifying information at all (for a copy of this rule, contact the Office of Human Research Protections, 1101 Wootton Parkway, Suite 200, Rockville, MD, 20852, or http://hhs.gov/ohrp).

The greatest potential risk associated with online research is breach of confidentiality. Data collected on sexual behavior, divorce, abuse, family violence, and perpetration of violence are considered sensitive information. In most situations, researchers can eliminate this risk by not requiring identifiable information. However, there are situations when this is not possible. For example, much research requires that researchers follow participants over time and keep track of them for data collection. In this situation, numbers can be used as identifiers. These numbers should be familiar and memorable for your participants, such as the last four digits of their social security number or last four digits of a phone number. Further, if personal identifiers are used, they should not be stored in the same database as the study data, and they should not be stored on the same computer.

Confidentiality is breached when participant responses are shared (either purposely or unintentionally) with others not associated with the research. Cozby (2001) suggests that when there is a good chance that confidentiality could be breached, you should consider applying for a Certificate of Confidentiality from the U.S. Department of Health and Human Services. This certificate may be necessary if the data you collect could potentially be subpoenaed by the court (Cozby, 2001).

Participant anonymity can be compromised when investigating naturally occurring behaviors online (Kraus et al., 2004). For instance, researchers can investigate adolescent behavior and attitudes by examining blogs. However, if researchers choose to disclose a quote, they run the risk of breaching confidentiality. We can assume that individuals online often use pseudonyms to mask their identity, but more often real names are disclosed and information collected can be traced back to individuals through search engines (Bassett & O'Riordan, 2002). To reduce the risk of disclosure, researchers should choose to eliminate evidence that might compromise confidentiality by rephrasing quotes or disguising pseudonyms.

It could be argued that because individuals use pseudonyms in cyberspace, these should be sufficient disguise and privacy therefore need not be an issue. However, Frankel and Siang's synopsis (1999) of a workshop convened by the AAAS (American Association for the Advancement of Science) recommends that pseudonyms be compared to real-life identities, thus affording pseudonymous participants the same protection of confidentiality as those without pseudonyms.

As a researcher, you need to be aware that information provided online can be false. Identifying what is real and what is not real can be problematic. For example, if you are interested in studying sexism as posted on YouTube, you could examine video clips using key words or tags such as "sex," "male," or "female," and so forth. Many individuals use YouTube as the venue for their directorial debut, so their video clips cannot necessarily be trusted to depict real-life situations. How do you tell the difference? Be careful when conducting this type of research not to make inferences based on what you see online.

Researcher Integrity

The researcher is ultimately responsible for all ethical conduct in the research project. When weighing the risks and benefits of an online research project, you need to consider potential problems. Some problems can occur when conducting naturalistic observations online. For instance, while examining homemade videos on YouTube you might come across something that is clearly against the law. What do you do? What are your rights and responsibilities? What are our participants' rights and responsibilities?

Stern (2003) stresses the importance of considering researchers' responsibilities, particularly when they come across disturbing information online. In a hypothetical situation, a group of researchers decide to examine Facebook pages, blogs, and Web pages to assess college students' coping behaviors. The researchers consider these Web pages as public domain and, therefore, not subject to IRB approval. While collecting data, the researchers come across some disturbing information detailing the frustrations of one twenty-three-year-old college junior from Joe's College. Researchers find an eighteen hundred–word manifesto and digital videos detailing the frustrations he feels, his anger toward his instructors, and his intention to get back at those who made his life hell. The researchers read this page as they would any other (as data) and move along to the next.

A few weeks later there is a school shooting at Joe's College where two instructors and three students are killed. The researchers realize they had stumbled upon his Web page weeks before. The national press disclose that the killer's intention to kill others could be found on his Web page and had someone noticed this, the massacre could have been avoided. The researchers then question their decision not to disclose information pertaining to the disturbing Web page. Did they have a responsibility to react in some way to this information? If researchers come across information suggesting an individual will harm themselves or others, then what is their duty? This particular topic regarding participant privacy and confidentiality continues to be debated. Stern (2003) suggests that researchers have a plan in mind for how to handle disclosures before conducting this type of research.

According to the American Psychological Association's *Ethical Code of Conduct*, the principle of ***integrity*** states that individuals conducting research should be "honest, fair, and respectful of others" while understanding how their own values or biases can affect research (APA, 1992). Researchers should never provide false information or mislead individuals. This principle corresponds with that of ***justice*** and *respect* as noted in Belmont Report. Researchers must be fair when distributing the benefits of the research as well as when bearing burdens and accepting any risks involved in the study. This principle originated because previous medical researchers had abused their power and taken advantage of discriminated or marginalized individuals. The Tuskegee Syphilis Study captures this element perfectly. In this study, which took place between 1932 and 1972 in Alabama, researchers denied treatment for syphilis to 399 poor African Americans because they wanted to examine the long-term effects of the disease. As a result of this study, public outrage led to the implementation of the principle of justice to ensure that participants are treated equally.

In order to ensure that all participants are treated equally and with justice and respect, the ethics code states that participants cannot be excluded from research because of their age, ethnicity, national origin, religion, sexual orientation, disability, language, socioeconomic status, or gender. All participants should be treated equally and researchers should respect all individuals and be aware of cultural, individual, social class, and sex-role differences associated with diverse populations.

Another aspect of research integrity is concerned with how data are interpreted, analyzed, and presented. Researchers are also expected to keep records of all raw data and reports and share their records with others if requested to do so. It is also unethical to publish or present the same information in more than one journal or conference as there may be concerns with copyright issues. Of primary concern during this final phase is researcher misconduct, which includes but is not limited to fabricating or falsifying data, which is considered fraud. *Fabrication* is defined as "making up results and recording them or reporting them" (U.S. Office of Science and Technology Policy [OSTP], 1999, as cited in Gray, 1999, p. 8). This can include manipulating, omitting, or changing research materials, data, or equipment, or using processes that lead to false reporting.

It is the researchers' responsibility to understand that plagiarism is a violation of ethical standards. According to the U.S. Office of Science and Technology Policy (OSTP), *plagiarism* is defined as "appropriation of another person's ideas, processes, results, or words without giving appropriate credit, including those obtained through confidential review of others' research proposals and manuscripts" (U.S. Office of Science and Technology [OSTP], 1999). This includes presenting published and unpublished information, ideas, results, words, or processes as your own work. Plagiarism appears to be a growing trend in college, and we cannot stress enough the importance of understanding the issue. Students are increasingly using the Internet to do their research and are not citing the appropriate Web pages as the source when they include the information in their reports. Information obtained online is not exempt from the rules of plagiarism.

Students often say, "I didn't know" when they are caught plagiarizing. This is no excuse. If you do not know whether you are plagiarizing someone's work, it is best to err on the side of safety and cite the author. Be sure to cite authors for their ideas, reports, or scientific findings. If the idea is not yours, then give credit where credit is due. You can also use quotes to capture other peoples' work, but a paper should not have too many quotes. Making minor changes in an existing document does not constitute your own work. It constitutes plagiarism. Therefore, if your paper uses the same words as or the original ideas of an author, then you need to cite that author. (*Citations* are references that include the author's name, date of publication, where it was published, and page number. For more in-depth information on the proper procedure for using citations, please refer to the *Publication Manual* of the American Psychological Association.) Each time you refer to an idea, theory, or work that is not your own, use citations. Davis and Smith (2005) provide some additional good suggestions on how avoid plagiarism.

Issues of authorship should also be addressed before your study is conducted. If there are multiple authors, researchers need to decide how credit for the article will be dispersed. Students working with faculty should always discuss publication credit as early as possible. We strongly suggest that students form a contract with the faculty member addressing each person's expected role and contributions to the research project.

Remember, integrity and honesty are the hallmark of all research conducted—from beginning to end.

SUMMARY

Whether or not a research project can be conducted is dependent upon the ethicality of the research. Ethics should be considered in all stages of research—from the planning stage, in the process of conducting the research, to interpreting and reporting results. It is your responsibility as a researcher to think through your research question and take appropriate action so that ethical problems can be eliminated or at least minimized.

Ethical standards are shared in all disciplines. This chapter focused on research with human participants, discussed the history of ethics, and revealed the need to establish a code of ethics. The National Research Act of 1974, developed by the Department of Health, Education, and Welfare, set out ethical guidelines for conducting research at the federal level. This led to regulations adopted by the National Commission for the Protection of Human Subjects of Biomedical and Social Science Research. This established institutional review boards (IRBs) or human subjects review boards (HSRBs). The ethics we currently adhere to can be attributed to the Belmont Report, a code that provides standards for assessing risk to participants. Readers are encouraged to contact their institutional review (IRB) or human subjects review board (HSRB) before conducting research.

One of the fundamental concepts of ethics is "beneficence and non-malfeasance." In order to "do no harm," researchers must conduct a "risk-benefit" analysis to determine whether the benefits of the research outweigh the risk of potential harm to participants. When assessing risk, researchers must determine whether there is minimal risk or greater than minimal risk to participants. When determining the potential risk factors, you must consider potential psychological harm or stress that your research might have on individuals when participating in your study. Participants should be aware of all possible risks and benefits of the research *before* participating. Informed consents are provided to potential participants as a vehicle to decide whether or not to participate in the study.

Sometimes deception is used in research. Deception is acceptable only when the benefits of the research outweigh the risks. If deception is used, participants must be debriefed and informed of the true nature of the research study. We encourage researchers to use debriefing statements in all research projects because they can encourage participants to give you constructive feedback about the study, alert you to participant stress, and allow you to reveal the true nature of the research project (a requirement).

Maintaining participant confidentiality is extremely important, particularly for online research. It is the researcher's responsibility to take all precautions to ensure participant confidentiality and professional integrity.

Professional integrity implies that researchers will be honest, fair, and respect others. Researcher responsibilities extend to how data are collected, interpreted, analyzed, and presented. Researcher misconduct includes fabricating or falsifying data. It is also the researcher's responsibility to understand what constitutes violations of plagiarism and avoid "lazy writing."

Conducting research is exciting and fun. However, it is the ultimate responsibility of the researcher to ensure that all ethical standards are followed.

KEY TERMS

institutional review boards (IRB)
human subjects review boards (HSRB)
beneficence and non-malfeasance
risk-benefit analysis
minimal risk
greater than minimal risk
psychological harm and stress
respect
informed consent

deception
public domain
debriefing statements
participant privacy
integrity
justice
fabrication
plagiarism
citations

DISCUSSION QUESTIONS

1. At what points during the research process should ethics be considered?

2. What is a risk-benefit ratio? Define and distinguish between minimal and greater than minimal risk.

3. In what ways can researchers protect participants from psychological harm and stress? Explain the purpose and elements of informed consent.

4. There are particular ethical issues to consider when conducting research online. Describe some of these problems and how researchers can prevent them.

5. What are researchers' responsibilities during the planning, execution, data interpretation, and communication stages?

NOTE

[1] The APA ethics code was first adopted and published in 1973, but revised in 1992 and 2002 and placed into action June 1, 2003.

CHAPTER

3

GETTING TO KNOW MICROSOFT EXPRESSION

LEARNING OBJECTIVES

- To learn how to use Microsoft Expression, the tool that will be used to create online surveys

- To be able to manipulate properties of Web pages, including page title, background color, and default type using Microsoft Expression

- To be able to add text to a page from a file and manipulate text font, size, and color

- To be able to explain how HTML tags help control the characteristics of type

- To discover how tables constrain text on a page and keep the appearance of text looking consistent on other computers and Web browsers

We assume in the text that you have finished installing Microsoft Expression on your computer, have a practice Web site, and a live connection to the Internet. If this is not the case, see the Introduction for instructions.

HOW THE INTERNET WORKS

This is a very abbreviated and nontechnical introduction to how the Internet works and what is necessary to create and view Web pages. The Internet is a way for computers to connect to each other and share information. These connections form a computer *network*, a group of computers that share a common language or protocol for exchanging information. The computer that you are using has hardware and software that enable it to connect to this network. The software is one of many variations of Web browsers, the most popular of which are Microsoft's Internet Explorer, Mozilla *Firefox*, *Opera*, and Apple's *Safari*. Today, the ability to connect to the Internet and share information is built into most electronic devices, from cell phones to computer gaming platforms.

Each computer connected to the Internet has a unique number, called an *IP address*, associated with it. In some cases, the number is permanently assigned and, in others, the number is assigned for the length of time you are connected the Internet. One such address is 207.46.19.190. This address is one of many associated with Microsoft's Web site. The computer uses these numbers to navigate the Internet, much as we use street addresses to find a house in a city. But people need something more easily remembered. *Domain names* are unique names that are associated with the numerical address. The domain name www.microsoft.com is linked to the above IP address. To reach www.microsoft.com you can type either the domain name or the IP address into the browser's address box.

In addition to users' computers, there are servers connected to the Internet. Web servers are sources of Web pages and other information. As you can see in Figure 3.1, when the user types a Web address into the address box, the browser software sends this request out to the Internet. The request works its way to the server that has that address. When it gets to the server, the server prepares a response to the request, sending the requested page back over the Internet to the browser. The browser interprets the code of the page and displays the page on the screen.

Hosting, Web Server Operating Systems, and Domain Names

Web servers run software that prepares responses to requests for pages and sends the pages back to the browser. There are two choices for a server operating system: Microsoft Windows Server and Linux-based servers. Windows Server is an operating system created by Microsoft. Windows-based servers have the advantage of working very closely and seamlessly with Microsoft Expression and making complicated tasks much easier. *Linux* is an operating system that is available to anyone at no cost (though the technical assistance and documentation may have a cost). Unfortunately, Microsoft

FIGURE 3.1 *Internet Model*

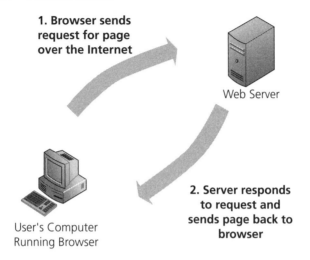

1. Browser sends request for page over the Internet

Web Server

User's Computer Running Browser

2. Server responds to request and sends page back to browser

does *not* make Windows Server available at no cost. Linux runs on a great many servers and does it quite well (some say better than Windows), but it lacks the tight integration with Microsoft Expression and more important, Linux servers cannot run Microsoft Access. *Microsoft Access* is a database program and part of Microsoft Office. We will use it to hold the results from the surveys that are created. We will have a great deal more to say about Access in later chapters. Though Microsoft Expression will work on a Linux server, for this text the *only* choice is a server that uses a Windows Server operating system. There are various versions of Windows Server (Server 2000, 2003, and so on). The version doesn't matter as long as it supports Access.

If you don't have a server connected to the Internet, then you can purchase the right to put your Web survey on another server. This process is called Web hosting and there are hundreds of companies around the world that will sell their server space to you. The most important characteristic needed for this project is that the server support Microsoft Access on the site. If you do a Google search on "Microsoft Web hosting Access databases," the result should be a list of acceptable hosting providers. Make sure the one you choose offers *unlimited* Access databases on the site. A note of caution: if you search for Web hosting providers, you'll see that some say they support "Microsoft Frontpage Server Extensions." This is necessary for Expression to work, but not sufficient; the hosting site must explicitly state that Microsoft Access is supported. If it does then the surveys can be created. If you are not sure, send a question to the site's customer support to verify that Access is supported before you pay for anything.

If you don't have one, you'll also need a domain name for your site. Pick a domain name based on its availability, memorability, and the degree to which it fits the purpose of the site. The site www.networksolutions.com, as well as many others, will allow you to search for an available domain name. At the end of the name are three-letter extensions that indicate, loosely, what kind of site it is. *Com* is the extension used by many businesses. *Edu* is only available to recognized educational organizations. *Org* is limited to nonprofit organizations. There are other extensions available as well. When you find a suitable domain name, you must purchase it. If you are purchasing a hosting package, some will also include a domain name registration with the package. The purchase is actually only a rental; you have the exclusive use of the domain name for the term of the rental.

The best case is when all of this work has been done already. Most users of this text will have access to a server through their educational institution or workplace. Talk with your computer system administrator to see if there is an existing server running Microsoft Server software and an existing domain name that you can use. It may be possible to create a subweb on an existing domain name. A **subweb** is part of an existing domain name. A suitable subweb name might be *surveys.xyz.edu—surveys* would be the subweb on the domain name *xyz*, and the extension *edu* indicates that it is an educational institution.

INTRODUCING MICROSOFT EXPRESSION

Microsoft Expression is the tool we will use to create, edit, and manipulate Web sites and pages. It provides many advantages to the user. First, it is created by Microsoft and is a part of the Microsoft Office suite of applications. It shares the same menu structure and basic interface with other Office programs. It is easy to get going with Expression because many of the functions (such as opening, saving, spell checking) in Expression are similar in Microsoft Word or Excel, which are widely used. Finally, Expression has a great deal of functionality built into it that allows the user to do complicated tasks in just a few button clicks. This makes the job of building online surveys much easier.

In the introduction to this text, we downloaded the files for the exercises and extracted them, installed Expression, and set several default settings on your computer. If you did not do these things at that time, then you should do them before proceeding to the exercises in the next section. You also need to have a Web site that you can use that meets the specifications outlined above, a username, and a password. The server administrator or your instructor should provide you with these.

EXERCISE 3.1. **Opening the Site in Microsoft Expression**

1. Using Internet Explorer (IE), navigate to your Web site.

2. On the IE menu, select **File > Edit with Microsoft Expression Web**.

3. When prompted, supply your username and password. Click **OK**. The site should open in Microsoft Expression.

As you can see in Figure 3.2, Expression opens a window with several window panes or sections. At the very top is a menu. Below the menu are toolbars with icons for performing various tasks. The default toolbar that displays is called the ***common toolbar***. This toolbar is similar to the toolbar in Word or Excel and contains frequently used icons that are the same in other Microsoft Office applications. If your window does not look like the one in Figure 3.2, reset it by clicking the menu choice **Task Panes > Reset Workspace Layout**.

Below the toolbar is a window with three main sections. On the left and right sides are pairs of ***task panes***. Task panes have specific information about the site, a page, or items on the page. The content of these panes will change depending on the activities being performed and the user's preferences. We will work extensively with these panes in later chapters. For now, it is enough to note that task panes show information about aspects of the site. Between the two sets of task panes is the ***document window***. The

FIGURE 3.2 *Expression Window*

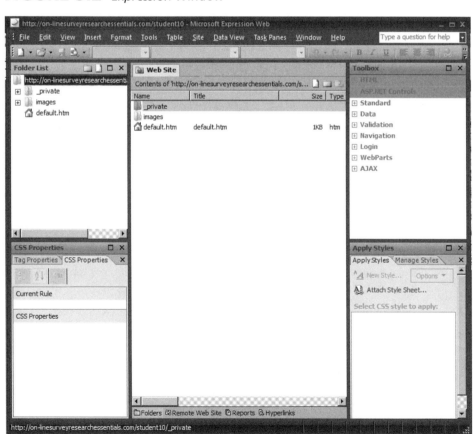

document window is where surveys and other pages will be created. The document window opens with a new generic page created by Microsoft Expression. At the bottom of the window is the status bar, which gives information about the current settings and activities of the program.

In the introduction we downloaded and extracted the files that will be used in the exercises. In Exercise 3.2 the files will be moved to the Web site.

EXERCISE 3.2. Adding Exercise Files to the Site

1. With the site open in Expression, select **File** > **Import** > **File** from the menu. The **Import** dialog box opens.

2. In the **Import** dialog click **Add File . . . .**

3. In the **Add File to Import List** dialog, navigate to the location on your computer where you extracted the *webs* folder which contains the exercise files for the text. Inside the *webs* folder select the file *default.htm*. Click **Open**. You are brought back to the **Import** dialog box and *default.htm* is added to the list of files to import.

4. Click the **Add Folder . . .** button.

5. Select the *chapter03 folder* and click **Open.** The files and folders will be added to the import list.

6. Continue selecting folders and adding them and their contents to the import list. Make sure that all of the folders are added, including the *images* folder.

7. When the list is complete, click **OK**. The files will be imported into the Web site. This may take a bit of time as there are quite a few files to import.

The items that were added are folders. However, because they are to be used on a Web server, we need to convert them to Web sites. The next exercise will accomplish this.

EXERCISE 3.3. Converting Folders to Web Sites

1. Figure 3.3 is a screenshot of the folder list in the upper left corner of Expression just after the folders were imported. Right click the *chapter03* folder.

2. In the shortcut menu select **Convert to Web** and then confirm by clicking **Yes**.

3. It will take some time, but the folder will change from a standard folder to one with a small globe in the folder. This is Microsoft's icon for a Web site.

4. Continue selecting every folder in the folder list (except for the *images* folder) and converting it to a Web site. You may see another folder titled *_private*. This should not be converted (Expression will not allow you to convert it).

At the conclusion of this exercise your folder list should look like Figure 3.4.

FIGURE 3.3 *Folder Task Pane Before Conversion to Web Site*

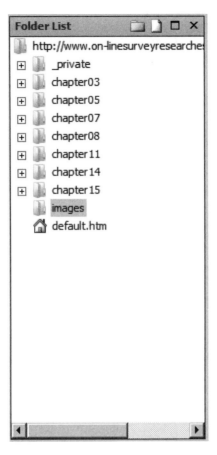

Your next task is to edit and then save a Web page. However, before you can do this simple activity, you need to understand filenames on a Web server. This issue of filenames is full of technical conventions. Compatibility with other servers and operating systems dictates that these conventions be followed.

Conventions for Filenames

1. Default page name: When a browser calls for a Web site such as www.fictitious-site.net, the page that it will display first is named either *default.htm* or *index. htm*. This is the name of the first page to be displayed in a site. The choice of names is determined by the server settings, so your server administrator will tell you which is correct. Both names are equally effective; the choice is merely a convention. After the page name is a period and a three-letter extension (in

FIGURE 3.4 *Folder Task Pane After Conversion to Web Site*

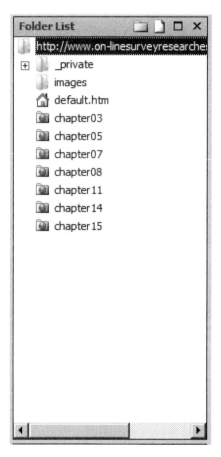

this case, *htm*). The extension tells the browser that this page was created using ***HTML*** (HyperText Markup Language). HTML is a coding language that tells the browser software how to display the information on the page and what to do with various elements on the page. As discussed, there are other extensions as well, and we will talk about them later.

2. No spaces: You should avoid including spaces in filenames. The name for a page should be one word. This is not absolutely essential, but it makes things clearer if spaces are avoided. In addition, some servers don't process filenames with spaces correctly.

3. No punctuation: Names can consist of letters or numbers, but almost no punctuation is allowed. The underscore (_) and the hyphen (-) symbols are allowed and can be used to create descriptive names that are one word. For example, *pageone.htm*

is an acceptable name, but it is hard to read. The name *page_one.htm* or *page_1.htm* is much easier to read.

4. Lowercase only: As a convention, page names should be in lowercase only.

5. *htm* extension: Normal Web pages will have the extension "htm."

EXERCISE 3.4. Edit and Save a Web Page

1. This exercise is the first exercise that is specific to Chapter Three. We will do this and all other exercises in the Web site for the chapter. To move to the Chapter Three Web site, double-click the *chapter03* Web site folder in the folder list.

2. To make a new page, click the first icon in the **Common Toolbar.** A new page should open in the document window.

3. Click anywhere on the empty page in the document window. In the upper left-hand corner of the page is a blinking cursor. This shows where the text will show on the page.

4. Type your name.

5. Click the menu choice **File > Save** or click the diskette icon in the **Common Toolbar.** At the bottom of the dialog box is the **Filename** text box. Type either the name *default* or *index*, as appropriate, in the box and click Save. You should *not* type the three-letter extension at the end of the filename. Expression will add it to the name when you hit Enter.

Other programs (such as Dreamweaver) create pages with the extension *html* after the page name. However, three-letter file extensions were used long before the Internet became popular and Microsoft continues to use them. Besides this historical note, it is very important to note that *page_1.**htm*** and *page_1.**html*** are two separate pages. They can coexist on a server, but you must type the page name and *exact extension* to see the appropriate one. The key to success is to be consistent. In this text, all regular HTML Web pages will be named *page_name.htm.* The browser doesn't care which is used. If all the pages are named with the extension *htm,* they will be correctly displayed on all browsers.

In the previous exercise, the page was created, named, and saved to the server. Now we need to check our work in a browser (a very important step).

EXERCISE 3.5. Previewing the Page in Internet Explorer

1. In Expression, select **File > Preview** in Browser. Select **Internet Explorer** from the list. Internet Explorer opens and the page is displayed. Your name should show in the upper left-hand corner of the browser window. This is the procedure that you should follow while working on pages. As you make changes, periodically save the page and preview it in a browser to make sure that changes are as you want them to be.

2. Go back to Expression, leaving the browser window open. Click immediately after your name and hit Enter.

3. Type your name again.

4. Save the file and preview it in a browser by hitting the F12 key. The page displays in a browser with your name showing twice.

5. Switch back to Expression and select both lines with your name. Either use the **Copy** button on the toolbar or right-click and select **Copy**.

6. Click below the text on the page and hit the **Paste** button or right-click and select **Paste.**

7. Save the page, but *do not hit F12 or use the menu commands to display the page.* Switch back to Internet Explorer and examine the document. Only two names should show in the window. Now either hit F5 (the Refresh key) or click **View** > **Refresh**. All four names should now display.

8. Switch back to Expression and select the last three lines of your name on the page. Copy and paste these on the page below the fourth. At this point, there should be seven copies of your name on the page. This time just hit F12 to preview the page in a browser. Because the page has not been saved, you are prompted to save it. Click **Yes** and the page will open in a browser with all seven names.

If you make a change to a page and don't see it in the browser, then the browser probably needs to be refreshed. Get in the habit of always refreshing the browser view of a page.

The text on the page is in the default typeface and size that is specified in Internet Explorer. Most people never change the default typeface in their browser, so it displays in the font Times New Roman. The size is the default type size. This combination is fine for many pages, but some contrast on the page makes it easier to read. In the next exercise we will use the style tags to change the way text is displayed on a page. *Style tags* are built-in formats that can be used to change the way text looks in a browser.

EXERCISE 3.6. Using Style Tags to Change the Way Text Is Displayed

1. Switch back to Expression and select all of the second name on the list by dragging across the text. On the **Common Toolbar** are three drop-down list boxes. The first has the style name **paragraph** showing. This means that the selected text is formatted as a paragraph.

2. Click the down arrow for the style list, and select **Heading1** <**H1**> from the list.

3. Save the page and preview it in a browser. The text of the second name should show in the browser as bold and approximately three times the size of the first name.

4. Switch back to Expression and select the third name. Apply the style **Heading2** <**H2**> to it. Select each subsequent name and apply the next style in the list until the six names have been formatted.

5. Save the page and preview it in a browser.

These style tags are also called *structural tags* because they change the structure of the page as it displays in the browser. The styles communicate a hierarchy in the text and add contrast to the text on the page. There are other ways of controlling the look of text on a page which we will cover in later chapters, but these style or structural tags are very quick and easy to use and are supported by all browsers.

EXERCISE 3.7. Creating and Saving New Web Pages

1. Select **File** > **New** > **Page** from the fly-out menu.

2. From the first column of the dialog box, select **General**. From the second column, select **HTML**.

3. Click **OK**. The dialog box should close and the new page should show in the document window. The page should automatically be given the filename *Untitled_1.htm*. You will want to give it a more descriptive name.

4. Select **File** > **Save** or **File** > **Save As . . . .** Because the page has not been previously saved, both commands do the same thing.

5. Near the bottom of the dialog box, select and delete the entire contents of the **Filename** text box and type **red_page** (let the program add the *htm* extension).

6. Click **Save**.

7. Repeat this process to create two additional pages. Give the pages the filenames **green_page** and **blue_page**. Expression will add the extension *htm* to both.

Modifying Page Properties

Web pages look different because the pages have page properties or attributes that cause the browser to display them in different ways. There are many page properties. In this section, we will illustrate three essential properties: the **page title**, default text style, and page background color.

EXERCISE 3.8. Modifying the Page Title

1. At the top of the document window, you should see several tabs. If you do not see the tabs, then double-click the filenames in the folder list to open the three pages created in the previous exercise. The tabs display filenames of pages that have been created. Click the tab labeled **red_page.htm**.

2. Right-click in the page and, from the menu, select **Page Properties**. On the **General** tab, select the text in the **Page Title** text box and delete it. In the same text box, type **This is the red page**.

3. Save the page and preview it in a browser. The title of the page just created should show in the ribbon at the top of the browser window and/or in the tab for the window depending on the version of IE you are using. All Web pages should have a descriptive title.

4. Repeat the above process with the *green_page* and *blue_page* using the appropriate color-related page title. Preview each page in a browser.

EXERCISE 3.9. Modifying Default Text Typeface

1. Switch back to the *red_page.htm* by clicking its tab. Type the following on the page (hitting the enter key as indicated): **Home** [Enter] **Red Page** [Enter] **Green Page** [Enter] **Blue Page**.

2. Save the page and preview it in a browser. The text should show at the left edge of the page in the default typeface Times New Roman.

3. Switch to the green page. Before typing anything on the page, click the down arrow for the type font list on the **Common Toolbar**. The font list is the second drop-down list on the **Common Toolbar**. Select **Arial, Helvetica, sans-serif**.

4. Type the four lines of text from step 1 above.

5. Save the page and preview it in a browser. All of the text on this page should now display in the typeface Arial or Helvetica.

6. Click the tab for the *blue_page.htm* page. Type the four words on the page in any typeface and save the page.

Typeface refers to the shape of the letters. There are thousands of typefaces available and new ones are created all the time. Graphic artists use typefaces to create a mood, add contrast, draw attention to something, or to set something off on a page. Every computer comes with some typefaces installed and programs will add new typefaces. There are many ways to categorize typefaces, but one basic way is as serif or sans-serif typefaces.

As you can see in Figure 3.5, the letter T in Times New Roman (on the left) has embellishments at the ends of the crossbar and down stroke of the T. These are called *serifs*. Originally these were added to mimic the shape of letters drawn by hand with a quill pen. Times New Roman and many other similar typefaces are called serif typefaces. The right-hand T is in the typeface Arial. It has no embellishments and has a clean, almost stark appearance. Arial is a ***sans-serif typeface***. *Sans* is a French word that means "without."

Which typeface should you use for your survey? It is a matter of style and readability. Books have long text passages and tend to be in serif typefaces, which are considered easier to read. Advertising and headlines are often in sans-serif typefaces

FIGURE 3.5 *Serif versus Sans Serif Text*

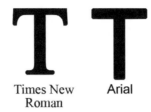

Times New   Arial
Roman

to get the reader's attention. In a survey, there will typically not be paragraph after paragraph of text, and the person taking the survey will already be paying attention. Either typeface can work, but the key is to be consistent throughout the pages and the site. Decide which typeface you will use and stick with it. In addition, there should be at most two typefaces in the entire site. Just because you might have fifty typefaces on your computer, it doesn't mean you should use all of them in a survey. Two is plenty.

When you set the default typeface on a Web page, the assumption is that the typeface resides on the browser's computer. Times New Roman has the advantage of being on every computer. Microsoft, Apple, and various publishers of Linux have included Times New Roman or some variation of it for many years. Arial is more problematic. Arial is a typeface that Microsoft owns, and Helvetica, which is a very similar, sans-serif typeface, is owned by Adobe, a major publisher of tools and typefaces for visual designers. Mac users all have Helvetica. When the default typeface on a page is changed, as in Exercise 3.9, the browser will look at the available typefaces and use the one that it has. If Arial is installed, it will be used to display the text. If it is not installed and Helvetica is, then Helvetica will be used. If neither is installed, then a generic sans-serif typeface will be used. The point is that the page designer may not have perfect control of the appearance of text on the browser.

The readability of a page is a function of many things. Certainly the content is important, as is the writing style. The layout on a page can affect readability as well. Part of the design of a Web page is the color scheme used for the text and the page background. The default color scheme is black text on white pages. This is fortunate because this is the most readable text and page color combination. Black and white have the maximum contrast and the resulting page is very readable. Unless there is some very compelling reason to change it (for example, if you are assessing the effect of type color and background color on comprehension), leave the default color scheme. If you must change it, then the next exercise will take you through that process.

EXERCISE 3.10. Modifying Text Color and Page Background Color

1. In Expression, click the **red_page.htm** tab at the top of the document window. Right-click the page itself and select **Page Properties**. Select the **Formatting** tab from the dialog box.

2. Halfway down the dialog box is the **Colors** section. Click the down arrow for **Background** colors. Select a red from the menu and click **OK**.

You may want to try various color schemes before you find one that will be easy to read—and remember, simple is better.

3. Save the page by right-clicking the tab at the top of the document window and selecting **Save**. The resulting page has a very intense red background. It would be hard to read a lot of black text with this background color scheme.

4. At the top of the document window, click the **green_page.htm** tab. Right-click the body of the document and select **Page Properties.**

5. Select the **Formatting** tab and click the down arrow for **Background**. The menu of colors appears, but this time we want a paler green than any that are available here. Click **More Colors . . .** at the bottom of the menu.

6. A palette of more than one hundred colors and shades of grey will display. Select any pale green that appeals to you.

7. Click **OK** twice. Save the page and preview it in a browser. The light green with black text is much easier on the eyes and the content is much more readable.

8. Click the **blue_page.htm** tab at the top of the window and modify the page background color to navy. Do not click **OK**.

9. Black text on a dark blue background would be very difficult to read. To improve readability, click the down arrow for **Text Color** and choose **white**.

10. Click **OK**. Save the page and preview it in a browser.

Though this color scheme is also difficult to read, the addition of the white text improves the readability. However, it must be restated that the goal of any survey is to communicate with respondents. Manipulating the page and text colors should be avoided. Black text on white pages is by far the easiest color scheme to read.

Hyperlinks

So far we have created pages that stand alone. The hallmark of the Internet is the ability to jump from one page to another in response to an action by the user. The most common way is to click a hyperlink. A *hyperlink* consists of two parts: the link that you click and the destination page you will be brought to in response to that click. We will begin with using text as the link.

EXERCISE 3.11. Creating a Hyperlink

1. In Expression, click the **red_page.htm** tab at the top of the document window.

2. Select the text *Home* on this page.

3. On the **Common Toolbar**, click the **Hyperlink** button. It is the button with the globe and a link of chain. If the **Hyperlink** button is not visible, click the menu choice **Insert >
Hyperlink**. Figure 3.6 shows the dialog box for a hyperlink.

4. In the dialog box, select the *default.htm* page.

FIGURE 3.6 *Hyperlink Dialog Box*

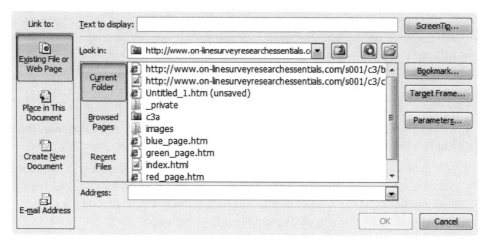

5. Click **OK**.

6. Select each of the subsequent text entries and add a hyperlink to their respective page.

7. Save the page and preview it in a browser. Click each link and confirm that the hyperlinks all work. Use the browser **Back** button to return to *red_page.htm*.

8. In Expression select all four of the hyperlinks on the red page and copy them.

9. Switch to the *default.htm* page. Select all of the text on the page and delete it. Paste the text for the four hyperlinks on this page. Notice that the typeface of the hyperlinks is the same as it was on the red page. The text retains the formatting of its source.

10. Copy and paste the hyperlinks onto the remaining pages. You will find that when you add the hyperlinks to the blue page, the links seem to disappear. This is because the default color for hyperlinks is blue. To fix this, change the page background color of the blue page to a lighter blue and save the page. Save all the pages and preview them in a browser. Verify that all hyperlinks work as expected.

In the above exercise, we created a functioning Web site with navigation that allows the user to move from any page to any other page in the site. Though crude, the site has a complete navigation system. However, in the rest of this text, navigation will be much less flexible. In most surveys the user will begin at the first page and work her way through the pages in the prescribed order. The use of hyperlinks and navigation will be very limited.

CREATING AND MODIFYING TABLES

In a browser window the way that text is displayed on a page is a combination of several factors. Plain text placed on a page will move and change as the size of the window changes. The line and paragraph endings will vary tremendously as the window changes size. In addition, the resolution setting of the computer monitor and video card play a significant role in how things appear on the screen. We want the page to look the same on any computer and in any browser. To overcome these problems, we will need a way of constraining text on a page so that it will be seen in the same manner no matter the browser window or resolution. Tables will be used to do this.

EXERCISE 3.12. Putting Text on a Web Page

1. In Expression, create a new page by clicking the **New Page** button on the **Common Toolbar** (the first button that looks like a piece of paper with the corner turned down).

2. When we downloaded and extracted the files for the text there were two folders. One folder, *webs*, had the structure of the Web site. The second, titled *exercise data*, has the files that will be used in the exercises. Double-click this folder and locate the *c3* folder. Double-click this folder and inside should be a document titled *mary1.doc*. Open the file in Word.

3. In Word, select all of the text and copy it.

4. Move back to Expression and right-click the page. From the menu, select Paste. The text should show in the upper left-hand corner of the page, to the right edge, and then wrap to another line on the page.

5. Save the page as *Mary_had.htm* and preview it in a browser.

6. In the upper-right corner of the browser window, locate the **Maximize/Restore** button (in the middle of the three). Maximize the window if it isn't already. Notice how the text flows across the window from edge to edge.

7. In the same browser window, locate what is now the **Restore** button (in the middle of the three) button. Click the button to restore the window and then, using the mouse, drag the border to resize the window. Decrease the width to about half of the maximum size. The text on the page will reflow on the Web page and the end of lines will change.

8. Drag the right side of the window to decrease its size again by about another half. The text should reflow again and the line ending should change. This is the same page and the same text, but, as a stimulus, each view is quite different. To be a consistent stimulus on any computer the text needs to be constrained.

Screen Resolution

In addition to the window size issue discussed above, the resolution of the computer screen plays a role in how things appear on the screen. Over the years, as the technology for computer screens has improved, so has image resolution.

Resolution is the amount of information that can be displayed on the screen and is measured by the number of pixels that can be displayed in the horizontal dimension (such as 1600) by the number of pixels in the vertical dimension (such as 1200). The word pixel (px) is a combination of the words picture and element, and it is a single dot of color on a screen. The higher the resolution, the more dots on a page and the more information that can be displayed and the richer the colors. Common screen resolutions in use today are 1600 × 1200 px, 1280 × 1024 px, or 800 × 600 px. The resolution of a screen depends on the computer's speed, video hardware, and display technology. Most new computers can display at higher resolutions. Very high-end computers support even greater resolutions than these. Today, the lowest or coarsest screen resolution that your site might encounter is 800 × 600 px. This is an old standard, but it is still used by about 10 percent of the computing population (JupiterOnlineMedia 2007; Refsnes, 2007). In survey research, we must aim for the lowest resolution that the survey is likely to encounter, and design pages that can be comfortably read at this resolution. Text and other elements on a page should be constrained to about 600 pixels in width. This allows for white space around the text and for the browser controls and edges. It happens that this is also about the width of text within standard margins of an 8.5 × 11-inch piece of paper.

Aim for the lowest resolution that your survey is likely to encounter.

EXERCISE 3.13. Creating a Table to Constrain Text on a Page

1. In Expression, click below the text on the page created above.

2. Add a table to the page by clicking **Table** > **Insert Table**. The resulting dialog is shown in Figure 3.7.

3. In the **Size** section of the **Table** dialog box, Set Rows to 3 and columns to 1.

4. In the **Layout** section set the **Alignment** to **Center** and check the box **Specify width**. In the text box, enter **600** and click the radio button **In Pixels**.

5. Set **Cell Padding** to 0 and **Cell Spacing** to 0.

6. In the **Border** section, set the **Border Size** to 1.

7. At the bottom of the dialog box, in the **Set** section, check the box to **Set this as the default for new tables**.

8. Click **OK**.

The resulting page is shown in Figure 3.8. This procedure creates a 600-pixel table centered on the page. The table has three rows and one column. The *cell padding*, the amount of space between the edge of each cell and the text within the cell, is 0 px and the *cell spacing*, the amount of space between the cells of the table, is also set to 0 px. The borders of the table are set at 1 px. These will be the default specifications for tables that we will use.

FIGURE 3.7 *Insert Table Dialog*

Insert Table
Size
Rows: 3
Columns: 1
Layout
Alignment: Center
Specify width:
Float: Default
600
In pixels
In percent
Cell padding: 0
Specify height:
Cell spacing: 0
0
In pixels
In percent
Borders
Size: 1
Color:
Collapse table border
Background
Color:
Use background picture
Browse...
Properties...
Set
Set as default for new tables
OK
Cancel

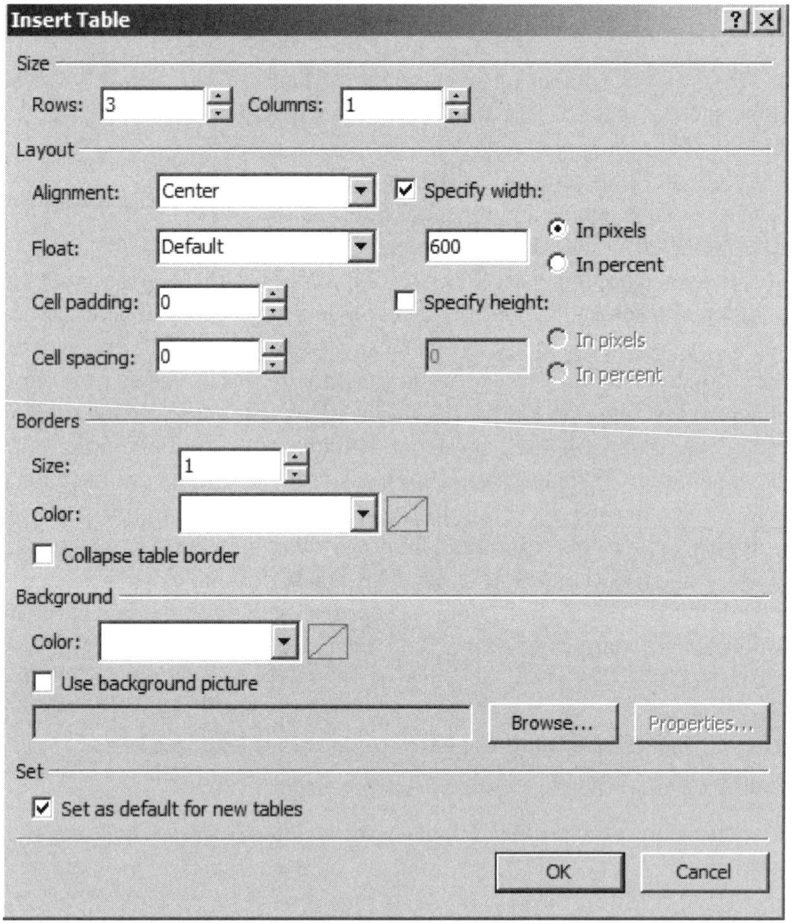

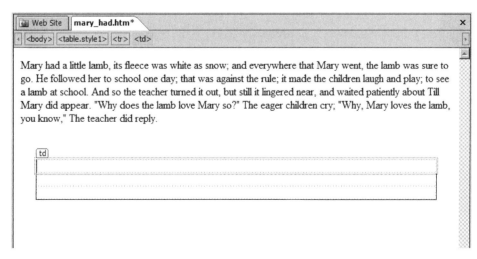

FIGURE 3.8 *"Mary Had a Little Lamb" Page with Table*

Web Site
mary_had.htm*
<body> <table.style1> <tr> <td>
Mary had a little lamb, its fleece was white as snow; and everywhere that Mary went, the lamb was sure to go. He followed her to school one day; that was against the rule; it made the children laugh and play; to see a lamb at school. And so the teacher turned it out, but still it lingered near, and waited patiently about Till Mary did appear. "Why does the lamb love Mary so?" The eager children cry; "Why, Mary loves the lamb, you know," The teacher did reply.
td

EXERCISE 3.14. Placing Text into the Table

1. Click inside the first row of the table. Type **Mary Had a Little Lamb**. Hit the Tab key. The cursor should move to the next row of the table.

2. Select all the text in the first row of the table. The properties of the text can be manipulated as in other Office applications. Click the **Bold** button to make the text bold. Click the **Centering** button to center the text within the cell.

3. Select the first line of the poem at the top of the page (through the phrase *the lamb was sure to go*). Cut the text from the top of the page and paste it into the second row of the table.

4. Select the next sentence of the poem (through the phrase *to see a lamb in school*). Cut and paste it into the third row of the table.

5. Click at the end of the third row of the table (this should be the last row) and hit the Tab key. As with other Microsoft applications, a new row is added to the table. The row will have the properties of the previous row.

6. Continue to select the text, a sentence at a time, cutting it from the top of the page and pasting each sentence into a row of the table.

7. Save the page and preview it in a browser. As in Exercise 3.12, view the page with the window **Maximized, Restored Down**, and in a narrow window (making sure that this window is less than 600 pixels wide).

As you can see in Figure 3.9 the text is contained within a table. When the window is resized the width and positioning of the text on the page doesn't change. When the window is too narrow to show all of the text, scroll bars appear to allow the user to scroll and see the text. Scroll bars are *not* something that is desirable, but it is the default behavior of all browser windows. And because almost everyone will view the page in a window that is at least 800 pixels wide, horizontal scrollbars should not be an issue.

FIGURE 3.9 *"Mary Had a Little Lamb" Inside Table*

Mary Had a Little Lamb
Mary had a little lamb, its fleece was white as snow; and everywhere that Mary went, the lamb was sure to go.
He followed her to school one day; that was against the rule; it made the children laugh and play; to see a lamb at school.
And so the teacher turned it out, but still it lingered near, and waited patiently about Till Mary did appear.
"Why does the lamb love Mary so?" The eager children cry; "Why, Mary loves the lamb, you know," The teacher did reply.

EXERCISE 3.15. Adding Finishing Touches to the Table

1. We added bold to text and centered it. Now we will apply styles within the table. Click anywhere in the text in the first row of the table (the row with the title of the poem). Click the down arrow of the Styles menu and select any one of the structural formatting styles discussed previously.

2. Save the page and preview it in a browser.

3. Table cells can have properties as well. Click in the first row and then right-click. Select **Cell Properties**.

4. Note in the **Cell Properties** dialog box, the **Horizontal Alignment** is already set to **Centered**. This was done with the **Text Alignment** button, but could also have been done as a **Cell Property**. Click the down arrow for the **Background Color** property at the bottom of the dialog box. Select a color that is appealing but not too overpowering.

5. Click **OK**.

6. Save the page and preview it in a browser. The title should show in a colored cell.

SUMMARY

This chapter has covered a great deal of material. We opened a Web site and added text to a page. We manipulated the style of the text by using styles and changed the default type styles for the entire page. We created new pages and added text to them. We then hyperlinked the pages together, creating a basic navigation system. Finally, we put text on a page inside a table which forced the text to appear the same no matter what size the window or resolution of the computer.

Some principles of working with pages were also established. One is that the first page of a site is named either *default.htm* or *index.htm* and this is determined by the server administrator. Page filenames should not include spaces. They can include hyphens or underscores to make filenames easier to read (*page_one.htm*). For our Web pages the three letters at the end of the name will always be *htm*. Hyperlinks are used to move from page to page. We demonstrated how to create text links. Other types of hyperlinks will be discussed later. Finally, all elements on a page should be constrained inside a 600-pixel table to keep them from jumping around in different browsers and screen resolutions. A 600-pixel table width will display well on any computer in use today.

KEY TERMS

Firefox
Opera
Safari
IP address
domain names

Web servers
Linux
Microsoft Access
subweb
Microsoft Expression

common toolbar
task panes
document window
HTML
style tags
page title

sans-serif typefaces
hyperlink
resolution
cell padding
cell spacing

DISCUSSION QUESTION

1. In a practice Web site, create a three- or four-page Web with each page linked to all others. Add some basic text to the pages. Experiment with different color schemes for the page and text on the page. Preview the pages in a browser. Which page and text color scheme is the easiest to read? Do any of the color schemes suggest an emotional feel as you look at it? Why might it be a good thing to avoid some color schemes?

CHAPTER

4

PLANNING YOUR RESEARCH STUDY

LEARNING OBJECTIVES

- To understand how research questions are formulated

- To be able to differentiate between descriptive methods and experiments—determining which is best for your research question

- To understand databases by sifting through existing literature using journals and abstracts

- To be able to define the variables to be investigated in your study

- To learn the important role played by scales of measurement

- To understand physiological and psychological measures and types of data collection

- To understand the roles of reliability and validity

- To be able to control for extraneous variables

- To be able to discuss additional considerations pertinent to high-quality research designs

FORMULATING YOUR RESEARCH QUESTION

Research questions naturally come from a question, problem, or observation. Research is an exciting field because there are so many possibilities and uncharted territories to explore in understanding human behavior. We see and experience things that make us question events, behaviors, attitudes, and observations. We ask such questions as

■ What causes this?

■ What is the relationship between X and Y?

Many people believe that research is a mysterious and difficult process. For some people, coming up with a research problem or question is not a difficult thing to do. For others, this task can seem a bit daunting. Most students tell us they have difficulty coming up with a research idea mainly because their interests are so diverse. If developing a research question seems overwhelming to you, let your passion lead. Peruse books and consider research topics that interest you. Go to the library and research your topic, but keep an open mind and use critical thinking to question what the authors may have left out. Researchers cannot measure everything and, therefore, they often focus on a few primary variables of interest which they believe may predict or cause behaviors or events. The complexities associated with human behavior make it extremely difficult to narrow down your variables to one or two and expect them to provide the complete answer to a research question; every study has its limitations. Scholarly journals in the behavioral sciences realize this and require authors to address the limitations of their study within the discussion section of their article, and authors must also provide ideas for future research that speak to these limitations. This is often where other researchers can obtain great ideas for their own research, so look for gaps in the research you read. You should find yourself asking, "The authors studied X and Y, but why didn't they examine Z?" Capitalize on this idea by creating a research project that can address some of the gaps. Are you a people watcher? Then observe behavior. Throughout this process, when you have a fleeting thought or idea, write it down, come back to it later, and then research the topic.

The implementation of the research process and choosing a design is what makes research a creative and more difficult endeavor. Once you have developed a research question, write down potential answers to that question. This is part of the process of developing a research *hypothesis*, a statement that helps organize information and identify expected relationships between variables. All hypotheses should be testable. There are many options to choose from when planning your research study. The design you choose will ultimately influence how you measure and interpret your findings.

Descriptive Methods or Experiments: Which Is Best for Your Research Question?

Your research question should dictate the research design you use. Research methods typically fall into two categories: descriptive or experimental methods. Questions that ask "what" or "how" are typically associated with descriptive (correlational) designs. For instance, "What do people think about X?" or "How do people respond to Y?" **Descriptive methods** examine relationships between variables. For instance, one might ask, "What is the relationship between attitudes toward obesity and hiring decisions in professional organizations?" or "How do organizational layoffs affect family dynamics?" Descriptive research methods do not manipulate independent variables but rather examine naturally occurring relationships between variables of interest. These include case studies (intensive research on one person or one group of people), personal interviews, observations, archival research, and surveys. If your goal is to understand a relationship between variables or make predictions based on the relationships between variables then you will use a descriptive method.

Predictions are statements referring to the future. For instance, bankers need to predict who will default on a loan. To do so, they would find variables most likely to be related to loan default (for example, prior credit history, length of employment, and so forth) in order to make a valid prediction. A **correlation** exists when two variables vary together. When scores on one variable (prior credit history) vary with another variable (loan default), we say the variables are correlated (or related). Researchers could then make predictions based on the relationships found. **Correlational designs** do not manipulate variables but rather seek to describe behaviors or events as they occur naturally and identify relationships between variables. For instance, using surveys, we may find that a relationship exists between attitudes toward abortion and self-reported levels of religiosity. In this situation, we are measuring individual attitudes to determine whether relationships exist. Descriptive analyses typically include frequencies, percentages, and correlations that describe relationships between variables. However, more sophisticated statistics can also be used (such as hierarchal linear modeling, covariance structure modeling) to examine relationships between variables.

When the basis of your research question attempts to understand causality or address the "when" or "why" of an event, then an **experimental design** is the most appropriate research design. For instance, "Why does X happen?" or "When I change X, how does this affect Y?" You'll notice that in order to answer either of these questions, the researcher must manipulate (or change) the independent variable to determine its effect on the dependent variable. The goal of an experiment is to ultimately decide whether a treatment or program (a change in the independent variable) created a change in the dependent variable.

Descriptive statistics allow researchers to describe events and identify relationships between variables. Experiments allow researchers to make causal inferences.

The control that an experiment provides makes it distinctive from surveys. Experiments are typically conducted in a laboratory setting where the environment and conditions are constant for all participants. The greater the experimental control, the more causal inferences researchers can make about whether or not their manipulation caused a change in the dependent variable. For example, we might investigate whether placement of advertisements on computer Web sites affects product purchases. In this experiment, we would want to determine whether strategically placing an ad in the upper right-hand corner of a computer screen would lead people to be more likely to purchase a product than if the advertisement was placed on the lower left-hand corner of the computer screen. We would create our study by manipulating the placement of where the advertisement will appear. Then, we would randomly assign half of our sample to receive only one advertisement condition—the top right-hand corner. The other half of our sample would receive advertisements on the lower left-hand corner of the computer screen. We would then monitor the purchases of the product from the ad. In this case, manipulation of the placement (independent variable) of the advertisement would determine whether it had an effect on consumers' behavior (the number of products purchased—our independent variable). Once you have a general idea of whether your research problem explores relationships or cause-and-effect, you can begin to dig deeper into the process.

Collecting Literature to Help Formulate Your Research Question

Formulating a research question is just the beginning of the research process. You can approach the research process one of two ways. First, once have a research question in mind, you should find existing research on your chosen topic to determine whether your question has already been studied by others. Second, you should read through the extant literature and create ideas based on identifying gaps or heed suggestions for research made by scholars. Either route will bring you to the next step of immersing yourself in the existing research literature.

A good literature review includes primary resources of peer-reviewed scholarly research.

While reading through the literature, you must be objective and examine all studies in order to obtain a comprehensive picture of the extant research. Good researchers will examine research that supports *and* refutes their expectations. Now, before you run to the Internet for answers, STOP! Not all information provided online is necessarily true or reputable. In order to obtain the best resources that will serve as the basis of your research question, you need to understand the difference between primary and secondary resources.

Books and scholarly journals can be found in college or university libraries and databases. This is the best place to start your literature search. Before you begin reading, though, you should be able to distinguish between primary and secondary resources. When you are reading the actual research study conducted by the researchers you are reading a ***primary resource***, in which authors will explain everything they did. Authors will go into detail regarding the research methodology used, the sample, all independent and dependent variables, statistical analyses, and interpretation of the study findings. The discussion section of the research article will summarize the research in layperson's terms and provide a list of limitations and directions for future research. If you are reading a source that mentions or cites original research conducted by someone else, or simply describes the findings of another research study, this is referred to as a *secondary resource*. You will often find the television news citing results from a poll, or a television show or magazine article that exalts the latest diet. These are considered secondary resources. Other examples of secondary resources can include encyclopedias, books that summarize previous research, newspapers, and magazines. We recommend that you use primary resources as the basis for your research study, but secondary sources can also be useful.

Secondary resources can be particularly helpful during the initial exploration process. Books, media, and magazines can provide ideas for research or references and can lead you to primary resources. It is likely that your discipline has something similar to an encyclopedia or handbook of psychology, such as the *International Encyclopedia of Social and Behavioral Sciences,* or the *Handbook of Social Psychology.* Similarly, encyclopedias, handbooks, and databases can be found for criminology and sociology. These are great resources to help you begin gathering relevant information on your topic. These resources tend to include classic and contemporary research and, best of all, provide a reference list at the end that will point you in the direction of appropriate primary resources. Likewise, references from a recent journal article that you find extremely relevant may lead you to other articles and primary resources that will widen your search even more. Keep in mind, however, that even though encyclopedias and periodicals may be great resources to get you started formulating your research question, do not cite them as references. These are only guides to get you started. When you are ready to conduct your own research, you will ultimately need to rely on primary resources.

During your literature search, be aware of possible *databases* to explore for information. For the behavioral scientist, there are reputable abstract databases available in your discipline (psychology has PsyINFO or PsyLIT; sociology and education have ERIC social science abstracts; criminal justice abstracts). These databases include scientific peer-reviewed research articles that use a specified set of descriptors to describe the research. The words *peer-reviewed* suggest that manuscripts of research studies were sent out to experts in the field to review before they were published. Experts make comments or suggestions and ultimately recommend whether the research should be published.

Another way to make your literature search more effective is to look at an *abstract*, a summary of the research. In the abstract should be a list of *descriptors* or key terms that identify exactly how that database describes the topic. For instance, if you are looking for previous research conducted on gender differences in organizational hiring practices, then it's possible the database indexing differentiates between the usage of the terms "gender" and "sex" (during a search) so be sure to find out what your database calls your topic. Using descriptors (or the database's thesaurus) is a key strategy to obtaining a thorough literature review. *Wild cards* are symbols used in a database that can bring up various forms of a word. Always ask the librarian (or refer to the database's help section to find out) what wild card it uses, as each database may have a different wild card (for example, in PsyINFO, the wild card is an asterisk, but it may be !, %, or something else in another database). If you are looking to find all the literature on child abuse, then you may want to use a wild card like "child*" This will bring up words like *children*, *child's*, *childlike*, *childcare*, and so on.

In our experience, students search for relevant articles and often return with overwhelming stacks of articles they must go through only to find that the majority of articles they have printed are only tangentially related to their topic, and that just a select few are actually helpful to their research topic. Before you print out stacks of articles, thoroughly examine the abstracts to determine whether a study merits closer attention. Some databases offer articles in full text, but many databases provide only the abstract and require you to take action to find these articles in your library. For this, you will need to obtain a list of journals available in your library (usually found in the online database). If the article is not available in your library, consider using interlibrary loan, a sharing system that can provide copies of the articles you request, usually free or for a nominal charge.

The Internet can provide a great deal of information on your research topic, such as governmental, national, or regional statistics on crime, illness, violence, and more, but be careful and pay attention to whether the sources you are using are primary or secondary. Do not rely too much on Internet resources, primarily secondary sources, as they are not peer reviewed, and therefore are subject to bias and inaccuracies. For instance, if you want to explore the prevalence or incidence of depression, there are very effective Web sites available that provide useful information. In this regard, the Internet can be very helpful. The Internet can include scholarly research, but, for the most part, you are safer utilizing databases within your discipline that provide abstracts or full scholarly articles on the topic you've decided to explore.

How can your research question be tested?

What is your theory?

Refer to your literature review for suggestions.

Once you have reviewed the literature pertaining to your topic, you should have a better idea of how researchers design studies to test similar issues. How can your research question be tested? What is your theory? Your literature review most likely provided you with possible theories that best explain your research study.

HOW TO CREATE A CLEAR AND TESTABLE HYPOTHESIS

Have you developed a research question and do you have expectations with regard to how your question will be answered? Congratulations, you have developed a hypothesis! You might also have more than one research question and therefore more than one hypothesis. Be sure to write a hypothesis to correspond to each research question. You will not be able to study everything, so think about what some of the potential problems or limitations of your study might be. For example, how might the variables you have chosen limit your study? Ask yourself the following questions:

- Is my question worth pursuing?

- Will anyone be interested in knowing the answer to my question?

- Will the answer to my research question help my workplace or other organizations?

- Will my study be of interest to the scientific community?

- How will society benefit by knowing the answer to my research question?

Research is not complete until you have figured out how to test your hypothesis and determined possible theories that may apply to your research. Good research is always guided by theory. When researchers make predictions, they also take into account the expected direction of the relationship between variables. While conducting your literature review, pay attention to theories used by researchers. Theories offer logical explanations for relationships found among various events and behaviors that occur; for example, one theory might be that violence and hate crimes can often be attributed to prejudice in the form of homophobia, racism, sexism, and so on.

Defining the Variables to Be Used in Your Study

Your hypothesis must be testable. Therefore, it must also be defined. If it cannot be defined, then it cannot be measured. Say you developed a research question designed to investigate the relationship between personality style and an individual's work salary. As currently defined, the term "personality" is vague. How would you define personality? Constructs such as intelligence, motivation, and personality are abstract concepts developed by researchers and used in theories, so how can you really measure them? There are many personality inventories created by various researchers, but which one will you use? Each personality inventory may be a little different and measure different characteristics. You would need to assess various personality inventories to find one appropriate for your study; choose one that is easy to score and has good reliability and validity.

Now that you have chosen which personality inventory is most appropriate for your study you have created an operational definition of the term "personality." For example, you can define depression using the Beck Depression Inventory (Beck & Steer, 1987). You can define phobia by measuring someone's heart rate as they approach the object they fear. Results of the Wechsler Intelligence Test (Wechsler, 1997) can measure intelligence, and counting the number of times a child strikes or pushes another child could be defined as "childhood aggression."

Next is where research creativity comes in. How will you *measure* the variables in your research question? During your literature review, you probably noticed different studies that may have assessed the same idea (or construct) differently. It is up to you to choose which definition clearly captures the construct you intend to measure. If your research question examines the existence of gender differences in depression, then defining gender may seem easy, but defining depression may take a little more investigation. There are literally hundreds of surveys designed to measure depression. A good place to start looking would be in your library's reference holdings for books designed specifically as references for these measures. For instance, one popular reference book, *Mental Measurements Yearbook* (Buros, 2007), can serve as a great resource tool for finding existing surveys on various constructs. This resource also includes information related to scale composition and references and describes the instruments' validity and reliability. Another place to find surveys is within research articles. When researchers create their own surveys, they often publish the full survey within the text or appendix of the article, and this is another good way to find measures.

During your search for the right instrument to measure the construct you have in mind, it is imperative that you use measures that have established reliability and validity. Evidence of reliability (consistency) of a measure can typically be found in the methods section of an article describing the measure. Validity (meaning your instrument measures what it is intended to measure) is usually a little more difficult to determine by perusing a research article. It is important that you research the instruments you intend to use before committing to using one that may be untested, unreliable, or invalid. If you choose an instrument that does not measure what you intend to measure, what good is it?

Commonly used instruments measuring personality characteristics, depression, anxiety, sexism, racism, and other attitudinal variables are often easy to find. If you find a valid and reliable tool that measures the concepts you are interested in, you do not have to write your own questions or survey to assess that construct. It is possible, however, that there is no existing measure designed to capture the construct you want to measure. In this situation, you would need to create your own measure (for an excellent in-depth discussion of online survey development see Dillman, 2007). You are charting new territory, but you don't have to go it alone. Don't be afraid to use existing research or theory and build upon it. Whether using an existing measure or building your own measure, you need to consider the type of measurements available to you.

Types of Measurement to Consider When Planning Your Research Study

You will want to consider the type of measurement that is most appropriate when developing your experiment or survey. For instance, you might be interested in examining accuracy. *Accuracy* could be measured as success, hit-or-miss, or frequency of the number of items correct. Another possible dependent measure is something researchers call latency. *Latency* refers to reaction time, or the time it takes from the point the independent variable is introduced to the time it takes to react to the stimulus. Duration is another option to consider. *Duration* is the amount of time it takes to complete a response once it's begun. Finally, *frequency* is the number of times a response occurs.

Measuring the Effects of Caffeine on Driving Accuracy

For example, you may want to study the effects of caffeine on response time and driving accuracy. You hypothesize that individuals who drink caffeine before driving will take less time to respond to a red light and have more accurate driving skills than those without caffeine. You obtain a sample of individuals and randomly assign them to either a "coffee" condition (given two cups of coffee before proceeding) or a "no coffee" condition. Then you ask participants to play a video game that simulates driving. The participants' cars sit at a traffic light and they are asked to proceed when the light turns green. To measure latency, you could measure how long it takes individuals to respond once the light turns red. Driver accuracy could be determined by counting the number of mistakes (such as objects hit, lights missed, and so forth) made during the simulated driving task. The number of mistakes could also be a measure of frequency. Fewer mistakes suggest greater accuracy. Finally, duration could be measured by examining the amount of time it takes for the individuals' response time to return to normal (caffeine leaves the system).

So far, we have considered modalities that are somewhat cut-and-dried. However, there are variables (or constructs) that cannot be observed directly, such as intelligence, fear, depression, or motivation. As a researcher, one major question you must ask yourself is, Which construct best represents what I need to measure for my dependent variable?

There are psychological and physical measures that can be used to measure your variables. *Physical measures* are those that you can physically examine and that have an accepted standard for how things are measured (such as height, weight, time, and so on). For instance, you can investigate the amount of time a person spends on a computer.

Psychological measures are agreed-on or accepted standard ways to assess more abstract concepts such as personality, beauty, achievement, or intelligence. These measures are used when researchers agree that the measure adequately reflects the concept. For instance, if you have participants rate the attractiveness of an individual or assess achievement on a task, you would need to agree upon how attractiveness or achievement is defined and therefore measured. You will need to identify what you believe (or what previous research has found) best illustrates the concepts of attractiveness or achievement.

Data Collection Using Physiological and Psychological Measures

Physiological measures are useful particularly when you are interested in understanding the underlying manifestations of a construct. One can measure the time it takes to respond to a stimulus or examine the effectiveness of something like biofeedback, which is often used to decrease anxiety or pain. For instance, electrodes can be applied to the chest of a patient with a migraine headache to assess his or her heart rate. Once the patient reaches a reasonable heart rate, measurements of pain can be taken to determine whether biofeedback actually reduces pain. With the appropriate equipment, this technique offers accurate, precise, reliable measures that are not based on subjective interpretations from researchers. Unfortunately, such equipment can be expensive and difficult to obtain and the unnatural condition of having electrodes attached in a research setting may influence participants' responses and ultimately affect research findings.

Self-report measures are one of the modalities most often used in survey and experimental research and certainly one of the easiest ways to assess feelings, attitudes, and beliefs. If you were to measure the general population's fear of a terrorist attack, the best way to do this would be to simply ask people. You could ask individuals to rate their fear of future terrorist attacks in the United States by using an 11-point scale where $0 =$ "not at all fearful" to $10 =$ "extremely fearful." Similarly, you can do this with any construct—pain, depression, sexism, traditional sex roles, a couple's commitment to each other, and so forth. Measuring attitudes are also a way to assess abstract constructs such as sexism, racism, and beliefs about abortion rights. Some of the benefits associated with using self-report measures to measure attitudes are that they are very easy to use and one of the quickest ways to collect data. However, there are problems and limitations when using self-report measures.

One of the primary criticisms of self-report is that people can lie. Sometimes individuals are not truthful, saying what they believe the experimenter wants to hear, what is politically correct, or exaggerating. Some surveys are designed to assess just such a problem. They measure things such as lying or social desirability and are often used in clinical research, particularly to assess "malingering" (faking the symptoms of mental disorders) or lying in response to clinical assessment questions. Researchers should always remind participants to be truthful when answering questionnaires and reiterate that their responses will be kept confidential. Ideally, these instructions will reduce some of these problems, but you should be aware that there are always limitations inherent in self-report measures.

With self-report measures you need to consider the type of items (individual questions) and answers you would like to collect. Questions on surveys can be open-ended or closed-ended. *Closed-ended questions* are questions whose response formats are determined by the researcher, where participants are provided with a predetermined set of responses to choose from. Because closed-ended questions force participants to limit their answers to the predetermined responses, sometimes the options provided by the researcher do not accurately reflect the true opinion of the respondent. In this situation, an *open-ended question,* which allows participants to answer a question in their own words, would be more appropriate. This format provides a much wider range of responses and richer data.

There are advantages and disadvantages with both open-ended and closed-ended question formats. You should be aware of the potential differences in responses you will get based on the format used. Let's say that when you asked individuals to choose which topic they believed was the most important issue facing America today—education, abortion, pollution, or terrorism—you found that 35 percent of your respondents believed that terrorism was the most important issue. Now, you assess another group of people using an open-ended format. Participants are asked to write down the most important issue they believe faces America today. The variability of these responses will be much broader and it is extremely likely that substantially fewer people will identify terrorism as the most important issue facing our nation. There are additional advantages and disadvantages associated with open- and closed-ended questions that we will expand upon in Chapter Five, where we will provide more information on survey item development.

Behaviors are responses to stimuli that can be measured through direct observation of participants in various settings and situations that occur naturally. Behaviors can be assessed anywhere. Observation of behaviors can occur in natural or laboratory situations. For instance, we can examine any behavior (such as laughter, hand-holding, kissing, or aggression) in public settings. Studies can also be conducted that examine behaviors online or in the media. For instance, a study could examine videos on YouTube that exhibit dishonest behaviors. Experiments can be set up by researchers in order to assess behavioral responses.

Structured observations are situations set up by researchers that would not normally occur in everyday life. Researchers manipulate a situation in order to determine how individuals will respond. Structured observations can take place in a laboratory or in natural settings. For instance, researchers may want to evaluate parent-child interactions when a child is frustrated and has a temper tantrum. In a laboratory situation researchers could set up a situation that would frustrate a child in order to observe his or her level of aggression, the severity of the tantrum, and the parents' reactions.

Field experiments are experiments that take place in a natural environment. Because it is considered an experiment, researchers will manipulate one or more variables to determine the effect on the dependent variable. For instance, famous social psychologists Latane and Darley (1970) studied the bystander effect via experiments in which they pretended to be robbers in order to evaluate whether others would intervene. Comedy shows are known to set up unusual situations in order to evaluate an individual's response and make a joke out of it. Some things to keep in mind with regard to observing behavior include participants' reactions to being observed. At first, participants may react differently if they believe they are being watched. However, if researchers (or cameras) are there on a consistent basis, most people will become accustomed to the repeated exposure of the observers' presence.

Some behavioral observation research may not be applicable for Internet research until technology allows us to measure particular behaviors that can be observed while participants are online. This technology is available for many researchers, yet the general public (our sample) most likely would not have the equipment to enable them to be observed. Though it may be difficult to obtain behavioral observations using online research, there is a treasure trove of data at your fingertips online.

One way to measure behaviors can be by examining ***archival data***. Analysis of archival data (already existing sources of information) is a great research resource that includes records that are considered public record (for example, sports or crime statistics, tax and death records) or can be found in news or media (television, online, magazines, books, movies, and so on). Archival data can also be private documents of measures that have already occurred such as sales records from an organization, absenteeism or tardiness, student grades, club membership lists, listservs, and so forth. Residual records left behind or recorded can be used to assess behavior. This includes all books, documents (including government documents), national records of violence and incidence and prevalence of mental illness, and other media forms (including all public Internet activity, such as blogs, IMs, log-on history, site hits, and the like). You could examine crime statistics in relation to weather patterns or census records. Or you could examine the use of humor on gravestones or in newspaper obituaries or personal ads. The options are virtually endless.

In order to conduct an archival analysis, researchers must first identify what it is they are measuring. What is the dependent variable and how will it be defined? One of the first things you would need to do is to create categories for variables of interest and then investigate the presence or absence of those categories or the frequency of occurrence of them. For example, we know that major depressive disorder affects almost fifteen million Americans and that as many as one in eight adolescents suffers from clinical depression (Center for Mental Health Services, U.S. Department of Health and Human Services, 1996). You could study depression in adolescents using blogs (Internet journals) or Web pages, but how could you do this? First, it is likely you would have developed a hypothesis. Because women are twice as likely to experience depression, you could hypothesize that female adolescents will exhibit more depression than male adolescents. You would first have to determine the time frame within which to work, how you will define and find your sample, and how you will obtain a random sample of blogs within a particular time period. You will then have to define depression. Which words would suggest an individual is depressed? You could then examine the presence or absence of those keywords as well as noting the frequency of keywords. In essence, you would be conducting a content analysis of the Internet blogs. A content analysis is the research procedure that identifies specific content to be collected. As you review all of these blogs, you analyze the content of each and then enter the data respectively. You would first make sure that your categories and definitions to be measured are clear, agree on the frequency method, duration, or interval score to obtain the data, and use multiple raters to establish reliability (consistency among raters, in this case).

Researchers examining this phenomenon should be aware of issues such as observer bias and expectancy effects. ***Observer bias*** can happen because researchers have a hypothesis that can actually bias their attempts at data collection. If the researchers in the previous example predicted that female adolescents would experience more depression than male adolescents, this hypothesis can bias the researchers' interpretation of the data. In essence, their expectations that females will exhibit more depression could render them unable to see factors that don't support their hypothesis. In order to avoid observer bias it is best to train research assistants who are blind to (that is, unaware of) the study hypothesis to identify the keywords and variables of interest and the context in which they are to be obtained. You would then choose a random sample of blogs from which to train your assistants. Assistants would then compare notes to determine whether all investigators were coding the same material similarly. This is called interrater reliability. *Interrater reliability* is the extent to which two raters agree upon *what* they are rating. In other words, this reliability provides an estimate of the correlation of scores between raters. This can be calculated by dividing the number of opportunities to agree by the number of times agreed and multiplying the result by 100. Interrater reliability of .70 is considered technically acceptable, although researchers should aim for interrater reliability of .80 or higher (this is called the "80/20 Rule") (Landis & Koch, 1977).

Conducting research and expanding theories into natural environments strengthens external validity (or the extent that your research results can be generalized to other situations). With the advent of reality television, you can examine many behaviors simply by watching the individuals on the shows and noting what they do in different circumstances. However, just as with the Internet, much of what is shown on the reality shows (such as "Top Chef" on Bravo) may not actually be real (that is, some shows are criticized for scripting what happens). Issues of validity should also be considered.

THE ROLE OF RELIABILITY AND VALIDITY IN PLANNING YOUR RESEARCH

We addressed the importance of reliability between observers but you must also consider the reliability of the measures you choose (for example, behavioral, physiological, or psychological self-report measures). As we mentioned a bit earlier, *reliability* refers to the consistency of a measure across time and populations. For example, if you were to take the SATs one month and take them again the next month, the results should be similar (consistent). If you were to give a survey intended for college students to a group of ten-year-old children, would the results be the similar? Probably not.

There are various types of reliability. For self-report measures, there is test-retest reliability and scale reliability. *Test-retest reliability* involves administering a test, item, scale, or instrument two or more times to the same individuals or administering the test to different populations. If scores on the tests are consistent (correlated to one another), the measure is said to have good test-retest reliability. *Scale reliability*, or *Cronbach's alpha reliability,* examines the relationships between items on a scale of a self-report

When planning your research study, examine existing measures for information pertaining to their reliability and validity.

measure. (For a more in-depth explanation see Cronbach, 1951.) A scale can be comprised of two or more items that are designed to measure a construct. For example, if you have five items designed to measure a construct called "content knowledge," then scale reliability will assesses the extent to which the five items are correlated. As with interrater reliability, a reliability of .70 or higher is considered acceptable for both test-retest and scale reliability measures (Cronbach, 1951; Nunnally & Bernstein, 1994).

Reliability is dependent upon the number of participants in your sample as well as the number of items you are correlating. It is also dependent upon the situation in which the testing occurs. For example, if one group of participants takes your survey in a laboratory environment with minimal distraction and moderated temperature and sound, then we can assume this is a good testing environment. However, if another group of participants takes the survey in a building that is under construction with many sound and temperature distractions, performance can certainly differ from one group to another. Therefore, it is very important to keep the environment constant in order to eliminate possible error or distraction.

A test's validity is also important. ***Construct validity*** pertains to the extent to which the measure truly captures the theoretical construct it is designed to measure. Studies examining depression and anxiety are often subject to scrutiny because both disorders have overlapping symptoms. Some authors argue that studies examining depression are actually examining anxiety and vice versa. If you found a measure designed to assess anxiety and a measure intended to assess depression, you could give both to your participants. If the two measures were very highly correlated, this would suggest that you were actually measuring the same concept (depression or anxiety); each would be indistinguishable from the other. When there are two different surveys designed to measure similar constructs that are highly correlated, we say the measures have high ***convergent validity***, which is the extent to which two measures are similar or converge. If this were to occur, you could find or construct a new anxiety measure that would not correlate too highly with depression. ***Divergent validity*** represents the extent to which two measures differ. Once you created your new anxiety measure, you could compare it with the old ones and hope that this time your measures are divergent. (If they were moderately or only mildly correlated, then you could say you obtained divergent validity.)

External validity refers to the extent to which the results of your study can be generalized to different situations or populations. When laboratory study results can be generalized outside of the lab, they are considered to have external validity. Many researchers conduct research on jury decision making. Laboratory experiments are often well-controlled and noted for their high internal validity but can lack external validity. Often, individuals are used as mock jurors to examine defendant blame in various crimes. Because researchers don't have access to real jurors, they use written scenarios depicting a crime or a video reenactment. The results found in those studies may not necessarily align to real juror environments and decision-making scenarios; these experiments have limited external validity. Furthermore, because of time, space, and financial constraints, few such studies use the same deliberation processes used in real cases. Even if research findings are found to be reliable across laboratory experiments, courts are skeptical of such research because of its lack of external validity. Studies can increase external validity by replicating research conducted in the laboratory in the real world. If results found in the laboratory can be replicated with different populations and real-world situations, we can then say the research findings have strong external validity.

Researchers must take caution to control for possible outside influences that could affect the results of their study. Therefore, experiments conducted in laboratories typically have highly controlled environments because researchers want to know whether the variable they manipulate led to the outcome. Experimenters are careful to control for alternative explanations that might affect the study's outcome. When a study has high *internal validity,* we can be more confident that the outcome of the study was due to the variable that was manipulated and not some alternative explanation.

Controlling for Extraneous Variables to Ensure a Quality Research Design

We mentioned the importance of limiting distractions that could affect participants when taking your survey. These distractions can cause the results of your study to change (that is, differences you find between the groups might be caused by the treatment *or* the environment). *Extraneous variables* are situations or unintended events that can affect the outcome of your study. While planning your study and developing hypotheses, you should always consider alternative explanations for your findings. Some extraneous variables can be controlled either statistically or by the experimenter; others cannot.

Experimenters cannot control for all possible problems or errors, but they can promote a study that controls for as many extraneous variables as possible. Experimenters should seek to provide a research environment free of distractions where all groups or conditions are treated equally (with the exception of the independent variable). This way, researchers can say it was the treatment (or manipulated independent variable) that caused the change in the dependent variable and not some other alternative explanation. Procedures for all studies should be the same for all participants. Even an experimenter's mood can affect the way participants perceive you and your study.

With online research, we cannot control the environment in which participants take the study. Some individuals may be in a relaxed and quiet environment while others are in a loud and hurried environment. Individual computers work differently. Some are faster

When planning a research study, consider all possible explanations that can influence your research findings. In order to control for extraneous variables, try to measure important variables that can influence your study and be sure to address all other potential confounds and limitations.

than others. Some online survey pages take longer to load and can frustrate partici-pants. Individual monitors can cause changes in the way the pages are loaded onto the computer and pages may not look the way the researcher intended. Our book will teach you how to eliminate or minimize these problems, but with online research there are additional areas where we lack control. Self-reports are based on human honesty. Just as some individuals misrepresent themselves on paper-and-pencil surveys, some individuals online may not represent themselves honestly both in their attitudes or demographic composition. Other potential errors associated with self-report are the general ability of participants to retrieve information from memory as well as the abil-ity to interpret the meaning of the question. Unfortunately, researchers conducting research online are limited in their ability to identify some of these problems. However, safeguards can be implemented to provide open-ended responses for participants to provide feedback or pose questions pertaining to their interpretation of the question.

Finally, if you think ahead when planning your study and measure potential alter-native explanations for the outcome of your study, you can then statistically control for extraneous variables. Many studies attempt to identify predictors of student achieve-ment in school. Socioeconomic status (SES) plays a significant role in student achievement, but it is also difficult to tease out the effects of biological and environ-mental influences. In an effort to examine this, researchers (Johnson, McGue, & Iacono, 2007) examined predictors of achievement in a sample of 614 adolescents from biological and adoptive families. Johnson et al. examined gender, parenting style, parental expectations of education, intelligence, genetics, and shared environmental influences. After statistically controlling for gender, parenting style, parental expecta-tions of education, and intelligence, they found SES continued to play a small but sig-nificant role in student academic achievement.

The more alternative explanations you can account for before you conduct your study, the more you can prepare for and actually study them. Many (but most likely not all) of the alternative explanations for your research findings can be examined if questions are added into your study to measure them. Researchers can examine the role of each of these variables statistically and how they affect research findings. Statistical programs allow us to control for effects such as SES or parent education. For example, if you do find a negative relationship between student achievement and teacher-student ratio, you can examine the role of the extraneous variables to deter-mine their effect on the original hypothesized correlation, thus controlling for extrane-ous variables.

ADDITIONAL CONSIDERATIONS FOR EXPERIMENTAL DESIGNS

The hallmarks of a good experiment are variable manipulation and experimental control. Experimenters manipulate an independent variable and investigate the effect that the manipulation had on the dependent variable by holding all other conditions constant. This is called *experimental control*. For instance, if researchers want to determine whether a new computer keyboard can facilitate faster typing, then researchers can manipulate only the computer keyboard. All other information remains the same (or constant).

Careful, systematic control to eliminate alternative explanations for research results is an essential component of the scientific method. A *control group*, a group of participants in an experiment that serves as a comparison for other groups (Graziano & Raulin, 2004), is always necessary in order to provide researchers with a basis for comparison. For example, if researchers develop a new drug they believe will cure cancer, they would have to compare the new drug with "existing therapies" or "no therapy" conditions. If experimenters find the new drug worked as well as existing therapies, then it did not work as well as they expected. If the new drug worked better than "no therapy" and "existing therapies," then they know the drug worked as expected. Without comparison groups, experimenters would not know whether the drug was effective. In experiments, manipulation of the independent variables is used as a control technique because it plays a key role in determining the time-order relationship necessary to make causal inferences. If researchers know the only difference between experimental groups is the variable being manipulated, they can assume the majority of alternative explanations have been ruled out as an explanation for the results and what is left is largely due to the variable manipulation.

Every participant comes into a study with his own biases and individual differences that can affect study outcomes. Let's say you were to examine whether problem solving is related to positive reinforcement in college students. We hypothesize that college students will be faster and more accurate when provided with encouragement. In one experimental group, the independent variable can be manipulated by offering encouragement and reinforcing students by telling them what a great job they are doing. In the other experimental group (control group), no reinforcement or encouragement is provided. In this situation, you would need to assume intelligence is related to problem solving, it is therefore important that participant groups be as equally balanced as possible. For this reason, experimenters randomly assign participants to an experimental condition (encouragement or no encouragement). The use of random assignment ensures that groups will be similar before the experimental treatment is administered. Therefore any changes in the dependent variable (time and accuracy of problem solving) can be attributed to the independent variable (encouragement or no encouragement).

When conducting experiments online, you have less experimental control over your environment. However, you can randomly assign participants to groups to ensure individual differences are balanced (see Chapter Ten for a more in-depth discussion of random assignment and balancing individual differences in experimental designs). Part of the process of planning your research study for an experiment includes considering how random groups will be established and how participants will be randomly assigned to conditions of your experiment.

SUMMARY

This chapter was intended to walk you through the first stages of the research process. When planning a research study you must first have a research question that is testable. Research methods tend to fall into two categories: descriptive or experimental. The goal of descriptive research is to simply describe what exists and ultimately attempt to predict behavior. Correlations describe how two variables are related. Surveys and naturalistic observations are typically associated with descriptive research. Experiments seek to make causal inferences. The goal of an experiment is to determine whether a treatment (independent variable) caused a change in the dependent variable. Researchers must have a clear idea of their independent and dependent variables when planning their study.

A literature review is essential to help solidify a research question. Be careful to obtain and reference primary resources (peer-reviewed scholarly journals) for information that will be helpful to you in formulating a research hypothesis and corresponding theory. Hypotheses can be constructed when there are clear operational definitions ascribed to all variables of interest. When trying to determine an appropriate operational definition for your variables, consider the types of measurement that can be used to conduct your study.

During the planning stage, you should realize that there are many ways to measure human behavior. One might examine accuracy, latency, duration, or frequency of behaviors. Your research question might be answered by assessing physical dimensions.

Whereas behaviors can be measured in a natural or structured environments, psychological measures are obtained via self-reports. Self-reports are most commonly used in surveys and experiments. Self-report measures can have items that are closed-ended or open-ended. Closed-ended questions are used most often in surveys because they are easy to analyze and interpret. Open-ended questions offer greater flexibility for researchers and participants but take longer to analyze and interpret. Archival data offer a source of information that researchers should consider when trying to find answers to their research questions. If archival data are considered, a content analysis can be conducted, but researchers should be aware of potential observer bias and take precautions to avoid this bias by hiring assistants who are blind to the research hypothesis.

Research reliability and validity are extremely important when planning your research study. Always use measures that have evidence of good reliability and validity, and be sure to consider whether the measure you choose will be appropriate based on the sample you intend to use. When planning your study, it is important to think of all the possible alternative explanations that could lead to your research results. As you plan, you should try to control for extraneous variables that can affect the outcome of your study. The more you control for extraneous variables, the greater the internal validity of your study. The more easily the results of a study can be generalized to different situations and populations, the greater its external validity.

Finally, remember that participants come into research studies with their own biases and individual differences, and these differences can affect study outcomes. Understanding the role of random assignment and random group designs can help balance these individual differences.

KEY TERMS

descriptive methods
correlational designs
experimental design
physical measures
primary resources
secondary resources
databases
abstract
descriptors
Behaviors
archival data
field experiments
reliability
convergent validity
divergent validity
test-retest reliability
predictions
peer-reviewed
control group

closed-ended question
accuracy
latency
duration
frequency
psychological measures
physiological measures
self-report measures
wild card
observer bias
interrater reliability
correlation
external validity
extraneous variables
scale reliability
construct validity
Cronbach's alpha reliability
experimental control
open-ended question

DISCUSSION QUESTIONS

1. What is the purpose of a research hypothesis and why is the research design you choose so important?

2. Define, compare, and contrast descriptive research methods and experimental research methods. How do the goals of each method differ?

3. Distinguish between the following types of measurement: accuracy, latency, duration, frequency.

4. Compare and contrast physical, physiological, behavioral, and psychological data collection techniques and consider which of these measures would be best to answer your research question.

5. Why are reliability and validity so important to researchers? Why are they important to your own research study?

CHAPTER

CREATING A SIMPLE SURVEY ON THE INTERNET

LEARNING OBJECTIVES

- To be able to understand the structure and flow of surveys
- To be able to design the form used for simple survey construction
- To be able to add form controls to capture user input
- To be able to define the importance of previewing the survey for completeness
- To be able to create variables that will hold participant answers to each question
- To be able to create a database to hold the data submitted
- To be able to connect the form to a database
- To learn the steps necessary to test the survey to make sure that it works as expected

In this chapter, we will be creating a satisfaction survey for a mythical health care facility, Fictitious Medical Center. We will assume you are employed by the center and your project is to collect data on patient satisfaction with the cleanliness of the center and helpfulness of the custodial staff. You will not be collecting any information about the patients' satisfaction with health services, costs, and so on, nor will you be collecting any personal identification information, thus there is no need to worry about protecting confidentiality. You have decided to create an Internet survey to accomplish this.

PLANNING THE SURVEY

An Internet survey is not just a single page on a Web server; it is a system of pages that work together to achieve a purpose. The first step in creating a survey is to understand the user's experience and the flow of information in the site; therefore, before we can create the survey, we must construct a plan. The *survey plan* or map should show all of the elements of the survey and should take into consideration all of the respondents' possible answers at each point in the survey. It should also show the sequence of pages that the respondent will see based on what they answer. The plan can be as simple as a pencil drawing or it can be done with flowchart software. Figure 5.1 was created with *Visio 2007*, a drawing and flowchart software package, but this sophistication is not necessary to create a usable map. A survey map should include page filenames, page titles, and a short description of the purpose of the page. It should also show the user's input and how an answer takes the user from one page to the next. With a completed survey plan, you can easily create the elements of the site structure (see Figure 5.1).

Internet surveys are not just one single page on a Web server, but are made up of a system of pages that work together to create the survey.

As Figure 5.1 indicates, the respondent enters the survey site from the *consent page*. As the name implies, the consent page lays out the purpose of the survey, the uses of the data, how the respondent's privacy will be protected, and any technical considerations (such as browser compatibility, settings, and so forth) that are required to successfully complete the survey.

Refer to Chapter Two to review key elements of a consent form.

At the end of the consent form are two links: **I Agree** and **I Disagree**. The **I Agree** link indicates that the user agrees to the terms of the survey and wants to begin. The **I Disagree** link indicates that the user does not agree and does not wish to complete the survey. Clicking the **I Disagree** link will bring the respondent to a *no thank you page*, which thanks them for their time and consideration in visiting the site and reading the consent form and provides alternate means for the respondent to contact the survey sponsor (e-mail, surface mail, phone number, and so on).

Clicking the **I Agree** link takes the user to the survey. The respondent sees a form with questions and various input devices to record opinions and satisfaction level and

FIGURE 5.1 *Survey Site Map*

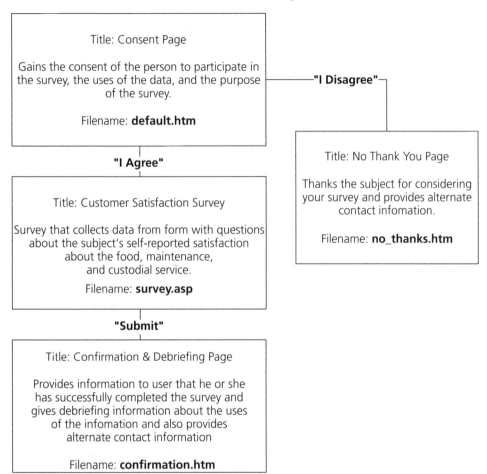

Customer Satisfaction Survey Flowchart

Title: Consent Page

Gains the consent of the person to participate in the survey, the uses of the data, and the purpose of the survey.

Filename: **default.htm**

"I Disagree"

"I Agree"

Title: Customer Satisfaction Survey

Survey that collects data from form with questions about the subject's self-reported satisfaction about the food, maintenance, and custodial service.

Filename: **survey.asp**

Title: No Thank You Page

Thanks the subject for considering your survey and provides alternate contact infomation.

Filename: **no_thanks.htm**

"Submit"

Title: Confirmation & Debriefing Page

Provides information to user that he or she has successfully completed the survey and gives debriefing information about the uses of the infomation and also provides alternate contact information

Filename: **confirmation.htm**

provide comments about the services. At the bottom of the survey, there is a *Submit button* that will trigger the processing of the information to the Web server. After clicking the **Submit** button, the user is brought to a confirmation page. The *confirmation page* indicates that he or she has completed the survey and the results have been processed at the server. The confirmation page thanks the respondents for their time, reiterates what will be done with the data, and provides alternative ways to reach the researcher with feedback. On some surveys, there may also be a debriefing statement that further discusses the intent of the research and outlines what the research is attempting to prove. At this point, the survey is over and the respondent can close the browser or go elsewhere on the Internet.

EXERCISE 5.1. Creating the Survey Site

Using the site map shown in Figure 5.1, you can now construct the survey structure.

1. Using Internet Explorer, navigate to the *chapter05* Web site. Open the site in Expression by clicking **File > Edit with Microsoft Expression Web**.

2. Expression should open the page *default.htm.* If not, create a new page by clicking **File > New**. On the page tab, select **General** and **HTML** and click **OK**.

3. On this page, create a table with the specifications as outlined in Chapter Three by clicking **Table > Insert Table**. Use the specifications: 3 rows, 1 column, and center alignment. Specify text box width as 600 px and select the **Pixel Option** button, set **Cell Padding** to 0 (zero), **Cell Spacing** to 0, **Border** to 1, with the color **red**, and check **set as default** for new tables.

4. Click **OK**.

5. Click in the first row of the table and type **Consent Form**. Select the text.

6. On the style drop-down list on the **Common Toolbar**, click the down arrow and select the style **Heading1 <H1>**.

7. Click at the end of the word *Form* and hit the Tab key. This moves the cursor to the second row. Type **Text for consent form goes here**.

8. Move your answer to the end of the text and hit the Tab key. This moves the cursor to the third row of the table.

9. Hit the Tab key once more to add a fourth row.

10. Click in the third row of the table.

Always have one additional row in tables!

The cursor is now located in the third row of the table, but you have added a fourth row. This is an important habit to get into because it makes working with tables much easier. At all times, you want to have at least one additional row in the table. This blank row provides a way to select the table without changing any of the content of the table.

EXERCISE 5.2. Splitting a Table Row into Columns

1. The cursor should be inside the third row of the table. Right-click and from the fly-out menu select **Modify > Split Cells**.

2. We want to divide this cell into two columns. In the split cell dialog box, make sure that **Into columns** is selected and the number of columns is 2.

3. Click **OK**.

Having two columns divides the row into cells and allows each cell to have different formatting. In this case, we want the alignment formatting to be different.

EXERCISE 5.3. Creating Agree and Disagree Links

1. In the first cell of the third row type **I Agree**.

2. Hit the Tab key to move to the second cell. Type **I Disagree**.

3. With the cursor in the *I Disagree* text, use the **Alignment** buttons on the **Common Toolbar** to align this text to the right in the cell. The layout of the page is shown in Figure 5.2.

4. Click in the *I Agree* text and apply the **Heading2 <H2>** style to the text. Repeat with the *I Disagree* text.

5. Click the **Save** icon. If the page was newly created, the page has not been saved and the **Save As . . .** dialog displays. In the filename text box at the bottom, make sure that it says *default.htm* or *index.htm* as appropriate for your server. Remember that this is the filename for the first page that displays in a Web site.

6. In the dialog box, below the filename box is a text box with the page title. Click the **Change title . . .** button and, in the resulting dialog box, type **Consent Form**.

7. Click **Save** to save the page.

8. Preview this page in a browser by clicking **File > Preview in a Browser > Windows Internet Explorer**. Verify that the page looks like Figure 5.2.

Next, we will create a page for the actual survey. Up to this point, all pages have been HTML pages. The survey is a dynamic page that accepts input from the user and, when the **Submit** button is clicked, sends the input back to the server for processing. The page we will use for this is an active server page. *Active server page* or *ASP* is a technology that has the built-in functions needed for easily creating and processing a survey. Active server pages use the extension *asp* at the end of the filename.

EXERCISE 5.4. Creating an Active Server Page

1. Select **File > New** on the **Page** tab, select **General** and in the second column, select **HTML**.

2. Click **OK**.

FIGURE 5.2 *Consent Page in Process*

3. Click the **Save** button on the **Common Toolbar**. In the **Filename** box type **survey.asp**. You will need to type both the filename and extension in the filename box.

4. Click the **Change title . . .** button and type **Survey** in the **Set Page Title** dialog box.

5. Click **OK** and then **Save**.

6. Click the page and insert a standard table (**Table > Insert table**). Specifications for this table are as discussed previously. Make sure that the horizontal alignment is set to **Center**.

7. In the first row of the table, type **Customer Satisfaction Survey**.

8. Center the text in the cell and apply a style of your choice.

9. Save the page.

 ## EXERCISE 5.5. Creating No Thank You and Confirmation Pages

1. Create a new HTML page with **File > New**. On the **Page** tab select **General**, and then from the second column, select **HTML**.

2. Create a standard table centered on the page and, in the first row, type **No Thank You**. In the second row type **The text for the no thank you page goes here**.

3. Apply the same styles used in the survey page created above.

4. Click after the text in the second row of the table. Hit the Tab key twice to add additional rows to the table.

5. Save the page by clicking the **Save** icon. The filename should be *no_thank_you.htm* and the page title should be *No Thank You.*

6. Create another HTML page with a standard table centered on the page.

7. In the first cell, type **Confirmation Page**. Center and apply the same style as on the page above.

8. In the second row, type **The text of the confirmation page goes here**. Hit the Tab key twice to add additional rows to the table.

9. Save the page as *confirmation_page.htm* with an appropriate page title.

10. Preview all four pages in a browser.

The pages should show in the browser as basic pages without much content. The next task is to link the pages together to create the flow that respondents will experience as they complete the survey.

 ## EXERCISE 5.6. Linking Pages with Hyperlinks

1. Close all browser windows. In Expression, save and close all pages.

2. Open the *Consent* page with the filename *default.htm* or *index.htm.*

3. Select the text *I Agree.* With the text selected, click the **Insert Hyperlink** button or click the **Insert** > **Hyperlink** from the menu.

4. From the dialog box, select the page *survey.asp.* Click **OK**.

5. Select the text *I Disagree.* Click the **Insert Hyperlink** button.

6. From the dialog box, select the page *no_thank_you.htm.* Click **OK**.

There is one more link to be made (between the survey and the confirmation page), but it is not a true hyperlink. It is activated only when the survey's **Submit** button is clicked. This link will be created after the survey is built.

7. Save all the pages and preview them in the browser. Test all of the links to verify that they work.

Adding Content to the Pages

Most people use Microsoft Word to write. It is a powerful and flexible word processing tool. When creating survey questions, scenarios, text, and the like, use Word or whatever tool you are most comfortable with. The text can then be brought into Expression and added to a Web page. However, when writing in Word or another word processor, avoid using extensive formatting in the text. It is better to create plain text and then apply formatting in Expression. Word can be used to make Web pages, but sometimes it does this in nonstandard ways that are not compatible with non-Microsoft browsers; Microsoft Expression does not do this. Also, if the formatting is added in Expression it is much easier to maintain a consistent look and style to the survey Web site. Though it is tempting to add formats in Word, resist the temptation. For Web pages, Expression is a much better tool.

You can write content in any word processor you feel comfortable with but be careful not to use extensive formatting throughout the text.

EXERCISE 5.7. **Adding Text to the Consent Page**

1. In the files that came with this text, locate the file *c5_consent_text.doc.* Open the file in Word or another word processor.

2. Select all of the text and copy it.

3. In Expression, open the *default.htm* page by double-clicking it in the folder list.

4. Select the text in the second row, *The text of the consent form goes here.* Delete it.

5. Paste the text copied from the document into the table cell. The text should have the formatting from the Word document.

6. Select all of the text just added to the page and click **Format** > **Remove Formatting**. The text should now show on the page without any formatting and be in the typeface

Times. If not in Times, you may need to select the text and change the font to Times New Roman.

7. Save the page and preview it in a browser.

EXERCISE 5.8.   Adding Text to the Confirmation and No Thank You Pages

1. In the files that came with this text, locate the file *c5_confirmation.doc.* Open the file in Word or another word processor.

2. Select all of the text and copy it.

3. Open the *Confirmation Page (confirmation_page.htm)* in Expression by double-clicking it in the folder list.

4. In the second row of the table is the text, *The text of the confirmation page goes here.* Select this text and delete it.

5. Paste the text copied from the document into the table cell. Select this text and remove the formatting. Sometimes the alignment of the table will go back to left aligned. To change the alignment of the table back to centered, right-click in the table and choose **Table Properties** > **Alignment** > **Centered**.

6. Save the page and preview it in a browser.

7. In the exercise files locate the file *c5_no_thank_you.doc.* Open the file.

8. Select all of the text and copy it.

9. Open the *No Thank You Page* (*no_thank_you.htm*) in Expression by double-clicking it in the folder list.

10. In the second row of the table is the text, *The text of the no thank you page goes here.* Select all of this text and delete it.

11. Paste the text copied from the document into the table cell. Select this text and remove the formatting. If needed, change the alignment of the table back to centered by right clicking in the table and select **Table Properties** > **Alignment** > **Centered**.

12. Save the page and preview it in a browser.

CONSTRUCTING THE SURVEY

The structure of the survey site is now complete, but there is no content. This section will introduce a methodology for creating a survey that will keep it well formatted in a browser. The survey questions and input devices will be added to the survey and a database will be created to hold the results of the survey.

In previous exercises, tables were used to contain text on a page. A standard 600-pixel table centered on the page was used to hold all text. Tables can also hold other types of objects. In this section we will use another table inside the main table to hold the question text and input devices.

EXERCISE 5.9. Adding the First Question to the Survey

1. In Expression, open the *survey.asp* page. The page should have a title at the top and three rows in the table.

2. In the files that accompany the text, locate the file *c5_survey_questions.doc.* Open the document with Microsoft Word or some other word processor and select all of the text in the document.

3. Copy the text and switch back to Expression.

4. Click at the bottom of the page below and *outside* of the table. Hit Enter twice.

5. Important Note: Paste the text on the page at this location using *only* the following procedure: **Edit** > **Paste Text** > **Select Normal Paragraphs with Line Breaks**. Click **OK**. This places the text at the bottom of the page with minimal formatting. We will use this area as a scratch pad, cutting text from the bottom and moving it into the survey table.

6. From the bottom of the page select the text beginning with the word *Instructions* through *Thank you again for your input.* Cut the text from that location and paste it into the second row of the table.

7. Hit the Tab key to move the cursor to the third row. Hit Tab again. This is to add one more row to the table. Remember that we always want an extra row in the table as we work with it.

8. Click inside the third row of the table. This is the location for the first question of the survey. Each question and answering device will be placed in a nested table inside the larger 600-pixel table. This will allow us to easily manipulate the formatting and location of the question in the survey. For this survey, most questions will have a 5-point answer scale and one additional choice to indicate that the question does not apply.

9. As shown in Figure 5.3, create a table in row three of the outer table. To add the table, choose **Table** > **Insert Table.** Set the specifications to 3 rows, 6 columns, 100% width, and red border color. Click **OK**. The bright border color is used to emphasize the boundaries of the question table. It will not show in the final survey.

10. At this point, there is a larger outer table on the page and another three-row table inside the third row of the outer table. This inner table will be called the *question table.* Click in the first row of the question table.

11. The first row of the question table is where we will enter the question. The row is divided into six cells, but it should be only a single cell. Use your mouse to select all of the cells in the first row by dragging through them. Merge these cells into one by selecting **Table** > **Modify** > **Merge Cells**.

FIGURE 5.3 *Table Definition Dialog*

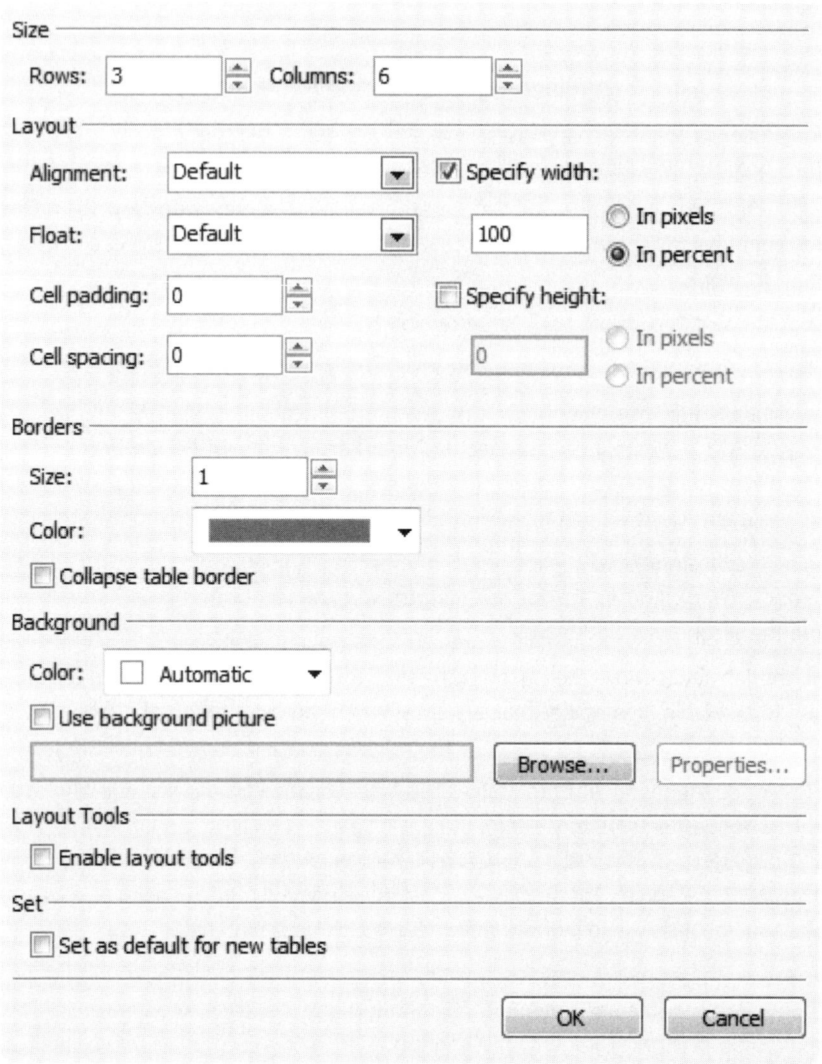

Size

Rows: 3   Columns: 6

Layout

Alignment: Default   ☑ Specify width:

Float: Default   100   ○ In pixels
⦿ In percent

Cell padding: 0   ☐ Specify height:

Cell spacing: 0   0   ○ In pixels
○ In percent

Borders

Size: 1

Color: ▼

☐ Collapse table border

Background

Color: ☐ Automatic ▼

☐ Use background picture

  Browse...   Properties...

Layout Tools

☐ Enable layout tools

Set

☐ Set as default for new tables

OK   Cancel

12. In the first row of the question table, type **1.** and cut the text of the first question from the bottom of the page. Paste the text into the first row of the question table.

Now we will add the answering device. We will use a 5-point scale from *Very Satisfied* to *Very Dissatisfied* and include one additional choice for *Not Applicable.*

13. Hit tab once to go to the second row of the question table. Type **Very Satisfied**. Tab to the next cell. Type **Satisfied**. Tab to the next cell and type **Neutral**. Continue with this procedure typing **Dissatisfied**, **Very Dissatisfied**, and **Not Applicable** in each cell.

The answering device for this question will be radio buttons. ***Radio buttons*** are round and come in sets and have a restrictive property that allows only one of the buttons to be selected at a time. This forces the respondent to answer with only one choice to this question; they cannot be both "satisfied" and "dissatisfied" with an aspect of the service.

14. Tab to the third row of the question table. As you can see in Figure 5.4, in the upper right corner of the Expression window is a task pane. It has the title ***Toolbox.*** In the toolbox are several headings. Locate the HTML heading. Click the plus (+) sign on the left to expand this section of controls. The form control devices that we will use to build the survey will display. Locate the round circle with a dot in it labeled **Input (Radio)**.

15. Left-click this input device and drag it onto the question table in the first cell of the third row. Repeat with the remaining five cells.

16. Save the page and preview it in a browser.

At this point your survey should look like Figure 5.5.

17. The question table needs some formatting attention. Select all the cells in the second and third rows. Click the **Centering** button on the **Common Toolbar**.

18. The cells of these two rows should be equal widths. To change the width of these cells, select the two rows and click **Table** > **Modify** > **Distribute Columns Evenly.**

Three of the cells have two words in them (*Very Satisfied, Very Dissatisfied,* and *Not Applicable*). These two-word answers can distort the spacing. To remedy this, you will have to add a soft return between the two words. A ***soft return*** forces the text onto two lines but doesn't add the extra space between paragraphs associated with a normal return.

19. Click immediately after the *y* in *Very Satisfied.* Hit the Delete key to remove the space and hold the Shift key down while hitting the Enter key. This Shift-Enter combination adds the soft return.

FIGURE 5.4 *Survey in Expression with Form Control Toolbox*

FIGURE 5.5 *Survey in Browser After First Question*

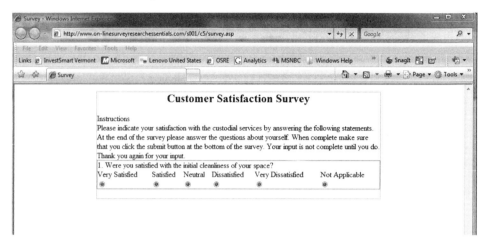

20. Repeat this with the other two-word text labels.

21. Save the page and preview it in a browser.

Though you have only one question done, most of the work on the satisfaction questions in the survey is done. In the next exercise, you will add additional questions and answer devices.

As a formatting rule you should skip a row between questions. This gives the respondent a visual cue about where a question ends and the next begins. Thus, the next question will go in the fifth row of the outer table. You could create the question table and answers from scratch as above. However, once it has been done it is a great deal easier to copy a question table and modify the text for the new question.

 EXERCISE 5.10. **Adding Additional Questions to the Survey**

1. Click in the fourth row of the outer table. Hit Tab twice to add two additional rows.

2. Click anywhere in the question table for the first question. Select the table by clicking **Table > Select > Table**.

3. Copy the table (**Edit > Copy**).

4. Click in the fifth row of the outer table and paste the question table into the outer table.

5. Select the entire question text in the second question table and delete the text.

6. Type **2** in the first row of the second question table.

7. Select the text for question two from the bottom of the page. Cut it from this location and paste it into the question area of the second question table.

8. Modify the text in the response area of question two. Change *Satisfied* to **Courteously** and *Dissatisfied* to **Discourteously**.

9. Save the page and preview it in a browser. At this point your survey should look like Figure 5.6.

10. Click in the last cell of the outer table. Hit Tab twice to add two new rows.

11. The answers to the third question are *Very Satisfied* to *Very Dissatisfied,* so we'll use question table one as the basis for this question. Copy the first question table and paste it in the second-to-last blank row of the outer table.

12. As before, delete the question text, add the next number, and cut and paste the third question text into this question table.

13. Continue until all of the satisfaction questions have been added to the survey.

14. Save the page and preview it in a browser. The survey should now look like Figure 5.7.

EXERCISE 5.11. **Using Other Types of Input Devices: A Text Box**

Question five asks respondents to elaborate on their answer. It asks the open-ended question, *Please explain briefly,* which requires a different input control to capture the input. We will use a text box for this.

1. In question five of the survey, click after the last radio button in the question table. Add another row to the question table with the Tab key.

2. Select all of the cells in the newly added row and merge them together (**Table > Modify > Merge Cells**) to create a single row in the table.

FIGURE 5.6 *Survey in Browser After Second Question*

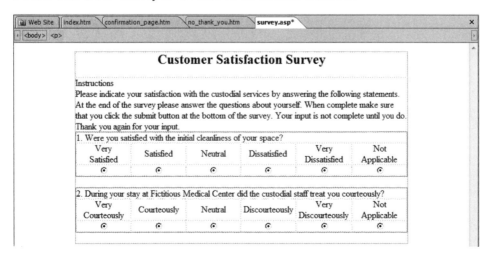

FIGURE 5.7 *Survey in Browser After All Likert Questions*

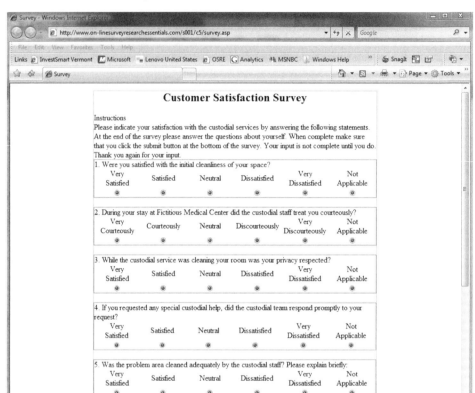

Remember that a text box can hold only 255 characters but text areas can have more than 255 characters.

3. Select the text *Please explain briefly*: and cut it from the question five text.

4. Paste the text into the row created in steps 1 and 2 above. Change the alignment for this cell to the left, click after the colon in the text, and type a space.

5. In the **Form Controls** toolbox, locate the **Input (Text)** control. Drag this out into the survey and drop it after the elaboration question text.

A text box allows the respondent to type anything and have it recorded in the database. A text box, however, is only for short text inputs. The box can hold a maximum of 255 characters. If it is likely that more text will be entered, then a ***text area box*** should be used. Text areas can hold more than 255 characters. An example of a text area will be used later in the survey.

EXERCISE 5.12. **Using Other Form Controls: Checkboxes**

1. The next question deals with the areas of the hospital that patients visited during their stay. There are six possible locations. Add two additional rows to the outer table of the survey. Click in the second-to-last row and create a question table with these properties: 4 rows, 2 columns, 100% width, and a red border.

2. Select the cells in the first row. Merge the cells together.

3. Add the next number and copy the question text from the bottom of the survey into the first row of the question table.

4. From the **Form Control** panel of the toolbox drag an **Input (Checkbox Box)** into the first cell of the second row of the question table. Type a space after the checkbox and copy the text *Medical/Surgical* after the first checkbox.

5. Continue with the remaining five options, adding a checkbox in front of each.

6. When done, select the three answer rows and distribute the columns evenly as before.

7. Save the page and preview it in a browser.

EXERCISE 5.13. **Additional Option Buttons**

1. Click in the last row of the outer table and add two additional rows using the Tab key.

2. Click in the second-to-last row and add a table inside the cell. The specifications for the table should be 1 row, 6 columns, 100% width, and the red border color.

3. Type the next question number and cut the question text *Gender* from the bottom of the page. Paste it into the first cell of the questions table.

4. The answer to the *Gender* question is limited to either female or male. The correct form control is a radio button. Tab to the next cell and drag a radio button into the cell. Type a space and then type the word **Female**.

5. Tab to the next cell. Drag a radio button control into the cell. Type a space and then type the word **Male**.

6. To improve the look of this question table, select all of the cells in this table and distribute them evenly.

7. Save the page and preview it in a browser. The page should look like the image in Figure 5.8.

The *Gender* question was placed in a table that had six columns, though the question had only two possible responses (female or male). This was done to keep the questions and answers looking uniform on the page. If only two cells had been used they would have been too widely spaced.

FIGURE 5.8 *Survey in Browser After All Questions*

Customer Satisfaction Survey

Instructions
Please indicate your satisfaction with the custodial services by answering the following statements. At the end of the survey please answer the questions about yourself. When complete make sure that you click the submit button at the bottom of the survey. Your input is not complete until you do. Thank you again for your input.

1. Were you satisfied with the initial cleanliness of your space?

Very Satisfied	Satisfied	Neutral	Dissatisfied	Very Dissatisfied	Not Applicable
◉	◉	◉	◉	◉	◉

2. During your stay at Fictitious Medical Center did the custodial staff treat you courteously?

Very Courteously	Courteously	Neutral	Discourteously	Very Discourteously	Not Applicable
◉	◉	◉	◉	◉	◉

3. While the custodial service was cleaning your room was your privacy respected?

Very Satisfied	Satisfied	Neutral	Dissatisfied	Very Dissatisfied	Not Applicable
◉	◉	◉	◉	◉	◉

4. If you requested any special custodial help, did the custodial team respond promptly to your request?

Very Satisfied	Satisfied	Neutral	Dissatisfied	Very Dissatisfied	Not Applicable
◉	◉	◉	◉	◉	◉

5. Was the problem area cleaned adequately by the custodial staff?

Very Satisfied	Satisfied	Neutral	Dissatisfied	Very Dissatisfied	Not Applicable
◉	◉	◉	◉	◉	◉

Please explain briefly: _____

6. Which areas of the hospital did you visit for any reason during your stay? (Check all that you visited)

☐ Medical/Surgical floor   ☐ Physical Therapy
☐ Maternity   ☐ Respiratory Therapy
☐ Pharmacy   ☐ X-Ray

7. Gender   ◉ Female   ◉ Male

EXERCISE 5.14. Using Other Form Controls: Drop-Down Box

1. Click in the last cell of the outer table and add two additional rows at the end of the table.

2. Select the second-to-last row and insert a question table with these specifications: 1 row, 1 column, 100% width, and red border color. Click **OK**.

3. Add the next question number, a space, and then cut the next question text, *Age Range,* from the bottom of the page. Move your cursor back into the question table and paste the text into the cell.

4. Click after the text and type a space.

This question deals with the age of the respondent. One option for this question would be a text box where the respondent would just type her or his age, but there are problems with this approach. First, does your research require that you have the exact age? A text box can hold anything—text, numbers, punctuation, and so on. If a twenty-two-year-old subject enters "twenty-two," is that information correct? It is, but the researcher will likely have to convert the resulting data to numbers prior to any analysis.

A way to collect just numbers is to use a drop-down box with possible ages from 17 to 85, for example. While this would be tedious to implement, the value that is stored in the database (a number) will be easy to use. Another way to implement this question is to use *age ranges*. A hypothesis might be that older people are more likely to voice dissatisfaction with custodial services. In this case, you would predefine age ranges and the respondent would have to select the range that includes her or his age. We will see the age ranges: *under 25, 26 to 45, 46 to 65,* and *66 and older.* The ranges should be inclusive, covering all possible ages. They should also be mutually exclusive (that is, a person should be allowed in one and only one category). The age ranges are what are of interest, but the value that is stored in the database can be anything. For this question we will use *1* for *under 25, 2* for *26 to 45,* and so on. To capture these age ranges, the survey will use a drop-down list box.

5. From the **Form Controls** Toolbox, drag a **Drop-Down Box** control onto the form and drop it after the question text. You will add the response choices to the control later in the chapter.

6. The list box does not look very good on the page. The bottom of the question text aligns with the bottom of the drop-down box, and it looks odd. A better design would be to have the drop-down box under the question text. To do this, click after the word *Range* but before the drop-down box and hit Enter.

7. Save the page and preview it in a browser.

The next question deals with the length of the person's stay at the facility. We will use four answer categories for this variable: *outpatient* (less than a day), *1–2 days, 3–6 days,* and *more than 6 days.* To collect this information we could use another drop-down box, but this can introduce a bias. The user must click the down arrow to see all the answers unless the drop-down height is such that they can all be seen. If only one or two choices can be seen without clicking the down arrow then they will be selected more frequently. Or the user may not realize that only one choice can be selected at a time, as a drop-down list can also be set up to allow for multiple selections. A different way to handle questions like this is to provide the choices in a list with radio buttons.

EXERCISE 5.15. Another Way to Present Categorical Answers

1. Add two additional rows to the outer table and, in the second-to-last row, insert a question table with these specifications: 5 rows, 1 column, 100% width, and the red border color. Select and cut the next question text, add the next question number to the cell, and paste the question text after the number.

2. Drag an **Input (Radio)** into the second row of this question table. Cut the first answer from the text below and paste it in the second row after the radio button.

3. Continue adding **Input (Radio)** buttons and cutting and pasting the answer text into the next three rows.

4. Save the page and preview it in a browser.

The next question in the survey is an open-ended question for the respondent to add any additional comments. These present the researcher with some analysis challenges because the answers do not fit neatly into categories. However, they are commonly used and an essential device in a satisfaction survey. To capture this data, a control that allows for input of any length is required. We will use a **text area** box. A text area can hold any amount of user input and will store it in the database when the **Submit** button is clicked.

EXERCISE 5.16. Using Other Form Controls: Text Areas

1. Click in the last row of the outer table and add two additional rows to the table. Click in the second-to last-cell and add an answer table with the specifications 2 rows, 1 column, 100% width, and red border color.

2. Type the next question number, a period, and a space in the first row of the question table. Cut the question text from the bottom of the page and paste it into the first cell of the question table.

3. From the **Form Controls** toolbox, drag a **Text Area** control and drop it in the second row of the answer table.

4. Save the page and preview it in a browser.

All of the questions have been entered on the page with controls to capture the respondent's input. There are two additional form controls that must be added to complete the survey. First, there must be a button at the bottom of the survey to trigger submitting the results to the server. And, second, a form control is needed to contain the entire survey.

EXERCISE 5.17. Adding the Submit Button and Creating the Form

1. Before completing this section of the survey, it is necessary to check the settings for Expression. In the Expression menu, click **View** > **Visual Aids**. From the fly-out menu make sure that **Show Block Selection**, **Visible Borders**, and **Empty Containers** are all selected (they will have an orange block to the left of the label).

2. Click in the last row of the survey and add two additional rows at the bottom of the outer table.

3. Drag an **Input (Submit)** button from the **Form Controls** toolbox and drop it into the second to last row of the outer table.

4. Double-click the button. In the dialog box, delete the contents of the name field and type **submit** in its place. In the **Value/Label** field, select the contents and replace it with **Click here to submit your responses**.

5. Verify that **Submit** is selected for the button type and click **OK**.

6. Save the page.

7. Click in the last cell of the outer table. Select the entire outer table by selecting **Table** > **Select** > **Table**.

8. Cut the table from the page by selecting **Edit** > **Cut**.

9. If in the quick select area there is a <**p**> tag, hold the mouse over it in the quick select are, click the down arrow and select **Remove Tag**. From the **Form Controls** toolbox, drag a **Form** control onto the page. The cursor should be inside the form on the page. Paste the survey table into the form by selecting **Edit** > **Paste**.

10. Save the page and preview it in a browser. The page will look like Figure 5.9.

The survey questions are now inside a form on the page. The form defines the boundaries of what will be processed by the server when a respondent submits the survey. Only input devices that are inside the form will be processed and saved. There should be only one form on a page and all parts of the survey should be inside that form.

At this point, the survey is established in terms of the layout, look, and flow of the questions. It won't actually work yet, but this is a good time to get feedback from your audience(s) on how it looks, the content, question wording, question order, and so forth. If this is an academic project, the okay of your advisor should also be secured. After all the constituent audiences give

Don't forget that this is the point at which you should obtain feedback on your survey from others to determine the ease of use and general understanding of the questions and question order.

FIGURE 5.9 *Completed Survey in Browser*

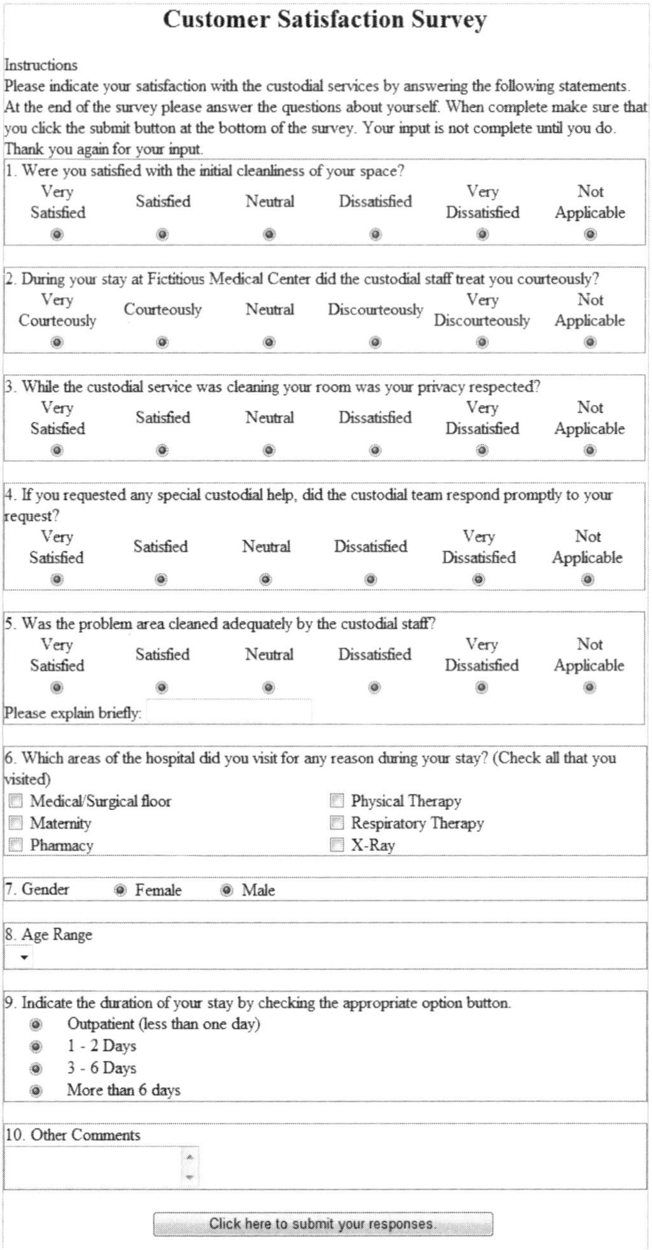

Customer Satisfaction Survey

Instructions

Please indicate your satisfaction with the custodial services by answering the following statements. At the end of the survey please answer the questions about yourself. When complete make sure that you click the submit button at the bottom of the survey. Your input is not complete until you do. Thank you again for your input.

1. Were you satisfied with the initial cleanliness of your space?

Very Satisfied	Satisfied	Neutral	Dissatisfied	Very Dissatisfied	Not Applicable
⊙	⊙	⊙	⊙	⊙	⊙

2. During your stay at Fictitious Medical Center did the custodial staff treat you courteously?

Very Courteously	Courteously	Neutral	Discourteously	Very Discourteously	Not Applicable
⊙	⊙	⊙	⊙	⊙	⊙

3. While the custodial service was cleaning your room was your privacy respected?

Very Satisfied	Satisfied	Neutral	Dissatisfied	Very Dissatisfied	Not Applicable
⊙	⊙	⊙	⊙	⊙	⊙

4. If you requested any special custodial help, did the custodial team respond promptly to your request?

Very Satisfied	Satisfied	Neutral	Dissatisfied	Very Dissatisfied	Not Applicable
⊙	⊙	⊙	⊙	⊙	⊙

5. Was the problem area cleaned adequately by the custodial staff?

Very Satisfied	Satisfied	Neutral	Dissatisfied	Very Dissatisfied	Not Applicable
⊙	⊙	⊙	⊙	⊙	⊙

Please explain briefly: [_____]

6. Which areas of the hospital did you visit for any reason during your stay? (Check all that you visited)

☐ Medical/Surgical floor   ☐ Physical Therapy
☐ Maternity   ☐ Respiratory Therapy
☐ Pharmacy   ☐ X-Ray

7. Gender   ⊙ Female   ⊙ Male

8. Age Range
[▼]

9. Indicate the duration of your stay by checking the appropriate option button.
⊙ Outpatient (less than one day)
⊙ 1 - 2 Days
⊙ 3 - 6 Days
⊙ More than 6 days

10. Other Comments
[_____]

[Click here to submit your responses.]

you feedback, rewording and reordering questions is easily done. To reorder questions, select the question table for the question, cut it from its present location, add additional rows to the outer table if necessary, and paste the question box into the new location.

DESIGNING AND CREATING THE DATABASE AND CONNECTING IT TO THE ONLINE SURVEY

The survey is now designed. All the pages of the site have been created and hyper-linked together according to the survey plan. Potential audience members have reviewed the content, question wording, order, and flow. Their feedback has been incorporated into the survey. All is ready to go, except that the survey is not yet ready to collect data. There are a number of back-end tasks that must be completed before the survey is truly ready to go. The tasks are called ***back-end*** because they do not directly affect the respondent but are essential to the functionality of the survey. First, variables need to be defined for each question and codes need to be established for each potential response. Processing must be set up to send the survey data back to the Web server and a database must be created to hold the data. The confirmation page must be linked to the submission of the form. The survey must be tested extensively to make sure that all questions are correctly coded and everything works as expected. And, finally, the survey must be polished to make it look presentable. The borders of the question and survey tables must be turned off to make the survey look finished, alignment of text must be standardized, and so on. Though much of the work of creating the survey form is done, there is still a great deal to do!

When a person completes the survey and clicks the **Submit** button, the results are sent to the server and stored in a database. The easiest way to think of a ***database*** is as a table. A table consists of rows and columns. In a database, each row is a single respondent's responses to the survey. Each column in the table is a variable which will store the input from a specific question in the survey. The survey collects data using form control elements. Each question has at least one control. The control elements are the way that a respondent will set values for each variable in the database. Actually creating the database is easy; Expression can create an Access database at the click of a button. However, the variables must first be specified for each question so that Expression knows what names to give to each of the columns in the database.

The following exercise is designed to activate a completed form of the survey. If you have worked through the entire chapter and are confident that you have done things correctly, you can skip this exercise. If you had trouble or did not finish creating the survey, then work through this exercise to have a completed version of the survey site for the next exercises.

EXERCISE 5.18. Getting Ready to Create Variables for Survey Questions

1. In the folder list for Chapter Five locate the folder titled *chapter5a.* Right-click the folder and select **Convert to Web**.

2. When the conversion is done, double-click the *chapter5a* folder in the folder list. The *chapter5a* Web will open in a new Expression window. This shows the site in Chapter Five after the first part of the exercise is completed.

3. Double-click the *survey.asp* page to open it.

Question 1 asks about the respondent's satisfaction with the custodial services. The answers are collected with a 5-point scale with choices from *Very Satisfied* to *Very Dissatisfied* and a sixth option for *Not Applicable.* Under each answer is an **Option** button. For this question, we want the respondent to click one and only one of the buttons in answer to the question. When a button is clicked, a value associated with the choice will be selected. When the data are submitted to the server, the value for that question will be saved in the database. Thus, each answer must have a code associated with it. The coding for these answers will be a *5* for *Very Satisfied, 4* for *Satisfied, 3* for *Neutral,* and so on, through *9* for *Not Applicable.*

Note that a variable name cannot have any spaces in it.

A variable is created when a form control object is *named*. There are specific rules for naming each variable. It is essential that these rules be followed to ensure that the survey works correctly. A variable name cannot have any spaces in it. The name must begin with a letter, but it can also contain numbers. The underscore or hyphen can be used to make the names easier to read (for example, *q1_elaborate*), but no other punctuation is allowed. To make it easier to understand the results, the variable name should be descriptive of the question. In most surveys after the question order is set the variables can be named *q1, q2,* and so on. Where further elaboration is needed the name should describe the purpose of the question, for example *q5_explain.* As a stylistic convention, the variable names should all be lowercase. Finally, each variable name must be unique. There can be only one *q1* in the survey and database.

Radio buttons are special control objects. They come in groups and have the property that only one may be selected at a time. When we create variables for radio buttons, there will be two pieces of information that are required. First, we must specify a group name. This will be the variable in the database. Second, we must specify the value for that choice. This is the value that will be stored in the database.

EXERCISE 5.19. Creating Variables for Survey Questions

1. In question 1 of the survey, double-click the radio button for **Very Satisfied**.

2. In the group name box type **q1**.

3. Tab to the Value box and type **5**.

4. We do not want to bias the respondent to a specific answer, so none of the radio buttons will be selected at first. Verify that **Not Selected** is set for the Initial State.

5. Leave the tab order box blank and click **OK**. The dialog box is shown in Figure 5.10.

6. Double-click the radio button for **Satisfied**. Repeat the steps above for the second choice. Since this response is still for the first question, the group name will still be *q1,* and the value *4.* Continue defining the remaining choices for question 1 with the appropriate values. The **Not Applicable** choice is a possible answer to question 1 and should have the value of *9.*

7. When all of the options have been coded for the first question, save the page and preview it in a browser.

8. Go back to the survey and repeat all of the steps for questions 2 through 5, using the same coding scheme. The most positive response will get *5,* next most positive will be *4,* and so forth, and *Not Applicable* will be a *9.*

9. Question 5 asks for elaboration on the answer. A text box has been added to this question to capture the elaboration.

10. Double-click the text box.

11. Text boxes hold text and get a single variable name. Each variable name must be unique. This text box elaborates the answer for question 5. So, in the **Text Box Properties** dialog box, delete the contents of the Name field and type **q5_explain**.

12. Tab to the **Width in characters** box. This property controls the width of the text displayed on the screen. Enter **65** for the width. Note that the amount of text that can be stored in the text box is not affected by the setting of *65,* only the amount of text that can be *seen* in the text box.

FIGURE 5.10 *Option Button Dialog Box for Question 1*

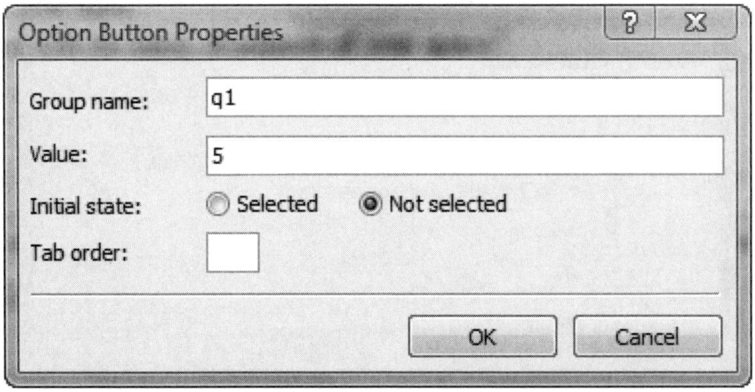

13. Verify that **No** is selected for **Password** field and click **OK**.

Question 6 deals with where the patients visited during their stay. The hypothesis is that people who see more of the facility are more likely to be dissatisfied with the cleanliness of the facility. There are six areas in the facility that are under investigation: medical/surgical, physical therapy, maternity, respiratory therapy, pharmacy, and x-ray. A patient could visit one, two, three, or all of these locations. Because any combination could be checked, a checkbox for each choice will be used. A checkbox can be checked or not and each choice is independent of the others (meaning any combination, all, or none of the boxes can be checked). Thus, a separate variable name is required for each checkbox.

14. Double-click the first checkbox in this question.

15. The first option in the dialog is **Name**. In this box, type the name **q6_med_surg**. The value is the data that will be stored in the database. We don't need to store the exact name of the floor, only a code that indicates it was a visited floor. When a floor is checked we will store the value 1. If it was not checked, it will remain blank. Type the number **1** for the value. Verify that **Not checked** is selected and the tab order is blank and click **OK**. The settings for the first checkbox properties are shown in Figure 5.11.

16. Continue on with the rest of the options for question 6. Name the checkboxes: **q6_pt**, **q6_maternity**, **q6_respiratory**, **q6_pharmacy**, and **q6_xray**. The value for each is 1.

17. Question 7 asks about *gender.* There are only two choices: *Female* and *Male.* Double-click the first radio button. Name the group **q7**. The value for this choice will be stored as **Female**. Click **Not Selected** for the initial state. Click **OK**.

18. Double-click the second radio button. The group name is *q7* and the value is *Male.* Click **Not Selected** for the initial state. Click **OK**.

FIGURE 5.11 *Checkbox Dialog Box for Question 6*

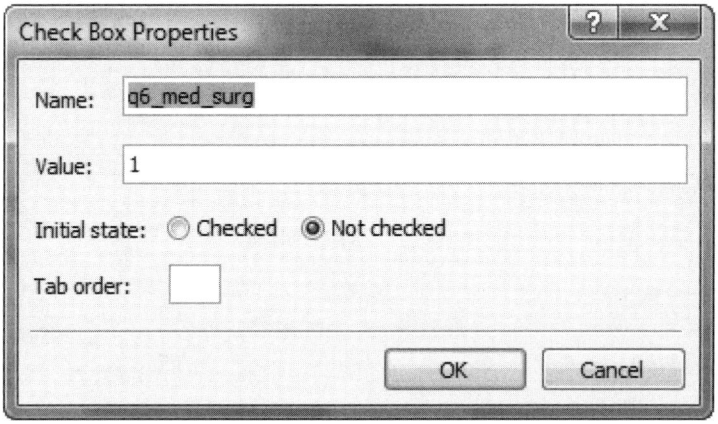

19. The next question deals with age and uses a drop-down list. A drop-down list must be named and the choices that show in the list must be specified. The question concerns the age of the respondent; age ranges will be specified. To add the ranges to the list, double-click the drop-down list. At the top of the dialog box, in the name box, delete what is in the box and type **q8**.

20. In the center of the dialog is the list area. Select the top line in the list and click the **Modify** button on the right of the dialog box. The **Modify Choice** dialog will open. At the top is the **Choice** box. This is the value that will show in the list when the respondent clicks the down arrow. Type **Under 25** in this box. The next line is a checkbox to specify the value. If it is not checked, the control will store the value in the **Choice** box. If checked then the researcher can store another value. Check the box and then, in the next line, type **1**. Verify that the **Not Selected** option is selected in the **Initial State** area and click **OK**. The first choice is added to the list.

21. Click the **Add** button and create the choice **26–45**. Store the value 2 for this range and verify that **Not Selected** is the state.

22. Continue, storing the **46–65** range as 3 and **66 and older** as 4. During the definition process, if you need to reorder the choices, select a line and use the **Move Up** and **Move Down** buttons as required to reorder the list.

23. The **Height** setting of the drop-down box refers to the number of lines in the text box that will be visible without clicking the down arrow. Drop-down lists are handy for questions with a great many answer choices. For example, if you ask respondents to input their home state, you'll need at least fifty possible responses (or more if you include Washington, D.C., Guam, and so on. You would not want all fifty responses to show without clicking the down arrow. However, the question at hand has only four possible responses. To show some, but not all of these would bias the results towards the choices shown. To remove this bias, the drop-down box should show all four choices. Type **4** in the **Height** box, verify that **Tab order** is blank, and **allow multiple selections** should say **No**, and click **OK**. The settings for this properties box are shown in Figure 5.12.

24. Save the page and preview it in a browser.

25. The next question uses a series of radio buttons. Double-click the first radio button and name it **q9**. The value of the first choice will be 1 and it should not be selected. Click **OK**.

26. Continue defining each choice for this question and using values of 2 through 4 for the remaining choices. None of the radio buttons should be selected.

27. Double-click the comments box at the bottom of the survey. The name for this control should be **q10**. The width of the control should be **65 characters** and the **Number of lines** that show on the screen should be 3. Click **OK**.

28. Save the page and preview it in a browser. At this point the survey should look like Figure 5.13.

FIGURE 5.12 *Drop-Down List Dialog for Question 8*

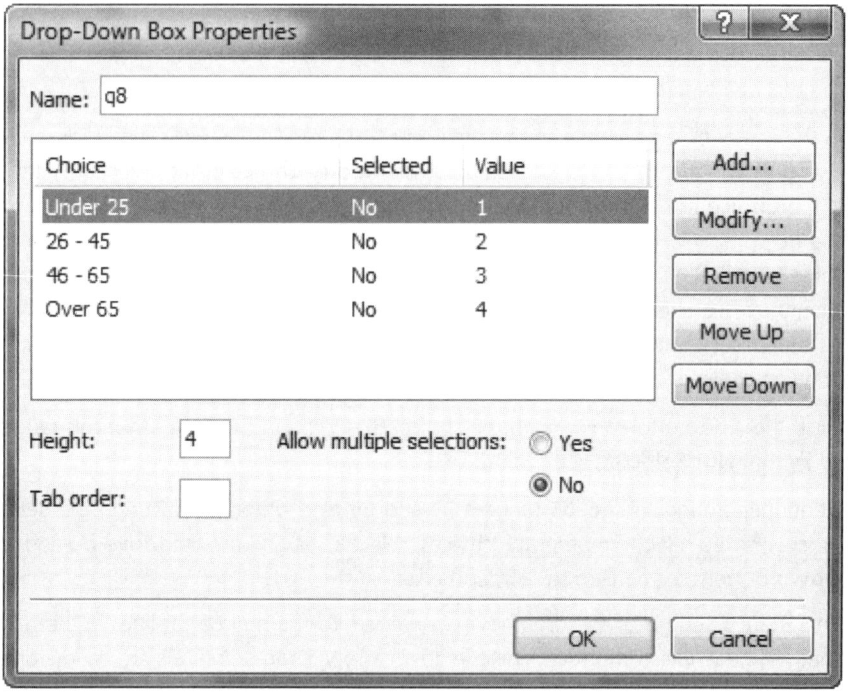

SPECIFYING THE SURVEY PROCESSING

All of the variables and coding values have been defined and specified in the survey and the survey looks good. The next step is to specify the processing that will be used when the survey is submitted. There are several options. All of the options are triggered when the **Submit** button is clicked. One option is to have the data e-mailed to the researcher. This is a good choice if the researcher only expects a few responses and the questions are not personal or controversial. The problem is that e-mailing is not a secure process. Any personal information in the survey could potentially be seen as it moves over the Internet. Another problem is that the researcher's e-mail account may not accept the e-mail. The researcher must ensure that *spam blockers* and *firewalls* are not refusing the submissions. Finally, the e-mail approach requires special setup on the Web server. Though not difficult, it does need to be done to allow e-mail submissions.

E-mail is not a good solution if there will be a great many respondents because the data are submitted in a form which is not easy to analyze. It must be copied from the e-mail and, for example, pasted into a spreadsheet to be further analyzed.

Another processing option is to have the submissions appended to a Web page on the Web server. Each submission becomes a new row on the Web page. This approach has many of the same limitations as e-mail submission. Unless special care is taken,

FIGURE 5.13   *Survey After Coding Completed*

Customer Satisfaction Survey

Instructions
Please indicate your satisfaction with the custodial services by answering the following statements. At the end of the survey please answer the questions about yourself. When complete make sure that you click the submit button at the bottom of the survey. Your input is not complete until you do. Thank you again for your input.

1. Were you satisfied with the initial cleanliness of your space?

Very Satisfied	Satisfied	Neutral	Dissatisfied	Very Dissatisfied	Not Applicable
⊚	⊚	⊚	⊚	⊚	⊚

2. During your stay at Fictitious Medical Center did the custodial staff treat you courteously?

Very Courteously	Courteously	Neutral	Discourteously	Very Discourteously	Not Applicable
⊚	⊚	⊚	⊚	⊚	⊚

3. While the custodial service was cleaning your room was your privacy respected?

Very Satisfied	Satisfied	Neutral	Dissatisfied	Very Dissatisfied	Not Applicable
⊚	⊚	⊚	⊚	⊚	⊚

4. If you requested any special custodial help, did the custodial team respond promptly to your request?

Very Satisfied	Satisfied	Neutral	Dissatisfied	Very Dissatisfied	Not Applicable
⊚	⊚	⊚	⊚	⊚	⊚

5. Was the problem area cleaned adequately by the custodial staff?

Very Satisfied	Satisfied	Neutral	Dissatisfied	Very Dissatisfied	Not Applicable
⊚	⊚	⊚	⊚	⊚	⊚

Please explain briefly:

6. Which areas of the hospital did you visit for any reason during your stay? (Check all that you visited)

☐ Medical/Surgical floor	☐ Physical Therapy
☐ Maternity	☐ Respiratory Therapy
☐ Pharmacy	☐ X-Ray

7. Gender   ⊚ Female   ⊚ Male

8. Age Range

Under 25
26 - 45
46 - 65
Over 65

9. Indicate the duration of your stay by checking the appropriate option button.
   - ⊚ Outpatient (less than one day)
   - ⊚ 1 - 2 Days
   - ⊚ 3 - 6 Days
   - ⊚ More than 6 days

10. Other Comments

Click here to submit your responses.

the page is not secure. Access to the Web page must be limited to the researcher. And it requires the same extra step to get the data into an analyzable form.

The best way to process most survey results is to save them in a database on the server. The database that we will use is Microsoft Access, which is easy to use and widely available. It is an excellent tool for the majority of surveys. The best reason for using Access is that Expression can create and locate the database on the Web server automatically. There are, however, two limitations to consider. First, Access has a storage limit of one gigabyte of data. This represents thousands of respondents, so in most cases this is not a real limitation. However, for very large surveys, this would be a problem. Second, Access can only accept approximately ten simultaneous connections at one time. After ten, the performance of the database degrades considerably. If the survey you are creating is likely to have a great deal of traffic, then a more powerful database would be required. In this case, talk with your Web server administrator and find out what options are available.

EXERCISE 5.20. Specifying the Survey Processing Method

1. The processing method is a property of the survey form. Right-click anywhere in the survey and select **Form Properties** from the menu. The dialog box for form properties is shown in Figure 5.14.

2. In the **Form Properties** dialog box are three options: **Send to a file or e-mail address**, **Send the results to a database**, or **Other**. The database option is what we will use exclusively. Select this option and then in the lower left corner of the dialog box, click the **Options** button.

3. As you can see in Figure 5.15, at this point no database exists and so we must create one. Click the button **Create database . . .** Expression will create a folder titled *fpdb* in the folder list to hold the Access database, a file (*global.asa*), which contains the information the survey needs to connect to the database, and of course the database itself. When you see the dialog that says all of this was done successfully, click **OK**.

4. Before proceeding, note the name of the connection that was created and the name of the table where the results will be stored. In Figure 5.16, the connection is *survey* and the table is *Results.* Near the bottom of the dialog box is a box to specify the URL of the confirmation page. You will need to type the name into this box directly. If you click **Browse** it will only show pages with the extension *asp.* Because the confirmation page is an HTML page, it will not show. Type **confirmation_page.htm** in this box.

5. Click **OK** twice.

6. Save the page and preview it in a browser.

Testing the Survey

The coding is now done and the survey is ready to collect data. To test that everything works as expected, you need to take the survey with a Web browser. However, this testing should be systematic and should verify that all of the coding is correct and

FIGURE 5.14 *Form Properties Dialog Step 1*

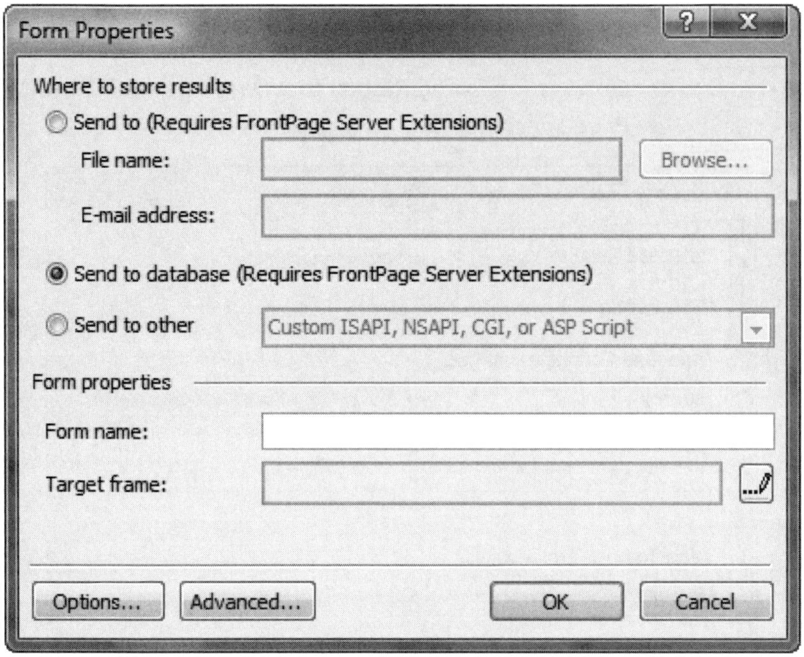

FIGURE 5.15 *Options for Saving Results to a Database Step 2*

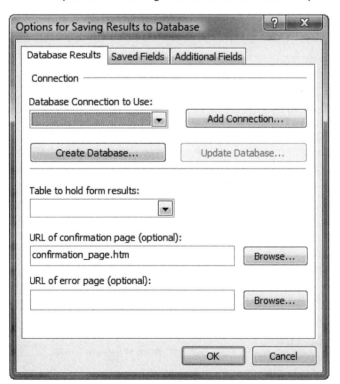

FIGURE 5.16 *Options for Saving Results to a Database with Confirmation Page Specified*

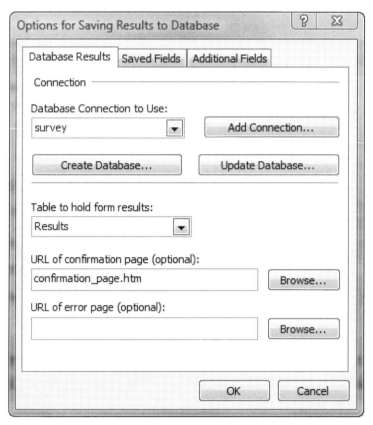

working. To do this, go through the survey multiple times, selecting and submitting each answer to each question. Start by always answering the first response to every question and submit the data. Then answer the second response, and so forth. After several passes, you will have answered all of the possible responses to all the questions. Make sure that you test the drop-down box, text boxes, and the text areas as well.

When piloting your survey, be sure to test every possible answer, going through the survey multiple times to ensure that all controls work.

Now, try the survey with other browsers. Complete the survey with Mozilla Firefox and the Opera browser and, if available, on a Mac computer with the Safari browser. If you don't have these browsers accessible on your computer, go to their Web sites and download a trial copy of them. Testing the survey is an important step, as it will verify that anyone can take the survey, regardless of browser or platform.

Viewing the Data in the Database

After the testing, it is time to view the data. Were the data saved to the database? Are all of the variables defined as you intended? If the complete data are in the database, then all is well. To check this we must open the site in Expression.

EXERCISE 5.21. **Viewing the Data in the Database**

1. Make sure that you have Access installed on the computer where you are working. Navigate to the survey site with Internet Explorer and open the site in Expression.

2. In the folder list, locate the folder titled *fpdb.* Double-click the folder. Inside the folder there will be a file with the *mdb* (Microsoft Database) extension. The file may have the same name as the connection that we created above, perhaps, *survey.mdb.* This is the database file. Double-click the file.

3. Double-clicking downloads a copy of the database file to your computer from the Web server. It may take some time, but once it gets to your computer it will open in Access.

4. Figure 5.17 is from Access 2007. On the left side of the window is a list of objects. Double-click the table where the responses are stored. You should see all of the data you submitted in a table. There will be a row for each submission and columns for each variable. Inspect the data and all of the variables to confirm that data are stored as you expected. Figure 5.18 shows the data from the survey in Access 2003.

Getting Ready for Deployment of the Survey

At this point, we have determined that all of the survey works and that the data from each question posts to the database. In addition, all of the questions are worded correctly and the order is as you wish. Now, what has to happen to deploy the survey to the world and collect data? First, the data that have been saved to the database must be erased so that only the data of new subjects will be in the database. Second, the survey must be cleaned up so that a respondent doesn't see questions inside boxes. Finally, if the survey is to be deployed to the general population from a different server, the site must be copied or moved to that server.

EXERCISE 5.22. **Erasing the Data in the Database**

1. In Expression, double-click the *fpdb* folder in the folder list. Inside is the database file. Double-click that file to download a copy to the desktop.

2. When Access opens, you may see a warning about **blocking unsafe expressions**. Answer **No** to this question. Then double-click the table where the results are stored.

3. As shown in Figure 5.19, select all of the database records by clicking the **Select All** button in the upper left corner at the intersection of the row and column headers. When they

FIGURE 5.17 *Access 2007 with Testing Data*

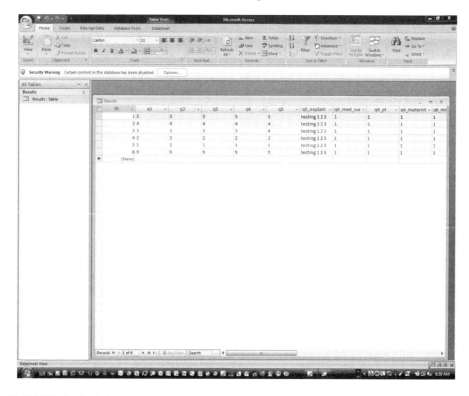

FIGURE 5.18 *Access 2003 with Testing Data*

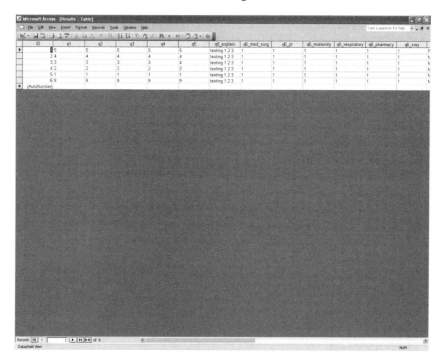

FIGURE 5.19 *Selecting All Testing Data in Access 2007*

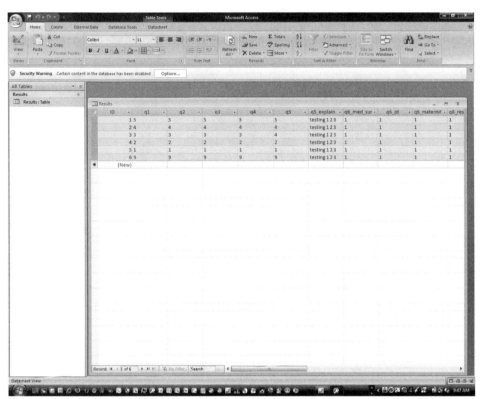

are selected, right-click in the selection and, from the menu, select **Delete Records**. When asked if we want to delete the records click **Yes**.

4. Close Access and the empty database will be uploaded back to the Web server.

EXERCISE 5.23. **Modifying the Survey to Eliminate the Boxes**

1. Open the survey page. Click inside the first question box.

2. Right-click inside the question box and click **Select > Table**. Right-click inside the now selected question table and click **Table Properties**. See Figure 5.20.

3. In the **Table Properties** dialog box change the size of the borders setting to 0. Click **OK**.

4. Continue with each question table, selecting it, then modifying the border size setting to zero.

5. When all of the question tables have been modified, click in the last row of the survey table (below the **Submit** button).

FIGURE 5.20 *Eliminating the Question Box Border Color in Table Properties Dialog*

6. Right-click inside the selection and select **Table Properties**. Change the **Border Size** setting to 0. Click **OK**.

7. Save the page and preview it in a browser. The survey should display without any borders.

8. Repeat this procedure for all of the tables on all of the other pages.

If the process described here seems cumbersome, you are correct. Having to select each box and turn the borders off is a pain. In Chapter Seven we will work with style sheets which will make this much easier.

When a survey is completely designed, coded, and tested, it is frequently the case that the survey will be moved to another server that doesn't allow development. This is done to improve the performance of the survey and restrict access to a survey while it is available on the Internet. The next exercise goes through how to move it to a production environment.

EXERCISE 5.24. Publishing the Survey to a Production Server

1. If necessary, open the survey site in Expression. Save and close any pages in the survey. In the folder list, select the top folder in the list.

2. Using any browser go to the address of the site where you will be publishing the survey. Select and copy the entire address for the new location.

3. From the Expression menu select **File** > **Publish Site**. When you do you should see a document window similar to Figure 5.21. If so, click the text at the top of the window *Remote Web Site Properties.*

FIGURE 5.21 *Publishing to Remote Web Site Dialog Step 1*

FIGURE 5.22 *Publishing Site to Remote Web Site Step 2 Specifying Location*

A dialog box for publishing will open. See Figure 5.22.

4. Verify that the **Remote Web site** tab is selected. Select FrontPage Server Extensions for server type.

5. In the **Remote Web site location** text box paste the address of the site that you are publishing to. Click **OK**.

6. As shown in Figure 5.23, in the left side of the document window is the **Local Web site** view. On the right side is the **Remote Web site** view where you are publishing the site. At the bottom of the window is a button to **Publish Web site**. Click that and the server should copy the pages, folders, and database to the *Remote Web site* location server.

7. When the operation is complete, close Expression and view the pages in a browser at the new location.

FIGURE 5.23 *Publishing Site to Remote Web Site Step 3 Prior to Publication*

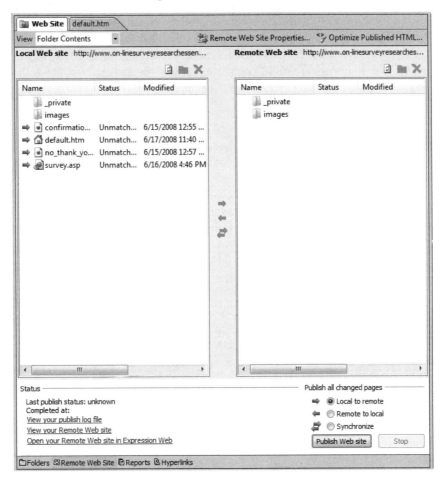

The preceding procedure applies only for the first time that a survey is published. On subsequent publications, Expression will remember the settings and bring the user directly to the publishing dialog (shown in Figure 5.23).

SUMMARY

You should now have a working survey that captures respondents' data and saves them to a database. Variables have been created for each input device and each choice has an associated code that will be stored in the database. The survey has been tested and you have verified that all the choices are stored in the database. The content of the survey has also been examined and it has been determined that it meets the needs of the researcher. What remains to be done?

Many things remain to be examined. Tighter control of the formatting options needs to be established so that the survey site has a consistent look throughout. Also, we need to learn about other types of surveys. Some surveys are more complicated and require balancing procedures to avoid biasing the responses by the order in which questions are presented. Finally, the survey needs some mechanism for advanced processing to avoid multiple submissions. These topics and more will be covered in the following chapters.

KEY TERMS

survey plan or map
Visio 2007
consent page
no thank you page
submit button
confirmation page
split cells
active server page (ASP)
survey.asp
form controls
input (radio)
soft return
input (text)
input (checkbox)
distribute columns evenly
drop-down box
age ranges
text area box
input (submit)
form control

back-end tasks
database
named form control object
group name box
spam blockers
firewalls
Microsoft Access
form properties
fpdb folder
global.asa
testing the survey
Mozilla Firefox
Opera browser
Safari browser
mdb file extension
blocking unsafe expressions
production server
publishing the site
local Web site
remote Web site

DISCUSSION QUESTIONS

1. You have been hired to test subject's perceptions of several new breakfast cereals. The cereals have the catchy names of Cereals A, B, and C. The dimensions which you are instructed to test are sweetness, crunchiness, resistance to becoming soggy in milk, and healthfulness. Construct a short survey to test these four dimensions for all subjects. Each person in the study will taste all of the cereals.

2. The people for whom you are doing the research in question 1 decide they want to know the demographics of the subjects in the study. If you have completed tasks for question 1, add the demographic questions to that survey. If not, then just create the demographic portion as a new survey.

CHAPTER

6

INTRODUCTION TO SURVEY DEVELOPMENT: EASY STEPS TO CREATING AN ONLINE SURVEY

LEARNING OBJECTIVES

- To be able to recognize the difference between interviews and questionnaires
- To be able to differentiate between survey methods and research designs: one-shot or cross-sectional research design, successive independent samples, and longitudinal designs
- To be able to determine which method and design should be used for your online survey
- To understand which questions should be considered when developing the survey
- To be able to explain important guidelines and question formats that will be helpful when designing an online survey
- To be able to describe the roles played by data and scales of measurement in collecting data
- To understand survey construction and the importance of piloting and editing your survey

A *survey* is an instrument that assesses an individual's self-reports of behaviors, thoughts, attitudes, opinions, or feelings. Surveys help researchers to (1) identify characteristics of a sample, (2) find relationships between variables, and (3) make broader statements about the population and ultimately make predictions—if the study is good and uses a good sample, procedure, and analyses. In this chapter, we briefly discuss various types of survey methods and designs to help you decide which is most appropriate for your research question. We will show you the process associated with creating a survey and demonstrate the importance of writing drafts and testing questions before putting your study online for the public.

SURVEY METHODS: INTERVIEWS AND QUESTIONNAIRES

With online research there are two main research methods that can be used. An *interview* is a research technique that assesses attitudes and behaviors typically in a one-on-situation and *questionnaires* or *surveys* obtain information by having participants read a list of questions and answer accordingly. Surveys are the most widely used research method for online research.

Interviews

The purpose of a personal interview is to put you, the researcher, in direct communication with respondents (Anderson, & Kanuka, 2003). Your research question may be broad in nature. For example, you might want to examine the personality characteristics of people that use Facebook or blogs. Or you may have a more specific research question in mind that you would like to examine. It may be important that your respondent answer questions in a particular order, or possibly you would like more open-ended personal responses to questions. In these situations, the researcher dictates exactly how questions will be administered. If you receive ambiguous responses such as "I don't know" or "I'm not sure," you can probe the respondent for additional information or provide clarification when needed.

Interviews can be semi-structured or unstructured (Anderson & Kanuka, 2003). A semi-structured interview guides participants along in the question-answer period. Interviewers ask questions in a specified manner, ensuring that each question is answered to the best of the respondent's ability. The *semi-structured interview* has a predetermined number of questions that will be asked of each respondent. One example is the research question "What do you consider to be sexually harassing behaviors?" An interviewer might begin by asking a respondent to list all behaviors they believe constitute sexual harassment. Then the researcher would follow this question with others such as "Have you ever experienced any of the behaviors you just mentioned on the job?" or "Have you ever exhibited this behavior toward others?" In a semi-structured interview, researchers guide the interview process because they have a particular research question in mind. In contrast, in an unstructured interview, the respondent guides the interview process.

Some refer to *unstructured interviews* as an open-ended because they offer researchers a look at the bigger picture. This strategy enables you to obtain a wide breadth of data. These types of interviews begin with only a few broad questions so that individuals can respond in their own way. Interpretation of the question is up to the respondent. This allows researchers to obtain nuanced answers they might otherwise have missed had they conducted a more structured interview.

You can obtain a great deal more data and assert more control in the administration of questions when using interview techniques. However, to decide whether or not an interview would best suit your research needs, you first have to consider what you would do with the data you obtain. Two important points are

- How will the data be coded?

- What are you really looking for?

You should also keep in mind that interviews take longer to administer and you must assess possible bias on the part of the researcher. Are you just recording information pertinent to the study, or are you changing the way you administer the survey based on the needs of the respondent? If you make changes in your interview procedure in order to "fit" a respondent, this will compromise the reliability and validity of your study. However, some new technology can rectify this problem. You can easily record questions to be given to participants to ensure all participants are given the same questions and in the same order. With online research the process of instant messaging (IM) can easily be used for interviews. E-researchers (Anderson & Kanuka, 2003) believe that with the advent of voice and video online interaction, interviews will become more common and eventually enable researchers to obtain face-to-face interviews with more diverse populations.

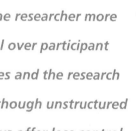

Semi-structured interviews allow the researcher more control over participant responses and the research study. Although unstructured interviews offer less control for the researcher, they can provide richer data.

Questionnaires: Types of Survey Methods and Research Designs

You may hear the term "questionnaire" or "survey." We will use these terms interchangeably throughout the text. When creating your questionnaires, you must first think about the type of design you would like to use. Survey designs can include one-shot or cross-sectional designs; successive, independent designs; and longitudinal designs.

One-shot or *cross-sectional survey research designs* are the most typical and economical design used in survey research. In this design, you obtain one or more samples from different populations all at once with the expectation that you can examine characteristics, attitudes, or feelings associated with the sample. You might focus on describing characteristics of a population or differences among two or more populations (Shaughnessy, Zechmeister, & Zechmeister, 2003). It is fast, inexpensive, and effective. Most Internet research surveys are conducted in this manner.

Characteristics of the samples can include basic demographic information such as age, gender, or ethnicity, or you can seek to determine differences in attitudes, personality, or social or behavioral characteristics. For instance, a one-shot survey can produce findings designed to examine the epidemiology of an event or disorder.

You might want to study the incidence of an event or condition. **Incidence** refers to the number of new cases of an event or phenomenon reported during a specific time period. If you are trying to figure out whether there is a change in the occurrence of diagnoses of attention-deficit hyperactivity disorder (ADHD) from 1980 to 2008, then you would be examining the incidence of that diagnosis. If you examine incidence of various disorders, you may find there is controversy associated with some diagnoses; this is certainly the case with ADHD. It is also particularly difficult to examine the incidence when a disorder may have been in existence for a long period of time yet has only been recognized and treated more recently (again, in the case with ADHD).

You might also want to study the prevalence of an event or condition. **Prevalence** is the frequency of an event or phenomenon in a particular population. Robinson, Sclar, Skaer, and Galin (1999) examined the prevalence of ADHD in children ages 5–18 by measuring the number of doctor visits resulting in diagnosis and the prescription of methylphenidate (Ritalin) between the years 1990 and 1995. The authors found almost one million (947,208) cases recognized as ADHD in 1990. In 1995, this number more than doubled to 2,357,833.

Surveys are also used to assess changes in attitudes or behaviors across time and to figure out the effects of some naturally occurring event, such as whether the institution of seat belt laws, or changing licensure laws regarding when juveniles can get their first license actually decreases motor vehicle deaths. For such studies, you would not necessarily want to use a cross-section of the population but rather a systematic sample of people across time.

Think of a **successive independent samples** study design as a series of cross-sectional surveys where the same questions are asked of each succeeding sample of people. Different people complete the same survey over a period of time. This design is best when the aim is to describe changes in attitudes over time—for example, if you wanted to examine America's sense of well-being over the last twenty years. You could examine multiple domains such as well-being and its potential relationship with issues important to a person's well-being—such as marriage, family, health, and so on. You could then obtain a sample of three hundred people from the year 2000, another three hundred participants from 2005, another three hundred participants from 2010, and so forth. This would be considered a successive independent groups design. You might notice, however, the primary disadvantage of this design is that the people surveyed in the year 2000 are not the same people surveyed in 2005, making it difficult to ascertain the reasons for any changes you might find. For example, individuals sampled in the 2005 sample experienced a significant historical change compared to the 2000 cohorts (such as the trauma of September 11, 2001). Another example might be if you followed incoming freshmen students each year to assess whether or not they were the

TABLE 6.1. **Assessment of Incoming Freshman First in Family to Pursue College Degree**

Freshman Class	2004	2005	2006	2007	2008
Are you the first in your family to attend college?	20%	22%	26%	32%	40%

first in their family to pursue a college degree. You might ask each incoming freshman class a series of questions each year, such as "Are you the first in your family to attend college?" (See Table 6.1).

If you wanted to assess whether changes in attitudes could be attributed to a particular event, you could assess attitudes after an important event. Let's say you wanted to examine fear of terrorism. If you obtained a sample of individuals and asked about their fear of terrorism before and after the 9/11 attack, you could assume ratings of fear would most likely be higher after the terrorist attack. However, one of the problems with this design is that the samples you obtain before and after the terrorist attack will be different, and because of this, you cannot say the reason fear increased after 9/11 was because of the terrorist attack. The samples obtained at each time period include different people. All we can say from such a study is that the fear is different. Perhaps there are additional reasons why individuals experience a heightened state of fear (for example mass media, personal experiences, and so on). However, if you are interested in determining how attitudes or behaviors change across time and you want to attempt to say why these changes happened, then you should consider using a longitudinal survey research design.

The primary difference between independent samples designs and longitudinal designs is that *longitudinal designs* follow the same people over time. Individuals are given the same questionnaire more than once to assess whether changes occur over time. For instance, you can assess participants' attitudes toward new software programs one month after trying the new software and then again after they have used the software for six months. The Minnesota Twin Study is one of the most famous longitudinal studies (Bouchard, Lykken, McGue, Segal, & Tellegen, 1990). Bouchard and his colleagues examined the extent that heredity was responsible for a wide variety of personality and psychosocial attributes. Researchers began their research by conducting a series of psychological tests on identical and fraternal twins reared apart. Ten years later, participants were evaluated again and researchers found heredity factors accounted for 64–74 percent of intelligence in identical twins and 39–55 percent of personality characteristics such as shyness, intimacy, and extraversion.

Longitudinal designs are the best methodological tools to study changes in individuals over time. With this design, you can assess the effects of a naturally occurring phenomenon such as divorce, job layoffs, terrorist attacks, prevention programs, disease, and the like. Though longitudinal designs are more methodologically sound, they are not used as often because they can take a substantial amount of time, are expensive to implement, and it is difficult to get people to commit to participating long-term.

When participants drop out of a study, researchers call this participant *mortality*, (or *subject attrition*). In longitudinal studies you often lose participants throughout the research process. People drop out for many reasons (for example, participants can lose interest or move). However, as a researcher, you need to pay close attention to which participants are dropping out and why they choose to withdraw from your study. For example, perhaps the phenomena you are studying might be the reason they are dropping out!

Additional problems associated with longitudinal studies include the way in which respondents complete the surveys. People do not like to be perceived as inconsistent. Therefore, participants might try harder to appear consistent each time they complete the survey. For example, if you're following people's diets over time, they might misrepresent what they actually ate. Events can occur that change people's attitudes. If you were assessing attitudes toward crime and one of the primetime TV news programs ran a weeklong series on crime in the city, this media influence might cause people to react differently to your survey.

Respondents might also react differently simply because they know they are being studied. This can be a problem not only for longitudinal studies. Developmental psychologists or sociologists might conduct an observational study to investigate the extent to which parents spank their children. Once parent and child participants come to the lab to be observed and know they are being observed, they are likely to react in a way that they believe is expected of them and not how they would normally behave if they were in their own homes or another natural environment. We can avoid this problem by having our participants become acclimated to the laboratory environment or observe them in their own natural environment. Eventually, participants will become acclimated to the observer and act the way they normally would act. You see this often with reality television shows. At first, individuals react to the camera, but after a few days, people's true personalities come to the fore.

Finally, in a longitudinal study, you need to realize that people mature over time. They can also get better or worse at the task you are evaluating. For instance, if you were studying motor coordination in preschool children aged 2–4, you might find that tying one's shoe or potty training comes more easily to some than to others. These problems are a normal function of maturation. Be aware of this when studying behaviors that can be affected by the normal maturation process.

Questions to Consider: What Information Are You Looking For?

When constructing your questionnaire, you should be asking yourself some basic questions. According to Shaughnessy and colleagues (2003) there are particular steps to take when creating your survey. The most important steps to consider when planning your survey include

■ What type of questions will best answer my research question?

■ What method (interview or survey) would be most appropriate?

■ Think ahead to what the results of your study might be. What results might you find using the research method and questions you're considering?

- Will these research results actually answer the question you intended?

- This is imperative: Don't rush this process! Most people have no idea of the work that goes into creating a research survey. It is a process that needs to be carefully thought through and implemented. If you create a survey that has mistakes or really does not measure what you intended to measure, then the whole process has been a waste of time.

What Method and Design Is Best for Your Online Survey?

We have outlined some options for online research possibilities. Now you must think about which approach would be most appropriate for you. When looking at these research designs and methods, you should also consider the type of data these surveys will produce. For instance, if you feel your research question lends itself to conducting an interview because more in-depth answers to your question are necessary, then you need to consider how you will analyze the data you receive from the interviews. You might consider using an online chat room for an interview and analyze respondents' answers to your questions using a design that allow you to control how questions are administered and to probe individuals for more information. You might also consider using a longitudinal design to follow particular individuals over time. All pertinent methods need to be carefully considered before creating your survey design. You might find using a one-shot or cross-sectional research design will be the most efficient and effective to answer your research question. Another important decision you will need to make is determining who will administer your survey. Will your survey will be administered by you, a trained assistant, or self-administered?

Also, keep in mind that if a survey exists that measures what you need and is known to be reliable and valid, there is no reason to create your own. In your research and literature review, you likely came across surveys conducted by others. Examine those surveys to determine whether they can be helpful. Some questions to consider:

If a survey already exists that measures what you intend to measure, and it has established reliability and validity, then we recommend using that survey.

- What method have others used to assess similar ideas?

- Did the researchers measure a construct you want to measure?

- Are the measures you reviewed considered reliable (have they been used more than once)?

- Can the measures you reviewed be considered valid (do they measure what they intended to measure)?

Find those surveys. If you want to measure depression, examine existing surveys that measure depression. If you are considering customer satisfaction, how has your firm measured customer satisfaction in the past? When you can, use instruments that already exist. If no survey exists to measure what you wish to measure, this chapter will provide suggestions and guidelines for general survey construction. (For those who would like a more comprehensive discussion of survey design we recommend Dillman, 2007.)

GENERAL GUIDELINES FOR FORMATTING AN ONLINE SURVEY

For any research method you choose, you need to consider the general formatting of the survey. What will the survey look like? The following are some general guidelines for creating your survey. Basic principles of Web design should be noted (e.g., see Niederst, 2001). We should assume your participants have minimal computer skills and, therefore, your survey must be simple, easy to use, and the arrangement of questions on each Web page should be logical and legible. Online surveys should also be visually attractive. A survey that is pleasant to look at can increase response rates. However, there is a fine line between attractive and too busy. Do not use too many colors as it can have an effect on transmission time and slow the loading of the survey. Change your font size or use bold or italics when needed to emphasize particular aspects of your questionnaire. Our experience suggests reader clarity can be enhanced by using a light or white page background and black text color. Be sure that colors of text, background, page, and layout are consistent throughout your survey.

Online surveys should be user friendly and easy to navigate. They should also be simple and visually attractive.

Questions with similar topics should be placed together, as should questions of the same type (such as yes-no questions, Likert-type, open-ended questions, and so on). As can be seen in Figure 6.1, if participants are asked to provide questions in a multiple-choice format, be sure the answer options are always available either at the top of each page or underneath each question so participants will not have to remember all response categories.

FIGURE 6.1 *Example of Responses Showing Under a Question*

Please rate your level of satisfaction with Microsoft Expression software:

- ○ Completely Satisfied
- ○ Mostly Satisfied
- ○ Somewhat Satisfied
- ○ Neither Satisfied or Dissatisfied
- ○ Somewhat Dissatisfied
- ○ Mostly Dissatisfied
- ○ Completely Dissatisfied

Participant instructions should explicitly state how respondents can respond to questions, deselect a response, or move forward or backward in a questionnaire. Participants can be notified how to do this at the beginning of the survey or within each question set. For instance, if respondents need to click a drop-down box or write in their answers using a text box, specific instructions should be included. Similarly, if you have a series of questionnaires with different response categories, you should have instructions for each section as necessary.

Choosing the Right Questions and Words for Your Survey

If you have looked for an existing survey to measure what you need and have found that none truly capture what you want to measure, then you must write your own questions. Though this need not be an intimidating task, be very cautious as to how your questions are constructed, for the words you choose can affect the data you collect. What is your research question? Do your questions cover the content area of interest?

There are two general question formats from which to choose—open-ended (or free response) or closed-ended questions. As we have seen, open-ended questions are those questions that allow respondents to write their answers freely. Think of an essay exam. Your history professor asks "What is the meaning of the concept 'natural aristocracy' and what leaders are associated with this term?" This type of question allows respondents more flexibility to write their responses in the manner they choose. Other examples might include "What behaviors do you think constitute sexual harassment?" or "With what aspects of the software were you satisfied?" With this format, you will receive a wider range of answers that allow your participants to express ideas, feelings, or reactions that aren't necessarily limited to preexisting categories. As a researcher, open-ended questions are easier to construct but need to be carefully worded. Answers to this question format will become text in your database. Analyzing this data can be complicated. When writing these questions a researcher must reflect on the following issues:

- What will I do when I get the responses?

- What key terms or ideas am I looking for?

- How will I analyze this data?

Remember that closed-ended responses provide specific response categories to choose from. Which categories you choose will depend upon the information you seek and the type of question it is. For instance, you can ask respondents to answer "yes" or "no" to the question "Are you a smoker?" However, some people who smoke in social settings may not consider themselves as smokers. This question could then be expanded to include "yes," "no," and "sometimes." Another word for this format is called *forced choice.* You are forcing individuals to choose one answer, when the correct answer may not actually be an option. Collecting demographic information such as "age" and "education" can easily be measured on a continuous scale. Other demographic information will likely require categories such "occupation type," "ethnicity," and "gender." Keep in mind that questions with preestablished categories such as these limit the statistical procedures you can use.

Finally, when using categorical data be sure that each category is mutually exclusive (Dillman, 2007). In Chapter Five, you created a survey where age options were "18–25," "26–35," "36–45," "46–55," and "55 and older." This is acceptable because each person fits in one and only one category. Not having exclusive categories (such as 18–25, 25–35, 35–45) would result in subjects' frustration and would make data interpretation very difficult. (Note: some ages appear twice. For example, respondents who were twenty-five would not know which category to choose.)

The most common use of closed-ended questions is learning about attitudes and opinions that individuals have regarding a topic or behavior. For this, you would set up your questions using a Likert-type rating scale. Likert-type scales allow you to measure the degree of agreement with a concept or idea. For instance, if you are interested in measuring the concept of satisfaction with the work environment, each item would relate to some aspect of job satisfaction. The scale would have a set of opposite conditions where participants can indicate their agreement or disagreement with the statement or rate the degree the scale matches their feelings. Likert scales can be formatted with the descriptors under the choices, to the left and right of the choices (see Figure 6.2), or above or below the choices (see Figure 6.3).

Forced Choice and Undecided Responses

Figure 6.3 shows that participants do not have the option to be "undecided" or have "no opinion." You can assume the number "3" used in the Figure 6.2 scale indicates a

FIGURE 6.2 *Examples of Formatting for Likert Scale Response Questions*

I believe my boss is fair.

1	2	3	4	5
Strongly Agree				Strongly Disagree

I believe my boss is fair.

Strongly Agree	1	2	3	4	5	Strongly Disagree

FIGURE 6.3 *Scale Showing No Undecided-Response Option*

Never	Almost Never	Rarely	Occasionally	Often	Almost Always	Always
1	2	3	4	5	6	7

neutral attitude, but that may not be accurate because this format forces participants to select a response that may not actually express their true attitudes. Researchers have noted the importance of recognizing the positioning of an undecided option (Dillman, 2007). When the undecided option was positioned in the middle or last place, researchers found participants were twice as likely to use the option when it was placed in the middle than when it was in the last position, suggesting participants were more likely to separate undecided options from neutral options (Willits & Janota, 1996, as cited in Dillman, 2007). If you prefer that participants avoid "undecided" options then you may want to place that option last; however, we recommend that this option be placed in the middle to better distinguish between neutral and undecided options.

Additional Tips for Creating Your Survey When creating your online study, consider your target sample. If your sample includes older adults, you may want to consider using a larger font size. If your survey includes children, be sure the vocabulary is age appropriate. Most surveys are written at an eighth-grade reading level. Use vocabulary that is simple, clear, understandable, and gets to the point. Your wording might seem clear to you, yet some people may find your questions ambiguous. The rule of thumb for question length is twenty or fewer words (Dillman, 2007; Shaughnessy et al., 2003). Furthermore, conditional information should be placed before the main idea of the question. Asking "If you work, would you consider carpooling?" is a better way to word the question than "Would you consider carpooling if you work?"

The consent form should be inviting and motivate respondents to answer your survey. Your consent form should include links to your e-mail address and that of your technical support contact person as well as a timetable of when the study will be completed and when results will be available online. In addition, participants should be urged to print out or save their consent form in case they have questions. Once participants have completed your survey, remind them to click the **Submit** button to make sure their survey gets submitted, appropriately. When the survey has been submitted, thank respondents for their participation on your last page.

There are unique features you can consider creating for your online survey (Thomas, 2004). First, you need to decide whether or not you will require participants to answer particular questions before allowing them to move on. This feature should be used very sparingly, if at all. Remember, with research in the social sciences, participants have the ethical right to skip any question they choose not to answer. Second, you may want to allow your respondents to follow up a question by providing additional information. If appropriate, provide subjects with a way to do this and encourage them to do so.

The statement "I believe my boss is fair and that I get paid fairly" is called a ***double-barreled question.*** It actually assesses two concepts (job enjoyment and pay satisfaction). This is confusing to the subject and difficult to analyze. You should ask these as two separate questions. Also, each survey item designed to assess a construct should have the same scale. For example, if I have five questions regarding job satisfaction, then all five questions should use the same 5-point Likert scale. You can also choose other rating scales that cover more information. A 7-point Likert scale can provide a wider range of response choices and more variability (see Figure 6.4.)

However, response choices should not exceed nine. Too many response options confuse participants (Thomas, 2004).

The definitions (or anchors) you assign to each of your questions can differ according to what question you are asking. An anchor is the definition you provide for your response scale (Thomas, 2004). All scale anchors should be presented uniformly. For instance, if you have a series of Likert scale questions, always present the questions in the same order (that is, "never" to "always" or "always" to "never").

If you have five questions that make up a job satisfaction scale, then you could add up the responses to those five questions and obtain an "overall job satisfaction score." The Likert scale commonly has response categories, such as "1" = "strongly disagree," "2" = "disagree," "3" = "neither agree nor disagree," "4" = "agree" and "5" = "strongly agree," and have rating scale anchors for each point on your scale. In the example above, each number has a corresponding definition (e.g., "1" = "strongly disagree"). However, you can also have only two or three anchors. (See Figure 6.5.)

If you are interested in obtaining information on the frequency of a behavior, you can use Likert-type questions, but be careful to stay away from relative terms such as "frequently" because some terms can mean different things to different people (Thomas, 2004). In this situation, participants could be presented with a drop-down box with response categories ranging from "never" to "always" or ratings such as "never," "once," "2–3 times," "4–6 times," "more than 6 times," and so on.

Another type of rating scale is called the ***semantic differential scale*** (Osgood, Suci, & Tannenbaum, 1957). This is a 7-point scale that includes a list of adjectives where one side of the scale is one adjective and the other side of the scale is its extreme opposite. Semantic differential scales are intended to provide another way to assess a person's feelings toward an object, event, or individual. You can use any adjective and its antonym that you would like.

FIGURE 6.4 *Seven-Point Likert Scale*

Never	Almost Never	Rarely	Occasionally	Often	Almost Always	Always
⊙	⊙	⊙	⊙	⊙	⊙	⊙
1	2	3	4	5	6	7

FIGURE 6.5 *Scale with Just Three Anchors*

Strongly Disagree		Neither Disagree nor Agree		Strongly Agree
⊙	⊙	⊙	⊙	⊙

Russell, Perkins, and Grinnell (2008) created a research study that used the semantic differential scale. The authors examined characteristics of individuals applying for a job interview. Either a male or a female applied for the job and either overused the words "like" or "uh" or did not overuse any words. Participants were asked to rate the extent to which the interviewee was professional or unprofessional, confident or not at all confident. They found job applicants who overused the word "like" were viewed as more unprofessional, less confident, and less intelligent than if they used the words "uh" or didn't overuse words. The original semantic differential scale designed by Osgood et al. instructed participants to place an X anywhere on the line that represented their evaluation. Current online research formats do not enable participants to place an X on the line. Therefore, we suggest that a scale ranging from –3 (unprofessional) to +3 (very professional) be used for online surveys (See Figure 6.6).

Finally, *checklists* can also be considered when determining question formats. You can make an adjective checklist, behavioral checklist, or other types of checklists. Adjective checklists can be used to assess how a person feels about a topic, event, or experience. Behavioral checklists can be used to assess what types of behaviors a person may have participated in or be interested in participating in. You can have participants check all adjectives or behaviors that apply. Dillman (2007) suggests refraining from using checklists that request participants to "check all that apply," though, as this format can lead to primacy and recency effects. Primacy effects refer to a participants' tendency to choose items presented first, and recency suggests that participants are likely to remember and respond to that which is most recent.

One alternative to the "check all that apply" option is to have respondents rank-order responses (see Figure 6.7). For instance, let's say schools are preparing their

FIGURE 6.6 *Question Showing a Semantic Differential*

Very Unprofessional						Very Professional
◉	◉	◉	◉	◉	◉	◉
-3	-2	-1	0	+1	+2	+3

FIGURE 6.7 *Question Asking for Rank Ordering*

Please indicate the summer class you would most like to participate in by ranking it as 1st, next most likely to participate in by ranking it 2nd, and your third most likely choice by ranking it as a 3rd preference.

	1st Preference	2nd Preference	3rd Preference
Archery	◉	◉	◉
Music	◉	◉	◉
Theater	◉	◉	◉
Swimming	◉	◉	◉
Cooking	◉	◉	◉
Mountain Biking	◉	◉	◉

summer school schedules and need to identify which programs will elicit the most student interest. Students are asked to place a "1" in the box they would most likely participate in, followed by a "2" for their second choice, and a "3" for their third choice, and so on.

As you might have guessed, closed-ended questions take more effort to create and put online. However, the ease of recording and scoring data will make it worth the effort. The results of closed-ended questions can be more easily summarized than those of open-ended questions. Some of the disadvantages include less flexibility for participants to respond. If a respondent's preferred answer is not available, he or she might choose an answer that does not truly represent how he or she feels simply because there was no alternative response that truly matched. As researchers, we dictate the responses our participants can choose. It is imperative that our questions and response choices be well chosen and consider the realm of possible answers.

Once you have chosen your question format, you must carefully consider how questions are worded. For example, you might get a different response from people if you asked "Do you get stressed frequently?" as opposed to "Do you get stressed occasionally?" In fact, Elizabeth Loftus (1979) conducted a great deal of research on the effect of wording and misleading information and found respondents reported having more headaches when they were asked "Do you get headaches frequently? If so, how often?" than if she asked "Do you get headaches occasionally? If so, how often?" Similarly, Loftus found participants were more likely to say a car was traveling faster when a test administrator said it "smashed" into another car than when they said it "collided" with another car.

Try to refrain from words and questions that might unduly influence respondents. This includes using *loaded* or *leading* questions, which can be emotionally laden with words such as "radical," "homophobic," or "racist." If you're wondering what words might potentially be emotionally laden, pilot your survey questions to your target audience and obtain feedback. Even questions that might appear harmless can affect individuals' responses. Let's say you wanted to assess attitudes toward potential presidential candidates. If you assessed the level of support for "Ms. Hillary Clinton" or "Hillary Clinton," the word "Ms." before the name might be enough to influence judgments of presidential support. Similarly, leading questions can introduce potential bias into your question. These types of questions include "Most schools are underfunded; what do you think about this?" Or "Most individuals believe in global warming; how do you feel about it?" In order to avoid this problem, be sure to include all possible opinions. For instance, you might ask, "Some people believe our schools are underfunded and others believe schools are not underfunded. What do you believe?" Or you can just ask, "How do you feel about global warming?"

Importance of Question Order

The order in which your questions are presented can influence participants' responses in various ways. The first questions you ask should capture respondents' interest and entice them to complete the survey. Typically, when you are asking for sensitive information, you may want to consider establishing a rapport with the participant by beginning with benign questions about demographics and then leading into more sensitive questions. Researchers call this *funnel ordering*—a natural flow of questions leading from general to specific information. An example of a general question might be "How do you feel about online research?" A specific question would be "Do you believe online samples are more representative of the population than paper-and-pencil surveys?"

Note that the content and order of questions in the beginning of the survey can affect a participant's responses to later questions. For instance, if you were to examine legal decision making in rape cases, you would need to consider respondents' own experiences regarding rape. However, in doing so, you must also be cautious of the placement of questions pertaining to victimization. Requesting respondents to first answer a series of questions about their own experience of sexual coercion or rape may arouse emotional issues that affect their later responses to questions regarding legal decision making. To account for this possibility, you would need to counterbalance the survey materials. Counterbalancing is a helpful technique used to control these types of placement-related variables. The above problem is best controlled by administering half of the surveys with the given questions in one order and the other half in the reverse order. In this particular case, half of the participants would receive questions pertaining to rape victimization before questions regarding legal decisions in a rape case, while the remaining half would be asked to complete the legal decision questions prior to the rape questions. In doing so, you come one step closer to eliminating the bias of questions that may have been perceived as emotionally laden as well as bias related to primary and recency effects. Most important, this technique allows us to statistically reveal any biases associated with the placement of your survey questions.

Response set is another issue to contend with when developing surveys. When participants are given a large number of questions with the same possible responses (all "yes" or "no" or all "strongly agree" or "disagree") they may simply begin to just check the same response throughout the survey, not paying attention to the actual question. In order to avoid this problem, you may want to begin your survey items in reverse order. Some of your items can begin negatively and some positively. For instance, the items in the list below are measured on a 5-point Likert scale from "never" to "always," where higher scores indicate greater media consumption:

1. I read the paper every day.

2. I read the news on the Internet every day.

3. I try to reduce the number of hours I spend watching television.

4. In the past week, how often have you listened to the radio?

5. If I watch the news, I get turned off from listening to other forms of media.

Some researchers change the anchor of particular questions to avoid the possibility of a response set. Therefore, before you can compute a total score of media consumption for each participant, you need to be sure that each response goes in the same direction. For questions 1, 2, and 4, above, if responses are "Always" then this infers greater media consumption. However, if responses to questions 3 and 5 are "Always" this infers less media consumption. Therefore, to ensure that higher scores indicate higher media consumption, you must reverse score questions 3 and 5 before obtaining a total "media consumption" score for your participants. **Reverse scoring** means reversing the scoring for those questions (3 and 5) that are in the opposite direction than the others. In this example, "1" = "never" and "5" = "always." Reverse scoring for questions 3 and 5 for this example would be 1 = 5; 2 = 4; 3 = 3; 4 = 2; and 5 = 1. If you are using a survey that already exists, be sure to obtain the original version of the survey. This should provide information pertaining to how to score the survey and whether particular items need to be reversed scored.

Finally, we must consider filter questions. **Filter questions** are those questions used to determine whether additional questions need to be asked. For example, if you were concerned about computer use, then you would first ask your participants whether they have a computer. If they answer "yes," then you can follow this up with more specific questions pertaining to computer use, such as a question regarding how much money they spent on computer software or hardware. Often, filter questions are necessary, but they should be used with caution because they can be confusing for the respondent. For instance, if you asked students about their involvement in a gang, you could ask them "Have you ever belonged to a gang?" If students say "yes," they proceed to answer additional questions pertaining to their gang. If they say "no," participants must be instructed where to go in the survey. (This is where hyperlinking will be effective. Refer back to Chapter Three to refresh your memory on how to implement hyperlinks.) Otherwise, participants might answer "no" to your more general question ("Do you have a computer?" or "Have you ever belonged to a gang?") and continue to respond to more specific questions.

Data and Scales of Measurement for Data Collection

When making a determination as to how you should ask your questions and in which format, you should also consider what you will do with your data once you've got it. One of the first things you will do is examine and describe your data. In order to describe your data, you must be aware of **measures of central tendency**, which is what researchers use to summarize a data set. When data are measured on a continuous scale (interval or ratio) you can use measures of central tendency (mean, median, and mode) to describe the data. The most common measure of central tendency is the mean. A **mean** is a measure that represents the average score. Some researchers examine the **median,** which is also an average score but represents the midpoint (or fiftieth percentile) of a score. The **mode** is the number that occurs most often in a data set.

Many statistics are based on the idea that the data are normally distributed. Therefore, it is extremely important to examine whether your scores are normally distributed first. A ***normal distribution*** assumes data will exhibit a bell-shaped curve that is a visual representation of the mean, median, and mode. A normal bell-shaped curve would present the mean, median, and mode as equal to one another. If the mean and median differ from one another then the distribution can become skewed in one direction or another (see Figure 6.8).

A ***skewed distribution*** refers to a disproportionate number of scores that fall toward the upper or lower end of the distribution (for more information on skewness, see Salkind, 2000).

Once your data can be described, you can use ***inferential statistics*** to identify relationships or causes. Inferential statistics determine whether your independent variables had a significant effect on your dependent variable. This includes the assumption that a random sample has been obtained and random assignment has been used. Let's say you wanted to assess customer satisfaction with a new software program. You would randomly assign half of your participants the old software program and half to the new software program. You could then assess customer satisfaction in both groups on a Likert-type scale where "1" = "not at all satisfied" and "5" = "extremely

FIGURE 6.8 *Histogram Bell Curve*

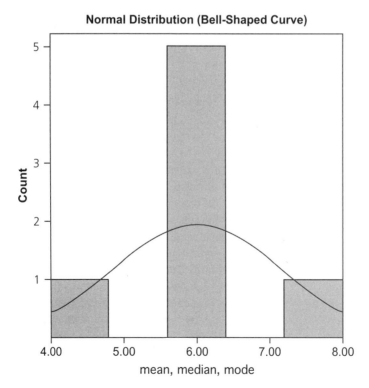

satisfied." If the new software program has significantly higher mean ratings in customer satisfaction, then we can assume that customers will be significantly more satisfied with the newer version of the software. In this case, you collected your data on an interval scale. This allows you to examine the average scores to determine whether scores differ among the two groups. (Similarly, you could have used a ratio scale, such as 1–10 in customer satisfaction.)

Perhaps you want to assess possible correlations between other possible variables measured with an interval or ratio scale and satisfaction scores. Measuring your dependent variable in this manner also allows you to investigate the extent to which your dependent variable is affected by possible interactions between a series of independent variables. For example, if you want to examine participant age and old and new software, you may hypothesize that younger individuals using new software will rate software satisfaction highest. If you originally measured age using a ratio scale, simply letting participants fill in their age, you can obtain a median score and categorize age into two groups (younger being equal to or lower than the median, and older being higher than the median). However, if your data are already collected on a nominal or categorical scale, this can limit your analyses to descriptive statistics. Remember, descriptive statistics can only describe the *nature* of your sample; they can only be computed to describe what is typical of groups or describe the characteristics of your sample. Nominal or ordinal data allows you to describe your data with percentages and frequencies. Ratio and Likert scales allow you to describe your sample with mean scores. (If you would like to make statistical inferences about your sample or perform statistical hypothesis testing, then you may want to consider using ratio or interval data when appropriate; see Chapter Fifteen.)

The Importance of Piloting and Editing Your Survey

The most important guideline of all is to be sure that you edit and **pilot** your survey before you actually put it online. Once you've rewritten your survey you must find a small sample of respondents to complete it and provide feedback. We cannot overstate the importance of this step, particularly when using online research. You may find that your questions are still ambiguous or that typing errors still exist. Consider this as a practice run. How does the survey look online? It may look different depending on the computers and browsers used. What you see may not necessarily be *exactly* what your participant sees. Today's Web tools are much better, but there are still some compatibility issues among different browsers and platforms. Participants should be able to navigate easily through your survey, move from page to page, and provide their answers quickly and efficiently without having to scroll down the screen vertically or horizontally. Will participants have difficulty linking from the consent form to the actual survey? Piloting your survey allows you to determine the most effective way to eliminate these problems.

 We cannot overemphasize the importance of piloting your study before presenting it to the public.

SUMMARY

This chapter was designed to help you with your first steps in developing an online survey. Before implementing your survey, you must first discern which method and research design are going to provide you with the information you need. Personal interviews, which can be semi-structured or unstructured, place researchers in direct communication with respondents and allow the researcher to control the flow of the responses. Using semi-structured interviews, researchers guide participants along a predetermined number and order of questions, whereas unstructured interviews are generally led by the participant and are based on an open-ended discourse with the researcher.

Survey methods are the most commonly used tool to assess attitudes and behaviors. A one-shot or cross-sectional design is most common in online research. Successive independent sample designs can be helpful when trying to assess attitudes or behaviors across time or to understand some naturally occurring event. Successive independent samples examine different individuals over various time periods. Longitudinal research designs look at attitudes or behaviors of the same people across a period of time. Unfortunately, longitudinal research is employed less often because of the expense and subject mortality associated with this design.

There are key issues to ask yourself before beginning any research study, and there are general guidelines to follow when formatting your online survey. First, you must decide whether the survey will be administered by you or a trained assistant. Second, if a survey already exists that measures what you intend to measure, be sure to use one that has established reliability and validity.

Most people who complete online surveys have limited computer skills. Therefore researchers should be careful to make their survey easy to use and visually pleasing. Be fairly simplistic and do not go overboard with too many colors or too much content on one page. Placement of questions should also be considered. When possible, try to group similar questions together—such as all Likert-type questions or "yes-no" questions. All surveys should be written at no more than an eighth-grade reading level. Consent forms should be particularly pleasing as they are intended to invite people to participate.

Choosing the right questions and wording is very important when constructing your survey. Open-ended questions ask all respondents to write down their answers freely (similar to an essay exam), whereas closed-ended questions are designed to force participants to make a choice in their response (as in multiple choice questions). Alternative response options you can consider when developing your survey include Likert scales using anchoring techniques, semantic differential scales, checklists, and rank ordering.

The order in which you present your questions can affect your research results. When there is a possibility that question order could affect participant responses, be sure to use counterbalancing techniques to avoid, or at least measure, this potential problem. If all questions have the same anchor, there is the potential for participants to go through the survey clicking the same response without paying attention to the question. This is called response set. In order to avoid this problem, researchers reverse-score particular questions. Filter questions are also used to determine whether additional questions need to be asked.

The type of data and scales of measurement to use should be considered when developing your survey. The type of data you collect will dictate your ability to analyze it. Measures of central tendency (mean, median, and mode) can be used to describe your data.

Finally, piloting your research is particularly important when using online research. Piloting provides researchers with important feedback regarding questions that may have typos, appear ambiguous, or be offensive to others. It is particularly important to pilot your survey with a sample similar to those who will be completing your final survey.

KEY TERMS

survey
unstructured interviews
semi-structured interview
questionnaires
semantic differential scale
incidence and prevalence
one-shot or cross-sectional survey
  research designs
successive independent samples
filter questions
inferential statistics
mode
forced choice

skewed distribution
longitudinal designs
reverse scoring
loaded or leading questions
response set
mortality or subject attrition
double-barreled question
measures of central tendency
mean
median
normal distribution
funnel ordering
counterbalancing

DISCUSSION QUESTIONS

1. Define "survey" and provide four examples of survey research designs. If relevant, identify which of these designs will be most appropriate for your research study.

2. Compare and contrast the primary differences between one-shot, successive independent samples, and longitudinal research designs, and describe the advantages and disadvantages of each design.

3. Why is it important to examine the reliability and validity of existing measures? Is there an existing measure that you can use for your own research?

4. Identify at least three unique guidelines associated with online research surveys that pertain to your own study.

5. Why is it necessary to be careful when choosing the correct questions and wording when creating a survey? Why is the order in which questions are presented important to consider, and what do these issues have to do with piloting the survey?

CHAPTER

7

USING STYLES, STYLE SHEETS, AND GRAPHICS

LEARNING OBJECTIVES

- To be able to use styles to control text and table attributes
- To be able to create an external style sheet and use it to format all of the text in a site
- To be able to use styles to control the look of tables in the survey
- To be able to create and use graphics in surveys as buttons, pictures, and stimuli

One of the most exciting developments in Web design has been the development and widespread adoption of the use of styles. A *style* is a collection of settings for objects on a page. An *object* can be text, graphics, a table, and so on. Styles can control almost every aspect of the object including type face, type style, alignment, color, background color, border color, and so forth. Expression creates styles automatically as the properties of objects are changed, but the style remains tied to that page. To be most useful in a site, the styles must be saved on a separate page and made available throughout the site. This is done by creating a *style sheet*, a set of styles that can govern all objects on a Web site. Using style sheets to control the appearance, placement, and behavior of objects makes creating and modifying sites much easier; it also helps maintain a site's consistent look across all pages. This section begins with an exploration of styles, creating new styles, creating an external style sheet, attaching a style sheet to a page or site, and applying the styles to objects on a page.

Style sheets help to control the appearance, placement, and behavior of objects on your Web site.

EXPLORING STYLES

EXERCISE 7.1. Exploring Styles

1. Navigate to the *chapter 7* Web site with Internet Explorer and open the *chapter07* Web site in Expression. Create a new page by selecting **File** > **New.** On the **General** tab, select **General** from the first column and **HTML** from the second. Click **OK**.

2. Save the page as *style.htm.*

3. Click the page, type your name, and hit Enter. Repeat this two more times so that there are three names on the page.

4. Select the first name and apply the **Heading 1**<**h1**> HTML style. (Click the down arrow in the first text box on the **Common Toolbar** and select **Heading 1**.)

5. Save the page and preview it in a browser. The page is shown in Figure 7.1.

6. Switch back to Expression. In the lower left corner of the document window are buttons for three views of the page. The first button for **Design View** should be selected now. Click the **Code View**. This view shows just the code that defines the page.

7. Click the **Split View** button. This option shows the page in **Design View** and also a view of the underlying code. If need be, drag the blue border between the two window panes to change the size of the windows to be approximately equal.

8. Select the first name in the list in the **Design View** pane. As you do, the code for the name will also be selected. In the code there is <**h1**> before the name and a </**h1**> after. These code elements are called **HTML tags** and they tell the browser how to display

FIGURE 7.1   *Text with HTML Style Applied*

the text. Tags come in pairs—one before the object and the other after it to close out and stop the property modification. In the highlighted example the <**h1**> style begins before the name and stops after it. There are many HTML tags that can be used on a Web page. Hyperlinks, images, and so on are all created with HTML tags. However, we will not have to apply these directly to the code. Expression adds the HTML code as we work in **Design View**.

9. With the **Split View** still open, select the second name in the list. On the **Common Tool-bar**, select the drop-down list for typefaces (this is the second drop-down list). Select **Arial, Helvetica, sans-serif** from the list. In the next drop-down list, select **x-large** from that list.

10. Save the page and preview it in a browser. The browser shows the first name in Times New Roman and the second name in the Arial typeface.

11. Switch back to Expression. Select the second name in **Design View**. The highlighted code now shows

```
<p class="style1">John Purcell</p>
```

The <**p**> is the code for a paragraph. Each of the three names on the page is a separate paragraph. Therefore, they begin and end with the <**p**> and <**/p**> tags. The tag for the second name includes the statement **class=“style1.”** This code means that the item has the properties that are defined in the style named *style1,* which was created automatically as the properties of the text were modified. We modified the typeface and its size, so the properties of *style1* change the typeface and the size. In Figure 7.2, lines 8 through 13 show the beginning and end of another HTML tag, the style tag. Inside the tags on line

FIGURE 7.2 *Code Showing Embedded Inline Style*

9 is **".style1"** (the period is what marks it as a style name). After the curly bracket, the two font attributes font-family and font-size are set equal to **Arial, Helvetica, sans-serif** and **x-large**, respectively. The style itself and the style section on the page were created automatically.

12. Click in the **Design View** window and select the third name in the list. From the menu, select **Format** > **Font.** In the **Font** dialog box change the font to **Arial, Helvetica, sans-serif** and, from the size list, select **xx-large**. In the **Effects** section, check **All Caps**, which formats the text in capital letters. Click **OK**. Save the page.

   In the style section of the **Code View** a second style is created with the name *.style2*. The new style runs on lines 13 through line 17. It modifies three attributes of the text.

13. In the **Design View**, select the second name in the list. On the **Common Toolbar** is a button that controls the color of text. Click the down arrow on the **Font Color** button and select **red**. Save the page.

   In the **Code View** a new line was added to *style1*:

   ```
   Color: #FF0000;
   ```

   This line defines the color of the text. After the colon is # which indicates that what comes next is a color. The **FF0000** is red expressed in hexadecimal. **Hexadecimals** are numbers expressed in **base 16**. Regular numbers are in **base 10**, so for base 16 additional characters are needed. Thus, a number can include letters as characters (FF in this case). Colors in computer displays are expressed as portions of the three display colors: red, green, and blue. There are three sets of values. The **FF** is the red portion of the color. The **00** is the green portion. And the final **00** is the blue portion. The most important aspect of this is that the style was updated automatically as the new font color attribute was modified. We don't need to worry about modifying the current styles because Expression takes care of the updating for us.

14. Click in a new line below the third name. Type your name, hit Enter, and type your name again. Select the first name that you just typed.

15. The styles that we have created exist in the page and Expression provides an easy way to access and use them. In the lower right corner of the Expression window is the **Apply Styles** window. The **Apply Styles** tab within it should be selected. Right-click **.style1**. From the fly-out menu select **Apply Style**. Your name should now be red and in a different typeface. Now select the next name and right-click to apply **.style2**. The name now shows in all caps. Finally, select all of the names on the page. Click **Clear Styles** in the window. The names should now revert back to the default font, size, and color, except for the first name. The first name was formatted with the structural tags <H1></H1>. When you clear styles, only styles created in the style dialog box will be cleared. Once styles are used, you should not use the structural style HTML tags

16. Styles can also be created from a menu. On the **Apply Styles** task pane click the tab **Manage Styles**. On that tab, click the button **New Style. . . .** The **New Style dialog**

allows you to define any of the attributes of text. At the upper left corner of the dialog in the selector box delete what is there and type **style3**. In the **font-family** box, select **Arial, Helvetica, sans-serif**. In the **font-size** box, type the number **38** and, then, in the box immediately to the right, select **pt** (or points) from the list. The size of the text will show as **38 points**. Click the last drop-down box on this page and select the color **red**. In the **Category** list, select **Background** and, in the **Background Color** drop-down box, select the color **yellow**. Notice at the bottom of the dialog box is a preview of the style that updates as more attributes are modified. Click **OK**. These settings are shown in Figure 7.3.

17. Select the fourth name, right-click **.style3**, and apply it to the text. Click off the text. The fourth name should show in large type that is red with a yellow background.

18. Save the page and preview it in a browser.

FIGURE 7.3 *Define Style Dialog for .style3 Definition*

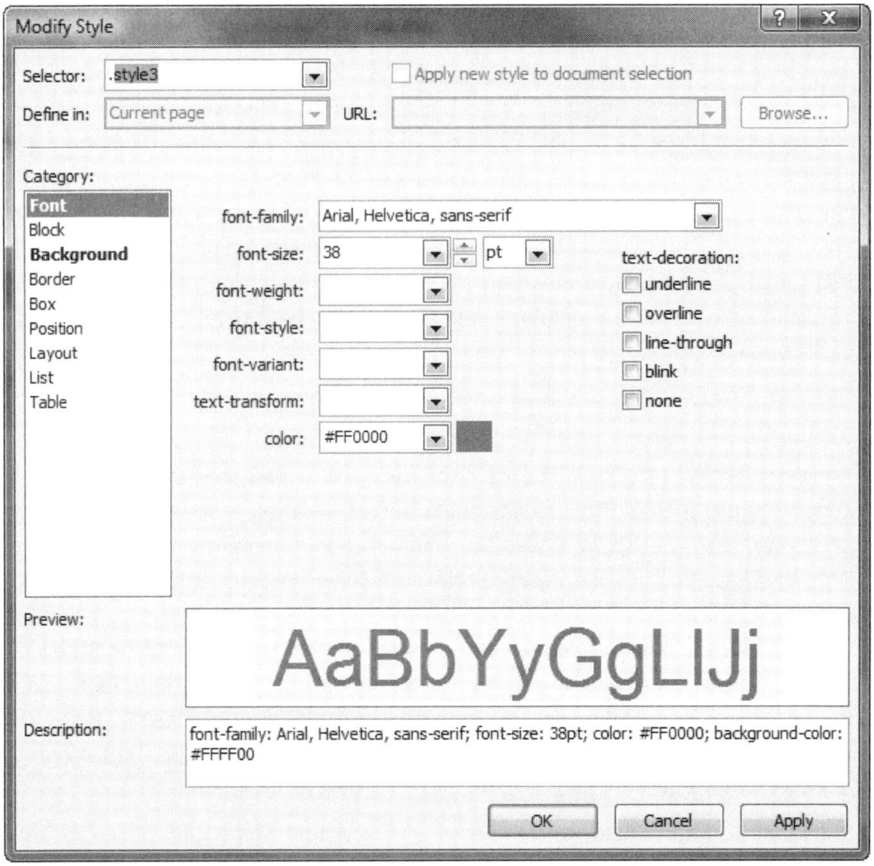

Styles are very powerful, but in this exercise, we have only defined a style in one page. To give all pages a consistent look, it would be best to have the styles defined outside of a page, making them available to use on *all* pages. Thus, if modifications need to be made, they can be made in one location and all of the pages will be updated. To achieve this, we will create a ***Cascading Style Sheet (CSS)*** page. A CSS page is a file that exists on the Web server and is a collection of styles that are created by the survey author. The meaning of the name *cascading style sheet* is somewhat technical, but "cascading" refers to how styles interact when applied on a page.

Cascading Style Sheets allow styles to be used on all pages.

WORKING WITH STYLE SHEETS

EXERCISE 7.2. **Creating a Style Sheet**

1. In Expression close any open pages.

2. It is important to create a new page for the style sheet using only this method: **File > New**. On the **Page** tab, select **General** from the first column and **CSS** from the second column (see Figure 7.4). Click **OK**.

FIGURE 7.4 *Creating a New CSS Page*

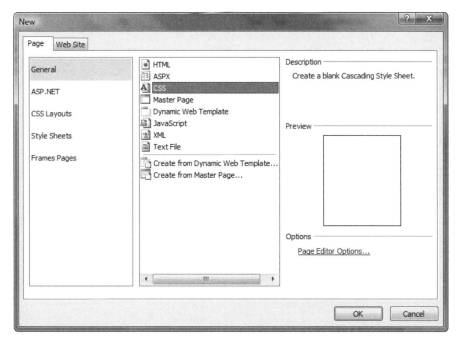

3. Save the page. Type **chapter7** for the filename. Don't enter an extension. Expression will add the *css* extension to the file. Click **Save**. The page is saved as *chapter7.css.*

4. There are only a few differences between defining the styles in a style sheet and what was done in the previous exercise. Click **New Style** in the **Apply Styles** pane in the lower right of the Expression window. In the upper left corner is the selector text box, type **question_text**. Click the drop-down list for **Define in**. Select from that list **Existing style sheet**. In the next text box, *chapter7.css* should be selected. If it is not, click the **Browse** button and select it. In the **font-family** list select **Arial, Helvetica, sans-serif**. Type **12** in the font-size box and **pt** in the **units** box to the right. The question text will be in Arial, 12-point font. These settings are shown in Figure 7.5. Click **OK**.

FIGURE 7.5 *Completed Style Page for question_text Style*

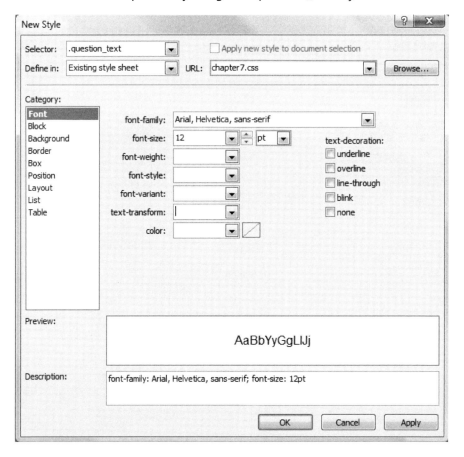

5. Create another new style in the style sheet called *answer_text* with the following proper-ties: **Arial, Helvetica, sans-serif, 9** points high, and, in the **Block** category, set the **Text Alignment** to **Center**. Click **OK**.

6. Save the style sheet.

7. In the folder list, double-click the page *unformatted_survey.htm* to open it. Resave the page with the name **formatted_survey.asp**. Remember to type the whole name and extension.

8. To have the styles available for use, the style sheet must be attached to the page. In the **Apply Styles** pane, click **Attach Style Sheet . . .** . In the dialog box, click **Browse** select *chapter7.css,* and click **Open**. Select **All HTML Pages** in the **Attach to:** section and ver-ify that it will be attached as a **Link**. Click **OK** and then **Close**.

    The *formatted_survey.asp* page is a very simple three-question survey of very plain text.

9. The **Apply Styles** pane should now show the two styles, *question_text* and *answer_text,* from the external style sheet.

10. Click anywhere in the title of the *formatted_survey.asp* page. In the **Apply Styles** pane, right-click the style *question_text* and select **Apply Style**. The title should now show in the *question_text* style.

11. However, we would like to have this text show as a title on the page. To do this, we will create a new style. In the Styles pane click **New Style . . .** .

12. In the **Selector** text box type **headline**. In the next box, the style should be defined in an **Existing Style Sheet** and, if necessary, click **Browse** and select the **chapter7.css** style sheet page. Click **Open**.

13. The font-family is **Arial, Helvetica, sans-serif,** font-size is **40 points**, font-weight is **bold**. Click the **Block** category, select text-align as **Center**. When all settings have been defined, click **OK**. Select the **chapter7.css** tab and Save the page.

14. Switch back to the *formatted_survey.asp* page. Click in the title on the page and, in the **Apply Styles** pane, right-click the **headline** style. Click in the text in the first line of the table. (Do not select the text; just click anywhere in it.) Right-click the **Headline** style and select **Apply Style**. The title should now show in Arial, bold, and large type.

15. Click in the text for the first question. Right-click the **question_text** style and apply it to this text.

16. Select the entire second and third row of the first question table. (This is the row contain-ing the descriptions of each response and the radio buttons.) Right-click the style **answer_text** and apply it to the selection. Notice that the alignment style (**Center**) is applied to all objects (text and radio buttons) in these rows.

17. Repeat both procedures for the remaining two questions in the survey. Save the page and preview it in a browser. The formatted survey is shown in Figure 7.6.

FIGURE 7.6 *Completed Survey Formatted with Styles*

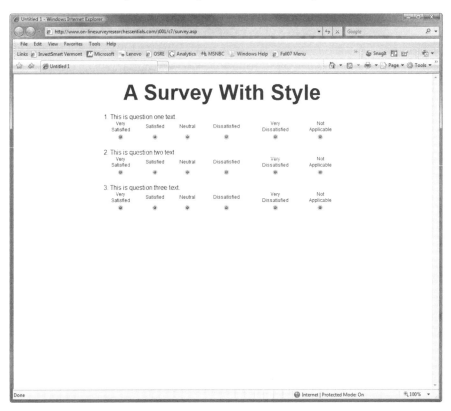

The use of style sheets allows you to easily change the look and feel of the survey.

Why bother with styles and style sheets at all? Because it makes controlling the survey's look and feel much easier. Suppose you tested your preliminary survey with several people and some of the respondents said there was not enough contrast between the questions and the answers. To remedy this problem, you decide to make the question text bold.

EXERCISE 7.3A. **Modifying a Style**

1. In the **Apply Styles** section under the heading **chapter7.css**, right-click the style **question_text**. From the menu select **Modify Style**.

2. In the **Font** category, click the down arrow for **font-weight**. Select **bold**. Click **OK**.

3. All three of the questions on the survey should now show in bold type.

In previous exercises we used a larger table to contain the entire survey and inner tables for each question and answer. To highlight this fact, the borders of the tables were colored red. In the next exercise we will color the outer table's border red and the inner question table border green. We will do this using a style sheet.

EXERCISE 7.3B. **Creating a Style for a Table and Modifying the Question Text Style**

1. Click anywhere in the *question 1* text. At the top of the document window you'll see a succession of words and tags surrounded by less-than and greater-than symbols (< >). This is called the **Quick Select** area. As you can see in Figure 7.7 some of the items are <**body**>, <**table**>, <**tr**>, <**td**>, and <**td.question_text**>. These are the HTML tags in the page. The **Quick Select** area allows us to quickly and accurately select items on the page. Starting from the right end of the list, select the <**table**> tag. The entire first question-and-answer table should now be selected.

2. In the **Apply Styles** pane, click the button **New Style**. In the selector box, name the style **question_table**. Define the style in an **Existing Style Sheet** and verify that **chapter7. css** is selected just to the right of the **Define** box.

3. In the **Category** list, select **Border**. As the name implies, this category puts a border around what is selected. In the drop-down box for **border-style**, verify that **Same for all** is checked. Click the down arrow for **top** and select **solid**. Though not necessary, you can define the **border-width** in the next drop-down box. Finally, in the last drop-down box for **border-color**, click the down arrow and select **green**. At his point, a green box should surround the text in the **Preview** area at the bottom of the dialog. Click **OK**.

4. The new style should be in the style list in the **Apply Styles** pane. With the first **question table** still selected, right-click the style **question_table** and apply it. Click anywhere outside the table to deselect it. There should now be a green border.

5. Repeat this process for the remaining two question tables. Make sure that you use the **Quick Select** area to select the question table.

FIGURE 7.7 *Question 1 Table Selected*

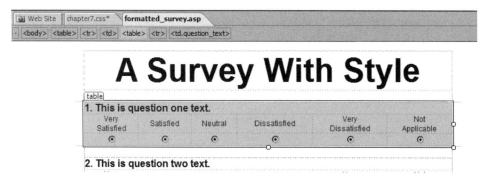

6. Click in the last row of the table, which should be outside of any questions or answers. In the **Quick Select** area, click the <**table**> tag. By clicking it, the outer table should now be selected. Make a new style called **survey_table** in the style sheet whose only property is a red border. Apply the **survey_table** style to the outer table.

7. Save all the pages and preview the survey in a browser. The formatted survey is shown in Figure 7.8. In Expression, save and close any open pages.

When the survey is ready for deployment to the population, the borders of all tables should be turned off. In the previous chapter, this was done manually for each question table. The advantage of using styles with a style sheet is that the borders of all tables can easily be turned off at one time. To do this use the procedure outlined in Exercise 7.3B and turn the border off for the question and survey tables.

WORKING WITH PICTURES AND GRAPHICS

Remember, smaller graphic file sizes take less time to transfer over the Internet.

Pictures and graphics serve a vital function in Web surveys. They can be stimuli in a research study, make pages look more interesting, identify the sponsoring organization for the study, or function as buttons.

Graphics or pictures that are going to be used on the Web need to be saved in a format that is compatible with

FIGURE 7.8 *Completed Survey Formatted with Borders On*

A Survey With Style

1. This is question one text.

Very Satisfied	Satisfied	Neutral	Dissatisfied	Very Dissatisfied	Not Applicable
⦿	⦿	⦿	⦿	⦿	⦿

2. This is question two text.

Very Satisfied	Satisfied	Neutral	Dissatisfied	Very Dissatisfied	Not Applicable
⦿	⦿	⦿	⦿	⦿	⦿

3. This is question three text.

Very Satisfied	Satisfied	Neutral	Dissatisfied	Very Dissatisfied	Not Applicable
⦿	⦿	⦿	⦿	⦿	⦿

the Web. The file sizes need to be as small as possible to minimize the time it takes to transmit them over the Internet from the server to a browser. A smaller file can move faster. If loading a graphic takes a long time it could mean the difference between someone completing the survey or bailing out before completing it. However, the file cannot be *too* small. As the file gets smaller, some of the detail in the graphic can be lost. Graphics on the Internet are a balance between small file size and image quality. The key is to achieve the optimal balance.

Photographs taken with a digital camera are usually saved in the file format *jpeg*. **JPEG** is a format that was designed to give an excellent picture quality with a some-what small file size. A JPEG file is compatible with most picture editing programs, such as Photoshop. They have the file extension *.jpg* and this is the format of choice for photographs.

JPEG and GIF are formats that are used for graphics.

The other main image format used on the Internet is the **GIF**. A GIF is a format that reduces the size of the file even more than a JPEG. It does this by minimizing the number of colors that are in each file. A GIF is best for drawings and illustrations that have few colors (most photos have a wide range of colors, shadows, and subtle grada-tions of color). A GIF will take out most of these details and reduce them to a few col-ors. Images will appear flatter and more homogenous—not good for photographs, but very effective for other things. For instance, GIF is the best choice for buttons, ban-ners, and small illustrations. Files saved as GIFs have the file extension *.gif*.

As it comes directly from a digital camera a JPEG's file size that is too large to work on a Web page. JPEGs must be compressed to further reduce the size. In addition, images may also need to be cropped to change the size of the image or to make the sub-ject of the photo clearer. Expression has built-in tools that allow you to do simple photo editing. For more complex tasks, you may need Photoshop or the assistance of a graphic or Web designer. The next exercise will use Expression's tools to edit a photo.

EXERCISE 7.4. Uploading and Editing Photographs

1. Create a new page in the Web site and save the page as *photo.htm*.

2. Click the **Attach Style Sheet . . .** button in the **Apply Styles** pane and browse to the **chapter7.css** style sheet. Attach the style sheet to this page.

3. Create a standard survey table on the page with the specifications of 3 rows, 1 column, 600 px wide, centered on the page, and no border around the table.

4. Click inside the table and, on the **Quick Select** menu, select the table tag (<**Table**>). Apply the **survey_table** style to the table.

5. Click inside the first row of the table and type **My Dog Sam**. Apply the **headline** style to the text.

6. Click in the second row of the table. This is where the picture will be placed. On the menu select **Insert** > **Picture** > **From File**. In the files for *chapter 7*, locate the image *sam.jpg* and select it. Click **Insert**.

7. If you see a dialog box titled **Accessibility Properties**, type **My Dog Sam** in the **Alternative Text** box and click **OK.** The alternative text allows blind people to surf the Net with a screen reader that will read this description and say it out loud.

8. Save the page (see Figure 7.9).

When you click the Save button a new dialog box opens as shown in Figure 7.9. In the Save Embedded Files dialog box, a thumbnail of the image should show on the right side. On the left should be the name of the picture (sam.jpg) and, next to it, the location where the image will be saved on the Web.

9. If this doesn't show the folder *images/* (meaning the image will be saved in the *images* folder), click the **Change Folder . . .** button and select the images folder on your Web site. Click **OK** when you have the image folder selected. The graphic will be uploaded to the server and stored in the images folder.

It is important to do this. In the course of creating a complicated survey site, there may be many image files. The above procedure puts all images into a separate folder and keeps things neat and organized.

FIGURE 7.9 *Save Embedded Files Dialog Box*

10. In Expression, there is a separate toolbar with tools for manipulating photos. To bring it or any other toolbar into the window, click **View** > **Toolbars** and select **Pictures** from the fly-out menu. The **Pictures Toolbar** should show somewhere on the screen. It may be at the bottom of the window or it may be under the **Common Toolbar**. If you want to move a toolbar, left-click the left edge of the toolbar and drag it to the location that you prefer.

11. Click the picture. As shown in Figure 7.10, this selects the picture and begins the editing process. The picture is selected when there are small circles in the corners and midpoints of the photo. The first task will be to crop the picture.

12. With the picture selected, click the cropping tool on the **Pictures Toolbar** (it looks like two interlocked Xs.) As you can see in Figure 7.11, when you click the button, a dashed line with dots at the four corners and at the midpoints of each side should appear on the picture. Using the dots, drag the white box so that Sam is centered in the picture, or use

FIGURE 7.10 *Page with Photo Selected*

FIGURE 7.11 *Photo-Cropping Dialog Box*

the mouse to draw a box around Sam, leaving plenty of lake above his head and the small tree on the right side. When the cropping is as you wish, hit Enter. The image is cropped to the smaller size. If the image after it has been cropped is not to your liking, click the **Restore** button on the **Pictures Toolbar** to restore the original image, and then crop it again.

13. Though the photo may show what you want it to show, it may still not be the correct size for the Web page. To increase or decrease the size of the image, right-click the picture and select **Picture Properties . . .** from the menu. Click the **Appearance** tab in the dialog box (see Figure 7.12).

14. To resize the image, check the **Specify Size** check box and check the **Keep Aspect Ratio** check box (if needed). The **aspect ratio** is the ratio of the picture width to the height. With this checked, the image will stay in the same proportions when it is resized. You should always keep a photo at the same aspect ratio. If you don't, the results will be distorted. Set the width of the image to 600 and verify that **in pixels** is selected. Leave the

FIGURE 7.12 *Picture Properties Dialog Box*

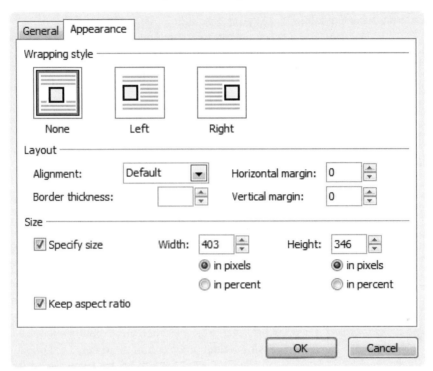

height setting alone; it will automatically adjust as needed (because of the **Keep Aspect Ratio** setting). Click **OK**.

15. Because the picture size was increased, it may look a bit blurry. With the image still selected, click the **Resample** button. The image should sharpen up.

16. Save the page and preview it in a browser. The **Save Embedded Files** dialog box may appear. This is because the cropped image is now actually a new unsaved picture. If necessary, click **OK** and the image will be saved again in its new cropped size.

The resampling process also reduces the size of the file for the Web. The image is now compact enough to travel over the Internet quickly, but large enough to look good when it gets to the browser. If images are used as stimuli in an experiment, they should be the same size. If one stimulus is larger, it will bias the results to that stimulus condition. Also, the size of the main element in the images should be roughly equal. In the exercise above, if the hypothesis was that dog pictures would influence people's ratings of product packages more than cat pictures, the images of the dog and cat should be roughly equal in size.

17. There are also other tools for making rudimentary adjustments in contrast and brightness, orientation, and so on. Click Sam's picture and experiment with increasing and decreasing the contrast and brightness of the picture. When you are done experimenting with the picture, save the page. When you do, the photo edits will be made. If you do not like the results of your editing, close the page without saving. Note that as soon as you save the page the **Save Embedded File** dialog box will open and prompt you to choose an action for the photo. If you are not sure whether your picture edits are what you want, you can also click the **Rename** button. Give the edited graphic another name. You will now have both the edited and unedited versions available on the server.

Graphics as Buttons and Banners

Most surveys need, at minimum, an **I Agree** button and an **I Disagree** button. These buttons are used on the consent form. In the files for this chapter are these two buttons. They were created in Photoshop using the procedure outlined in Appendix 1.

Do not use Interactive Buttons in Microsoft Expression. Using these buttons can lead to compatibility issues with other browsers and can be distracting for respondents.

There is another source of buttons for Web pages in Microsoft Expression. If you click the menu choice **Insert** > **Interactive Buttons** there will be a menu with many animated and colorful buttons. *Do not use these buttons!* While creating an Internet survey, the mission is not to create a jazzy Web page; it is to create an effective and uncomplicated survey. Interactive buttons require more processing by the browser and there may be compatibility issues with other browsers. They also take the respondent's attention away from completing the survey. It is better to use a plain graphic button like the agree-disagree links.

Banners are graphics at the top of a page that may reflect the ownership of the survey or indicate the client that sponsors the survey. From a technical point of view, they are just graphics, and the rules for graphics and photos apply to these as well. They should be the smallest possible file size to minimize the time it takes to travel across the Internet but large enough to communicate the idea that they represent.

As we mentioned earlier, a banner or button should not be saved as a JPEG. The JPEG format is primarily designed for graphics with many colors. Most buttons and banners have only a few colors. The better format is the GIF. If you are making the banner or buttons with a program like Photoshop or Adobe Illustrator you should save them as GIF.

EXERCISE 7.4.   Adding Buttons to a Page

1. Open *default.htm*. This is the consent page that a respondent will see upon first entering the site. Click anywhere in the title at the top of the page.

2. In the **Style** pane, right-click the **Headline** style and apply it to the title.

3. Create a style called **bodytext** in the style sheet. The style should specify the font as **Arial, Helvetica, sans-serif** and the size should be **11 points**. Click OK.

4. Select all of the text in the middle of the consent page. Apply the style **bodytext** to all of this text.

5. Delete the words *I Agree* and *I Disagree* from the page.

6. In the files for this chapter are graphics for these two buttons. Click in the first cell of the second-to-last row. To bring the graphic into the Web, select **Insert** > **Picture** > **From File . . .** then navigate to the location for the *chapter 7* files and select *i_agree.gif*. Click the **Insert** button and **OK**. The **I Agree** button should now show on the page.

7. Click in the second cell of the same row. Insert into that cell the *i_disagree.gif* graphic. Use the **right alignment** button to position the graphic at the right edge of the cell.

8. Save the page. The **Save Embedded Files** dialog box should appear. If necessary, click the **Change Folder** button. Select the *images* folder and click **OK** twice. The graphics should upload to the site and the page should save. The page should look like Figure 7.13.

FIGURE 7.13 *Completed Consent Form Formatted with Styles*

Consent Form

This survey is designed to collect information about your satisfaction with your recent stay at Fictitious Medical Center. We are particularly concerned with your experiences with the custodial staff and the cleanliness of the facility.

The information collected will not be viewed by anyone other than the survey researcher. The results will only be reported in total and no individual inputs will be discussed. No personal information will be collected, except for demographic information which will be used for research purposes only. The identity and privacy of participants will be safeguarded at all times.

This information is collected to improve the service at Fictitious Medical Center. We would like your honest input. If you would like to discuss this or any other topic at length there is contact information below and at the end of the survey.

This survey is best viewed using an Internet Explorer 4.0 or Netscape 4 compatible browser (most browsers meet this requirement). No cookies will be added or used in this survey.

By clicking I Agree you are indicating that you are over 18 years old and agree to the conditions stated above. If this is not the case, click I Disagree.

If you would like to discuss your input contact us at survey@fictitiousmed.org. We can also be reached by phone at 800-555-1212. Thank you for your consideration.

I Agree   I Disagree

9. When respondents click the **I Agree** button, it should take them to the survey page. We need to make the **I Agree** button a hyperlink. The process is identical to making a hyperlink out of text, but first you select the image. Select the **I Agree** button and then click the **Insert Hyperlink** button on the **Common Toolbar**. From the page list select the page *formatted_survey.asp* and click **OK**. Create a hyperlink to the *no_thank_you.htm* page with the **I Disagree** button.

10. Save the page and preview it in a browser. Test both hyperlinks.

11. To insert the banner at the top of the page, click in the first row of the table for the consent page. Select **Table** > **Insert** > **Row Above**. Click in the new first row of the table.

12. Insert the banner GIF image (*c7_banner.gif*) into the first row of the table.

13. Save the page and preview it in a browser. When prompted save the GIF image in the *images* folder.

At this point you should be able to add the banner file to any page of the survey.

Using a banner in a Web survey is purely a matter of preference. If the survey is for a corporate client, the client will probably insist on some logo or identifying banner. For academic research, it doesn't add much and it could make the survey slower to load. It could easily be left out.

SUMMARY

In this chapter, we taught you how to use styles and style sheets to govern the appearance of objects in a Web site. The use of styles can create a common and consistent look and feel on all pages throughout the site. Styles were created, applied, modified, and resaved to an external style sheet. The sheet was saved on the Web server and attached to all of the pages in the site.

We also covered inserting graphics. Graphics come in two basic formats on the Internet. The JPEG format is used for photographs and the GIF format is used for illustrations or buttons with few colors. Expression has photo tools for basic photo editing and cropping. When the page is saved, the edits are also saved into the image file.

Most image editing tasks can be done using these basic tools. If more complicated tasks are needed and you are not comfortable with a more advanced editing tool, a graphic or Web designer can usually help in a few short minutes.

KEY TERMS

styles
object
style sheet
heading1, <h1>
Design View

Code View
Split View
<h1> and </h1>
HTML tags
Arial, Helvetica, sans-serif

<p>
class="style1"
All Caps
Font Color button
Apply Styles window
Clear Styles
New Style dialog
pt or points
Manage Styles
Cascading Style Sheet (CSS)

Attach Style Sheet
Quick Select area
pictures and graphics
JPEG or jpg
GIF
Save Embedded Files
pictures toolbar
Keep Aspect Ratio
Resample

DISCUSSION QUESTION

1. Either take a picture of someone with a digital camera or find a photo on the Internet and download it to your computer. What is the file type of this image? In Expression, create a new page and put a standard survey table centered on the page. In one of the rows, split it into two columns. Insert the photo into the left cell of this row. Crop this photo so the person is the main focal point of the image. Reduce the size of this photo to be 300 px wide and keep the same aspect ratio. Save the page. When prompted, name the photo *image1.jpg*. Now insert the original photo into the right cell of this row. This time, crop the image to intentionally distort the main feature of the picture. You might make the person larger or off-center in this second image. How could this simple manipulation of the images result in biased results in a survey? How could you guard against this happening?

CHAPTER

CREATING MORE COMPLICATED INTERNET SURVEYS

LEARNING OBJECTIVES

- To be able to create style guidelines for longer surveys

- To be able to "chunk" survey questions to limit the amount of information presented at one time

- To be able to use internal hyperlinks to allow respondents to move through a survey from chunk to chunk

- To be able to add progress indicators to give respondents feedback on their progress

The surveys created thus far were very simple surveys with only a few questions and no special stimuli associated with them. Research often demands more complicated surveys and the presentation of text and pictures to stimulate the respondent. This chapter will discuss the preparation of longer surveys and offer some style guidelines to ensure that the survey has the best chance of success.

STYLE GUIDELINES

There has been a great deal written about style considerations for Web surveys. There are technical considerations that have to do with the medium of the Internet and there are psychological considerations that have to do with the respondent. A comprehensive set of guidelines for the preparation of Internet surveys has been written by Schonlau (Schonlau, Fricker, & Elliott, 2002). These guidelines provide some very practical style principles for surveys:

1. List Only a Few Questions per Screen and
2. Eliminate Unnecessary Questions

Some of these guidelines (such as number 2) apply to any survey, whether online or paper. It is always a good idea not to ask unnecessary questions. Some of these guidelines

1. List only a few questions per screen.
2. Eliminate unnecessary questions.
3. Use graphics sparingly.
4. Be aware of how respondents may interpret questions in light of accompanying graphics.
5. Use matrix questions sparingly.
6. Reduce response errors by restricting response choices.
7. Force answers only on rare occasions.
8. Make error or warning messages as specific as possible.
9. Always password-protect Web surveys.
10. Ensure that respondents' privacy and their perception of privacy are protected.
11. Provide some indication of survey progress.
12. Allow respondents to interrupt and then reenter the survey.
13. Carefully handle respondents who fail a screening test.
14. Give respondents something in return.
15. Take advantage of the media's presentation capabilities.

are unique to Internet surveys. The purpose of the first guideline is to limit the amount of information that the respondent sees at one time and to prevent the need for scrolling to see the entire question or passage. Internet users do not like to scroll, either up and down or left to right, to see text. In prior chapters, we have restricted text width to a 600 px table so users would not have to scroll right or left. In this chapter, we will introduce a method to further "chunk" information in a survey. **Chunking** divides the information presented on a page into sections. Each section should contain about 4–5 questions, which is an amount that fits on one screen and that people can reasonably complete in a short time. When they are done with a chunk, they can click a button and move on to the next chunk. The chunking can be based on some contextual break or come just after a stimulus.

3. Use Graphics Sparingly and 4. Be Aware of How Respondents May Interpret Questions in Light of Accompanying Graphics

Be careful when using graphics to choose graphics and illustrations that will not bias your research sample.

Using graphics sparingly reduces the possibility of distracting the respondent and also keeps the overall size of the survey to a minimum. This will maximize the survey's loading speed in a browser. Graphics also have an influence on how questions are interpreted. A picture of a man may introduce bias when the survey is viewed by men as opposed to women, and vice versa. That may be the purpose of the research. If so, then the graphic would be integral. Otherwise, be careful not to introduce a potential bias if it is not part of the research.

5. Use Matrix Questions Sparingly

A matrix question presents a table of questions in the first column and a set of responses to each on the right. There are usually many answer choices in these types of questions and they can appear intimidating in a survey. Schonlau suggests that these may be too overwhelming and should be avoided. An example of this is given in Figure 8.1.

6. Reduce Response Errors by Restricting Response Choices

Restricting response choices means providing a set of responses that limit what the subject can enter in answer to a question. For example, as shown in Figure 8.2, the question is "Please indicate your date of birth." One way to design this question would be to provide a text box where participants could type in their date of birth. Possible responses might be February 14, 1951; Feb. 14, 1951; 2/14/1951; 02/14/1951; 02/14/51; Valentine's Day, 1951; and so on. All of these responses are equivalent, but would need to be interpreted and translated to one uniform format prior to analysis. Another way to set this question up would be to have three drop-down boxes—one for the month, one for the day, and one for the year. In this way, the subject's choices have been restricted, but the analysis is much less time-consuming.

FIGURE 8.1 *A Matrix Question*

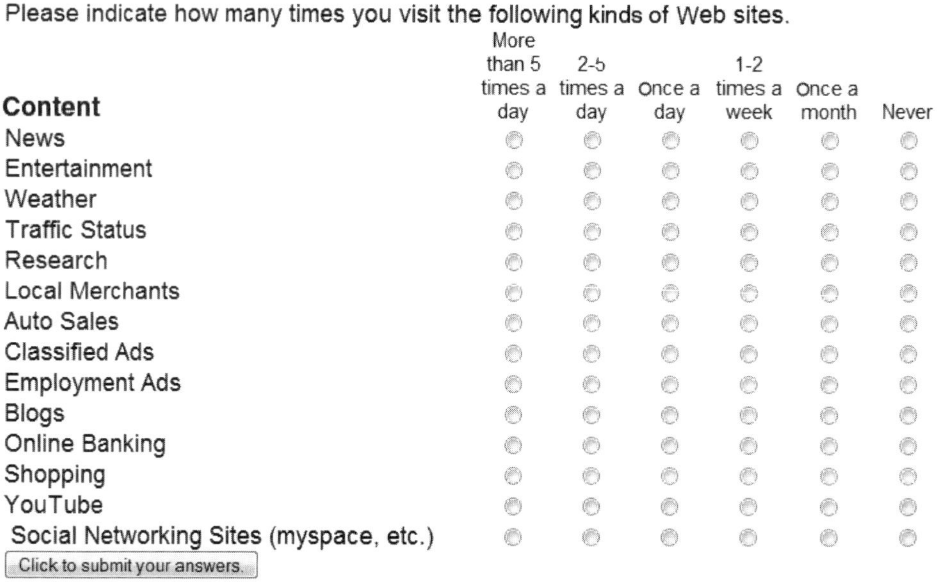

Please indicate how many times you visit the following kinds of Web sites.

Content	More than 5 times a day	2-5 times a day	Once a day	1-2 times a week	Once a month	Never
News	○	○	○	○	○	○
Entertainment	○	○	○	○	○	○
Weather	○	○	○	○	○	○
Traffic Status	○	○	○	○	○	○
Research	○	○	○	○	○	○
Local Merchants	○	○	○	○	○	○
Auto Sales	○	○	○	○	○	○
Classified Ads	○	○	○	○	○	○
Employment Ads	○	○	○	○	○	○
Blogs	○	○	○	○	○	○
Online Banking	○	○	○	○	○	○
Shopping	○	○	○	○	○	○
YouTube	○	○	○	○	○	○
Social Networking Sites (myspace, etc.)	○	○	○	○	○	○

Click to submit your answers.

FIGURE 8.2 *Two Ways of Collecting Date of Birth*

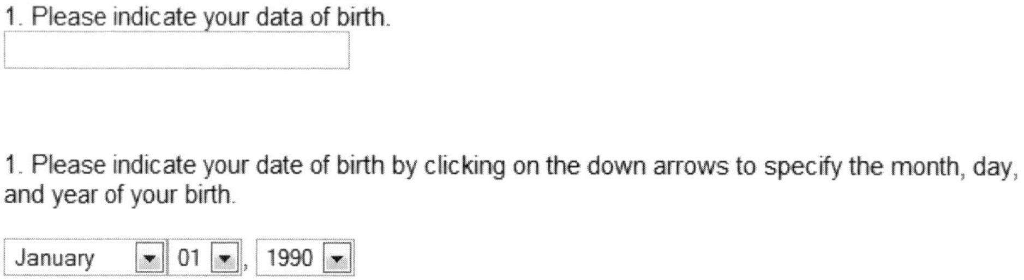

1. Please indicate your data of birth.

[   ]

1. Please indicate your date of birth by clicking on the down arrows to specify the month, day, and year of your birth.

[January ▼] [01 ▼], [1990 ▼]

7. Force Answers Only on Rare Occasions

Forcing an answer means not allowing a subject to opt out of answering or voicing an opinion on a question. Figure 8.3 shows the same question with unforced and forced answers. Option 1 gives the subject the option of being "neutral" or not answering the question. Option 2 does not. You must take a stand and be either "satisfied" or "dissatisfied." You can leave the question blank, but that raises questions about how to interpret the answer. Forcing should be used in rare situations.

FIGURE 8.3 *Example with and without Forced Answers*

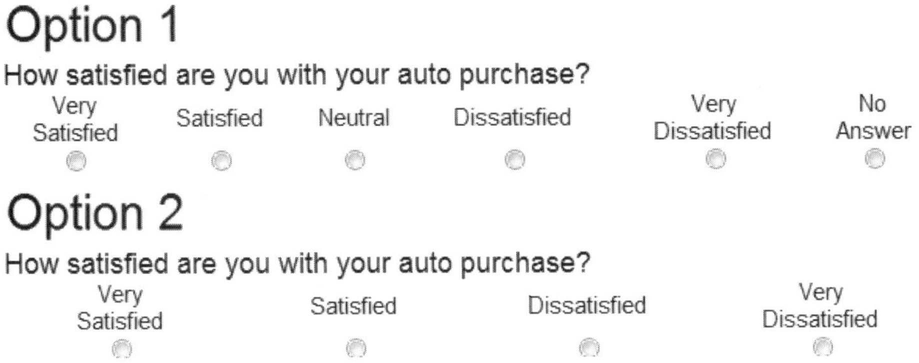

Option 1

How satisfied are you with your auto purchase?

Very Satisfied	Satisfied	Neutral	Dissatisfied	Very Dissatisfied	No Answer
◌	◌	◌	◌	◌	◌

Option 2

How satisfied are you with your auto purchase?

Very Satisfied	Satisfied	Dissatisfied	Very Dissatisfied
◌	◌	◌	◌

8. Make Error or Warning Messages as Specific as Possible

We will not be writing custom errors messages in our surveys. If you must write a *custom error message*, then make sure that it is specific to the question that caused the error and clearly describes to the subject what actions must be taken to correct it. Finally, there should be a visual indicator in the survey to indicate what caused the error.

9. Always Password-Protect Web Surveys

Though Schonlau and colleagues (2002) recommend password protection, understand that utilizing password protection presents considerable problems for the researcher. It adds another layer of technical expertise that must be mastered that is beyond the scope of this text. A second database must be created to hold usernames and passwords. Input forms and scripts for entering and retrieving names and passwords must be created. Authentication of the user with the database must be programmed and the survey must be restricted from unauthenticated users. Password protection forces the researcher into providing or capturing usernames and passwords, and there must be a way for the participants to get their initial username and password from the researcher. This means that a participant must visit the site at least twice to respond to the survey. Capturing and transmitting passwords should be done in a secure Web site, which adds the expense of a secure SSL connection. There must also be a mechanism for retrieving a forgotten username and password. All of these steps complicate the process of completing a survey and will drive the response rate down. Password protecting a survey presents major challenges to the researcher and should only be used if absolutely necessary.

10. Ensure That Respondents' Privacy and Their Perception of Privacy Are Protected

Ensuring privacy and respondents' perception of privacy is a paramount task for the researcher. As stated in Chapter Two, the privacy of subjects' inputs must be clearly

If sensitive identifying information is to be collected, it must be done in a secure manner and the site must use a secure connection to prevent the information from being stolen as it travels on the Internet.

stated and kept secure at all times. The consent page is where privacy procedures should be spelled out and those measures should be strictly adhered to by all researchers involved in the study. Collected data should be kept safe and, if identifying codes are used, they should not be stored on the server or on the same computer at any time. Physically separating the codes from the data helps ensure that the two cannot be linked should a computer be hacked into or stolen.

11. Provide Some Indication of Survey Progress

A *progress indicator* is a graphic that gives the subject feedback about their progress through the survey. Sometimes this is a graphic or text that says how much is left to finish the survey. Research indicates that the presence of progress indicators reduces the number of missed items (Heerwegh, 2004) and creates a more positive experience completing the study (Conrad et al., 2005). Indicators are easily implemented and we will illustrate their use later in this chapter.

12. Allow Respondents to Interrupt and Then Reenter the Survey

Allowing subjects to leave and then reenter a survey presents considerable problems for the researcher. Some are technical in that the subject must be identified in both sessions so that the data from each session can be merged. Some problems are research concerns. If a subject leaves the study and comes back, will the results be different than if it was completed in one session? If subjects leave and come back, would they have had time to think about the stimuli? The stimuli might change in the intervening time. Respondents may not come back, increasing the incomplete responses. For most social science research a survey is more appropriately done in one session.

13. Carefully Handle Respondents Who Fail a Screening Test

Screening questions are used to target only the subjects that are desired. For example, a researcher studying attitudes towards clothing may only be interested in female participants. A gender question would provide a way of screening respondents. But how would you implement the survey with this screening question? One way is to have the subject answer the question and, if the answer is "male," take the respondent to a "thank you" page, ending the survey. Another way is to have everyone complete the survey and then, in the analysis, eliminate the responses of males or those who skipped the gender question. The second approach doesn't offend anyone and is a cleaner design. We recommend using this approach.

14. Give Respondents Something in Return

The use of rewards and incentives for completing a survey is a standard practice for traditional surveys. It increases response rates by on average 13 percent (Church, 1993) and response rates are higher when the incentive is presented to the subject prior to taking the survey (James & Bolstein, 1990), but using such payments in a Web-based survey presents some challenges. The incentive cannot be presented to the subject "in cash"; there is no way of e-mailing a physical dollar. One method that shows promise is through the use of prize drawings. Upon completion of the survey, a respondent is entered into a drawing pool for an item worth a set monetary value. This increases completion rates and reduces incomplete participation patterns (Bosnjak & Tuten, 2003). If you can afford to offer incentives for completion, then it is a good idea.

15. Take Advantage of the Media's Presentation Capabilities

The Internet makes using photographs and graphics in a survey very easy. If the research question is best presented with these media, then by all means use them. And they can be presented with little increase in the cost of implementing the survey. Take advantage of it!

CHUNKING QUESTIONS

The survey that we will be working with in this chapter was created by a student to determine the factors a jury might consider when sentencing an offender. The survey consists of a long presentation of text followed by questions about the respondents' perceptions of the offender and the sentence they would give to the offender. The layout of the study is given in Figure 8.4.

EXERCISE 8.1. Chunking the Text and Questions in a Survey

1. With Internet Explorer navigate to the *chapter08* Web site and open it with Expression. Open the page *survey_start.asp*. Save the file as *survey.asp*.

The page consists of an outer table with a red border containing the entire survey and each question in a table with a green outline. Styles are used throughout the survey to control the format of text and the border color of the tables. At the top of the survey are six paragraphs of text that are to be read before answering the questions. Six long paragraphs of text is quite a bit to read at one time on a Web page. The user would need to scroll down to move through the entire text. That much scrolling might frustrate users and cause them to exit the survey.

2. Click at the top of the survey in the statement *Please read the following information*. Add fourteen additional rows to the outer table above the first row by clicking **Table > Insert > Rows or Columns**, verify that the rows option is selected, enter 14 for the number of rows, select **Above selection** for the location, and click **OK**.

3. Select the statement *Please read the following information* and move it to the first row of the table.

FIGURE 8.4 *Survey Map*

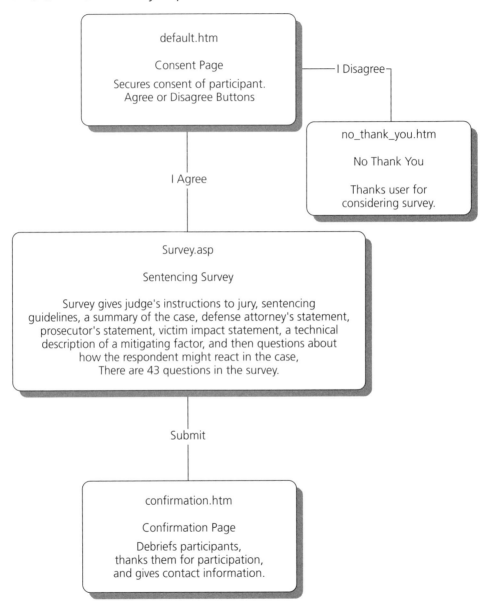

4. Select the next paragraph that begins with the heading *Judge's Instructions* and the paragraph after that ends with *robbery or burglary*. Cut this text from its present location. At the top of the survey, skip a row and paste the text into the third row of the table.

5. Select the text that begins *In order to determine* **. . .** through *defendant's punishment should be*. Cut the text from its present location and paste it into the fifth row of the table.

6. Select the text beginning with the heading *Case Summary* and the following paragraph through *police officers*. Move this text to the seventh row. Make sure that you always skip a row between the text chunks.

7. Continue until all of the paragraphs at the beginning of the survey are in separate rows of the table with blank rows between. If there is any extra punctuation, returns, or text left after all the moving is done, delete it. There should be one blank row between the paragraphs and the first question.

8. Save the survey.

9. Click in the blank row under the *Judge's Instructions* paragraph (that is, the fourth row of the table). In the *chapter 8* files is an image titled *next.gif*. This is a simple button with the text *Next Section*. We will use this button to move respondents through the survey. Insert this button in the fourth row (**Insert** > **Picture** > **From File**). Locate the graphic file, select it, click **Insert**, and click **OK**).

10. Click the graphic and copy it.

11. Paste a copy of the button in each blank row of the top section, including the row above the first question.

12. Save the survey. When the **Save Embedded Files** dialog box appears, if necessary, click the **Change Folder** button. Click the *images* folder of the Web site. Click **OK** twice. This step will upload the image file from your computer to the Web site and save the page.

13. Each cell in a table has properties associated with it. The next action requires that the vertical alignment of the table cells that contain the *Next Section* graphic be modified. Click in the fourth cell of the outer table. It contains the first instance of the **Next Section** button. On the **Quick Selector** bar at the top of the document window, click the entry for <**tr**>. This is the HTML code for a table row. In the lower left corner of the Expression window is the **Tag Properties** pane. This pane allows you to see the property settings of an object that is selected. In the properties pane find the **valign property** (the properties are listed alphabetically). **Valign** is the vertical alignment of the selected cell. Click **valign property** and then click the down arrow in the column to the right of this property name. From the list, select the property **top**. This will align all of the contents of this cell at the top of the cell.

14. We could move through the survey and change the **valign property** for each cell, but a style can do the same thing. In the **Manage Style** task pane click the **New Style** link. In the New Style dialog change the selector name to *next_section_cell*. The **Define In** box should be set to **Existing Style Sheet**. The URL should be *chapter8.css*; click browse to select this.

FIGURE 8.5 *Creating a Block Style*

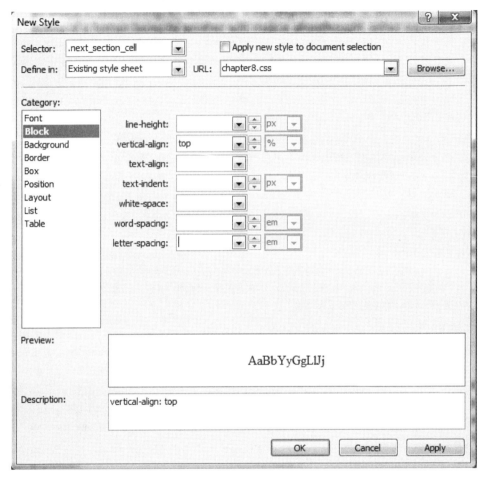

15. In the Category list, select **Block**. Click the down arrow for the vertical-align property and select **Top**. Figure 8.5 shows the completed style definition.

16. Click **OK**. Save the page and click **Yes** to save the style sheet as well.

17. Click in each cell with the *Next Section* graphic. Use **Quick Select** to select the <**tr**> tag. Apply the **next_section_cell** style to each cell.

18. Save the page.

Internal Hyperlinks (Bookmarks)

Internal hyperlinks, sometimes called *bookmarks*, are links on a Web page that, when clicked, take the user to a different location on the *same* Web page. An internal hyperlink can be anchored by text or a graphic. When the hyperlink is clicked, the bookmarked location will be in the upper left corner of the browser window. To create an internal hyperlink, first establish the bookmark's landing location and then create a hyperlink to that location.

Internal hyperlinks can be very helpful and serve as bookmarks that link the user from place to place on the same Web page.

EXERCISE 8.2. Creating Internal Hyperlinks

1. Move to the top of the survey and click in the fifth row. Click just before the text *In order to determine* . . . (to the left of the *I*). It is sometimes helpful to click in the text and then use the arrow keys to move the cursor to the beginning.

2. To insert the bookmark, click **Insert > Bookmark.** In the **Bookmark** dialog box, type a descriptive name for the location in the **Bookmark name** text box, which in this case is the word **judges**.

3. Click **OK**.

4. Click just to the left of **Case Summary** in the seventh row.

5. Insert a bookmark at this location, named **case summary**. Bookmark names can be one or more words and upper or lowercase.

6. Continue adding bookmarks at the beginning of the text just after the **Next Section** buttons. They should be named **defense attorney, prosecutor, victim impact, and appropriate sentence**. The final bookmark should be just to the left of the *I* of question 1 of the survey. Name this bookmark **q1**.

7. Save the page.

After completing this task, the bookmark list should look like Figure 8.6. To view the list, click **Insert > Bookmark**.

8. To link to the bookmarks, select the first **Next Section** button (in row four). With the button selected, click the **Insert Hyperlink** button on the **Common Toolbar**. In the **Insert Hyperlink** dialog box, select the **Bookmark . . .** button on the right side. Select the bookmark *judges* from the list.

9. Click **OK** twice.

10. Proceed to the second **Next Section** button and hyperlink it to the bookmark *case summary*.

11. Continue this process until the final bookmark is linked to **q1**.

12. Save the page and preview it in a browser. Test each internal hyperlink and verify that it takes the user to the correct specific location in the page.

The survey questions should also be chunked to prevent the user from seeing too many at a time and getting discouraged. In addition, when the questions switch to

FIGURE 8.6 *Bookmark List Through Question 1*

a different topic, such as demographic questions, these should be set off from the others. We will next add bookmark locations and buttons to the question part of the survey.

Choosing the location of the bookmarks is not a precise process. There should be about 400 px of information on the screen at one time. To accomplish this, you should have a **Next Section** button and a bookmark every 4–6 questions.

13. Select any of the **Next Section** buttons and copy it. Click in the blank row above question 4. Paste a **Next Section** button in this location.

14. Click inside the cell where you just added the button, select the row with the **Quick Selector** mark, <**tr**>, and apply the **next_section_cell** style to the cell.

15. Click to the left of *4* in the question and name this bookmark location **q4** (**Insert > Bookmark,** name *q4*).

16. Select the *Next Section* graphic and hyperlink it to the bookmark *q4*.

17. Continue adding buttons, formatting with the cell style, inserting bookmarks on the following question number, and hyperlinking the button to the next question. Add them at the following locations: button above q7; bookmarks at q10, text descriptions before q13, q18, q22, q26, q30, text line above q33, q36, and q40. Add buttons in the row immediately before the bookmark, apply the style to that row, and create a hyperlink to the bookmark following.

18. When done, save the page and, when prompted, save the style sheet. Preview the page in a browser. When you get to the last button, it will appear that the link doesn't work. This is not the case. We have one more step in the chunking process.

19. We used a style for each cell that has a button. The style has been applied to every cell that has the button in it. Move down to the cell with the **Submit** button. Click inside this cell, but not on the **Submit** button. Select the table row with the **Quick Selector** bar and apply the **next_section_cell** style to this cell.

20. Move to the top of the page and select the first **Next Section** button. Select the table row using the **Quick Selector** bar and apply the **next_section_cell** style to this cell.

21. In the **Manage Styles** task pane, right click the **next_section_cell** style. From the menu select **Modify Style . . . .**

22. Select the **Position** Category from the list. Set the **Height** to 2000 and verify that px is showing in the units box next to it. This change will have the effect of making every cell with a button 2000 pixels high. Click **OK**.

23. Save the page and, when prompted, save the style sheet. Preview the page in a browser. Test each button to verify that the chunking was successful. Some of the chunks will be too large. We will address this in the next exercise.

EXERCISE 8.3. Testing the Survey for Compatibility

The chunking process is essential to ensuring that the survey can be viewed and completed in any browser at any screen resolution. Today, it is unlikely that anyone coming to your site will be using a computer with a maximum resolution of less than 800 × 600 px. Therefore, this is the lowest resolution we will use for testing. If the chunking works at this resolution, it will work at any resolution greater than this.

1. Preview the survey in Internet Explorer at the 800 × 600 resolution (**File** > **Preview** in Browser. Select **Microsoft Internet Explorer 7.0** (800 × 600).

This preview should show that most of the questions are generally visible at the 800 × 600 resolution and that most of the chunks are the right size, but there are some problems. The *victim impact* statement is too high to see, and the button and the chunks that begin with questions 13, 17, 31, and 35 are also too high. One solution to this problem is to redo the chunking and have fewer questions in each chunk.

The *victim impact* statement has a heading and then a paragraph of text. The heading is separated from the text by space. The space is there because the heading and text are separate paragraphs. The HTML code automatically adds the extra space between paragraphs. A solution to the size problem of the *victim impact* statement is to put the heading in a new row of the table just above. A table row takes less vertical space than two paragraphs in the same cell.

2. Click in the table cell containing the victim statement. Click **Table** > **Insert** > **Row Above**.

3. Select the heading text and cut it from its present location. Click in the new row and paste the heading into it. If necessary, delete any returns in the previous cell. Check to see that this eliminated the extra space.

4. To move the bookmark, open the bookmark list (**Insert** > **Bookmark)**, select the *victim impact* bookmark. Click the **Clear** button.

5. To set the new bookmark, click just to the left of the *A* in the heading phrase *A victim impact statement* . . . . Insert the new bookmark at this location (**Insert** > **Bookmark**. Type the name *victim impact* in the **bookmark name** field, click **OK**.

6. Save the page and preview it in a browser. Verify that all of the chunks are visible in a 800 × 600 browser window.

The survey now needs progress indicators. The indicators that we will use were created with Photoshop and are just simple graphics. We will add these graphics at the appropriate location in the survey. There are nineteen bookmark locations in the survey. The indicators that we have are for 25%, 50%, 75%, and 90% done. These indicators should therefore be located near the **q1** next section button, after the **q9** button, after the **q22** button, and after the **q32** question respectively.

EXERCISE 8.4. Adding Progress Indicator Graphics

1. In Expression, click the *survey.asp* page and scroll down to the **Next Section** button after *q1*.

2. Click in the row that has the *Next Section* button. Click **Table** > **Modify** > **Split cells** . . . . Verify that **Split into columns** is selected and that the number of columns is set to 2. Click **OK.**

3. Click in the right cell of this row. Click the **right align** button.

4. Insert the *25% done* graphic. (**Insert** > **Picture** > **From file**) In the files for this chapter, locate the graphic *25_percent.gif*. Select it and click **OK**.

5. Locate the **Next** button after question 9 in the survey and repeat the procedure above. Insert the graphic *50_percent.gif*.

6. Locate the **Next** button after question 21 and repeat the procedure. Insert the graphic *75_percent.gif*.

7. Locate the cell after q32 and repeat the procedure. Insert the graphic *90_percent.gif*.

8. Save the page and preview it in a browser.

EXERCISE 8.5. Changing the Look of the Survey

The survey is almost complete. To test it, let's assume you ask several friends to take the survey and give you feedback about any aspect they found to be a problem, and they told you the following:

- The green and red boxes are distracting.

- The size of the text in the opening paragraphs is too small and there isn't enough space between the lines to see it easily.

- The question text doesn't need to be bold.

Since all of the survey elements are controlled by styles, changing the look of the survey involves modifying the styles.

1. Right-click the style **survey_table** in the **Apply Styles** pane. From the menu, select **Modify Style . . . .**

2. Select the border category and set the **border style** to **none** and delete the color code in the border-color area. This dialog box is shown in Figure 8.7.

FIGURE 8.7 *Modifying the survey_table Style*

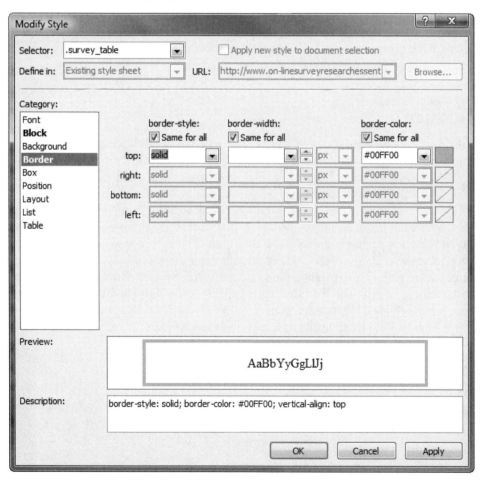

3. Click **OK**.

4. Turn off the border on the **question_table style** as well.

5. Right-click the **question_text** style. Select **Modify Style . . .** from the menu.

6. Change the font weight to be **normal**. Click **OK**.

7. Right-click the **body** style. Select **Modify Style . . .** from the menu.

8. In the **font** category change the font-size to **12 points**.

9. Click the **Block** category. Set the line-height property to be **16 points**. If the text is 12 points and the line-height is 16 points, this will leave 4 points of space between each line.

10. Save the page and preview it in a browser. Check each chunk to verify that it fits and looks good in the browser.

11. Add an additional button, style, bookmark, and hyperlink after question 16.

Open the consent (*index.htm* or *default.htm*) and confirmation (*confirmation.htm*) pages. Notice that the pages look different. Because the pages use styles and we modified the styles, every page in the site has been updated.

SUMMARY

This chapter introduced a way to "chunk" information to limit the amount of text that shows on a screen. Using a simple table and skipping a row between each major piece of information, adding buttons, internal hyperlinks, and finally, linking the buttons to the internal landing spots allows us to limit the content to screen-sized parts. By expanding the size and vertical alignment of the cells between the chunks, the monitor displays only a chunk of information at a time and the respondent clicks a button to move to the next chunk. This simple technique overcomes the problem of needing to scroll down through the survey.

In addition, graphics were added to the survey at appropriate locations that indicate the progress of a respondent through the survey. These graphics were provided by the author, but they can be easily made with Photoshop. A very basic introduction to using Photoshop is given in the Appendix.

KEY TERMS

chunking
bookmarks
internal hyperlinks

valign (vertical alignment)
progress indicators

DISCUSSION QUESTIONS

1. Some surveys show only a single question at a time on the screen. Use a survey from another chapter or a new survey that you made up and work out how this could be done.

2. Preview in a browser the survey created in Exercise 8.2. Roll the mouse over one of the **Next Section** buttons that are linked to an internal hyperlink. At the bottom of the browser window is the status bar. When the mouse is over the button, the destination of the link should show in the status bar. How does this *internal* hyperlink differ from a regular hyperlink? Examine the code of this hyperlink. How does Expression create an internal hyperlink?

CHAPTER

SAMPLING PROCEDURES

LEARNING OBJECTIVES

- To be able to understand the importance of using a representative sample in research

- To be able to differentiate between populations and samples

- To be able to define sampling error and its important

- To be able to estimate sample sizes, confidence intervals, and margin of error

- To be able to identify probability and non-probability sampling procedures

- To be able to sample behavior that considers situation, time, and events

- To be able to understand why randomization, balancing, and counterbalancing are important

- To be able to obtain an online survey sample

UNDERSTANDING POPULATIONS AND SAMPLES

You have decided to conduct your own online research study. Now you must consider who your sample will be. Who is the target audience you intend to investigate? One of the major goals of research is the ability to generalize results to larger populations. If

Researchers strive for external validity using representative samples.

you developed a survey intended for older adults ages forty-five and up, would that survey be appropriate for younger adults? If you surveyed a small sample of older adults, could you then generalize the results of your study to *all* older adults? The answer is no. In order to generalize the results of your study, you need to consider sampling procedures. The sampling procedures you use dictate the extent to which the results of your study can be generalized or considered representative of the population you have surveyed.

As researchers, our aim is to obtain a representative sample that ultimately enables us to generalize to larger populations. A ***representative sample*** is one that truly exhib-

Consider these questions when planning your research study:

1. What are the characteristics of the people to whom you would like to generalize and how accessible are these individuals?

2. How sure do you want to be that your sample represents the larger target population?

its the characteristics of the population you are studying, thus increasing your study's external validity. Being able to generalize to other populations is essential to all research but is particularly important in survey research. For instance, if you created a survey designed to assess attitudes toward tax increases in the community, you would want to obtain a simple random sample with which to test your survey to determine whether the measure has acceptable validity (it measures what it is intended to measure) and reliability (consistency). However, if you took that same survey and asked fourth-graders to complete it, you would probably find the measure had poor reliability and validity for individuals in this age group. Fourth-graders do not know— much less care—about tax increases, and, therefore, their responses would likely not make sense. This would suggest that the external validity of this community survey would be limited to adult community members in the town you sampled.

Most researchers will obtain a sample of the population they are interested in testing. A ***population*** can be defined as all possible participants of interest to your study. For example, if you were interested in surveying student attitudes toward drug testing in high school, your population of interest would include all high schools in the world. For practical purposes, let's suppose your population would be all high school students in the United States. Unfortunately, it is still virtually impossible to obtain feedback from this entire population. Instead, researchers obtain a sample of high school students. A ***sample*** is a subset of individuals from the population. In this case, a sample could be obtained by surveying students in high school in the town or state where you live. The larger the sample, the more likely your results will be representative of the population of high school students as a whole.

Sample Sizes, Confidence Intervals, and Margin of Error

Sample size, confidence intervals, and margin of error are all important ingredients to consider when understanding and interpreting research results. Your goal is to obtain a sample that is representative of the general population, but *how big should your sample be*? To answer this question there are two things you must ask:

1. What are the characteristics of the people to whom you would like to generalize and how accessible are these individuals? If you want your sample have homogeneous (similar) characteristics then your sample size can be smaller. If you need the sample to be heterogeneous (dissimilar), with greater variability, then you may need a larger sample.

2. How accurate would you like to be? In other words, how sure do you want to be that the participants you've sampled actually represent the population?

The answers to these questions will help you determine the appropriate sample size needed for your study.

One additional consideration should also be the time and budget you have to conduct your study. This, too, may affect your sample size choice. Overall, a good rule of thumb is the larger the sample, the better. For instance, if you would like to generalize your results to all college students in the United States, you will have to obtain quite a large sample using one or more of the sampling techniques discussed in this chapter.

Homogeneous populations share similar characteristics. Statistically speaking, random samples of the population should have the same general characteristics (such as age, gender, socioeconomic status, and so forth) of the population of interest. The more similar your populations are, the smaller the sample size you will need. Keep in mind that although "homogeneous" suggests that the population members are similar, the samples will not be exactly the same. Each random sample will have slightly different characteristics (Leedy & Ormrod, 2005).

A *heterogeneous population* is diverse or dissimilar. The greater the diversity of the population, the larger the sample you will need to represent the true nature of the population. If you assessed attitudes toward drug testing and sampled two hundred high school students from one state and two hundred students from another state, the results will differ slightly because of the samples' different characteristics. This is referred to as sampling error.

Sampling error is a term that refers to the variability among samples or the characteristics of samples due to chance. Statistical theory assumes error between the population mean and sample mean because samples are not always representative of the population. Therefore, researchers cannot conclude that their sample will generalize to the greater population. However, researchers *can* use probabilities to make inferences regarding how their sample represents the population.

Researchers make estimates because they do not know the population mean and therefore can only estimate the sample mean. There are three statistical assumptions you can make, though. The first assumption is based on the fact that an infinite number of samples will create a normal distribution. Remember, a **normal distribution** (bell-shaped curve) is one in which the mean, median, and mode are all equal (Salkind, 2000). Second, the population mean is based on obtaining samples that constitute the normal distribution. Third, we can assume that the standard deviation of the normal distribution characterizes the population (Leedy & Ormrod, 2005). If we use proper sampling techniques, we can estimate the general characteristics of the population of interest. Statistical theory and statistics based on the normal distribution allow us to surmise what the population is like, if a good sampling technique is used. The better the sampling technique used and the larger the sample size, the greater the inference that can be made to the larger population.

Researchers make estimates based on the probability that a given event will occur. When determining how large a sample must be to represent the population, researchers estimate the variability of the characteristics of the population using an approximation of the size of the standard deviation for the population of interest. This allows us to calculate confidence intervals that represent how confident we are that our sample mean is close to the population mean. *Confidence interval* is a term used by researchers when making determinations as to how similar the sample mean is to the true population mean. For instance, assume your research found that 63 percent of your Internet sample recently made major purchases online. Researchers like to be confident when they state whether their sample is similar to the population. In fact, scientists often use a 95 percent confidence interval so that they can be 95 percent confident that when they say their sample is homogeneous to the population, there is only a 5 percent chance of making an error. When p = the probability of an event occurring (or not occurring) using a 95 percent confidence interval (p < .05—or one chance in twenty—that differences found are not due to chance), you can say that the population value is most likely between 58 percent and 68 percent. You actually don't know what the population value is, but you can obtain a good estimate using the sample value. Though 95 percent is considered the norm when making determinations of homogeneity, you can choose to be more confident. For instance, you can choose to be 98 percent confident and the margin of error would be ±2.

What is the right sample size for your study?

Sample size is based on the amount of sampling error you are willing to accept.

As you have only your sample and not the whole population with which to work, you can assume some potential for error. The confidence interval tells you approximately how much your sample value is prone to error. This is your **sampling error** (also known as the **margin of error**). A small sampling error suggests there is little difference between your sample and the population (Salkind, 2000).

Now that you have a basic understanding of confidence intervals and sampling error, you can determine your sample size with greater precision. For those who would like to delve deeper into sample size calculations, mathematical formulas can be computed calculating a sample size based on the amount of sampling error you are willing to accept (see Cozby, 2001; Dillman, 2007; or Fowler, 1984 for more in-depth explanations). For example, general rules of thumb for a $\pm$ 5 percent confidence interval suggest that, if the size of your population is between 2,000 and 5,000, you would need approximately 300–350 participants in your sample. If your population is between 10,000 and 50,000, your sample should consist of 350–400 respondents. Finally, if your population consists of over 100,000 people, then your aim should be to sample approximately 400 people. Keep in mind that for confidence intervals (such as $\pm$ 2 percent), your sample should be double the sizes mentioned here. If your confidence levels are higher (such as $\pm$ 10), then your sample can be half of what was recommended for 95 percent confidence intervals.

For those less likely to compute the mathematical calculations, following are some general guidelines for sample sizes (see Gay and Airasian, 2003, as cited in Leedy & Ormrod, 2005, p. 207):

1. When the sample size is fewer than 100, include the entire population.

2. If the population constitutes approximately 500, then 50 percent of the population should be sampled.

3. When the population approximates 1,500, then 20 percent of the population should be sampled.

4. If the population size reaches 5,000, then a sample size of 400 should be sufficient.

Understanding Random Sampling Procedures

Randomization enables researchers to extend and generalize results to the general larger population. If your goal is to generalize results to the greater population of interest, you should consider a random sample. In *a **random sample***, every person in your chosen population has an equal chance of participating in your study. If we can also assume that selections are independent of one another (they do not affect each other), then there is no systematic bias that results in one group or person being more likely to be selected than another. If selection is truly random, we can assume that individual differences (such as age, ethnicity, and intelligence) are balanced within the sample and that each person completing the study has his or her own individual beliefs and biases. Yet, if we utilize a random sample, it is assumed that these individual differences would balance out across your sample, ensuring greater representation.

Randomization is a crucial component that enables researchers to generalize results. Sampling bias is something that should be considered as a limitation for all online research.

In order to generalize results to the larger population, random samples must be obtained. Generally, however, samples obtained by researchers are not representative, but biased. Bias can include any conditions that can influence the data (Leedy & Ormrod, 2005). Online research is particularly susceptible to *sampling bias*, which refers to unfairness that occurs when researchers access certain groups to the exclusion of others within the same legitimate population of interest. Researchers conducting online surveys and experiments should assume participants responding to the research may not represent the general population. For example, if researchers e-mail a random sample requesting participation in a survey, they must realize that individuals without access to the Internet cannot be surveyed. This biases the sample. We must also consider those individuals who were e-mailed the invitation to participate but did not respond (nonresponders). Might these individuals have different characteristics than those who did respond? Despite the attempt to obtain a random sample, online researchers must realize that prejudice creeps into all aspects of sample selection, making it difficult to generalize to the larger population. Be sure to keep sampling bias in mind as a limitation when interpreting and communicating research results.

Non-Probability Sampling Approaches: Convenience and Purposive Sampling

There are two approaches to sampling individuals from a population: non-probability sampling and probability sampling. *Non-probability sampling* is a sampling technique where there is no way to estimate an individuals' inclusion in the sample. Non-probability approaches are most often used in basic survey research, yet these approaches are limited because they do not create a random sample.

There are two types of non-probability sampling procedures. The first is called *accidental* or *convenience sampling*. Convenience samples are obtained from individuals willing and able to respond to your study. This sample might be a group of people standing outside your door or in the cafeteria, willing and able to take your survey. Most media polls (or television show polls such as *American Idol*) are made up of convenience samples—people who willingly respond to vote for their favorite candidate. Thus, it hardly constitutes a representative sample. Unfortunately, online research will by nature most often consist of this type of sample. However, there are safeguards and alternatives available to make your online sample more representative that will be addressed later in this chapter.

Sometimes there are particular groups of people you might want to survey. *Purposive sampling* is a technique where you choose the people you want to include in your study based on particular characteristics they may have. Let's say you create a survey designed to investigate how often people between the ages of eighteen and twenty-four make purchases over the Internet. Or perhaps you want to assess love and commitment in couples who have been married over ten years. In both cases you have specific populations in mind; you want to handpick your respondents. Purposive sampling is used quite often in scholarly research simply because hypotheses are often made to assess particular characteristics associated with a research topic. Convenience sampling and purposive sampling are the two most often used approaches to sampling, but because of the nature of the techniques, these approaches limit how representative your sample is and how the research findings can be generalized. In order to better generalize your findings you can choose probability sampling techniques.

Probability Sampling Techniques: Simple Random, Stratified, and Cluster

In a *probability sampling* technique, each participant has an equal chance of being included in the study. There are three probability sampling approaches: simple random sampling, stratified random sampling, and cluster sampling. *Simple random sampling* is the most basic technique, in which every person has an equal chance of being included in your sample. If you estimate there are ten thousand people in your proposed population, then you coordinate a randomized system so each person has an equal chance of being included. For instance, suppose you want to survey homeowners in your town to determine how they feel about proposed increases in the homestead tax. You would first need a sampling frame from which to choose your sample. A *sampling frame* is the actual population of people (or clusters of people) from which your sample with be drawn, which, in this case, is a list of all homeowners in your town. Utilizing a list of ten thousand homeowners obtained from your town clerk's office, you would then devise a randomized system so each homeowner has an equal chance of being included in your study. For example, you might choose to include every third person from the list of homeowners. Based on the guidelines for sample sizes, we would like to obtain a sample of at least four hundred people.

There are many ways to choose a random sample from the sampling frame. *Systematic sampling* was the most common procedure used in the past (Dillman, 2007). This technique is based on numeric intervals. For example, if the town has ten thousand homeowners and you would like to sample one thousand participants, then you could select every tenth person. In this situation the sampling interval is ten. You would then write down numbers from one to ten on a piece of paper and toss it into a hat. The number you choose from the hat will dictate where you begin the selection process. For instance, if you choose the number three then you would select every tenth interval starting with the third (that is, 3, 13, 23, 33, 43, and so on) until your sample has been selected.

Simple random sampling procedures are similar to systematic sampling but do not rely on intervals. For instance, numbers can be assigned to each homeowner from your sampling frame on a piece of paper and tossed into a hat to select respondents. Another option is to choose every third person on the list of homeowners to participate.

However, there are less arduous options available to researchers via more advanced computerized sampling lists.

Check online for randomizers to help randomize your sample selection.

Computers can now generate random lists of telephone numbers with similar dialing prefixes in order to study specific geographical areas of interest. This would be considered a random sample as long as most people in that area have telephones. Similarly, Internet addresses can be generated randomly. For online research, you would need to consider whether these households had Internet access. (If many people do not have Internet access, the sample would be biased.) There are also companies offering phone numbers or e-mail addresses of individuals. Another more recent development that makes randomization easier is the Randomizer (www.randomizer. org). This system, sponsored by the social psychology network, creates a randomized list for just about anything you would like to do. It has five capabilities:

1. Creating a random sample of one hundred participants from a population of five hundred

2. Randomly assigning subjects to experimental conditions

3. Assigning participants in random block designs

4. Creating random samples of telephone numbers

5. Randomly ordered survey items

There are other online systems developed as basic random number generators. These can be used to generate random numbers, such as lottery numbers or random databases, allowing researchers and mathematicians to use fictitious data to examine mathematical theory (otherwise known as Monte Carlo Studies).

Another form of probability sampling is ***stratified random sampling***. In this procedure your population is divided up into subpopulations called strata, and random samples are selected from each stratum. There are two approaches when considering how samples should be drawn. The first and more commonly used stratified random sampling technique is to select an equal number of participants from each stratum. For instance, if you were investigating college students' attitudes toward having a "dry campus" (no alcohol on campus), researchers would sample equal numbers of freshman, sophomores, juniors, and seniors.

The second approach is to select participants on a proportional basis. To assess student attitudes toward a dry campus, you would likely consider that the college population may include more freshmen and sophomores than juniors and seniors. In this situation, you would draw the sample based on the proportion of individuals in each stratum. Let's say you would like to sample 500 students on campus. You would first have to obtain your sampling frame, or list of students attending the college, intended for sampling. In this case, a recent registrar's list of enrolled students would be sufficient.

If the whole student body consisted of 3,000 students and 30 percent were freshman, 35 percent were sophomores, 20 percent were juniors, and 15 percent were seniors, you could randomly choose 150 freshman students (30 percent of 500), 175 sophomore students (35 percent of 500), 100 juniors (20 percent of 500), and 75 seniors (15 percent of 500). This sampling technique is particularly useful when strata represent relatively homogeneous segments of the population. This approach increases representativeness of your sample, so it is helpful to use when you want to make general statements about portions or populations you have sampled. This is generally considered a more complex approach to sampling, and scholarly researchers tend to use it when representativeness is crucial to their study. But what do you do when no sampling frame is available? What if there was no list from which to randomly choose your sample?

Cluster sampling is used when the population is too large to obtain a random sample and there is no sampling frame available. Let's say you want to study people who work at insurance agencies, or you need a national sample of adolescents. In each case, there is no sampling frame. *Cluster sampling* refers to sampling participants who are already part of an existing group (or cluster); the sampling unit is some aggregate—or cluster—of people in the population. If we want to examine college students' attitudes toward a dry campus we can assume that student classrooms on campus make up clusters of students. If we acquire samples of students in required classes, this suggests we will ultimately get a representative sample of students for that campus.

Observing Behavior: Situation and Time Sampling Considerations

When research involves behavioral observation, time and situation sampling are necessary to obtain a representative sample. Researchers who observe behavior must have clear operational definitions of what is being measured. Researchers cannot examine all behaviors, so they carefully plan which behaviors will be measured. Furthermore, in order for researchers to gain a representative sample of behavior and generalize research findings, observations must be made over various times and situations. Using the scientific method, observations must be made either systematically or randomly.

Time sampling is one technique where researchers study behavior at random or systematic time intervals. For example, say you were interested in conducting a study that examines the use of online tutoring designed for adolescents. You would carefully define tutoring as "an interaction between two people where educational information is requested and exchanged by another." Now you must decide at what times you will sample. For example, if you chose to conduct your research at noon each day for seven days, this sampling time frame would not be representative. In fact, online tutoring is more likely to be used when students are doing homework after school.

You have three options. You could choose a random sample of times to go online and collect data or choose time intervals systematically (such as every third or fifth hour of the day) to collect a more representative sample of online tutoring behavior. Second, you would use random time sampling to observe behavior, randomly choosing days and time periods throughout the day. In order to examine online tutoring behavior using random time sampling, you would randomly choose six thirty-minute time intervals throughout the day. Different time intervals would be chosen each day. Thus, behaviors would ultimately be represented throughout the day. Third, a combination of systematic and random time sampling can be used. One of the advantages to using systematic time intervals is that particular behaviors (such as tutoring) can be targeted when they occur most often. Obviously, this method is not random. Therefore, one of the best approaches would be to use random time intervals within systematic time intervals. For instance, you may decide that you will use a systematic technique to examine tutoring behavior after 4 PM from Monday through Friday, yet decide to use random time intervals (fifteen-minute intervals randomly distributed from 4 PM to 10 PM) to examine behavior.

Achieving a representative example of behavior is extremely important. That is why we must also consider various situations and events that can affect behavior. *Situation sampling* refers to sampling behavior in various situations—locations, circumstances, and conditions (Shaughnessy et al., 2003). For instance, you might want to find out whether adolescents are using online tutoring after school or during school and whether students are using online tutoring at home or while in the library. It may not always be possible to examine situational influences when conducting online research. However, situations should at least be considered when examining what can influence research results.

Finally, *event sampling* is conducted when behavior is monitored during a specific event, such as examining the use of online tutoring during the holiday season. Time, situation, and event sampling help to obtain a more representative picture of behavior.

The Importance of Randomization, Balancing, and Counterbalancing

Balancing and counterbalancing are more often associated with experimental research designs, but they are relevant to this chapter as well. If your goal is to examine different groups of people or characteristics of people, then you need to consider using balancing techniques. For example, if you intend to investigate problem-solving skills in older versus younger adults, then you need to be sure that your samples are equal, and that they are not different in particular characteristics that might affect the results of your study. If your problem-solving task includes assessing motor coordination, then you would want to be sure both groups are homogeneous with regard to motor coordination response. In order to ensure that participant characteristics are equal across groups, you must balance individual variations among different groups of people. Balancing groups is particularly important for experimental designs and is addressed in greater detail in Chapter Twelve.

When conducting survey research, you also need to consider *counterbalancing* your measures or surveys. We use counterbalancing to control the order in which a condition occurs. By systematically varying the presentation of materials we can control for order effects. Although used in experimental research, counterbalancing is more often used for survey research when you are administering multiple surveys. Often researchers in social science conduct surveys that examine many hypotheses and use various measures to assess whether there is support for such hypotheses. For instance, if you conduct research on attitudes toward stigma associated with mental illness, you might also investigate things that might be theoretically related to stigma, such as general knowledge of mental health, experience with individuals with mental illness, and other demographic variables. You might ask respondents to report whether they had received a psychiatric diagnosis, or if they know someone who has a mental illness. If your survey investigates topics that could potentially provoke emotional reactions, then you may want to consider using counterbalancing techniques. People might be emotionally affected simply by answering questions designed to assess whether they had a mental illness. Similarly, some men or women might become offended when asked whether they had been diagnosed with a mental illness. In addition, when there is a possibility that question order might affect participants' responses on later questionnaires, those measures should be counterbalanced (order effects). There exist several ways to address and control for order effects. Measures can be placed in random order, where each person receives the surveys in any random order. Or you might use any number of versions of the survey (typically two to four), where each version presents items in a particular order. By keeping track of which condition each participant received, you may statistically examine whether the ordering of the surveys affected participant responses.

Some Ideas for How to Obtain Your Online Survey Sample

Once you are ready to obtain your online sample, there are many options available to you. The first thing to consider should be the title of your study. You want to make the title attractive to potential respondents. Next, you should decide where you are hosting your study. If you are a behavioral science researcher at a school or university, you can most likely host your site on your school's server. Contact your information technology services staff and they will likely be able to provide further instructions. Behavioral science organizations, such as the Association for Psychological Science or the Web Experimental Psychology Lab, have up-to-date Web pages listing URLs for online research (www.psycho.hanover.edu/ or www.psychologie.unizh.ch/genpsy/). You can also use alternative sites, some of which provide additional services, including subject recruitment. These sites (such as www.surveyresponse.com or www.surveymonkey.com) typically charge a fee for data collection but can provide purposive samples, recruit participants, and administering incentives as part of their packages. Both of these services have templates that offer easy survey construction or allow you to put your own survey or experiment online.

If you are conducting your own research for a marketing firm or a business, consider creating your own Web site. Making your own Web site enables you to have a stable homepage (one that doesn't come and go), which makes it easier for returning persons to find your site. Research and homepages can also be registered with search engines such as Google or Yahoo. If you do this, keep in mind that these search engines search by subject, so be sure to register your study using the most appropriate subject heading (see http://docs.yahoo.com/info/suggest/). Google can be a more powerful tool when links to your study are available. The nature of the search engine used in Google ranks pages depending on the number of links associated with your Web page, so if you create a Web site, you may want to consider asking colleagues to create links to your Web site to obtain a higher ranking on Google (Fraley, 2004). No matter which method you use, we strongly encourage you to refer back to Chapter Two to be sure your study follows ethical policies and procedures.

SUMMARY

This chapter has addressed how representative samples and sampling techniques can increase external validity. When putting your own online research study together, you should consider who should make up your sample. Will you use probability or non-probability sampling techniques? You should also have a good idea of how many individuals you need to sample to ensure that your sample accurately reflects the population you are studying.

In order to obtain a representative sample of behavior, researchers use time sampling. Time sampling techniques can be random, systematic, or combined. Situation sampling ensures that participants are observed over various situations and circumstances. Event sampling can also be used to examine behavior when particular events take place.

Finally, we examined the importance of balancing and counterbalancing conditions and questionnaires. In Chapter Twelve, we will expand on these topics as we discuss the development of experimental designs and the importance of increasing internal validity.

We have provided some information to help you decide how and where to make your research available in order to obtain participants for your study. You are now equipped to reflect upon who your sample will be and how to go about recruiting them.

KEY TERMS

representative sample
population
sample
sampling bias
confidence interval
sampling error (margin of error)
probability and non-probability sampling
time, situation, and event sampling
heterogeneous populations
accidental (convenience sample)

purposive sampling
random sample
simple random sample
stratified random sample
sampling frame
cluster sampling
counterbalancing
homogeneous populations
systematic sampling

DISCUSSION QUESTIONS

1. Why is sampling important, particularly when conducting research online?

2. Determine the sample size for your research study based on confidence intervals and margin of error.

3. Identify three non-probability and probability sampling procedures and explain which might work for your own research and explain how.

4. Describe a research situation where you would use time, event, and situation sampling.

5. Identify how randomization helps to balance individual differences and describe the situations under which counterbalancing should be used.

CHAPTER

10

DEVELOPING EXPERIMENTAL DESIGNS

LEARNING OBJECTIVES

- To be able to understand the basics of experiments and differences between subjects designs (independent groups designs)
- To learn the various ways to measure dependent variables
- To be able to understand the role of experimental control—the key to a good experiment
- To be able to balance and counterbalance conditions and use random groups designs
- To be able to understand the difference between simple experiments with two conditions and factorial designs
- To be able to pilot your experimental study

Surveys typically *describe* behaviors and attitudes. If you are interested in *why* or *how* things happen you may want to consider conducting an experiment because experiments examine cause and effect. This chapter details basic experimental designs, many of which can be implemented online as part of a well-constructed Web survey. *Experimental designs* use random assignment and experimental control to determine whether the independent variable affected the dependent variable. Experimental designs have three unique characteristics: (1) conditions include treatment and control—an independent variable is manipulated by the experimenter; (2) the experimenter utilizes methods to control for possible error; and (3) a *control group* is used to compare the effectiveness of a treatment. A *treatment (experimental) group* receives the treatment and the control group does not receive the same or any treatment.

INTRODUCTION TO EXPERIMENTS AND BETWEEN-SUBJECTS DESIGNS

There are two different types of experiments: between-subjects designs and repeated-measures designs. Each uses the scientific method to determine whether the independent variable(s) had an effect on the dependent variable(s). In a *repeated-measures design* (also called a dependent groups design) the same participants are measured more than one time (see Chapter Twelve). In contrast, a *between-subjects design* (independent groups design) is an experimental design that randomly assigns participants to only one experimental condition and participants are tested only once.

The distinguishing characteristic of an experiment is the systematic variation of an independent variable to produce changes in the dependent variable. The simplest experimental design is a two-group between-subjects design where participants are randomly assigned to one of two (independent) groups. Values assigned to the independent variable are called *conditions* or *treatments*. Participants are randomly assigned to only one of two experimental groups (conditions). Each group is mutually exclusive. This simply means that if you are in one group, you cannot be in the other group.

For example, if you would like to test whether artificial sunlight helps individuals with Seasonal Affective Disorder (SAD), you would first obtain a sample of individuals diagnosed with SAD. During the winter, you would conduct your study and randomly assign half of the participants to serve as your experimental group. The experimental group would be provided with an artificial sunlamp and instructed to use the lamp two hours a day for a two-month period. The control group would receive no treatment (no sunlamp). After completion of the treatment, both groups would be measured on the severity of SAD symptoms. If the participants who received sunlamps report less severe SAD symptoms compared to the control group, you can infer that sunlamps may be helpful in reducing the severity of SAD symptoms.

In the example above, the independent variable was "sunlamp" or "no sunlamp." However, independent variables can also include stable characteristics (characteristics

TABLE 10.1. **Experiments Include Treatment and Control Groups**

Treatment Group	Control Group
Receives experimental manipulation (sunlamps)	Receives no experimental manipulation (no sunlamps)

that cannot be manipulated, such as gender, IQ, ethnicity, and so forth). Many researchers combine stable and manipulated independent variables to create a between-subjects factorial design. For instance, you might hypothesize that women who use sunlamps will have less severe SAD symptoms compared to men that do or do not use sunlamps. Here, there is one variable (sunlamp or no sunlamp) that is manipulated and one stable variable (gender) that is not manipulated.

Various Ways to Measure Dependent Variables

The primary goal of an experiment is to determine whether systematic variation (manipulation) of an independent variable can produce changes in the dependent variable. In between-subjects experiments, independent variables are categorical because you are comparing mutually exclusive groups. Dependent variables are typically measured on a continuous scale but can also be measured using other scales. Much of the research conducted examines multiple variables. Life is multifaceted; researchers often measure numerous variables in order to simulate this complexity.

When planning your study, consider scales of measurement that are appropriate for dependent variables of interest.

Thus researchers can examine how independent variables interact with each other to affect the dependent variable, providing them with greater flexibility to analyze more complex relationships between variables. The scale of measurement you choose for your independent and dependent variables ultimately affects how you analyze and interpret your data.

Good experiments typically involve measuring multiple constructs. Each measurement should be accurate, precise, reliable, and valid. Remember, well-conducted surveys can obtain greater external validity. In contrast, because they include a controlled environment and systematic manipulation, experiments tend to lack external validity. One way to increase the external validity of experimental findings is to use multiple methods to test your research hypothesis. This can include using a combination of methods such as online surveys, experiments, observation, or archival data. When multiple methods are used and results are similar, your experiment will have greater external validity.

Understanding the Role of Experimenter Control: The Key to a Good Experiment

Online surveys can provide information about people or behaviors, but they are simply describing relationships between variables. With large representative samples, well-conducted surveys can have good external validity, but often lack internal validity. Similarly, although experiments aim to infer cause and effect, one experiment can never "prove" that one thing causes another, because there will always be problems associated with internal and external validity. The two main characteristics of a good experiment include (1) determining whether the independent variable had an effect on the dependent variable and (2) establishing experimental control and internal validity. Internal validity was briefly introduced in Chapter Four. In the context of experimental designs, internal validity refers to the extent to which experimenters can be confident that the change in the dependent variable is due to the effects of the independent variable and not some other variable. A study has internal validity when you can say the independent variable alone was responsible for changing the dependent variable. To ensure internal validity, you need experimenter control. Good experiments are identified by examining internal validity, reliability, sensitivity, and external validity (Shaughnessy et al, 2003).

Experimental control leads to greater internal validity. Extraneous variables (confounds) are any variables that are not controlled or a flaw in the experiment.

Every research study has limitations because we cannot account for all possible alternative explanations that could ultimately affect research findings. These alternative explanations should be considered before and after conducting your study. A researcher can control for confounds (***extraneous variables***). Confounds are (1) variables that are not controlled or (2) experimental errors that lead to flaws in the experiment. The more we control for confounds, the greater the internal validity. For example, if we conduct research in a laboratory (a very controlled environment where all participants are treated similarly, with the exception of how the independent variable is manipulated), we need to consider whether the findings from the laboratory could be generalized to other situations and populations in more natural environments.

When planning your study, you can anticipate possible threats to internal validity. When evaluating your results, you must address additional factors that may have contributed to the findings. Let's say you conduct a research study to examine whether a new reading curriculum for students in grade school increases student achievement. Students are randomly assigned to one of two groups. One group participates in the new reading curriculum and the other group continues with the old reading curriculum. The reading curriculum is implemented in urban and suburban areas. You find that students in the suburban areas received significantly higher reading scores than students in the urban areas. Before making conclusions, you should consider the possible reasons why students in the suburban areas had higher reading scores. Was the program implemented similarly in each school? Perhaps the teacher-to-student ratio was higher in suburban schools as compared to urban schools. Students in suburban schools may have received more resources (such as books or workbooks), or parents of students living in suburban areas may have higher socioeconomic status or levels of education. It is our job as researchers to think about the possible alternative explanations for results before any study is conducted; thus we can attempt to measure and control for variables that influence research findings.

Another potential problem associated with experiments is the experimenter's own expectations of the findings. You must implement controls to offset your own biases that might affect the results. For instance, if you conduct an observational research study on gender differences and aggression and hypothesize that boys will be more aggressive than girls, it is possible that your own biases could taint the research findings. *Confirmation bias* is a social psychological term that suggests that we tend to search for behaviors that confirm our hypotheses. Without even realizing your own biases, you might observe more aggressive behaviors in boys because that is what you expected to find. *Experimenter effects* refer to any potential biases the experimenter brings into the study. Experimenters can intentionally or unintentionally treat individuals differently or interpret behaviors differently depending on their own biases. In order to control for this possibility, you should employ research assistants who are "blind" to your research hypothesis. If the research assistant collecting the data does not know what your hypothesis is, then you reduce the potential for experimenter bias.

To avoid potential problems with confirmation bias and experimenter effects it is best to have a research assistant who is blind to the hypothesis of the study.

In one famous research study, a professor constructed an elaborate maze to test the intelligence of rats. One group of his assistants was told that the rats exhibited average intelligence. The second group was told the rats were superior in intelligence. The last group was told that the rats were "stupid." Not surprisingly, research assistants found intelligent rats performed better in the maze than the average rats, and stupid rats performed the worst. The point here is that the professor randomly assigned the rats to each condition. In reality, the rats did not differ in intelligence. The simple act of telling the assistants beforehand influenced their perceptions of what constituted intelligent behavior. This research supports the fact that researchers collecting data should be blind to the conditions they are measuring.

Your after-school reading study would be considered reliable if you conducted the study with multiple after-school programs and schools and found that the samples did not differ in reading scores, and that those schools with reading programs scored consistently higher in reading achievement scores than those schools without the reading program. In essence, reliability is consistency of findings over time and samples. If you obtain the same findings, you can attribute those findings to the new reading program, and not to chance. The *sensitivity* of an experiment refers to the strength of the effect on behavior. In our example, how much difference did the new reading program make? As a researcher, you would want to know the extent to which the new reading program was effective. Even if the program had a small or negligible effect, you would need to know the size of the effect.

If you recall, an experiment has external validity when the results can be generalized to other groups, individuals, situations, and so on. Threats to external validity can include experimenter effects and reactivity. The simple fact that an experimenter is present and paying attention to an individual can affect the outcome of a study. This is called *reactivity (demand characteristics)* and is another threat to external validity. Let's say you are conducting a research study to assess the amount of verbal self-disclosure in chat rooms. You go online at random times of the day and week, and tell others in the chat room that you are conducting research on the number of verbal interactions between individuals in chat rooms. All of the sudden, many of the participants begin to talk to you about their families and friends and their experience in the chat room. Simply by being present in the chat room, interactions of verbal disclosure can increase. You can reduce this problem by simply observing the amount of verbal disclosure in the chat room without participating, or you can become a disguised participant in the chat room.

Be aware of threats to internal and external validity when planning your research project. Extraneous variables and experimenter effects threaten internal validity. Experimenter effects and reactivity threaten external validity.

The famous Hawthorne effect was the result of a research study conducted by a Harvard business professor, Elton Mayo, whose intent was to examine how changing environmental cues could influence employee productivity. Mayo examined the effect of lighting and work hours in the Hawthorne plant in the Western Electric Company in Chicago between 1924 and 1932 (Roethlisberger, 1977). Participants in the plant were assigned to either low lighting and longer work hours (experimental group) or no change in lighting and shorter work hours (control group). Mayo examined the effect of these two variables on work productivity. Workers were aware of Mayo's presence. Mayo unexpectedly found that work productivity was greater in the experimental group but that it also increased in the control group. Though there is some controversy with regard to why productivity increased (for example, Parsons, 1974), it was speculated that results were not due to the variables that were manipulated but rather the special attention the workers received while in the research study. The lighting and work hours were of less importance. The participants reacted to the presence of the experimenter.

Please refer to Chapter Two to refresh your memory on the ethical issues involved with being a disguised participant.

There are some options available to reduce experimenter effects. Let's say you conduct a research study examining the effectiveness of a new medication for migraine headaches. You randomly assign one group of individuals to the treatment group that receives the new medication for migraine headaches. The control group does not receive the new medication. Participants in the control group receive a *placebo* (an inert substance that looks like the drug but has no therapeutic effects) so that participants in both the treatment and control conditions experience the same awareness and expectations of taking the drug. In order to reduce experimenter effects, you should be blind to which participants receive the new medication and which receive the placebo. In order to reduce reactivity, participants also should not know which condition (treatment or control) they are in; therefore, participants are also blind to the treatment being administered. This is called a ***double-blind procedure*** and limits both experimenter effects and reactivity.

In order to increase reliability, we consider extraneous variables, but there are other ways to utilize experimental control. Additional key ingredients to experimental control are holding conditions constant and balancing and counterbalancing conditions.

Experimental Control: Holding Conditions Constant, Balancing, and Counterbalancing

There are strategies researchers use to eliminate possible alternative explanations. Holding conditions constant is one strategy to ensure that the independent variable is the only factor that differs systematically across groups. In order to do this, you need to hold constant all possible extraneous explanations. ***Holding conditions constant*** simply means that all variables—the setting of the experiment, experimental stimuli (except for manipulation), participant instructions, room, or interviewers—are all the same. The ideal experimental situation would be one in which all participants were treated exactly the same with the exception of the manipulated independent variable. Individuals would complete the experiment the same exact way, in the same room, with the same instructions, same interviewer, temperature, and so forth. This controls for many possible alternatives. However, you can never account for or anticipate *all* possible alternative explanations. Holding conditions constant is one of the largest limitations for online researchers. You cannot control for the setting, room, temperature, or distractions of your online participants.

Each person in your experiment is different and comes to your study with different experiences, biases, and so on. If you conduct an experiment without using random sampling, it is possible your experimental group will have different characteristics from the control group. If the groups differ before the experiment is administered, how would you know that it was the experimental treatment that made a change in the dependent variable? Let's say you conducted an experiment without random sampling that assessed problem-solving ability, and just by chance, your experimental group had higher IQ's than your comparison group. In this case, you could not attribute any differences to the experimental treatment because your groups differed in IQ—a variable that is related to the ability to problem solve.

Holding conditions constant, balancing, and counterbalancing are essential elements of experimental control.

Random group designs are necessary to ensure that individual differences (maturity, IQ, biases, attitudes, and so on) are balanced across experimental groups.

A *random groups design* helps establish external validity because everyone in the experiment has an equal chance of being included in the study; participants are randomly assigned to experimental groups. For example, you could hypothesize that student attitudes toward school can be influenced by receiving an incentive such as ice cream. You obtain access to one hundred students at a local elementary school. Each student is randomly assigned to an experimental group that receives ice cream before completing the attitudes toward school survey or to the control group that completes the survey without receiving ice cream. You then assess whether students who had ice cream before you administered the survey reported higher levels of school enjoyment. You could randomly assign students using different methods. In this case, you have only two conditions (experimental and control group) to compare. You could simply flip a coin and direct students to the experimental or control group, or, as each student formed a line to participate in the study, every other person in line would receive the ice cream. Another option could be to have the students form a line and assign all odd-numbered students to one group and all even-numbered students to the other group. These methods of random assignment are appropriate for experiments with only two conditions (experimental or control). Random assignment becomes more complex with more treatment conditions, particularly when the experiment requires an equal amount of participants in each condition. Parametric statistics (statistics used for inference testing) are based on the assumption that there are an equal (or similar) number of participants in each experimental group. Using a coin toss or assigning every odd- or even-numbered individual into an experimental condition would not ensure an equal number of participants to groups. To obtain an equal number of individuals in each group, then you may want to use a random assignment technique called block randomization.

Block randomization is a technique used to balance participant characteristics and potential confounds by randomly assigning participants to groups in such a way that your groups are equal in size. Before you administer your experiment, a block randomization schedule must be created. The schedule is a block made up of the number of conditions in your experiment. Let's say you have four conditions in your experiment. You want to assess depression levels after participants receive either psychotherapy alone, psychotherapy with drugs, drugs alone, or no therapy or drugs (control group):

Group 1: Psychotherapy alone

Group 2: Psychotherapy with drugs

Group 3: Drugs only

Group 4: Control group (no therapy or drugs)

You hypothesize that participants receiving therapy and drugs will report lower depression levels than other groups. Your first block will consist of four participants and each person in the block will be randomly assigned to a condition. The number of blocks you create depends upon the number of participants you need in each group.

Most researchers recommend a minimum of ten to fifteen people per condition. In this case, you have four conditions, and you would like to have ten people in each group. Therefore, you would need forty participants, or forty blocks in our randomization schedule. We suggest using Randomizer (www.randomizer.org) to obtain your schedule, or you can simply create one by using a table of random numbers, typically found in the back of a statistics or research methods text (see Chapter Twelve for more in-depth discussion of random block schedules).

Balancing participants across random conditions ensures that individual differences are controlled and participants are randomly assigned to experimental conditions. We discussed the importance of counterbalancing (systematically varying the presentation of conditions) with regard to surveys. Counterbalancing controls for possible *order effects (sequence effects)*. Order effects are changes in scores that can be attributed to participation in earlier treatments. The concept of order effects suggests that simply presenting your stimuli in a specific order can affect an individual's response. For example, you may have a lengthy survey, or you may put the most important aspect of your research last all of the time. It is possible that people might get fatigued by the time they reach the end, and may not be paying as much attention to the study questions as they did when they began. Thus, you may be worried that fatigue might be an issue, and you may then want to counterbalance your conditions so that the important aspects of the study are balanced within your study. Another order effect to be aware of is that participants often improve with practice. If you are measuring performance, you have to consider whether performance on one task might affect performance on the next task. Finally, an order effect can occur when one aspect of the first treatment (or survey) carries over into the next treatment. In this situation, behavioral scientists in particular need to be aware of whether their survey questions might influence responses to future surveys. There are many counterbalancing techniques to deal with this and other order effects.

Most researchers conducting survey research often counterbalance individual surveys (or conditions) within their study. You can do this by changing the order in which the surveys (or conditions) are presented. Be sure to collect data to determine whether the order of the surveys affected your dependent variable. For example, if you were to hypothesize that attitudes toward sexism were related to decisions of blame in a rape case, you might set up a study where participants would read a rape scenario and then complete their verdict decision regarding the case. Respondents would then be asked to complete a sexism survey. In this situation, it is possible that simply reading the rape scenario first and providing a verdict can influence responses to the sexism survey that followed. To counterbalance this potential confound, half of the participants should be asked to complete the sexism survey before reading the rape scenario and provide a verdict decision, and the other half should complete the sexism survey after reading the rape scenario.

Researchers should keep track of potential order effects of the survey to determine whether groups differed from each other (for a more in-depth discussion of counterbalancing techniques see Graziano and Raulin, 2004).

Conducting Simple Experiments with Two Conditions

There are different types of between-subjects designs. The simplest independent groups design compares only two groups or conditions. One group is typically designated as a control group and the other is the treatment group. Experiments need a control group as a basis for comparison with the treatment group, which receives the experimental manipulation or treatment. When hypothesis testing, researchers examine whether the treatment (manipulated independent variable) has an effect on the dependent variable, and it is often assumed the treatment group should differ from the control group. For instance, we may want to determine whether males differ from females in their attitudes toward learning new statistical software. (See Table 10.2.)

This might be referred to as a two-group or a single-factor design. The term *factor* is another word for independent variable. If we examine gender as an independent variable, our factor would be gender with two levels—males and females. So we have two groups and one factor. If we examined two independent variables—gender and drug treatments—we would have two factors (independent variables). Each independent variable has a condition. **Condition** refers to the number of levels of the independent variable. For example, if gender is the independent variable, there is one independent variable (gender) with two levels or conditions (male and female). This can be expanded to include all experiments. For instance, we can have one variable called "treatment" that has four conditions or levels (four different treatment groups to examine). This is called a multi-group design. In a **multi-group design** there is one independent variable with more than two groups (levels).

Previous literature suggested that childhood maltreatment can have debilitating effects on intellectual and physical growth. In order to assess the effect of maltreatment in criminal populations you obtain a random sample of the following four treatment groups:

Group 1: No childhood maltreatment

Group 2: Mild childhood maltreatment

Group 3: Moderate childhood maltreatment

Group 4: Extreme childhood maltreatment

TABLE 10.2. **Single-Factor Experiment with Two Levels**

Independent Variable: (Gender)	
Males	Females
Dependent Variable: Satisfaction with new software	

Here, you have four mean scores (groups) to compare and each of these groups consists of different people. Therefore the independent variable is categorical (with four groups) and the dependent variable (intellectual or physical growth) is measured as interval or ratio. Yet, you have only one independent variable (childhood maltreatment type). (See Table 10.3.) To assess whether there are significant differences in the mean scores, you can compute a one-way ANOVA (Analysis of Variance, see Chapter Fifteen) that computes the variability between subjects divided by the variability within treatments. A *factorial design* (complex design) includes more than two independent groups.

Factorial Designs and Exploring Interactions Between Variables

Behavioral science research always attempts to examine the complexity of life. Typically, there is more than one variable that is affecting one's intellectual and physical growth. Boys and girls grow at different rates. Therefore, a participant's gender might interact with childhood maltreatment to affect physical growth. Educational level of parents might affect intellectual growth. Ideally, you would explore possible effects of these variables either individually or as they interact together to create a more realistic representation of this example. Behavioral science research often investigates multiple effects of multiple independent variables. Factorial designs (or complex designs) allow us to explore the effects of more than one independent variable on a dependent variable. Multiple independent variables are examined to determine their effects on the dependent variable. Each independent variable can be explored individually, or you can determine how the variables interact with each other and ultimately affect the dependent variable. An interaction is the result of two or more independent variables combined to produce a different outcome than each variable individually.

Experiments comparing two groups are the simplest between-subjects design. A multi-group design will produce more information. Factorial designs let us explore the effects of more than one variable.

Interactions occur when the effects of one factor (independent variable) differ as a function of a level of another independent variable. These results combine to affect

TABLE 10.3. **Multi-Group Design (Single-Factor with Four Levels)**

Independent Variable: Child maltreatment condition			
No childhood maltreatment	**Mild childhood maltreatment**	**Moderate childhood maltreatment**	**Extreme childhood maltreatment**
Dependent Variable: Intellectual and Physical Growth			

TABLE 10.4. 2 × 4 Experimental Design

MALE	No childhood maltreatment	Mild childhood maltreatment	Moderate childhood maltreatment	Extreme childhood maltreatment
FEMALE	No childhood maltreatment	Mild childhood maltreatment	Moderate childhood maltreatment	Extreme childhood maltreatment

the dependent variable. For example, if you hypothesize that gender and childhood maltreatment interact to affect physical development, you are expecting an interaction between the two factors of gender and childhood maltreatment.

This would exemplify a 2 × 4 design indicating there are two levels of the first factor (gender) and four levels of the second factor (childhood maltreatment condition). (See Table 10.4.) More specifically, we might anticipate that boys with extreme childhood maltreatment might be significantly smaller in stature compared to boys and girls with less or no childhood maltreatment. Therefore we are predicting an interaction between the two independent variables. We might also hypothesize that girls and boys with highly educated parents and the least childhood maltreatment will demonstrate significantly greater intellect. The point is that—just as in real life—examining two or more variables enables experimenters to better capture the complexity of real life and the interactions of those variables that create the outcome.

The Importance of Piloting Your Experimental Study

In Chapter Six, we referred to the importance of piloting your research study. However, an *experimental pilot* refers to testing the strength of the experimental manipulation and helps identify problems before you put your study online. *Manipulation checks*, which are always conducted at the conclusion of a well-conducted experiment, are questions posed to participants that are designed to assess whether respondents correctly identified experimenter manipulations. Say you conducted an experiment to investigate whether participants would hire an individual based on their sexual orientation and gender. You could manipulate the gender of the interviewee (male or female) and the sexual orientation of the interviewee (homosexual or heterosexual). Your research design is a 2 (gender of interviewee) × 2 (sexual orientation) independent groups design. At the conclusion of the study you provide questions designed to serve as a manipulation check. Questions are forced choice (for example, "What was the gender of the interviewee in the scenario you just read?" and "What was the sexual orientation of the interviewee in the scenario you just read?). This will allow you to determine how many participants made errors identifying your manipulation. If a large percentage of individuals are making errors on the manipulation check questions, it is possible that your experimental manipulation is not strong enough.

By examining accuracy for each condition, researchers can examine whether manipulation check accuracy rates differ depending on the condition participants were in or if accuracy levels were low across conditions. If researchers found that accuracy was lowest in one condition compared to others, they would examine whether there was a problem with that condition. Scoring for accuracy is easier if forced-choice question formats are used, but open-ended formats can also be used. Researchers must be careful to measure which questions respondents may be answering incorrectly.

Once the research study has been constructed and is ready to go online, you must first pilot the experiment to flush out potential problems. In addition to determining whether there were obvious problems associated with various browsers or links to the study, you need to know whether the manipulation is strong enough to be understood by study participants. Think of manipulation checks as another form of experimental control. If you use an experiment that manipulates independent variables, you should always use manipulation checks. If participants appear to answer manipulation checks incorrectly, you should first consider whether there is an error in the presentation. If the majority of people in the pilot study got most of the manipulation check questions wrong, you should seriously rethink whether the manipulations of the independent variables were strong enough to produce the anticipated effect in the dependent variable. For example, if a pilot study found more than 5 percent of participants got one or more of the manipulation questions wrong, those participants most likely would be excluded from analyses. However, if 40 percent of participants got the manipulation check questions wrong, it is clear you need to reexamine whether the manipulation was clear or strong enough to be identified by participants. Manipulation checks are an extremely important step in conducting good research and experimenters should be sure to identify and report the number of participants who answered the manipulation check questions incorrectly.

SUMMARY

This chapter discussed simple two-group experiments and multi-group experiments and stressed maximizing internal and external validity using experimental control. Experiments aim to infer cause and effect, but one experiment can never "prove" that one thing causes another. Based on the experiment's conclusions, researchers can make strong *suggestions* that X causes Y, but we can never control for all possible extraneous variables.

In experiments, there are treatment and control groups. The independent variable is always considered categorical in nature; an individual is in one treatment group or another. How you choose to measure your dependent variables depends on what your research question is. Dependent variables can be measured using self-reports of attitudes or behaviors, latency, duration, observation, or physiological measures, or by using archival data.

Experimenter control is the hallmark of a good research study. Yet, even with careful consideration, researchers cannot control for all threats to internal or external validity. There is really no way to eliminate all possible confounds. Good researchers are aware of this and think of all possible explanations of results.

Experimenters should strive for internal validity in their research design.

Manipulation checks can be used to determine the effect of the manipulation of your independent variable on your participants. However, there will always be some amount of experimenter or subject error. Alternative explanations should always be considered when planning, developing, interpreting, analyzing, and writing up your research results. Researchers should be aware of types of potential experimenter effects and contamination, and be aware that these threaten to validity.

Remember that the more you strive to obtain greater internal validity, the less external validity your study will have.

Piloting your experiment is essential. Conducting manipulation checks is just one way you can assess the integrity of your variable manipulations.

Before making broad conclusions regarding your research, consider whether the effects could be generalized to other people, settings, events, and so forth. Will the results you find in the laboratory be replicable into the real world? Will results be reliable and consistent across various populations and situations? As a researcher you can't control for everything, but you can be aware of alternative explanations for your experimental results.

KEY TERMS

experimental designs
treatment group
control group
repeated-measures design
between-subjects designs
conditions (treatments)
factorial design
interactions
confounds
sensitivity
placebo
factor

multi-group design
experimenter effects
double-blind procedure
reactivity
holding conditions constant
random groups design
block randomization
order effects
manipulation checks
experimental pilot
confirmation bias

DISCUSSION QUESTIONS

1. How do surveys and experiments differ? Describe the three unique characteristics associated with experimental research designs.

2. How do between-subjects designs differ from repeated-measures designs?

3. Why is it important to identify how your dependent variables will be measured? Describe which type of measurement is most appropriate for your research study.

4. Why is experimenter control important? Explain how variable manipulation, holding conditions constant, and balancing increase internal validity. How can individual differences be balanced across experimental groups?

5. Briefly explain the difference between experiments with two or more conditions and multi-group experiments.

CHAPTER

INTRODUCTION TO WEB PROGRAMMING

LEARNING OBJECTIVES

- To be able to understand JavaScript programming language
- To be able to use simple JavaScript programs to control the display of the survey
- To be able to create multiple versions of a survey to counterbalance for order biases
- To be able to use JavaScript to randomly assign participants to conditions
- To be able to use hidden variables to store the values in the database

The surveys that we have created thus far were relatively simple, with a single survey page that opened in a normal browser window that allowed the user to move forward and back through a Web site, print pages, adjust window size, scroll up and down a page, and so on. What if you do not want the user to be able to do these things? If the survey was to assess reading comprehension in different conditions, you may not want the respondent to be able to go back and reread a paragraph while answering the questions. Can you modify the first browser window to prohibit the user from going back to a prior page or changing things? The answer is no. Since the beginning, browsers have been designed to prohibit Web pages from modifying the computer that is viewing the page. This is a good thing. If a page could modify the computer that is viewing it, we would have a whole new crop of Internet viruses to worry about. But, if you create a *new* window, then you have control over all its properties. The way to do this is by writing a simple JavaScript program.

JAVASCRIPT PROGRAMMING

JavaScript is a programming language that can be used in Web pages to allow for more creative survey techniques. JavaScript is easy to use and learn. In this chapter, the language will be introduced at a very basic level. All of the scripts that will be used are written and provided with the files for the chapter. When this chapter is complete you won't be an expert at JavaScript programming, but you will have some specific tools to get the job done.

JavaScript enables researchers to use more creative strategies for online research.

We'll begin by looking at the code for a blank Web page. A Web page is composed of three main sections. Figure 11.1 shows the code. On the left are line numbers for each line. We will use these numbers to explain the specific statements.

Line 1 of the code is a declaration of the type of page that Expression has created, and, on the same line, is a reference to the Web site (www.w3.org) where the standards used to define the page reside. Line 2 begins the page by stating that it uses HTML code. This is done with the opening *<HTML> tag*. As discussed in Chapter Seven, the tag tells the browser how to display the content of the page, and HTML tags are always enclosed in angle brackets (< >). The tag on line 2 also has a modifier that tells where the standard for the structure of the page is found. Lines 4 through 7 define the head section of the page. The page is read by the browser software from top to bottom, so the *head section* of the code loads into the computer's memory first. Any scripts (which we will add in just a bit) found in the head section will be loaded as well. Another element of a Web page that is found in the head section is the *page title* (line 6). This is the title that shows in the browser window's top banner. Line 6 has the tags <**title**> and <**/title**>. Between these tags is the title of the page. In this case the title is *Untitled 1*. Lines 9 through 11 define the body of the Web page. In this case, the body of the page is blank, so the only codes that show are the opening (<**body**>) and closing (<**/body**>) body tags. The *body* is where all the

FIGURE 11.1 *Code View of a Simple Web Page*

```
 1 <!DOCTYPE html PUBLIC "-//W3C//DTD XHTML 1.0 Transitional//EN" "http://www.w3.org/TR
 2 <html xmlns="http://www.w3.org/1999/xhtml">
 3
 4 <head>
 5 <meta http-equiv="Content-Type" content="text/html; charset=windows-1252" />
 6 <title>Untitled 1</title>
 7 </head>
 8
 9 <body>
10
11 </body>
12
13 </html>
14
```

content of the page resides. When you add text on a Web page through Expression, the text is automatically inserted into the body section. Line 13 marks the end of the HTML code with the closing HTML tag (**</HTML>**) and is the end of the Web page.

EXERCISE 11.1. Creating the First JavaScript Page

1. Open the *chapter11* Web site and create a new page. The filename for this page is *script1 .htm*.

2. In Expression, switch from the **Design view** to the **Split view** by clicking the **Split view** icon in the lower left corner of the document window. This allows both the design view of the page and the code to be displayed.

3. In the files for this chapter, locate the text file *script1.txt*. Open the file by double-clicking it and select and copy all of the text in the file.

4. In Expression, place the cursor on line 4 of the code, immediately after the opening head tag (**<head>**). Hit Enter. Paste the code into the new blank line.

5. Save the page and preview it in a browser. The code for this page is shown in Figure 11.2.

This page represents a tradition in programming texts. The tradition is that the first program that is created in a text writes *Hello World* to the screen. Besides keeping up with tradition, this page does some other interesting things. First, as stated, the body of the page is to hold the content, but on this page, the body section is blank. The text on this page was written by the script. We will not do much writing of content to a page via a script, but, as shown, it can be easily done. Line 5 begins the script with the opening script tag (**<script>**). The tag has a modifier that says the language for the script is JavaScript. There are other languages that could be used (Jscript, Visual Basic, and so on.), but we will use JavaScript throughout. This line also tells the browser that what comes next is a script. Line 6 contains a code that writes a statement directly to the Web page. The statement begins with *document.write*. A ***document*** is what is inside a browser's window. ***Write*** is an action or method that is built into a document. What it writes to the screen is enclosed in the parentheses and double quotes. In this script, *Hello World* will be written to the page. At the end of the line is a semicolon; each line in a script ends with a semicolon. Line 7 is the closing script tag (**</script>**). When the page loads, the script runs and the message is written into the browser window.

EXERCISE 11.2. Adding Text to a Script Page

1. Switch back to Expression. In the **Design** view, type your name on the page.

2. Save the page and preview it in a browser. If you do not see your name on the page, refresh the browser by hitting the F5 key or **View > Refresh**.

This modification illustrates how the browser executes the text. The script is executed first and then the text in the body of the page is written to the window.

FIGURE 11.2 *Code View for script1.htm Page*

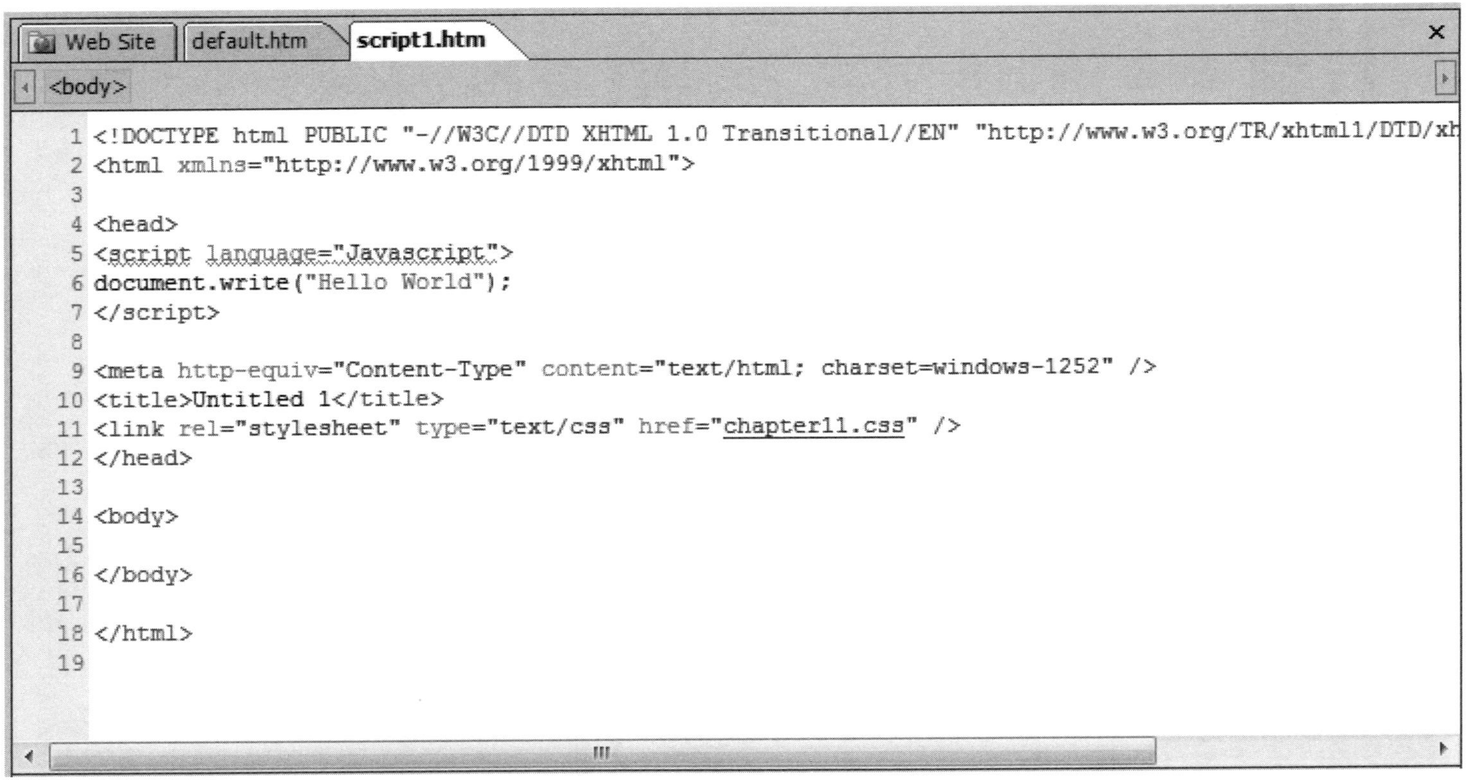

```
     Web Site   default.htm   script1.htm

 1   <!DOCTYPE html PUBLIC "-//W3C//DTD XHTML 1.0 Transitional//EN" "http://www.w3.org/TR/xhtml1/DTD/xh
 2   <html xmlns="http://www.w3.org/1999/xhtml">
 3
 4   <head>
 5   <script language="Javascript">
 6   document.write("Hello World");
 7   </script>
 8
 9   <meta http-equiv="Content-Type" content="text/html; charset=windows-1252" />
10   <title>Untitled 1</title>
11   <link rel="stylesheet" type="text/css" href="chapter11.css" />
12   </head>
13
14   <body>
15
16   </body>
17
18   </html>
19

<body>
```

JavaScript is a language that is "event driven." Things happen with JavaScript when an action or *event* happens. An event is some action in the browser window. In the above script, the event was the page loading into the browser. An event might also be clicking a button or checking a check box. A script can be made to run in response to an event by modifying the script slightly. We must redefine the script as a *function*, a script (or block of code) that is designed to do a specific task. It is written in the **Head** section of the page and is triggered by an event.

EXERCISE 11.3. Creating a Web Page with a Function

1. Create a new HTML page and name it *script2.htm*.
2. In the chapter files, double-click the file *script2.txt*, select all of the text, and copy it.
3. In Expression, paste the text into the head section of the page.
4. Click the page in the **Design view** and type your name.
5. Save the page and preview it in a browser. The code for this page is in Figure 11.3.

A largely blank page shows with your name in the upper left corner. Did the script run? Not yet. Unlike on the previous page, this script is a function. Line 5 begins the script and defines the language it is written in. Line 6 begins with the word *function*. After the word function is the name that is given to the function. This function has the name **hello()**. The parentheses are needed to indicate that this is the name. Function names are case sensitive, need to be one word, and must begin with a letter, but they can have numbers after the first character. For example, **Hello()** and **hello()** are different functions. Finally, at the end of line 6 is an opening curly bracket ({). This marks the beginning of the code that makes up this function. Line 7 contains the code to write *Hello World* on the screen, and line 8 contains the closing curly bracket (}), which ends the function. Line 9 ends the script. The function requires an event to "trigger" it. In this case the event will be the user clicking a button.

EXERCISE 11.4 Adding a Button to the Page and Defining a Behavior

1. Click the page in Expression under your name. In the files for this chapter is a button called **run_script.gif**. Insert this button onto the page (**Insert > Picture > From File**. Locate the *chapter 11* files and *select run_script.gif* and click **Insert**). The button should show on the page.
2. Save the page. When you save it, the **Save Embedded Files** dialog box will appear. Click the **Change Folder** button and save the button in the images folder. Click **OK**.
3. Preview the page in a browser. The only thing on the page should be your name and the button.

Expression makes the programming of events easy. In Expression, we will define a behavior for the button using a menu. Expression will take care of the coding.

FIGURE 11.3 *Code View for script2.htm Page*

```
 1  <!DOCTYPE html PUBLIC "-//W3C//DTD XHTML 1.0 Transitional//EN" "http://www.w3.org/TI
 2  <html xmlns="http://www.w3.org/1999/xhtml">
 3
 4  <head>
 5  <script language="Javascript">
 6  function hello() {
 7      document.write("Hello World");
 8      }
 9  </script>
10  <meta http-equiv="Content-Language" content="en-us" />
11  <meta http-equiv="Content-Type" content="text/html; charset=windows-1252" />
12  <title>Untitled 1</title>
13  </head>
14
15  <body>
16
17  <p>John Purcell</p>
18
19  </body>
20
21  </html>
22
```

4. Open the task pane for behaviors by clicking **Task Pane > Behaviors**. The behaviors task pane should open in the lower right corner of the Expression window.

5. To create a behavior, the object that the user will interact with must be selected. Click the button. In the **Behaviors** task pane click the **Insert** button. A menu with many possible behaviors appears. Select **Call Script** from the list.

6. The **Call Script** dialog box will appear. In the dialog box, type the name of the script that will execute, hello(). It is essential to type the opening and closing parentheses; they are part of the name. Click **OK**.

7. In the **Behaviors** task pane, the event **onclick** shows with the action **Call Script** to the right of it. As the selected object was a button, Expression assumes that this is the desired event. These two components, an event and an action, make up a behavior. If you wish to see what script is being called by the behavior, double-click Action. The dialog showing the function name should appear. Adding the behavior to the page should modify the code in line 24 (see Figure 11.4). Line 24 is what causes the button to appear on the page. The modifier **onclick=FP_callJS('hello()')** was added. The modifier specifies the event, **onclick**, and, in response to this event, executes the function **hello()**. The actual mechanism for this (**FP_call()**) is built into every browser.

8. Save the page and preview it in a browser. Click the button.

An event and an action constitute a behavior.

The script is executed and the page is rewritten with the text *Hello World.* Your name disappears because the script redefines the whole page, and the script does not include writing your name. This simple script was done for illustration purposes. In the next section, we will use a script to open a window and control its properties.

EXERCISE 11.5. Creating a Script That Opens a New Window and Loads a Page

1. To begin this exercise a page needs to be created. In Expression, create a new page with the filename *page3.htm*. On the page, type **Page 3** and apply the **<h2>** style to the text.

2. Save the page and close it.

3. Create another page and save it as *script3.htm*. While saving it, give the page the title **Run Script 3** (without the quotes).

4. Create a table on the page with the following specifications: 3 rows, 1 column, center alignment, 600 px wide, and a green border. Click **OK**.

5. Click in the first row and type **Run Script 3**. Apply the **<h1>** style to the text and center it in the table cell.

6. Click the second row of the table and split this row into three cells (**Table > Modify > Split Cells**). Enter **3** for the number of columns, verify that **Columns** is selected, and click **OK**).

FIGURE 11.4 Code for script2.htm Behavior

```
 1  <!DOCTYPE html PUBLIC "-//W3C//DTD XHTML 1.0 Transitional//EN" "http://www.w3.org/TR/xhtml1/DTD/xhtml1.
 2  <html xmlns="http://www.w3.org/1999/xhtml">
 3
 4  <head>
 5  <script language="Javascript">
 6  function hello() {
 7      document.write("Hello World");
 8      }
 9
10  function FP_callJS() {//v1.0
11      eval(arguments[0]);
12  }
13  </script>
14  <meta http-equiv="Content-Language" content="en-us" />
15  <meta http-equiv="Content-Type" content="text/html; charset=windows-1252" />
16  <title>Untitled 1</title>
17  </head>
18
19  <body>
20
21  <p>John Purcell</p>
22
23  <p>
24  <img alt="" src="images/run_script.gif" width="130" height="60" onclick="FP_callJS('hello()')" /></p>
25
26  </body>
27
28  </html>
29
```

7. Click in the first cell of the second row. Insert the graphic *run_script3.gif* into this cell (**Insert** > **Picture** > **From File**; Select *run_script3.gif* and click **Insert**). If asked to enter alternate text enter *Runs Script 3*. Save the page. When asked, make sure that the graphic will be saved to the images folder on the server and click OK.

8. Locate the file script3.txt in the files for this chapter and open it. Select all of the text and copy it.

9. In the **Code** or **Split view**, locate the **opening head** tag (<**head**>). It should be about line 4. Click after the head tag, hit Enter, and paste the script text into the page at this location. The code view of this page is shown in Figure 11.5.

This script also contains a function. The first line of the script (line 5) defines the script and specifies the language. Line 6 defines a function with the name *script3()*. Line 7 uses a new concept. The word *var* begins the line. **Var** (which stands for variable) is a special term that defines a variable. A variable in a program is like a variable in algebra—it can be anything. In the next section of this line, we name the variable *newW*. The equal sign implies, "using the variable 'newW,' create a new window; into that window, load 'page3.htm' and name the new window 'newWin.'" When a script creates a window, it must specify, at a minimum, which file to load into the window and a name for the window. Line 8 closes the function and line 9 closes the script. We have the function, and now the function must be triggered by an event. The event will be clicking the button.

An event such as clicking a button is needed to trigger a function.

EXERCISE 11.6. Adding the Event to Trigger the Function

1. Click the *run_script3.gif* button on the page. In the **Behaviors** task pane click the **Insert** button. From the menu, select **Call Script**. In the call script dialog box, type **script3**(). Click **OK**.

2. Save the page and preview it in a browser. Click the button and *page3.htm* should open in a new window.

The window that opened is just a regular browser window. With the simple addition to the script, we can control the properties and size of the window.

EXERCISE 11.7. Modifying the Script to Control the Window Properties

1. Create a new page with the filename *script4.htm*. Create a standard table on the page as before.

2. Click inside the first row and type **Script 4 Page** at the top of the page and set the page title to be *Script 4 Page*. Save the page.

3. Open the script file *script4.txt* and copy the entire contents. Paste this text in the head section of the page on a new line.

FIGURE 11.5 *Code View for script3.htm Page*

```
1  <!DOCTYPE html PUBLIC "-//W3C//DTD XHTML 1.0 Transitional//EN" "http://www.w3.or
2  <html xmlns="http://www.w3.org/1999/xhtml">
3
4  <head>
5  <script language = "javascript">
6  function script3(){
7  var newW = window.open("page3.htm", "newWin");
8  }
9  </script>
10 <meta http-equiv="Content-Language" content="en-us" />
11 <meta http-equiv="Content-Type" content="text/html; charset=windows-1252" />
12 <title>Run Script 3</title>
13 <style type="text/css">
14 .style1 {
15     border: 1px solid #00FF00;
16 }
17 .style2 {
18     text-align: center;
19 }
20 </style>
21 </head>
22
```

4. Save the page.

The script is much the same as the last version. The only difference is that the window.open section has modifiers for setting the height and width of the browser window (height=400; width=300).

5. Click in the second row of the table and insert the *run_script4.gif graphic* If asked, add the alternate text, *Script 4*. Save the page and, when asked, make sure that the graphic is inserted in the images folder on the Web server. Click **OK**.

6. Select the button and click **Insert** from the **Behavior** task pane. From the menu, select **Call Script**. In the dialog box, type **script4()**.

7. Save the page and preview it in a browser. Click the button and a smaller window should open.

Note that when the size of the window was specified, other aspects of the window were disabled. The scrollbars, menus, borders, and so on of a window are often called "chrome." When the script opens a window of a specific height and width, the page displays in a window without much of the "chrome"—the menu, toolbar, favorites menu, and scrollbars don't show in the window. For our purposes, the survey window must be large enough to fit the 600 px table that we have used to contain the survey. There should also be a bit extra, for a border, to make it easy to read, so we will use 700 px for the width of the survey window. The height should be large enough to show one "chunk" of information in the survey, yet not so large that the bottom runs off the window on an older computer. As discussed earlier, the smallest or coarsest screen that a user should encounter is 800 px wide by 600 px high. If we use 550 px for the survey window height, that should accommodate any survey nicely.

The survey must be large enough to fit a 600 px table that holds the survey and a 550 px for survey window height should be appropriate.

This scheme of opening the survey in a new window is not perfect. It works well in Internet Explorer, but there are other browsers to consider. Firefox, Opera, and Safari are also used by a great many users. How does the survey look in these browsers? The results with other browsers are mixed. The basic functionality is there, but there are some aspects that are not the same. Internet Explorer and Firefox are the most successful at rendering the pages without the chrome. Both open the new window without scrollbars and menus and load the page into it. The window in both browsers does not have scrollbars, scrolling, or support for the wheel mouse. The latest Opera browser (version 9.5) creates a window without scrollbars, but the wheel mouse is supported. Safari is a browser written by Apple. The Windows version (version 3.1.1) has the same features as Safari for the Mac. The chrome is largely gone, but the form controls are rendered differently.

What is the answer to getting a clean window for presenting surveys? There isn't a good one. At this time, having the page open in a new window that is 700 px wide,

550 px high, and has a minimum of chrome is the best solution. It is not completely compatible with all browsers, but it works well in the most popular ones. A statement should be added to the consent page stating that the survey is best seen using either Internet Explorer or Firefox.

CREATING MULTIPLE VERSIONS OF A PAGE TO ELIMINATE BIAS

Some research involves using several survey instruments and the order in which they are presented may introduce a bias into the results. Assume that you are presenting three instruments to a respondent: instruments A, B, and C. There are six possible permutations of the three instruments. You could present them in the following orders: ABC, BAC, ACB, BCA, CBA, or CAB.

To remove order bias in this research, we need to create six surveys with the instruments in one of the orders outlined above. Respondents could then be randomly assigned to one of the six surveys. This counterbalance would effectively remove any bias that results from the order in which the instruments were presented. Figure 11.6 summarizes how the site will work.

This exercise is based on a real research situation. The survey had over eighty-five questions. We will approach the problems in a conceptual way to illustrate the problems. Of course the researcher had to actually create the full versions of the surveys.

Mathematicians tell us that there are 3! (factorial) permutations. This can be calculated by multiplying 3 × 2 × 1 to get 6. If there were 4 instruments, 4! would be the number of survey versions required or 4 × 3 × 2 × 1 = 24.

EXERCISE 11.8. Creating the First Survey Version

1. In Expression, close any open pages.

2. Create a new page and save it with the filename *default.htm* or *index.htm* as appropriate. Create a 600 px table with 3 rows and 1 column, centered on the page. Do *not* add a border to the table. Type **Consent Page** in the first row of the table and set it as the page title. Save the page.

3. Save the page created in step 2 as *no_thank_you.htm*. Type **no_thank_you** in the **file-name** box, click **OK.** Substitute **No Thank You** in the first row of the table and as the page title. Save the page.

4. Save the page created in step 2 as *confirmation_page.htm*. Substitute **Debriefing and Confirmation Page** in the first row of the table and as the page title. Save the page.

5. Create another page and save it as *survey1.asp*.

6. Attach the style sheet **chapter11.css** to all the pages in the site.

7. On the *survey1.asp* page, create a 600 px table with 4 rows and 1 column, centered on the page. Do not add a border to the table. Click inside the table and, with the **Quick Tag**

FIGURE 11.6 *Survey Map for Multiple Versions Site*

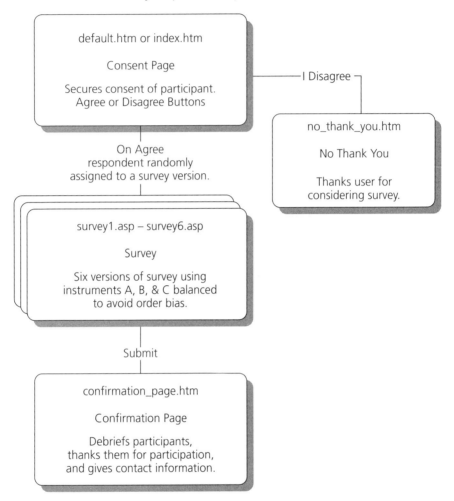

Selector, select the entire table. Apply the **survey_table** style to the table. In the first row, type **Survey Version 1**. Select the text and apply the style **title** to the text. Save the page.

8. From the **Form Control** toolbox, drag a **Form control** onto the page and drop it into the second row of the outer table.

9. With the cursor inside the form in the second row, insert a table with 4 rows, 1 column, and 100% width. Select the entire table using the **Tag Selector** and apply the style **question_table** to the table. Click in the first row of the new question table.

10. Insert a table with 4 rows, 1 column, and 100% width. Use the **Tag Selector** to select the entire new table and, from the **style** menu, apply the **instrument_a** style. Type **Instrument A** in the first row of the table and **Question 1 of Instrument A** in the second row of the table.

11. Click in the second row of the question table (it has a green border). Insert a 4-row, 1-column, 100% width table. Using the tag selector, select the table and apply the style **instrument_b** to it. Type **Instrument B** in the first row of the table and **Question 1 of Instrument B**. in the second row of the table.

12. Click in the third row of the question table. Insert a 4-row, 1-column, and 100% width table. Using the **Tag Selector**, select the table and apply the style **instrument_c** style to it. Type **Instrument C** in the first row of the table and **Question 1 of Instrument C**. in the second row of the table.

13. In the fourth row of the question table, drag and drop an **Input (Submit)** button from the **Form Control** toolbox. Double-click the button and change the **Value/label** to **Click Here to Submit Your Data**. Click **OK**. Center the button in the table row. Save the page. Hit the Tab key to add one more row to the question table.

14. Save the page and preview it in a browser.

15. From the **Form Control** toolbox, drag and drop an **Input(text)** control into the cell under the *Question 1 of Instrument A* text. Repeat for each of the other question areas. Save the page and preview it in a browser. The resulting page is shown in Figure 11.7.

FIGURE 11.7 *Completed Survey 1.asp Showing Instruments A, B, and C*

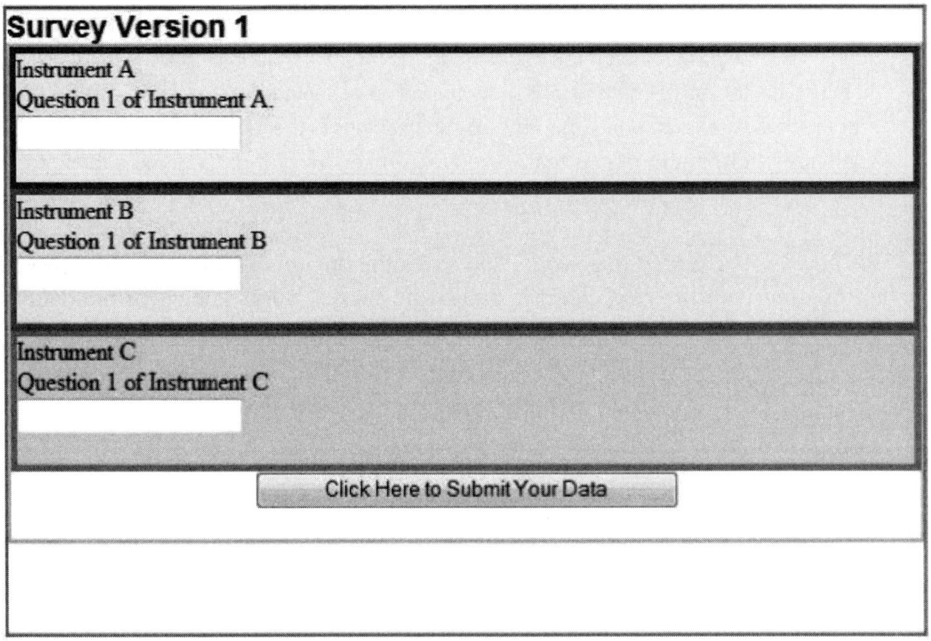

At this point, we have a survey created with proxies for the three survey instruments in use. Each has a single question with a text box. Because this is just conceptual, one question for each instrument suffices. The next task is to define the variables and link the survey to a database.

 EXERCISE 11.9. **Defining the Variables and Creating the Database for survey1.asp**

1. Double-click the text box in the instrument A table. In the dialog box, give this the name *a_q1*. Set the width in characters to be 65 and click **OK**.

2. Repeat for the text box in the other instrument tables, naming them *b_q1* and *c_q1*. Save the page. With this naming convention, each instrument retains the original numbering, but the database has unique variable names for each input device.

3. Right-click in any instrument areas in the survey. From the menu, select **Form Properties**. Select the option **Send to Database**. Click the **Options** button in the lower left corner. In the next dialog box, select **Create Database**. When this is done successfully, click **OK**. Before proceeding, note the name of the connection (usually *survey1*) and the table that will hold the results (usually *results*). In the **URL of confirmation page** box, type **confirmation_page.htm**. Click **OK** twice and save the page.

4. The survey is now ready to test. Preview the survey in a browser, fill in each of the text boxes with some text, and click the **Submit** button. You should see the *confirmation_page.htm* page after the submission.

5. After submitting data with the survey form, check to see that the data are in the database. Double-click the *fpdb* folder in the folder list. Inside the folder, double-click the database file that contains the survey data. It will show the name of the connection from step 3 above with the *mdb* extension. Verify that the column headings in the results table match the variable names from the form and that there are as many rows of data as you submitted. If everything checks out, then close the database file.

We now have a survey that works and saves the data to a database on the server. Do not proceed with the next exercise unless the survey works and saves the data as expected. This first version of the survey uses the three instruments in the order ABC. Figure 11.8 shows the remaining versions that must be created.

FIGURE 11.8 *The Possible Ordering of the Three Instruments*

Filename	Survey1.asp	Survey2.asp	Survey3.asp	Survey4.asp	Survey5.asp	Survey6.asp
Order	ABC	BAC	ACB	BCA	CBA	CAB

EXERCISE 11.10. Creating Version 2 of Survey

1. Save the *survey1.asp* page as *survey2.asp*. Modify the title in row 1 of the outer table and the page title to be *Survey Version 2*.

2. Click in the table row that contains the **Submit** button, but do not click the button itself. Add three new rows above this row (**Table** > **Insert** > **Rows or Columns**. Number of rows should be 3 and location **Above**. Click **OK**).

3. When reordering the instruments, it is best to work from the bottom up. The order for the *survey2.asp* version is BAC. Click inside the *instrument C* table. Select the entire table using the **tag selector**. Cut the table from its present location. Move to the row two rows above the **Submit** button and paste the *instrument C* table into that row.

4. Repeat with *instrument B* and *instrument A* tables. When all the moving and repositioning is done, delete any extra empty rows in the survey by clicking in the empty row and selecting it in the **Quick Select** area (click the tag <**tr**>—for table row) and then hit the Delete key on the keyboard.

5. Save the page, preview the page in a browser, and submit at least one set of data to verify that all is working. After the data have been submitted, open the database and verify that the data are saved to the database file. Close the database.

During the analysis, it might be useful to test whether there are differences between the six versions of the survey. To do so, the survey version must be stored in the database. The respondents will not know which version they are taking, so they cannot type it into a text box; you must program it into the form. You also don't want the respondent to see the version number—they don't need to concern themselves with it and it may confuse them. To prevent this, you will need to program the value into a **hidden field**, which is like any other field in a survey form except that it has a fixed value and is not seen by the user.

EXERCISE 11.11. Creating a Hidden Field in a Form

1. Right-click anywhere in the instrument area of the survey and select **Form Properties** from the menu. Click the **Advanced . . .** button at the bottom of the dialog box. In the **Advanced Form Properties** dialog box, click **Add**. In the **name** box, type **version**. In the Value box, type the number of the survey version, **2**. This will create a new variable called *version* in the database and store in it the value 2. Click **OK** twice.

2. In the **Form Properties** dialog box, click the **Options . . .** button. Because a new variable was added to the form, the database is not in sync with the form. Any time the form changes, the database must be updated. To remedy this, click the **Update Database . . .** button. When you get the *successfully updated* message, click **OK** three times to get out of the **Form Properties** dialog box.

3. Save the page and preview it in a browser. Enter some data and submit to the server.

4. Open the database and verify that the new variable was added to the database and that the value was set at **2**. This new variable will be at the right end of the data display in Access. Close the database.

The database has the data from the three text boxes even though the boxes were in a different order. The Web server doesn't care about the order in which the data are entered; it saves the data depending on the names of the fields on the form, regardless of the order.

5. Open *survey1.asp* and add the hidden field named *version* with the value of 1. Enter test data and verify that they were stored in the database correctly.

6. Create the remaining four survey versions using the same procedure. Make sure that you add a hidden field to each page with the appropriate value. It is not necessary to update the database each time. Once updated, the database is ready to receive the version number from any survey page. Test each version to verify that it saves the correct data in the database.

There are now six versions of the survey balanced for the order of presentation of the instruments that save data and the version number of the survey to the database. To complete the task of creating the research site, you must assign respondents to a survey version randomly. The map in Figure 11.6 shows the respondent going to the default page for the site first and then being randomly assigned from that page. We'll begin the next exercise with the default page.

EXERCISE 11.12. Updating Each Page and Hooking Pages Together

1. Close any open pages and double-click the *default.htm* page. Click in the table row under the title. Type the following: **Consent page text goes here**. Select this text and apply the **question_text** style to it.

2. Move to the third row and use the **tag selector** to select the entire row. Split the row into two cells by clicking **Table** > **Modify** > **Split Cells . . .** . Verify that **Into columns** is selected, that **2** is the number, and click **OK**.

3. Click in the first cell of the third row. Insert the graphic *random_agree.gif* in that cell.

4. Click in the second cell of the third row. Insert the graphic *random_disagree.gif* in that cell. Right-align the **disagree** button in the cell.

5. Save the page and put the graphics into the image folder.

6. If the person disagrees with the consent information, then they will click the **disagree** button. This will take them to the *no_thank_you.htm* page. Create a hyperlink from this button to the *no_thank_you.htm* page.

7. There are six versions of the survey, so we need to assign a subject to one of the six versions. In the *script_files* folder, locate the file *random_6.txt*. Open the file, select all of the text, and copy it.

8. In Expression switch to the **Split view** and paste the text into the head section of the *default.htm* page. Save the page. The code for this script is in Figure 11.9.

This script, though it looks complicated, creates a function that does just two things: it generates a random integer between 1 and 6 and, on the basis of the value of that number, the script triggers one of six functions. The function opens the respective survey in a new window.

FIGURE 11.9 *Code View of Random Assignment Script*

```
 1 <!DOCTYPE html PUBLIC "-//W3C//DTD XHTML 1.0 Transitional//EN" "http://www.w3.org/TI
 2 <html xmlns="http://www.w3.org/1999/xhtml">
 3
 4 <head>
 5 <script type="text/javascript">
 6 function pickWin(){
 7     var randNum = Math.random();
 8     var randPage = randNum*6;
 9     var pageNum = Math.ceil(randPage);
10
11     if (pageNum == 1) {
12         openWin1();
13         }
14     if (pageNum == 2) {
15         openWin2();
16         }
17     if (pageNum == 3) {
18         openWin3();
19         }
20     if (pageNum == 4) {
21         openWin4();
22         }
23     if (pageNum == 5) {
24         openWin5();
25         }
26     if (pageNum == 6) {
27         openWin6();
28         }
29 }
30 function openWin1() {
31     window.open("survey1.asp","newWin","width=700,height=550");
32 }
33 function openWin2() {
34     window.open("survey2.asp","newWin","width=700,height=550");
35 }
36 function openWin3() {
37     window.open("survey3.asp","newWin","width=700,height=550");
38 }
39 function openWin4() {
40     window.open("survey4.asp","newWin","width=700,height=550");
41 }
42 function openWin5() {
43     window.open("survey5.asp","newWin","width=700,height=550");
44 }
45 function openWin6() {
46     window.open("survey6.asp","newWin","width=700,height=550");
47 }
```

The *random number* section of the script needs a bit of explanation. On line 6 a function, **pickWin()**, is created. On the next line a variable, called **randNum**, is created and a random number is assigned to it. The number is generated using a built-in math operation. **Math.random()** generates a random number between 0 and 1. Each time the page is loaded or refreshed, a number is regenerated. Line 8 creates another variable to hold the random number multiplied by the number of versions of the survey (in this case, 6). The value of this new variable is now between 0 and 6, but it has about 8 decimal places after the number. To get an integer number, the number must be rounded. There are three rounding options: **Math.round()**, **Math.ceil()**, and **Math.floor()**. The **.round** method is the typical rounding routine; numbers greater than .5 are rounded up, less than .5 are rounded down. This generates values from 0 to 6. However, it does not generate six equal probability distributions for the six versions. Because of the rounding, the probability of getting a 0 or a 6 is half of the probability for the other values. **Math.floor** and **Math.ceil** work correctly: **floor** always rounds down and **ceil** always rounds up. **Ceil** will take any value less than 1 and will round it up to 1. Any value that is greater than 1 will be rounded up to 2, and so on. This will give us the desired range for the numbers. Line 9 uses the ceil method to round the random number to an integer.

The next group of code tests the value of the number. Lines 11 through 13 create a test of the value generated in line 9. The test is to evaluate if the variable **pageNum** is equivalent (using the operator ==, the *comparison operator*) to 1. If **pageNum** is equivalent to 1, then the code on the next line will execute (**openWin1()** in this case). If they are not equivalent, then the program will jump out of this test and go to line 14 and do the next test. The functions that are executed are given below the six testing codes. Each function opens a window with specific properties and puts one of the surveys into that window. In general there must be a test and a function for each survey version.

In the files for this chapter are several other *random_XX.txt* files. These files are scripts you can use to randomly assign respondents to XX surveys. The difference in each is the number used to generate the random number in the fourth line, and the number of statements that are shown to test for each value. There is also a corresponding function that opens a window and inserts the version of the survey into the window. Each version of the survey should be named *surveyX.asp*, where *X* is the number of that survey version.

9. Before the page will work, the function **pickWin()** must be tied to some event. The event will be clicking the **I Agree** button. Select the **I Agree** button and in the behavior task pane and click **Insert**. From the menu, select **Call Script** and, in the next window, type the name **pickWin ()**. Click **OK**.

10. Save the page and preview it in a browser. Click the **I Agree** button and note the version of the survey that opens. Close the survey window and click the **I Agree** button again. Continue clicking the button and noting the survey number that appears. Verify that all six of the survey versions appear. A common error is to have a script that doesn't generate numbers for all of the versions of the survey. It may take a bit for all six versions to appear.

Because the numbers are generated randomly, there is an equal probability of any one version coming up at any time.

The survey works and the six versions are randomly assigned. Each version saves data to the database and the coding, question wording, flow, and appearance are in good shape. What remains is to turn off the border and fill colors from the various tables.

EXERCISE 11.13. Editing the Table Styles

1. If necessary, open the site in Expression. Locate the **Manage Styles** task pane in the lower right corner of the Expression window. If it is not there, select **Task Panes** > **Manage Styles** to turn it on.

2. Right-click the **survey_table** style in the task pane. Select **Modify Style** from the menu. Select the **Border category** from the list on the left and set the **Border style** to **none** and click **OK**.

3. Right-click the **instrument_a** style in the task pane. Select **Modify Style** from the menu. Select the **Border** category from the list on the left and set the **border style** to **none**. Select the **Background** category and delete the color number in the **background color** box.

4. Repeat this procedure for the other two instrument styles.

5. Right-click the **question_table** style in the task pane. Select **Modify Style** from the menu. Select the **Border** category from the list on the left and set the **Border style** to **none** and click **OK**.

6. The survey site is now ready to deploy.

SUMMARY

The conceptual model of the research site is complete. Six versions of the survey instrument were created and they are counterbalanced to remove order bias. If instrument tables are used for each section and all the questions are kept inside the instrument sections, then producing the six versions is easily done.

To complete the survey site, all that remains is to create the survey questions themselves, code each response, and place the instruments inside the tables. This should be done in the first version. The survey can then be coded, connected to a database, and tested to verify that it all works. After this is done, each version of the survey can be recreated.

KEY TERMS

JavaScript
<HTML> tag
tag

head section
page title
document

<script> and </script>	fpdb folder
function	hidden field
event	random number
onclick events	Math.random()
var or variable	Math.round()
window properties and modifiers	Math. ceil()
Firefox	Math.floor()
Opera	comparison operator
Safari	

DISCUSSION QUESTION

1. Notepad is a very rudimentary word processor that is included with every version of Windows. Programmers like it because it does not add anything else to the text that you create. It allows you to use different fonts, but most programmers don't use anything beyond the default typeface. In this exercise we will use Notepad to write a simple script. To open Notepad, click the Start button > **All Programs** > **Accessories** > **Notepad**.

A. Type the following into Notepad exactly as it is written.

```
<script>
var1 = 12;
var2 = 3.3;
varProduct = var1*var2;
document.write(Math.round(varProduct));
document.write(Math.ceil(varProduct));
document.write(Math.floor(varProduct));
</script>
```

B. Save the file as *extra_script1.txt*.

The purpose of this script is to multiply two numbers, 12 and 3.3, and write the result to the screen. The second, third, and fourth lines each create a variable and set it equal to a value—12, 3.3, and the product of 12 and 3.3, respectively. If you multiply these two numbers together with a calculator, the product is 39.6. The next three lines use the three methods discussed in the chapter (**round, ceil,** and **floor**) to modify the product variable and then they write the answer to the page.

C. In Expression, create a new page and save it as *extra_script1.htm*. Switch to the code view, copy the script from Notepad, and paste it into the head section of the *extra_script1.htm* page. Think about what the results look like. After you have guessed, preview the page in a browser. You should see output in the upper left corner of the page that looks something like *404039*. What does this mean? It means that everything worked, but the script doesn't go far enough. The first two digits are 40; this is indeed the answer 39.6 rounded. The next two digits are 40; this is 39.6 rounded to the ceiling. The final two digits are 39; this is the number 39.6 rounded to the floor.

Why are they not on individual lines on the page? Because we didn't tell the browser to put them on separate lines. We need to modify the script.

D. Switch back to Notepad and save the script file as *extra_script2.txt*. For each of the three *document.write* lines, add +"**
**" after the first closing parenthesis after *varProduct*. The first *document.write* line should read:

```
"document.write(Math.round(varProduct)+"<br>");"
```

Repeat this for the remaining lines, save the page, and preview it in a browser. You should now see each number on its own line.

What if you didn't get any results? You must have an error or a bug in your script. Look very closely at the code and compare it to the text above. One common error is to forget the semicolon at the end of the line of code. Another is to not have enough closing parentheses for the number opening parentheses that you used. Look hard at the text and you may see it. If not, in the files for this chapter are two script files *extra_script_1.txt* and *extra_script_2.txt*. If your script doesn't work, open the relevant Notepad file, copy the entire contents, paste the script into the page in Expression, and delete the code that you added. It should work now.

Congratulations! You now have an understanding of how computer programs are written.

CHAPTER

REPEATED MEASURES AND MATCHED GROUPS DESIGNS

LEARNING OBJECTIVES

- To be able to define within-subjects designs (repeated measures)
- To be able to differentiate between single-case designs and multiple-baseline designs
- To be able to explain a simple pre- and posttest design (research with two data points)
- To be able to understand a repeated-measures design with more than two data
- To be able to use matched pairs and quasi-experimental designs
- To be able to identify threats to internal validity
- To be able to use counterbalancing and random block design to counteract order effects
- To learn about complex and mixed designs

INTRODUCTION TO WITHIN-SUBJECTS DESIGNS (REPEATED MEASURES)

The experimental designs we've covered so far have included between-subjects designs, where participants are included in only one experimental condition. In repeated-measures designs, the same participants are assessed repeatedly, pre- and posttest or over multiple experimental conditions. There are three primary advantages of repeated measures: they require fewer participants than between-subjects designs, take less time to administer, and have greater statistical power.

Let's say that you have invented a new software program that proposes to increase work productivity for data-entry personnel. You have developed your program for maximum effectiveness. However, there is one thing you continue to wonder about. Font size and style are typically an individual preference, but your software program can only produce three font styles and sizes and you know, based on previous research, that letters that are physically different (for example, *A* and *a*) will take longer for participants to process than if they were physically the same (for example, *a* and *a*). For maximum work productivity you need to know whether the font size and style you ultimately choose for your final software system will produce the highest rates of data entry and maximum productivity.

Repeated-measures designs can be a more cost-effective approach depending on your research question. Repeated-measures designs lead to less within-group variability and greater experimental sensitivity.

In a between-subjects design, you can assign a group of individuals to each font size and style condition. That would make for nine different conditions (3 font styles $\times$ 3 font sizes). You would need a minimum of 90 to 180 participants (ideally twenty per condition, but a minimum of ten per condition). You know it is difficult to get data entry personnel as research participants, so a repeated-measures design is tempting. Then you consider the cost and time of administering the experiment across the nine conditions. If you had to provide instruction for each of the participants in all nine conditions, it would take quite a while. A repeated-measures design may be better. Then you realize repeated-measures designs increase statistical power. Because the same individuals are participating in all conditions, you can minimize individual differences, hence minimizing within-group variability. Less within-group variability means greater experimental sensitivity, so fewer people are needed to participate and to determine whether differences exist. (Remember, with between-subjects designs, your hope is that any differences between groups you find are due to the independent variable.)

Computing analysis of variance (or ANOVAs, see Chapter Fifteen) to examine between-group differences takes into consideration the individual differences between the groups and calculates additional error variability between the groups. In repeated-measure designs, you can assume that any changes between groups can be attributed to the change in the independent variable because participants were exposed to all conditions.

Any change in the independent variable would not be caused by individual differences between groups because scores in all conditions came from the same person. This reduction in error variability allows us greater statistical power (experimental sensitivity) and shows the true effects of the independent variable. There are many different forms of repeated-measure designs. The easiest is the single-case design, followed by multiple-baseline designs. We also examine pre- and posttest designs and more complex repeated-measures.

Single-Case Designs

So far, this book has focused on research using groups of people in order to determine mean differences among groups or to determine average scores. Some researchers believe using mean or average scores loses sight of the individual. Think about it. How often have you read research that the average person "does this" or "does that," and you think to yourself, "Gee, *I* don't do that!" Quite often, mean scores or typical scores do not reflect the individual in your sample. In addition, sampling larger groups of people often leads to larger error variance (and potential for error) in your results (Sidman, 1960).

One of the simplest repeated-measures designs is the single-case design. A *single-case design* (sometimes known as *applied behavioral analysis*) introduces an independent variable (or treatment) to one person (N = 1) and measures that person repeatedly. This research can be conducted with one or more individuals but typically examines one behavior of interest to determine the effectiveness of a treatment.

Single-case designs are used most often by clinicians or medical doctors. These designs are helpful when examining rare diseases or mental illness—especially when testing a new theory on a single participant. If the theory and results are replicated over several individuals, then a larger study can be conducted based on preliminary data received through the single-case design. For instance, you may want to test the effectiveness of a new treatment aimed at reducing self-mutilating behaviors among adults. You could graph your participants' behavior before and after the treatment to determine whether your new treatment decreased self-mutilating behaviors. You will observe patient Jo.

Single-case and multiple-group designs are dependent upon obtaining baseline information to compare behavior before and after treatment is administered.

There are several ways to conduct single-case designs. In the first situation, you conduct general observations of Jo's behavior. Your initial observations will serve as a *baseline*, which provides information about behavior before intervention is presented. In order to determine a baseline, you observe Jo's self-mutilating behavior for ten days, recording the number of such behaviors for each day. You would then introduce an intervention designed to reduce the undesired behavior. The ABAB reversal design is the simplest single-case design that provides some experimenter control. *ABAB reversal design* is an experimental design where a treatment is introduced and then taken away two or more times (see Figure 12.1).

If you think of the A as the control group and the B as the experimental group (or treatment), you would first obtain A—the baseline data to determine the frequency of self-mutilating behaviors before intervention is introduced. B would be the intervention (treatment) to reduce the self-mutilating behaviors. The intervention measure is then taken away and self-mutilating behaviors are recorded again. It is likely the behavior will return to baseline without the intervention.

One of the primary ethical issues associated with the ABAB reversal design (and certainly in this situation) is the dilemma of withholding treatment. What if the treatment actually worked and it helped the participant? It is not ethical to allow the self-mutilating behaviors to continue when the treatment is stopped. Another potential problem with this design occurs when participants begin to anticipate the treatment and respond before it is administered. Having received the treatment, participants can carry over the effects of the first condition into the next condition; it is difficult to "unlearn" a behavior once it has been established. With the ABAB design you may find differences when treatment is administered, but there are significant limitations, because you will still be studying one person, in one period of time, and in one situation. There is always a chance that there will be no changes after treatment has been administered or that the behavior will not return to baseline as expected. If you suspect these could be potential problems for your research project you may want to consider using a multiple-baseline design.

FIGURE 12.1 *Sample Results of ABAB Experimental Design*

Multiple-Baseline Designs

Multiple-baseline designs allow you to control for some of the problems just mentioned by reversing the treatment and baseline conditions over different situations, behaviors, or individuals. Using multiple baselines across participants is similar to using the ABAB design, but it assesses a small number of people with treatment conditions introduced at different times. Let's say a teacher has a discipline problem in her class. She notices the class is disturbed primarily by three students: Jo, Sally, and Phil. The teacher believes her new time-out approach will help stop discipline problems. By administering the independent variable (that is, the treatment of time out) at various times, she can control for possible confounds in the experiment. In other words, if you see a pattern of behavior changing in the desired direction each time a treatment is administered, then it can be safe to assume the treatment is effective and the effects are not due to some other extraneous variable. As you can see in Figure 12.2, time out did not affect Jo's behavior, but it was effective in reducing discipline problems for Sally and Phil.

Multiple-baseline designs allow researchers greater experimental control by assessing individuals repeatedly over time and in various conditions.

You can also obtain multiple baseline measures across situations. Most likely, you will want to know whether the behavior change you are measuring can be generalized across situations. For instance, most young children cry and whine. In fact, crying and whining are behaviors that most children do and most parents try to prevent, at least in

FIGURE 12.2 *Sample Results of Multiple Baseline Studies*

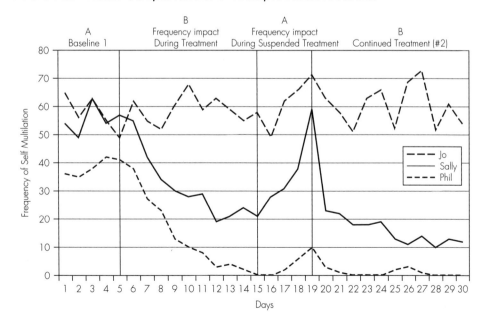

public. When crying and whining begins, parents can introduce a treatment such as ignoring the child. Parents may find that this treatment works well at home, but you may want to determine whether the treatment also works in different situations such as school, grocery stores, restaurants, and the like.

Multiple baselines across behaviors can also be used to assess treatment effectiveness with various behaviors. For example, behavioral therapy to treat obsessive-compulsive disorder (OCD) can be used to reduce or eliminate repetitive thoughts or behaviors. Let's say a client with OCD has compulsions to wash his hands seventy-five times a day and check the stove and coffeepot fifty times a day. Again, baseline measures are obtained and behavioral therapy treatment is introduced multiple times as you assess the effectiveness of the treatment across each behavior (handwashing, checking the stove and coffeepot). If you see a systematic improvement across behaviors, you can assume treatment was successful. Again, there is the potential that behavior may not return to baseline after intervention. If this occurs, it is best to repeat the process of "no treatment-treatment" conditions to determine whether changes did occur. It is also possible that behaviors will remain the same after intervention, suggesting that intervention did not work, or behaviors may increase or decrease in the desired direction yet not return to baseline after treatment was administered. In this situation, it is likely the intervention was successful. However, a good researcher will investigate all other possible explanations for behavior. Generally, single- and multiple-case designs do not entail statistical analyses. Researchers tend to eyeball the data to get an idea of the effectiveness of the treatment. Statistical analyses are conducted with repeated measures with two or more groups.

Simple Pre- and Posttest Designs (Research with Two Data Points)

A simple **pretest/posttest** repeated-measures design is a common research technique that measures individuals before and after an intervention or treatment. Researchers obtain a random sample and administer a pretest. Upon completion of the pretest, treatment is introduced, followed by a posttest. This design allows researchers to examine changes in mean scores from pre- to posttest on specified measures. Let's say your boss believes a class in meditation will help increase productivity and reduce stress in the workplace. Your boss has you and others in your department attend a workshop on stress reduction. On the first day of the workshop the presenter asks you to complete a questionnaire (pretest) measuring your current stress level. The workshop begins (the treatment is meditation) and ends. Upon completion of the workshop the presenter asks you to complete the stress questionnaire again (posttest). Your boss is interested in knowing whether stress scores reduced significantly from pre- to posttest; he wants to know whether a change in stress occurred by examining mean scores for the pretest and comparing them to mean scores of the posttest. If there is a significant change (reduction) in mean scores from pre- to posttest, then your boss can attribute this change to the effectiveness of the stress reduction workshop.

Pre- and posttest designs test individuals two times (two data points)—once before treatment begins and after treatment is complete.

Occasionally you may want to conduct a pre- and posttest research study that does not use mean scores but rather categorical information. For example, let's imagine that smokers are invited to a "stop smoking" seminar. At the beginning of the program participants are asked whether they smoke (yes or no). A week after the program is administered; participants are asked whether they still smoke (yes or no). Statistical analyses for categorical pre- or posttests use non-parametric statistics, and, in this case, a McNamar test. (For more in-depth information on non-parametric statistics see Chapter Fifteen and Siegel and Castellan, 1988).

Repeated Measures with More Than Two Data Points

Sometimes it is necessary to conduct experiments that measure participants repeatedly. For instance, some individuals believe they can identify criminals simply by looking at them. You want to test a hypothesis that individuals can identify real criminals compared with noncriminals simply by looking at photos. Participants are shown a series of ten photos in which there is one true criminal and the rest are individuals known to be innocent. Participants are asked to rate how confident they are that each picture is the actual criminal (on a scale from 0 = "not at all confident" to 7 = "extremely confident"). For each photo there will be an average confidence rating. Researchers can then assess whether mean scores were higher for the true criminal and provide support for the hypothesis that individuals can distinguish criminals from noncriminals.

A repeated-measures design with more than two data points measures individuals more than two times and relies upon the average rating between all data points.

A study by Pryor, Reeder, Patel, and Monroe (in press) showed participants a series of pictures of a person standing next to an individual who was obese or thin. The authors theorized that simply being near a stigmatized individual would evoke negative evaluations of the nonstigmatized individual. They called this phenomenon "stigma by association." In their first study, the researchers showed participants sixteen pictures of men standing next to an overweight female "relative" and sixteen pictures of men standing next to a thin female "relative." Participants rated the attractiveness of the man standing next to the woman in each picture. Results found that men standing next to thin female relatives were rated as significantly more attractive than men standing next to overweight female relatives. In this repeated-measures design, participants were asked to complete ratings for each of the thirty-two photographs (sixteen thin, sixteen overweight), and researchers then averaged the scores for individuals standing near thin or overweight individuals.

Consider another example. Drug addicts sent to prison are unable to continue their drug use, and in many cases, are unable to smoke cigarettes. During initial incarceration, many individuals experience withdrawal due to addiction. A study is conducted to assess whether acupuncture is a helpful technique to alleviate inmates' withdrawal symptoms. Drug addicts often experience extreme cravings, headaches, body aches or flu-like symptoms during withdrawal. Upon entering prison, inmates experiencing withdrawal complete a comprehensive intake screening inquiring about their current status regarding symptoms such as drug cravings, headaches, and so on (pretest or baseline data). Participants are then instructed to attend daily acupuncture sessions. Upon completion of each acupuncture session, participants rate the severity of withdrawal symptoms and cravings on a short survey. Four weeks later, they are asked to complete the comprehensive survey again. If there is a significant reduction of symptoms following the pretest you can assume the acupuncture program was successful in helping to reduce drug cravings and withdrawal symptoms. Keep in mind, though, that there are always alternative explanations as to why withdrawal symptoms may dissipate. For instance, it is likely that symptoms of withdrawal dissipate naturally over time. If you suspect alternative explanations can potentially confound your study, adding an appropriate control group (such as addicts who do not receive acupuncture) is the best course of action. If the control group also demonstrates the same pattern of reduction in withdrawal symptoms, then the acupuncture program may not have been successful. If participants receiving acupuncture actually had significantly fewer symptoms than the control group, you could then attribute the success to the acupuncture program. An appropriate control group is truly the key to a good research design.

Understanding Matched-Pairs Designs

Matched-pairs designs actually match participants on important dependent variable characteristics that create comparable groups. Matched pairs are particularly useful when there are a limited number of participants and comparable control groups are difficult to obtain. In a good experiment, it is imperative that the control group be similar to the experimental group. In the previous example, withdrawal symptoms of drug addicts were assessed. If you used a control group of individuals who did not experience drug addiction and withdrawal, the comparison would not make sense because individuals who are not addicted to drugs would not experience the same symptoms.

The purpose of a matched-pairs design is to match participants on variables that are relevant to the study. The appropriate research design to assess the effectiveness of the acupuncture program would include all inmates experiencing drug withdrawal. Inmates would then be matched on various variables of interest (such as gender, type of drug addiction, and so forth.) and randomly assigned to either the experimental group that receives acupuncture or the control group that receives no acupuncture. Then you would examine differences between the two groups. This allows you to control for threats to internal validity.

When conducting research, you want your control group to be similar to your experimental group, sharing similar characteristics. For example, if you examine differences in problem-solving ability among individuals, you would need to consider a person's intellect. You could examine differences in problem-solving skills between those with high and low intellect. To do this, you would first need to obtain a measure of intellect for each person. Then, based on that measure, participants would be divided into high- and low-intellect groups. To obtain matched pairs, you would randomly assign one individual from the high intellect group to the experimental condition and one individual from the high-intellect group to the control condition (no treatment). You would do the same with the low-intellect group. When participants are matched on one or more variables of interest they are related (or correlated). ***Correlated groups*** contain aspects of between- and within-subjects designs. You have a control group (an element of between-subjects designs), yet your control group has attributes that are matched (or correlate) to the experimental group. Hence, matched groups are considered to be a within-subjects design because they are correlated (Jackson, 2008).

Quasi-Experimental Designs

When a study does not have the experimental control often associated with a true experiment, it is most likely a quasi-experimental design. A ***quasi-experimental design*** is a type of experiment conducted in the real world, not a laboratory, and therefore lacks experimental control and is called *quasi*-experimental. Often, these designs are used in real-life situations to determine the effectiveness of particular treatments, laws, or programs.

Studies that use quasi-experimental designs are considered applied research because they are conducted in real-world situations with real-world consequences.

For example, suppose you were asked to examine the effectiveness of a new after-school program. You have access to student academic records and standardized test scores. The school hires you to determine whether their after-school tutoring program has increased student grades and standardized test scores. You decide to use a matched-group design and match students based on gender and grade level. However, random assignment is not an option. Students have already begun to participate in the program. Because the groups are already formed, you lack the experimental control of random assignment. Without random assignment, internal validity is threatened. This would be considered a quasi-experiment because, although you can compare student grades and test scores between those who attend and do not attend the after-school program, there are a variety of other variables that can affect the outcome.

One of the hallmarks of a quasi-experimental design is a non-equivalent control group. Non-equivalent control groups can never be equivalent like true experimental control groups because participants are not randomly assigned.

Quasi-experimental designs include pre- and post-test designs as well as non-equivalent control group designs and time-series designs. ***Non-equivalent control group*** designs use groups already in existence and compare them. This design is a quasi-experimental procedure that compares control and treatment groups that have not been randomly assigned. Because the groups are not randomly assigned, you must assume the control group included in the research study is not equivalent to the experimental group. ***Time series designs*** (or ***interrupted time-series designs***) are a type of quasi-experimental design that is an expansion of the simple pre-post test design and the same individuals (or event of interest) are tested multiple times before and after some event (or manipulation) has taken place. The event of interest can occur naturally in the environment (for example, massive layoffs in the community or a hurricane) or can be manipulated by the researcher.

Perhaps you want to investigate the impact of massive layoffs in the community on children of employees who are laid off. You could study child well-being or academic achievement before and after the layoffs occurred to determine whether the layoffs actually affected the children. Or consider another situation—often states enact new laws, such as when states changed the speed limit from sixty-five or seventy-five miles per hour (mph) to fifty-five mph, researchers could examine whether car accidents resulting in death decreased after new speed limit laws were implemented. In order to assess this, researchers could examine the number of traffic accidents resulting in death in the years before the speed limit changed via public records (archival data) and after the speed limit changed. In order to improve the validity of a time-series research study, a non-equivalent control group should be used to compare groups over a period of time before and after treatment began.

Despite the fact that time-series designs are an improvement over simple pre- and posttest designs—because they test multiple points in time—all of these quasi-experiments examine groups already in existence and therefore lack random assignment. When random assignment is not possible or you compare naturally existing groups, you lack experimental control. Lack of random assignment leaves you with greater threats to internal validity. (For a more in-depth review of quasi-experimental designs, see Graziano and Raulin, 2004 or Shaughnessy et al., 2005).

Important Considerations and Threats to Internal Validity

All experiments have *threats to internal validity* that should always be considered. A threat to internal validity is anything that compromises the extent to which changes in the dependent variable can be attributed to the experimental manipulation. Remember, in any experiment, the goal is to control for as many extraneous variables as possible so you can say that the independent variable caused a change in the dependent variable. Based on the nature of the experiment, some of these threats to internal validity pose more of a potential problem than others. Repeated-measures designs come with unique threats to validity and some are more prevalent than others. Use your best judgment to determine whether these threats might be a problem in your own research.

Any changes in the dependent variable can also be due to shared history among participants. *Historical events* are shared events that occur outside of the study. Certainly, elderly individuals have had different historical experiences than young adults and their histories must be considered. For example, you may want to study a new treatment program intended to reduce work-related stress. You conduct a pre- and posttest to measure stress and then introduce your new stress reduction program. However, during the posttest, you see that work-related stress actually increased instead of decreased. Before you assume your program did not work, you need to assess what could have happened during the data collection process. After you explore this, you find that the organization where you held your stress reduction program had started to lay off workers. This certainly would give the workers added stress that was not a result of your program. In this example, participants shared a similar history that affected the results of the study and compromised internal validity.

Just as people have shared histories, they also mature psychologically, socially, and physically over time. **Maturation** refers to any change that can be attributed to the passing of time. Maturation can be a significant problem to researchers who are studying individuals over a period of time where significant physical and mental maturation can take place. Let's say you have a new shoe-tying technique that you believe all preschoolers can easily master. You conduct five instruction sessions over a period of eight weeks, teaching three- and four-year-olds how to tie their shoes. You find, after the eight-week period, that almost all of the four-year-olds and a small number of three-year-olds can tie their shoes. Before you get excited thinking that your shoe-tying technique worked, you must consider that your small participants could have matured physically and cognitively as well and developed that skill within the time period with or without your new technique. Maturation would certainly explain why the four-year-olds tended to do better than the three-year-olds. In order to ascertain whether your technique worked and was not a function of maturation, you would need to add a control group. If the control group performed differently, then your technique might be valid after all.

Sometimes, it is necessary to select individuals to participate in a study because of scores on a test. **Regression to the mean** is a statistical term that can occur when participants are selected based on extreme scores. When individuals are chosen to participate in a study based on their extreme scores, upon retesting, their scores will regress to the mean. For example, if you wanted to examine problem-solving skills of depressed and nondepressed individuals, you would need to assess them before the research study began. Based on their responses, they would be considered "severely depressed" or "not depressed." However, everyone has bad days (or good days) and, if you were to test them again, participants with extreme scores would most likely be lower or higher depending on the original direction of their scores.

Participant mortality is a typical problem with longitudinal research. Participants may drop out of the study for various reasons. Be careful to pay attention to which participants are dropping out. It is possible that the conditions associated with your experiment may cause higher mortality rates than other conditions.

Finally, testing participants over and over again can have its problems. **Testing** more than once can affect the results of subsequent tests; testing repeatedly can lead to better or worse performance. If you test participants often (hourly, daily, weekly, monthly) using the same tests, there are two potential outcomes. Both are the result of practice effects. Individuals can do better on a task simply because of practice, or they may get fatigued completing the same task over and over again and may perform worse even though they are capable of doing better. If your study entails testing many times you can avoid practice effects by changing your test to a similar task or test that is equivalent in difficulty level.

When conducting repeated-measures designs, instrument accuracy and precision are essential. Sometimes researchers need to study differences in nanoseconds; even a minor difference in calibration of instruments can be a problem. If the instrument you use for your study is faulty then this can cause **instrumentation effects**, which refer to changes in tests or instruments that can affect the results of the study. The measuring devices you use must be consistent and accurate. Sometimes the instrument effect can be attributed to the researcher. Researchers can get tired collecting data and miss observing behaviors. As mentioned earlier, using multiple raters to collect data should be considered to ensure that instrumentation is not a problem. In order to avoid some of the common pitfalls associated with testing effects, researchers should also consider the order in which the stimuli are presented.

Finally, **diffusion of treatment** can occur when participants are placed into an experimental condition and then change their behavior because of real or perceived information they have obtained about the other research conditions. Treatment is diffused to the control group when participants take matters into their own hands and attempt to try their own treatment. For example, if participants in a new diet pill study are placed into either a control group that receives no diet pill or into a treatment group that receives the new diet pill. Individuals in the control group feel a little cheated because they found out they were not receiving the "magic" diet pill. In response, individuals in the control group increased their diet exercise routine. When the researchers examined weight loss between the control group and experimental group, they found there were no differences between the two groups. Researchers might infer that the diet pill did not work. However, they should consider the possibility that a diffusion of treatment took place that actually affected research results.

Counteracting Order Effects

Because participants are measured two or more times in a repeated-measures design, testing effects can be problematic. Participants can anticipate upcoming presentations, get tired, or improve with practice. To eliminate some of these problems, researchers counterbalance conditions.

Counterbalancing To reiterate the importance of counterbalancing, let us explain some of the implications associated with making false assumptions based on research results that are not counterbalanced. Let's say you wanted to assess how young children processed color. You studied one hundred children in the age range of three to ten years old. You presented fifteen cups in various colors to each of the children and had each child describe the color of the cups (such as red, orange, white, and so on). Results of your study found that younger children made more errors when discriminating the color blue. Based on the research results of this study, you could have easily concluded that younger children cannot see the color blue and that our ability to distinguish color increased with age. However, you realized that, since the blue cup was always the last cup presented, perhaps the younger children became tired or disinterested and made more errors by the time they got to the blue cup. Sure enough, when you counterbalance the conditions of the cups, presenting the blue cup earlier, you find that young children do not make more errors with the color blue.[1]

Researchers must counterbalance conditions in repeated measures experiments. When there are only two conditions, it is easy to systematically vary the conditions. *ABBA counterbalancing* is one option to control for practice and testing effects. With the ABBA counterbalancing technique, participants are presented with stimuli in one order (AB) followed by the next order (BA). However, one of the drawbacks with this technique is that participants come to expect the conditions in a particular order. In other words, you must assess the control condition (no treatment) and then present the treatment to participants to determine whether changes occur after treatment is implemented. To counterbalance this situation, half of your participants should receive the experimental condition first and half receive the control condition first. However, when there are more than two or three conditions, counterbalancing can get complicated. For example, when you have two conditions (X and Y) there are two possible orders for these conditions (XY and YX), but if you add another condition (Z), you have six possible orders (XYZ, XZY, YZX, YXZ, ZYX, and ZXY).

Complete counterbalancing techniques assume there are an equal number of participants in each group (or condition). When an experiment has a large number of conditions, you will have difficulty trying to obtain enough participants to complete all possible conditions. As the typical experimental condition will include between twenty and forty individuals, it would take a very large, impractical number of participants to fill all possible conditions using this technique. An alternative to this approach is to simply randomize the order in which conditions are presented to each participant.

Random Block Designs. Random block designs are a technique used to control or reduce sequence effects. A random block design should be created before your research is presented to participants to control for order effects. Participants should be randomly assigned to conditions. You can do this on your own or you can use Randomizer (www.randomizer.org; see Chapter Ten for more information.) Let's say you have five conditions and you know you will have twenty-five participants. To obtain counterbalancing for the five conditions you would have 120 possible orders ($5! = 5 \times 4 \times 3 \times 2 \times 1$) in which the stimuli could be presented. However, because you only have twenty-five participants you can have only twenty-five different orders. Therefore, you opt for twenty-five random blocks. This *incomplete counterbalancing approach* or (partial-counterbalancing approach) is used most often because of the difficulty in obtaining large numbers of participants to complete all possible orders. Partial counterbalancing techniques are used most often when there are more than three or four conditions in the experiment. Let's say you would like to conduct a study to assess social prejudice. You vary five different pictures of individuals based on race (Caucasian, African American, Asian, Hispanic, Nondescript). Participants are then asked to rate each individual picture on perceived intelligence. You have five conditions and you could assign each a letter (for example, 1 = A, 2 = B, 3 = C, 4 = D, and 5 = E). Then, you use a table of random numbers in the back of your old statistics book or simply put the letters in a box or hat and blindly pull them out one at a time. Do this twenty-five times. This provides a *random block schedule* (a group of random blocks that include one trial of each condition in the experiment) for how to present your stimuli to your participants.

Using Randomizer for the same study just mentioned, you simply answer the questions presented to you accordingly. In your situation, Randomizer asks, "How many sets of numbers do I want?" You have twenty-five participants, so you want twenty-five sets. The next question requests, "How many numbers per set?" For your five conditions, you would need five numbers per set. Finally, Randomizer asks your number range. Again, you have five conditions, so your number range is 1 through 5 (see Table 12.1). So, the presentation of conditions to the first participant would be condition 4, 1, 5, 2, and 3.

Another partial counterbalancing technique used quite often is a ***Latin square***. This design is a counterbalancing technique used in repeated-measures experiments that uses an N × N matrix where each experimental condition appears equally as often in every position. There are some general rules associated with using this design. A Latin square is created by producing the same number of orders as conditions. If you had five conditions, you would have five possible orders (five across and five down), of which each condition must be presented once. Moreover, each condition should precede and follow every other condition once and appear once in each ordinal position (order or succession). Don't worry. It's easier than it seems. If you look at Table 12.1, you will notice that we have A, B, C, D, and E on the top line across. We then begin the next line across with B, C, D, E, and A, and so forth. You can also randomize these conditions further, but that is beyond the scope of this book. (For more information on Latin squares, see Shaughnessy et al., 2003, pp. 250; or Winer, Brown, and Michels, 1991, pp. 674–679).

Latin Square 5 × 5	**Latin Square 4 × 4**
Participant 1: A, B, C, D, E	Participant 1: A, B, C, D
Participant 2: B, C, D, E, A	Participant 2: B, C, D, A
Participant 3: C, D, E, A, B	Participant 3: C, D, A, B
Participant 4: D, E, A, B, C	Participant 4: D, A, B, C
Participant 5: E, A, B, C, D	

A Note about Complex and Mixed Designs

You will recall, as discussed in Chapter Ten, that complex designs examine two or more independent variables of interest, enabling us to examine how variables interact with each other. Factorial designs assess whether one level of one independent variable is dependent upon another level of another independent variable. ***Mixed designs*** are complex designs that include a combination of between-subjects and within-subjects variables. Suppose you wanted to conduct a research study to examine gender (between

TABLE 12.1. Example of Random Block Design

Set 1:	4	1	5	2	3
Set 2:	5	3	4	2	1
Set 3:	4	5	3	1	2
Set 4:	5	4	1	3	2
Set 5:	3	1	5	4	2
Set 6:	4	5	3	1	2
Set 7:	1	2	3	4	5
Set 8:	1	2	4	3	5
Set 9:	3	1	4	2	5
Set 10:	5	1	4	2	3
Set 11:	2	3	1	5	4
Set 12:	5	2	4	1	3
Set 13:	4	1	2	3	5
Set 14:	3	1	5	2	4
Set 15:	2	1	3	5	4
Set 16:	2	3	4	1	5
Set 17:	5	3	4	2	1
Set 18:	2	5	1	3	4
Set 19:	4	5	1	2	3
Set 20:	5	1	3	2	4
Set 21:	5	3	2	1	4
Set 22:	4	1	5	3	2
Set 23:	2	5	1	3	4
Set 24:	3	4	2	1	5
Set 25:	3	4	2	5	1

Source: randomizer.org.

subjects) and racism (rating perceived intelligence of five racial conditions (within-subjects). You ask participants to look at a series of an equal number of men and women of various races and rate each of the five racial conditions (Caucasian, African American, Asian, Hispanic, or Nondescript). Then, you ask participants to rate each individual picture on perceived intelligence on a scale where 1 = "not at all intelligent" and 10 = "very intelligent." In this design, there is a between-subjects variable (gender) and a within-subjects variable (ratings of perceived intelligence on five different races). By examining these two variables together, you can determine whether there are possible interactions between gender and racism. For instance, are males and females rated lower in perceived intelligence based on race?

An experiment can combine as many variables and combinations of variables as needed for the research study. Keep in mind that the more independent variables you have in your study, the more complex the results will be, thus leading to more difficult statistical interpretation. The best experiments are those that are simple, yet unique. Complex and mixed designs offer greater flexibility, experimental control, and the ability to examine interactions between variables that more often mirror real-life situations.

SUMMARY

This chapter highlighted several additional repeated-measures experimental design models as well as threats to internal validity. Within-subjects designs assess the same people repeatedly. The three primary advantages of repeated measures include: the need for fewer participants, less time to administer, and greater statistical power. Single-case and multiple-baseline designs are options appropriate for clinicians and medical doctors and are used primarily for theory development. The ABAB reversal design is one way to present treatment conditions in single-case and multiple-baseline designs. Multiple-baseline designs are used to assess individuals across participants, situations, and behaviors. Simple pretest and posttest designs are used to assess individual changes as a result of a treatment. If there are significant changes in the expected direction from pre- to posttest then it is possible that the treatment had an effect.

More complex repeated-measures designs with more than two data points can be very effective. Matched-pair designs are useful when you need an appropriate control group, which must be similar to the experimental group. With a matched-group design the control group shares similar characteristics to the experimental group and participants are randomly assigned to treatment or control conditions. Quasi-experimental designs are experiments conducted in real-world environments (regarding treatments, laws, programs) that don't offer the option of random assignment and lack internal validity. Non-equivalent control group and time-series designs are considered quasi-experimental.

Threats to internal validity include historical events, maturation, regression to the mean, subject mortality, testing, and instrument failure. Order effects are particularly important to consider for repeated-measures designs. Counterbalancing varies the presentation of the experimental conditions. Thus it is extremely important to control for order effects. Complete counterbalancing techniques assume there will be an equal number of participants in each group and are more appropriate for three or four experimental conditions. A random block design offers a complete counterbalancing technique. Incomplete (partial) counterbalancing techniques are used most often when there are more than three experimental conditions. Complex designs are factorial designs that include two or more independent variables. Mixed designs include a combination of between- and within-subjects variables. Complex and mixed designs offer more flexibility, experimental control, and the ability to examine more complex interactions between variables that often mirror real-life situations.

KEY TERMS

single-case designs
baseline
applied behavioral analysis
ABAB reversal design
multiple-baseline designs
pretest/posttest
matched pairs
correlated groups
quasi-experimental design
non-equivalent control group
time series designs
Latin square

maturation
regression to the mean
testing effects
historical events
instrumentation effects
diffusion of treatment
ABBA counterbalancing
complete counterbalancing
random block design
incomplete counterbalancing
random block schedule

DISCUSSION QUESTIONS

1. Describe three primary reasons researchers would choose to use a repeated-measures design.

2. Under what circumstances are single-case and multi-group repeated-measures designs used and what methods of experimental control can be used in these designs?

3. Distinguish between a simple pretest and posttest design and repeated-measures with more than two data points. What information can such repeated-measures provide over and above pretest and posttest designs? How could a matched-pairs design be used to provide greater experimenter control?

4.　What is a quasi-experimental design and what are the advantages and disadvantages associated with this design? Identify at least five threats to internal validity in repeated-measures designs.

5.　What options do researchers have to control for order effects?

NOTE

[1] The author remembers reading a very old study similar to the example and has searched diligently, but without success, for its source.

CHAPTER

13

ADVANCED JAVASCRIPT PROGRAMMING

LEARNING OBJECTIVES

- To be able to create a timing program in JavaScript

- To be able to use other events to trigger scripts

- To be able to program to write data to a form field

- To be able to create a hidden field from a text box

- To be able to set and test a cookie to prevent multiple submissions from the same computer

It is often useful to measure how long a page or picture is viewed by a respondent. For example, there may be a relationship between how long a person sees a stimulus and his or her attitudes about the subject in the stimulus. A hypothesis might be that the longer a juror views an evidentiary photo of a victim, the greater the sentence they would give to a criminal. To test this hypothesis, timing scripts are added to a Web page and started as the photo comes into view.

EXERCISE 13.1.   Creating a Simple Timing Script

1. Open the *chapter13* site in Expression and create a new page titled *script1.htm.*

2. In Expression, view the page in the **Split View** mode to allow you to see the page in **Design View** as well as the underlying code. Right-click the page in **Design View** and select **Page Properties**. Modify the **Page Title** to be **Timing Script 1**. Click **OK**.

3. Click the page in **Design View** and type **Timing Script 1**. Save the page.

4. Click under the text at the top of the page and insert the graphic *start1.gif* from the chapter 13 exercise files. Save the page and when the dialog box appears, place the graphic into the images folder on the Web server.

5. In the files for *chapter 13* is a file titled *script1.txt.* Locate it, open it, and copy the entire text.

FIGURE 13.1 *Code View for script1.htm Timing Script 1*

```
1  <!DOCTYPE html PUBLIC "-//W3C//DTD XHTML 1.0 Transitional//EN" "http://www.w3.org
2  <html xmlns="http://www.w3.org/1999/xhtml">
3
4  <head>
5  <script type="text/javascript">
6  function start_timer1() {
7  var currDate = new Date();
8  var start1 = currDate.getTime();
9      document.write(start1);
10     }
11 </script>
12
13 <meta content="en-us" http-equiv="Content-Language" />
14 <meta content="text/html; charset=windows-1252" http-equiv="Content-Type" />
15 <title>Timing Script 1</title>
16 </head>
17
18 <body>
19
20 <p>Timing Script 1</p>
21 <p><img alt="Start" height="30" src="images/start1.gif" width="150" /></p>
22
23 </body>
24
25 </html>
26
```

6. In Expression, locate the opening **Head** tag (<**Head**>) in the **Split View** and click after it. Hit Enter and paste the text into the code. Save the page. The code for this page is shown in Figure 13.1.

In line 6, the script creates a function called **start_timer1()**. Line 7 creates a variable called **currDate** and assigns the value of today's date. A date is more complicated than one might suppose. It is composed of the month, day, year, time, and time zone. For this exercise, only the time portion is needed. Line 8 creates a new variable called **start1** and assigns just the time portion of the date to it. The **getTime()** portion of the line determines the time portion of the variable. Line 9 uses the *document.write* code discussed previously and writes the **start1** variable to the screen.

7. The event that will initiate the timing script is the clicking of the **Start** button. View the page in the **Split View** mode and select the **Start** button. If the **Behaviors** task pane is not visible in the lower right window, click **Task Panes > Behaviors**. In the **Behaviors** task pane, click the **Insert** button. From the menu, select **Call Script**. In the dialog box, type the name of the function, **start_timer1()**. Click **OK**.

8. Save the page and preview it in a browser. Click the **Timer Start** button. The window will display a large number similar to *1187715473985*. This number is the number of milliseconds (one thousandths of a second) from midnight, January 1, 1970 to today. The number increases by one each millisecond. This script gives us a precise way of determining the time when the button was clicked. To capture viewing duration, you will also need another button to get the end time.

9. Create a new page with the name *script2.htm*. Modify the page title and at the top of the page type **Timer Script 2**.

10. Click under the text on the page and insert the graphic *start1.gif*. Hit Enter twice and add the graphic *stop1.gif*. Save the page and, when prompted, put the graphics in the *images* folder on the server.

11. In the files for this chapter, locate the file *script2.txt*. Open the file and select and copy the entire text. Paste the text into the head section of the *script2.htm* page.

12. Save the page.

This script creates two functions. Both functions are identical except that the script names (**start_timer1()** and **stop_timer1()**) and the variable names (**start1** and **stop1**) are different.

13. Select the **Start** button and add the behavior to trigger the **start_timer1()** script when the button is clicked. Select the **Stop** button and call the function **stop_timer1()** when it is clicked.

14. Save the page and preview it in a browser. Click the **Start** button. The value is written to the screen. Use the back arrow of the browser and return to *script2.htm* and click the **Stop** button. Another value is written on the screen, but the first is now gone.

Using start and stop times will allow you to investigate how long a participant studied a stimulus. This is a valuable tool for between-subjects and repeated-measures designs.

The **Start** and **Stop** buttons should have both generated a time value when clicked, but only one is written to the screen at a time. This is not the desired behavior. The scripts need to be modified to show both the start and stop times on the screen.

VARIABLE SCOPE

The *scope* of a variable refers to where in the script the variable is created and where its value will be retained. The **start1** and **stop1** variables were both created within their respective functions. The function executes, the variables are created, values are assigned and written to the screen, the function ends, and the variables are deleted from the computer's memory. The variables in this case are *local variables*—they go away when the function ends. Once the function stops, the value of the variable cannot be used in another script. To see both the start and stop times and to calculate duration, the variables need to retain their values after the functions end. To do this, the variables must become global variables. *A global variable* is created outside of a function. When a specific function ends, the value of a global variable is retained. This will give you the ability to show both times on the same page.

EXERCISE 13.2. Modifying the Scope of the Variables

1. Create a new page with the name *script3.htm*. Modify the page title and on the page, type **Timer Script 3**.

2. Click under the text on the page and insert the graphic *start1.gif*. Hit Enter twice and add the graphic *stop1.gif*. Hit Enter twice again and add the graphic *show_times1.gif*. Save the page and, when prompted, put the graphics in the *images* folder on the server.

3. In the files for this chapter, locate the file *script3.txt*. Open the file, select and copy the entire text. Paste the code into the **head** section of the page.

4. Save the page. The code for this page is shown in Figure 13.2.

In the **Code View** on lines 6, 7, and 8, three variables should have been created: **start1**, **stop1**, and **duration1**. They were created outside of any function. These variables and their values will persist as long as the page is in a browser window. Their values are now available to other functions; they are global variables.

There are three functions in the script. The first two record the start and stop times and the third writes all of the values to the screen. The only difference between these scripts and the previous versions are that the variables **start1** and **stop1** were created outside of the scripts. They were assigned a value within the script. The last function is titled **timer_sequence1()**. Line 19 creates and names the function. Line 20 assigns to

FIGURE 13.2 *Code View for script3.htm Timing Script 3*

```
 5 <script type="text/javascript">
 6 var start1;
 7 var stop1;
 8 var duration1;
 9 function start_timer1() {
10 var currDate = new Date();
11     start1 = currDate.getTime();
12     }
13
14 function stop_timer1() {
15 var currDate = new Date();
16     stop1 = currDate.getTime();
17     }
18
19 function timer_sequence1() {
20     duration1 = stop1 - start1;
21     document.write("Start Time: " + start1);
22     document.write("<br>");
23     document.write("Stop Time: " + stop1);
24     document.write("<br>");
25     document.write("Duration: " + duration1 + " in milliseconds" );
26
27 }
28 </script>
```

the global variable **duration1** the difference between the global variable **stop1** and the global variable **start1**. Lines 21 through 25 write the results out to the screen. In line 21, the label *Start Time:* is written to the screen. Next the statement has a plus sign and the name of a variable. The plus sign tells the program to concatenate the text and the variable's value on one line. (*Concatenation* is the joining of two text items together.) The plus sign is the operator for this. The text in the first part of line 21 is enclosed in parentheses, but variables are not. Line 22 writes the HTML code (**
**) for a new line on the page. This is the same as hitting the Enter key. The remaining lines write the label *Stop Time:* and its variable, a new line code, and the duration and its label.

5. Select the **Start** button and create a behavior that calls the script **start_timer1()** when it is clicked. Select the **Stop** button and create a behavior that triggers the script **stop_timer1()** when it is clicked. Select the show times button and create a behavior that triggers the script **timer_sequence1()** when it is clicked.

6. Save the page and preview it in a browser. Click the **Start** button, then the **Stop** button and finally the **Show Times** button. Timer results should now show on the screen.

7. Save the page and test the buttons.

8. The duration is displayed in milliseconds, but we would like it to display in seconds. In the code, locate the following line:

```
document.write("Duration:"+duration1+"in milliseconds");
```
Delete this line from the code. Open the file *script3a.txt,* select and copy the text, and, in Expression, paste the statement in the same location as the line above. The new statement writes the label and then calculates the duration in seconds (by dividing the variable by 1,000). Make sure that the pasted line is above the closing curly bracket (**}**).

9. Save the page and preview it in a browser. Click each of the three buttons in sequence and note the output on the screen. The duration should now be expressed in seconds.

You now have scripts to mark points in time when an event (such as a button being clicked) occurs, but most often you will want to store these time values for use in data analysis. Writing the information to the screen doesn't store it in the database, and, as soon as you leave the page, the values go away. To store these values, the data need to be inserted into a form field and stored when the form is submitted.

A note of caution: In the next section, it is important to follow the directions precisely. Forms and fields must be named exactly as indicated for the scripts to work correctly. Watch spelling and capitalization. These are the most common errors and they are also the hardest to spot.

To write data values to the database, the page must have a form and text boxes to hold the values. As before, the scripts need events to execute the scripts. For now, we will use button clicks to trigger the scripts.

EXERCISE 13.3.   Writing Data to Form Fields

1. Create a new page and save it as *script4.asp.* Note that the extension on the page changes to an *asp* page. Change the page title only to **Timer Script 4**.

2. From the **HTML tools** in the toolbox, drag a **Form Control** onto the page. Click inside the **Form Control** and create a new table with the following specifications: 5 rows, 2 columns, 600 px wide, center alignment, and add a border color.

3. Click in the first row of the table and type **Timer Script 4**.

4. In the first cell of the second row, insert the button *start1.gif.* In the first cell of the third row insert the button *stop1.gif.*

5. Drag a text box from the **Form Control** toolbox and drop it into the second cell of the second row. Drag another text box onto the page and drop it in the second cell of the third row. Save the page.

6. To program a script to refer specifically to the elements in the form, the form must have a name. Right-click anywhere inside the form. From the menu, select **Form Properties**. In the dialog box, click in the field for **Form Name** and type **form1** (with no spaces in the name). Click **OK**.

7. Double-click the text box to the right of the **Start** button. Name this text box **start1**. Double-click the text box to the right of the **Stop** button. Name this text box **stop1**.

8. In the files for this chapter, locate the file *script4.txt*. Open it, select all of the text and copy it. On the Web page, click after the opening **head** tag, hit Enter, and paste the text into the page. Figure 13.3 shows the script section of the page.

This script is almost exactly the same as in *script3.htm,* except for one addition. On lines 10 and 16 are statements:

```
document.form1.start1.value = start_timer1.
```

This code writes the start and stop times into the text boxes. A *document* is what the browser displays in a window. Within that document is another object. Because it is part of the document the objects are separated by periods. The name **form1** was given to the form in step 6. The next period says that what follows is about something on the form. Its name is **start1** and it is the text box to the right of the button. The next period separates the **start1** from its properties. **Value** refers to what is in the text box. The equal sign sets that text box to the time value. Line 16 does the same thing for the stop time.

9. In the **Design View** of Expression select the **Start** button. Add a behavior to the button that calls the script **start_timer1()**. Select the **Stop** button. Add a behavior to the button that calls the script **stop_timer1()**.

10. Save the page and preview it in Internet Explorer. Click each button on the page in order. The text boxes should contain the time values for when the **Start** and **Stop** buttons were clicked.

The page stores the start and stop times in the text boxes, but they are just written into text boxes. To save the values, the form needs to be submitted to the database.

FIGURE 13.3 *Code View for script4.asp Writing Results onto Form*

```
 4 <head>
 5 <script type="text/javascript">
 6
 7 function start_timer1() {
 8 var currDate = new Date();
 9 var start_timer1 = currDate.getTime();
10     document.form1.start1.value = start_timer1;
11     }
12
13 function stop_timer1() {
14 var currDate = new Date();
15 var stop_timer1 = currDate.getTime();
16     document.form1.stop1.value = stop_timer1; |
17     }
18
19 </script>
20
```

11. Drag an **Input(Submit)** button into the table inside the form. Double-click the button and, in the **Value/label** box, type **Click to Submit Your Data**. Click **OK**.

12. Right-click inside the form and select **Form Properties**. Select **Send to Database . . .** and then click the **Options** button in the lower left corner. Click **Create Database**. When the popup says you have done this successfully, click **OK** three times.

13. Figure 13.4 shows the page at this point. Save the page and preview it in a browser. Click the **Start** and **Stop** buttons and then submit the data to the server. An auto-generated confirmation form should show after the data has been submitted. Verify this by opening the database and examining the data.

14. The scripts work and the data are saved to the database. However, it would be better if the text boxes were not shown to the respondents. They may confuse the user and the user may try to modify the values stored in the text boxes. To prevent this, you need to modify the properties of the text boxes. In Expression, click the first text box. In the lower left corner of the Expression window is the **Tag Properties** task pane. In the **Attributes** section is the **Type** attribute. Now it reads **Text**. Click the down arrow and select **hidden**. Select the other text box and make it **hidden** as well.

15. Save the page and preview it in a browser. Click both buttons and submit the data to the database. When the confirmation page displays, you should see that values were submitted. Verify that the data were saved to the database by opening the database and inspecting.

16. What if you want to time how long someone looks at the survey overall? The time would need to start when the page opens and stop when the form has been submitted. This change is easily made by changing the events that trigger the scripts. Save the *script4.asp* page as *script5.asp*.

17. Delete both of the buttons on the page. Click anywhere in the page and create a new **Behavior**. In the text box, type **start_timer1()**. Click **OK**. In the **Behaviors** task pane, verify that the event is **onload**. As soon as the page has loaded into the computer's memory, it will execute the script and record the start time in the hidden text box.

18. Click the **Submit** button. Add a behavior to this object. From the menu, select **Call Script**. Type **stop_timer1()** in the dialog box. Click **OK**. Verify that the event for this script is **onclick**.

FIGURE 13.4   *Page to Capture Start and Stop Times*

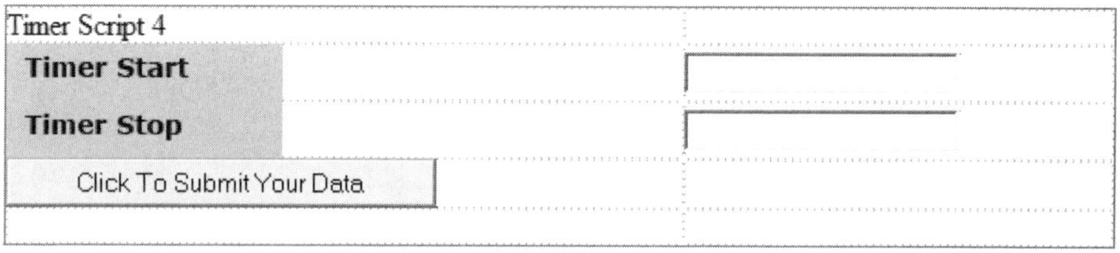

19. Save the page and preview it in a browser. Submit the data. The auto-confirmation page shows that both **start** and **stop** times were submitted.

This timing script was first created for a student who had four stimulus photos on her survey. She wanted to measure how long each photo was examined by the respondent. There were four timer **start** and **stop** scripts and eight text boxes within the form to hold the times. The first button brought the first picture into the browser window (using internal hyperlinks) and also started the first **start_timer** script. At the bottom of the picture was another button. When the respondent clicked that button the browser would move to questions about that picture and also execute the **stop_timer** script. This scheme went on through all four pictures and questions. At the end, the respondent clicked a **Submit** button that sent all the data to a database.

USING COOKIES TO PREVENT MULTIPLE SUBMISSIONS

In the surveys we have created thus far, the participant reads and agrees to the consent document and clicks a button to indicate that agreement. The survey appears and the subject completes the survey. At the conclusion of the survey, the participant clicks the **Submit** button and the data are sent back to the server. A confirmation

Cookies can prevent rapid resubmission of data.

page is shown in the browser. What is to stop the participant from hitting the browser's **Back** button and resubmitting the data another time . . . and another and another? Would such behavior happen? We hope not, but, given the anonymity of the Internet, it is certainly possible. Such behavior would clearly confound your research results and potentially sink the project. This section will demonstrate how to make resubmission more difficult.

Cookies have been part of Internet browsers' technology for many years. They are somewhat controversial because users erroneously think that cookies stored on their computer can collect and send personal information about the user to a third party. This is not the case. A *cookie* is merely a piece of text that is placed on the computer in a restricted area of the browser; only the site that created the cookie can read it and write to it. An Internet browser can read the text when it revisits the site again and thus know a bit about the user from their last visit, but the behavior of cookies is very limited. Some pages use cookies to store preferences for viewing a site or perhaps remember a favored type size for viewing. Cookies also have an expiration date built into them. If no date is set, then they expire and go away when the browser closes. The cookie will prevent the rapid resubmission of data, but if the browser is closed, someone else can use that computer to complete the survey. Cookies are an easy and efficient way to make it much more difficult to submit a survey multiple times.

Figure 13.5 shows a general flow for a survey. Participants read the consent page and, if they agree, click the **I Agree** button. If they don't agree, they click the **I Disagree** button. This takes them to the no thank you page, where they are thanked and given the researcher's contact information. Clicking the **I Agree** button takes them

FIGURE 13.5 *Survey Map of Set Cookie Survey*

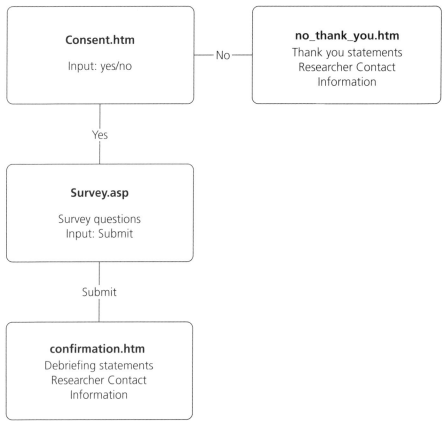

to the survey itself, where they may view stimuli and answer questions. At the conclusion, they click the **Submit** button which sends the data back to the server, and the confirmation page is displayed. The confirmation page has debriefing statements, a *thank you* statement from the researcher, and contact information. If a person were to attempt to resubmit the data, it is at this point that they would attempt to go back to the survey page.

Resubmission depends on having the **Back** button available. If the survey and confirmation pages appear in separate windows, then it will be more difficult to go backwards. Further, if a cookie is set as the confirmation page loads, then a page could test for the presence of the cookie. If one is found, then users would be prevented from going ahead in the survey. We will use this plan to build a survey that will minimize resubmissions. Figure 13.6 shows this modified flowchart with the cookies setting and testing.

FIGURE 13.6 *Survey Map Showing Where Cookie Is Set and Tested*

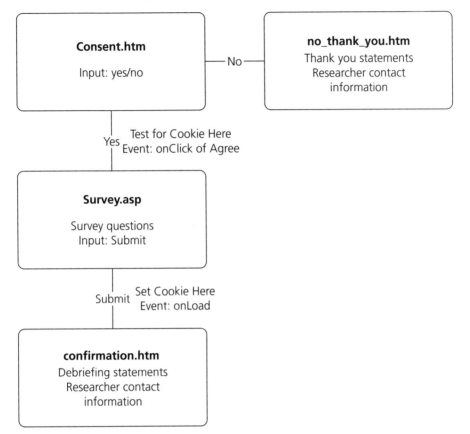

EXERCISE 13.4. **Creating the Survey's Pages**

1. In the *chapter 13* Web site, we will create pages with the specifications indicated in Figure 13.7.

2. *Consent page:* Create the table for this page and then select both cells of the first row. Right-click in the selected cells and merge them into one cell.

3. Click in the second row of the *consent.htm* page. Type **Consent text goes here**. Select both cells of this row, right-click the selected cells, and merge them into one cell. Click in the third row, first cell. Insert the **I Agree** button. In a similar manner, insert the *i_disagree.gif* into the second cell on the third row. Right-align the **I Disagree** button in the cell. Save the page and, when prompted, place the images into the *images* folder.

4. *Survey page:* Create the *survey.asp* page and drag a form onto the page. Inside the form create the table per the specifications. In the first row of the table, type **Survey**. In the

FIGURE 13.7 *Specifications for All Pages for Cookie Embedded Site*

File Name	Page Title	Table Specifications	Text in top line of Table
consent.htm	Consent Form	4 rows, 2 columns, 600 px wide, centered, red border around table	Consent Form
survey.asp	Survey	4 rows, 1 columns, 600 px wide, centered, red border around table	
no_thank_you.htm	No Thank You Page	4 rows, 1 columns, 600 px wide, centered, red border around table	No Thank You
Confirmation.htm	Confirmation and Debriefing	4 rows, 1 columns, 600 px wide, centered, red border around table	Confirmation and Debriefing

second row of the table, insert a second table that is 100% wide with 3 rows and 2 columns and has a green border.

5. Click in the first cell of this table and type **Name**. Drag a text box into the second cell of this cell. Select both cells of the second row and merge them. Insert a **Submit** button into the third row. Center the button in the cell.

6. Double-click the text box. In the properties dialog box, give the box the name *name* and the width of 50 characters. Click **OK**.

7. Double-click the **Submit** button and change the **value/label** to **Click to submit your data**.

8. Finally, right-click inside the form and select **Form Properties**. Select **Send** to database. Then click **Options**. Click **Create Database ....**. When the popup comes up indicating that you have successfully created the database, click OK.

9. In the **Options for Saving Results to Database** dialog box, type **confirmation.htm** into the URL of the **confirmation page** text box. Click **OK** twice and save the page. Test the form to ensure that data are saved to the database and that the confirmation page shows after submission.

10. *No Thank You* page: Create the *no_thank_you.htm* page and put the table on the page. In the first row, type **No Thank You**. In the second row, type **Thank you statement goes here**. In the third row, type **Researcher contact information goes here**. Save the page.

11. Create the *confirmation.htm* page and create a table on it per the specifications. Click in the first row and type **Confirmation and Debriefing**. Click in the second row and type **Confirmation statement goes here**. Click in the third row and type **Debriefing and contact information goes here**. Save the page.

12. The confirmation page is where the cookie will be set. In Expression, switch to the **Split View** mode of the page. Click in the **code** section of the document and locate the

opening head section tag (**<head>**). After this, hit Enter. Locate the file *setCookie.txt*, open it, select and copy all of the code and paste the code into the page. The code for setting the cookie is shown in Figure 13.8.

13. The event that will trigger the cookie setting function is the **onload event**. Click anywhere on the page outside of the table in the **Design View**. Click the **Insert Behavior** button, select **Call Script**, and in the text box type **setCookie()**. Click **OK**. In the **Behaviors** task pane verify that the event is **onload**. Save the page.

This script adds a cookie to the page. Line 6 creates the **setCookie()** function. Line 7 creates a variable, **d**, and sets it equal to today's date. Line 8 creates another variable and sets it to only the time portion of today's date. Line 9 sets the cookie. The cookie is the text *survey=* that ends with a number that is the time portion of the date. An example of a cookie from this page would be *survey=1203356054047*. The cookie is set with a new time each time the *confirmation.htm* page loads.

The test for whether or not there is a cookie will go in the consent page. There are four possible outcomes for the test.

1. The cookie could be blank. This means that the browser has not visited the confirmation page. As a result the script should take the browser on to the *survey.asp* page.

2. The cookie is not blank but was not set by the survey. There are other ways that a page can set a cookie. One is if the site uses Web analytics software to track visitors. The cookie from this software will exist, but it will not have the correct form of a cookie as set by our script. As a result the browser should go to the survey.

3. The cookie is from this site and has the correct form, but the cookie was set before a built-in duration. Because the cookie was set, but too long ago, the action should be to take the browser to the *survey.asp* page.

FIGURE 13.8 *Code View of Cookie-Setting Script*

```
1  <!DOCTYPE html PUBLIC "-//W3C//DTD XHTML 1.0 Transitional//EN" ".
2  <html xmlns="http://www.w3.org/1999/xhtml">
3
4  <head>
5  <script type="text/javascript">
6  function setCookie() {
7          var d = new Date();
8          var t = d.getTime();
9          document.cookie = "survey=" + t;
10 }
11 </script>
```

4. The test could yield that the cookie is present and of the correct form, but the time duration has not elapsed. The time duration should be sufficiently long so that someone would have to wait an annoying amount of time before resubmitting. If the duration has not elapsed, a warning message should be displayed and, when the person clicks **OK** on the message, the browser should be redirected to another page.

EXERCISE 13.5. Adding the Testing Script to the Consent Page

1. Open the page *consent.htm* and view it in **Split View** mode. Locate the opening head tag **<Head>** and click after it. In the files for this chapter, locate the file *testCookie.txt*. Open the file, select all of it and hit Enter, and copy it. Move back to Expression and paste the script into the page after the **head** tag. The code for this page is shown in Figure 13.9.

Although this script is somewhat complicated it follows the four conditions just outlined and gives the action indicated. Lines 5 and 6 begin the script and create the function **openWin()**. Line 7 creates a variable and sets it equal to the cookie. Line 8 creates another new variable, then reads the cookie text, counts the first seven characters, and sets the variable equal to the result. Lines 9 through 12 test for the first condition (cookie not there). The test is on line 9. If the cookie text is exactly equal (==) to nothing (""), then, on

FIGURE 13.9 *Code View of Cookie-Testing Script*

```
 5 <script type="text/javascript">
 6 function openWin(){
 7     var c = document.cookie;
 8     var testStr = c.substr(0,7);
 9     if(c == "")
10         {
11         var newW = window.open("survey.asp","newWin","height=550,width=650");
12         }
13     else if(testStr != "survey=")
14         {
15         var newW = window.open("survey.asp","newWin","height=550,width=650");
16         }
17     else if(testStr == "survey=")
18         {
19         newArray = c.split(";");
20         var first = newArray[0];
21         newArray1 = first.split("=");
22         var time = newArray1[1];
23         var d = new Date();
24         var tNow = d.getTime();
25         var timeTest = tNow - time;
26         if(timeTest < 10000)
27             {
28             alert("Someone has submitted a survey from this computer recently. If you are a new
29             window.location.replace("http://www.google.com");
30             }
31         else
32             {
33             var newW = window.open("survey.asp","newWin","height=550,width=650");
34             }
35         }
36 }
37 </script>
```

line 11, create a new window that is 550 px high and 650 px wide, and has the name *newWin*. Inside should be the *survey.asp* page.

Lines 13 through 16 test the next condition (cookie is present, but not the survey cookie). Line 13 tests the variable created previously (line 8). If the text is **not equal** (*!=*) to *survey=,* then the cookie was not set by the survey and the browser should go to the survey now (which it does in line 15).

For the third case, you use lines 17 through 30. The initial test is on line 17. If the **testStr** variable is exactly equal to *survey=,* then it must have been set by the survey. Lines 18 through 22 break the cookie apart into its components. Line 19 creates an array or matrix and uses the **split** command to split the cookie at every location of the ";". When cookies are created, they have the form of *name=value;name2=value.* The semicolons separate one part of a cookie from another. Lines 20 and 21 do the same thing again. They create a second array and break the first part of the cookie into its parts. If the cookie begins with *survey=1203356054047,* line 21 splits this and puts the *survey* into the first location in the matrix and *1203356054047* into the second. The time component of the cookie is now separate from everything else in the cookie. Line 22 creates the variable time and attaches the time portion to it.

Now we need to know what time it is now. Lines 23 and 24 do the same thing as the **setCookie** function. It creates a variable **d** and sets it to today's date. Line 24 creates a new variable **tNow** and sets it to just the time portion of the date. So, **tNow** is the time portion of today's date and **time** is the time portion indicating when the cookie was set. Line 25 creates a new variable, **timeTest**, and sets it to the value that comes from subtracting the time when the cookie was set from the time now. Line 26 is the point of all this. If the difference is less than some value (in this case 10000), then it has been too short a time period and the browser should not go to the survey. Note that the value of 10000 is only for testing purposes. It is a measurement in milliseconds—10000 represents 10000 milliseconds or 10 seconds. Not a very long time! In practice, this value should be perhaps 10 to 15 minutes. This would be 10 minutes $\times$ 60 seconds $\times$ 1000 milliseconds per second, or 600000. Thus, the actual value might be between 600000 to 900000. If it has not been long enough between attempts to take the survey, an alert box should show on the screen. Figure 13.10 shows the alert box.

The user reads the message and clicks the button. Line 29 now sends the browser window to the Google Web site. This line uses the method **replace** to do this. At the same time, replace also erases the history of the browser. This means that the **Back** button is rendered inoperative. Lines 31 through 35 cover the last situation. The cookie was set by the page, but it has been long enough so that it is unlikely that it is a resubmission. In this case, the user should be directed to the survey. Line 33 does just that.

2. Select the **I Agree** button. Click the **Insert behavior** button and select **Call Script** from the menu. In the text box, type **openWin()**. The testing function will be executed when the respondent clicks on the **I Agree** button. Save the page and preview it in a browser.

Test the pages with each scenario. The first time through, there will be no cookies, so the survey will open. After completing the survey and submitting it, close the confirmation

FIGURE 13.10   *Alert Box Message When a Person Attempts to Send Data Too Soon*

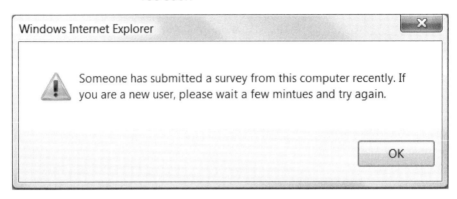

page window and immediately click the **I Agree** button again. This should be within the duration and the alert message will show. Finally, go through the survey again and close the confirmation page, but wait for at least a minute after. Click the **I Agree** button and you should also be directed to the survey.

SUMMARY

This chapter covered some frequently requested features. First, we created a timing sequence and illustrated its use by timing the viewing of a stimulus. The script introduced the use of JavaScript methods and writing the value from a function to a text box in a form. That field was then converted to a hidden field, which allows the researcher to save items to a form without the subject being aware of the values that are saved. Finally, we created a script that sets a cookie and then another that tests for the presence of a cookie. If the cookie is present and not too old, then it prohibits the respondent from taking the survey again. If the cookie is absent or past the expiration time, then the respondent is taken to the survey.

KEY TERMS

variable scope
global variables
concatenation

form

onload event
cookie
If statement
not equal to

DISCUSSION QUESTION

1. Use the timing scripts from this chapter to time two button clicks. How could this script be used to record the length of time someone takes to read a text passage? What would be the event that triggers the script? How would the data be stored in the survey?

CHAPTER

14

ADVANCED JAVASCRIPT PROGRAMMING II

LEARNING OBJECTIVES

- To be able to use scripts to carry information from one Web page to another using query strings

- To be able to split off the information in a query string and saving the value in a database

- To be able to use a script to create jumps in a survey to move to other parts of a page based on users' input

If you go to most e-commerce Web sites (for example, http://www.llbean.com) and begin to browse items, a curious thing happens in the Web address line of the browser, which started as *http://www.llbean.com*. Select just one category and the address changes to something like *http://www.llbean.com/webapp/wcs/stores/servlet/Category Display ?categoryId=26&storeId=1&catalogId=1&langId=-1& feat=ln.*

USING QUERY STRINGS

Clicking just one item (which in this case happened to be the men's department) changed the address so that it contains a great deal of information about who clicked on the page, where they want to go, and what language it should be displayed in. All of this information was communicated in the codes that are part of the address. About halfway through the Web address is a question mark. After the question mark is a name (the first is categoryID), an equal sign, and a value (26). This information is one of four chunks of information in the Web address that are joined together with amper-sands (&). Everything from the question mark on is called a *query string* and can be used to move information from one Web page to another.

Query strings are helpful and used to move infor-mation from one Web page to another. Query strings are particularly important when keeping track of participant identi-fication is necessary.

When the Web was created, each page was intended to function by itself. Originally there was no way to retain information across Web pages; designers referred to the Web as being stateless. It quickly became apparent that this was a limitation, so various techniques were developed to carry information from one page to another. One very useful technique is the query string. Text is appended to the Web address, car-ried to another page and stripped off the address line and used to bring information to the second page.

Why is this useful? Consider the following sce-nario encountered by a student. You have a survey with a fixed population of all of the members of a profes-sional organization. Each member has a membership ID and you have a list of names, member IDs, and e-mail addresses. It is important that as many members as possible complete the survey, so you plan to send reminders to members who have not taken the survey. Therefore, you need to keep track of the IDs that have completed the survey. E-mails were sent out with an invitation to complete the survey and a hyper-link to the survey at the bottom. The hyperlink included the membership ID in the Web address. An example of a hyperlink might be

http://www.fictitious.biz/survey.asp?memberID=101

The member is to click the link and the survey will open in a browser. The page will then take the query string, split it into its parts, and store the membership ID in a form field. When the member submits his or her data to the database, the membership ID is stored as well. The researcher can get the information from the database and determine who has completed the survey. The researcher can then send a note encouraging those who have not replied to do so.

It is important that researchers inform respondents that they are using their membership ID to record whether they have taken the survey. The ID can uniquely identify the user and, in a sense, you are exposing the identity of the subject. There must be statements in the consent page that state why you are using their ID number, how you will use their IDs, and how you will protect their identity. The subject needs to know this before agreeing to participate in the survey. Only the researcher should have access to the membership list, which must be safeguarded and obviously not be kept on the Web server.

You will not need to use an e-mail for the next exercise. It complicates the task. Just put a hyperlink on a Web page, which has the same effect. The participant clicks the link and a browser opens the specified page.

Remember that participant confidentiality is the researcher's responsibility. Therefore, if membership IDs (or any other personal information) will be used, participants must be informed of this.

EXERCISE 14.1. Using Query Strings to Pass Information from One Page to Another

1. Open the *chapter14* Web site in Internet Explorer and then open it in Expression.

2. Open the *default.htm* page at the site. If your server required an *index.htm* page, then save the default page with that name. At the top of the page type **Home Page for Chapter 14**. Save the page and preview it in a browser.

3. In Internet Explorer, select the entire contents of the address line. Copy it.

4. In Expression, click in the page under the text and paste the address onto the page. Delete the page name from this address (either *default.htm* or *index.htm*). Immediately after the address type (without spaces or quotes): **survey.asp?memberID=101**. Hit Enter.

5. Save the page and preview it in a browser. The link to the page on my server is shown in Figure 14.1. Your link will look different because of the different Web address.

   When the user clicks on this hyperlink, a survey will open in a browser and the membership ID will be part of the address. The next task is to get the ID out of the address.

6. Create a new page. The filename is *survey.asp.* and the page title is **Query String Survey**. Save the page.

7. Drag a **Form Control** onto the page from the **Form Control** toolbox. Inside the form, create a table with 4 rows, 2 columns, 600 px width, and a green border. Click **OK**.

8. Select the two cells in the first row and merge them into one cell. In the first row, type **Query String Survey**. Tab to the next row.

FIGURE 14.1 *Modified Page Showing Hyperlink with memberID=101 Added*

Home Page for Chapter 14

http://www.on-linesurveyresearchessentials.com/c15/survey.asp?memberID=101

9. Type **Name** in the first cell. Drag an **Input (Text)** control into the second cell of the first row. Click in the first cell of the third row and type **Membership ID**. Drag another **Input (Text)** control into the second cell in that row. Drag an **Input (Submit)** button into the first cell of the fourth row. Save the page.

10. Double-click the text box next to the word *name*. In the Name field of the dialog box, type **name**. Set the width to 40 characters. Click **OK**.

11. Double-click in the text box next to the word *memberID*. In the Name field of the dialog box, type **memberID**. Set the width to 20 characters. Click **OK**.

12. Double-click the **Submit** button. Change the **value/label** field to **Click Here to Submit Your Data**. Verify that **Submit** is selected as the **Button type**. Click **OK**.

13. Right-click inside the form. Select **Form Properties** from the menu. Select the **Send to database** option in the **Where to store results** section of the dialog. Click the **Options...** button in the lower left corner of the dialog box. In the second dialog box, click **Create Database**. Do not enter a page for the confirmation page. Note the name of the database connection and the table name that has the results. Click **OK** twice.

14. In the **Form Properties** dialog box, type **form1** in the **Form name** text box at the bottom of the dialog box. (Remember that we need to name the form to refer to it in a script.) Click **OK** and save the page.

15. Preview the page in a browser and manually enter information in the **name** and **memberID** text boxes. Verify that the data are saved in a database.

    When viewing the survey page from now on, it is essential that the page be entered by clicking the hyperlink on the home page. There must be a **memberID** query string in the address for the script to work. As you work, save the page and then use the link from the home page to preview it.

16. View the page in **Split View** mode. In the code, locate the opening head tag (<head>). Click after the tag and hit Enter. In the files for this chapter locate the script file *script1.txt*. Open the file, select all of it, copy it, and, in Expression, paste the text into the **head** section of the *survey.asp* page. Save the page (see Figure 14.2).

This script is a bit more complicated than any previously used. It creates a function called **get_memberID()**. This function separates the **memberID** portion of the page address from the query string and puts it into the text box on the form. It uses the

FIGURE 14.2   *Code View of Script to Read memberID, Split It Off, and Store in Text Box*

```
1  <!DOCTYPE html PUBLIC "-//W3C//DTD XHTML 1.0 Transitional//EN" "http://www.w3.c
2  <html xmlns="http://www.w3.org/1999/xhtml">
3
4  <head>
5  <script type="text/javascript">
6  function get_memberID() {
7      var member = location.href;
8      var newArray = member.split("?");
9      var id = newArray[1];
10     var newArray2 = id.split("=");
11     var memberID = newArray2[1];
12     window.form1.memberID.value=memberID;
13 }
14
15 </script>
```

method **split()**, which we have used in a previous exercise. The **split()** method takes a string of text and divides it at a specified character, and the results go into an array. Each line of an array can hold text. The first position of the array holds the text to the left of the character in the split operation. The next line of the array holds the text to the right of the character. Just to make things a bit more complicated, the lines of the array are numbered. The first line is **array[0]** and the next line is **array[1]**. The square brackets ([and]) indicate that it is a line in the array that is referred to in an expression.

Line 7 of the script creates a variable called **member** and sets it equal to the address of the Web page (which also includes the query string). Line 8 creates an array called **newArray** and then it splits the address at the question mark. The value in **newArray[0]** is the left part of the Web address and **newArray[1]** holds the query string part. The value of **newArray[1]** is **memberID=101**. Lines 9 and 10 do the same thing again with the text string **memberID=101** Line 9 sets the variable id to the query string part of the address. Line 10 splits id at the equal sign =. Line 11 creates a new variable, **memberID**, and sets it equal to the right side of the id string. The value of this is now **101**. Line 12 puts the value of the memberID into the **memberID** text box on the form.

When users click the **Submit** button, their memberID will be saved in the database. But you do not want the users to see this. After testing the form and verifying that the memberID is stored in the database, we will make the memberID text box hidden.

17. Before the page will work correctly, you have to tie the function entered above to an event. The event will be when the page loads into the browser. Click anywhere in the page outside of the form. In the **Behaviors** task pane, click **Insert**. Select **Call Script** from the menu. In the dialog box, type **get_memberID()**. Click **OK** and save the page. Verify that the event is **onLoad**.

FIGURE 14.3 *Confirmation Page Showing memberID Submitted to Database*

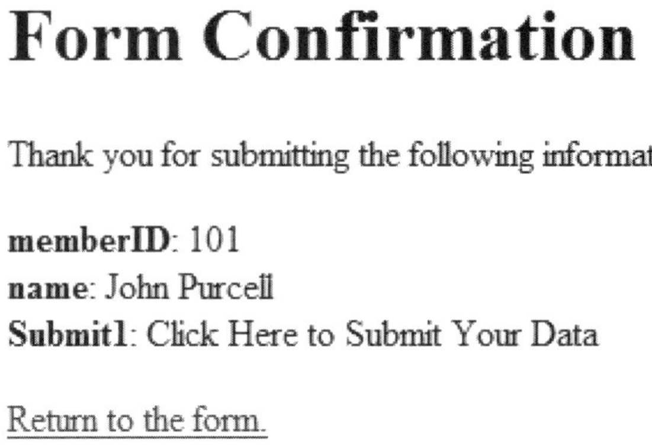

Form Confirmation

Thank you for submitting the following information:

memberID: 101
name: John Purcell
Submit1: Click Here to Submit Your Data

Return to the form.

18. Open the home page in a browser and click the hyperlink. The memberID value should be in the second text box. Enter a name in the name text box and submit the data. The Expression generated confirmation page should list the variables and their values. The memberID value should be correctly stored in the database (see Figure 14.3).

19. After you have verified that the link and survey work as expected, it is a good idea to change the property of the memberID text box to hidden. On the *survey.asp* page, select the **memberID** text box. In the lower left corner of the Expression window, locate the **Tag Properties** task pane. With the text box selected, locate the property **type**. Click in the box to the right of the name, click the down arrow, and, from the list, select **hidden**. The text box should not show on the form.

The exercise above works well for a list of member IDs, but what if you are working with a group that doesn't have IDs? Or what if you don't want to send an e-mail to the participants prior to their completing the survey? With any longitudinal or repeated-measures research, it is necessary that the repeated measurements be paired during the analysis. The above method would work, but if you don't want to send out e-mails, you could have the respondent enter an ID number each time they take the survey. The following exercise creates a login page where the respondent can enter an ID, which will then be passed to the survey.

EXERCISE 14.2. **An Alternative Way to Capture and Store a Participant ID**

1. Create a page with the title *Login Page* and the filename *login.htm*.

2. Drag a form onto the page. Inside the form, create a table that has 5 rows and 1 column, centered alignment, and a red border.

3. In the first row of the table, type **Login with Member ID**. In the next row, type **Please enter your member ID number in the box and click the button at the bottom of the form**.

4. Right-click in the third row and select **Modify > Split Cells**. In the dialog box, set it to split the row into 2 columns. Click **OK**.

5. Click in the first cell of the third row and type **Member ID**. Drag a text box into the second cell of the third row. Double-click the text box and name it **memberID** and set its width to 25. Click **OK**.

6. Skip the fourth row. In the fifth row, insert the picture *c14_submitID.gif*. The file is in the files for this chapter. Save the page and, when prompted, place the picture in the *images* folder.

7. View the page in **Split View** mode. In the **Code View**, locate the opening head tag (<Head>). Click after the tag and hit Enter. Locate the file *script2.txt* in the files for this chapter, open the file, select all of the text, copy it, and paste it into the login page after the opening head tag. The code is shown in Figure 14.4.

8. The event that will trigger the function is clicking the button. Select the button and click **Insert** in the **Behaviors** task pane. Select **Call Script** from the list and in the text box type **memberID()**.

9. Finally, we need to name the form on the login page so that we can refer to it in the script. Right-click inside the form and select **Form Properties**. Near the bottom of the dialog type **form1** in the **Form name** text box. Figure 14.4 shows the script inserted in the page.

Line 7 creates a variable called **membershipID** and sets it equal to the value that the member inputs into the form field. Line 8 begins with an *if() statement* to test a value that was submitted. It states that *if the value is exactly equal to (==) nothing* (this is indicated by two double quotes or " "), *then show an alert message that reminds the user to enter his or her ID*. On line 11 begins an **else{** statement. This means that, if the above test is not true (that is, the value of the variable is something, not nothing), then (on line 12)

FIGURE 14.4 *Code View of Script to Ensure that memberID Is Present*

```
5  <script type="text/javascript">
6  function memberID() {
7      var membershipID = document.form1.memberID.value;
8      if(membershipID == ""){
9      alert('Please Enter Your Member ID.');
10     }
11     else{
12     var survey_page;
13     survey_page="survey.asp"+"?"+"memberID="+membershipID;
14     window.location.replace(survey_page);
15     }
16 }
```

create another variable called *survey_page*. Line 13, sets the **survey_page** variable equal to the text *survey.asp,* then *?,* then the text *memberID=,* and finally the value stored in the variable **membershipID**. Remember that the plus signs join the text together (concatenate). The text must be inside double quotes, and the variable name places the value of the variable onto the end. Line 14 then replaces the login page with the value of the variable **survey_page**, which is the survey created in the previous exercise (*survey.asp*) with the **membership ID** added to it via a query string.

10. Save the page and preview it in a browser. Enter a **member ID** and click the button. When you get to the survey page, click the **Submit** button. The confirmation page will show the Membership ID value. Now try the login page without entering an ID. You will get an alert box reminding you to enter your number.

EXERCISE 14.3.   Creating a Jump in a Form Based on User Input

Many times you'll want the survey to ask one set of questions when subjects answer a screening question one way and another set of questions when they answer the screening questions another way. This is called a ***jump*** and can be easily programmed into a script.

Note that neither approach verifies that the number is the correct member ID. To do so requires a great deal more work, a database with member usernames, ID numbers, and so on. For the purpose of this exercise, it is assumed that respondents will be able to remember their IDs.

1. In Expression, close any open pages. Create a new page. Give the page the title **Jump** and save it with the filename *jump.asp*. View the page in **Design View**.

2. Drag a form onto the page from the **Form Control** toolbox. Click inside the form and create a table on the page with 8 rows, 1 column, 600 px width, center alignment, and a green border. Save the page.

3. Click in the first row and type **Jump in a Survey**. Apply a style to the text.

4. Click in the second row and type the word **Gender**. Type a space and then drag an **Input(Radio)** button and drop it after the word. Type a space and type **Male**. Type a space and then drag another **Input(Radio)** button and drop it after the word *Male*. Type a space and type **Female.**

5. Skip a row and click in the fourth row. Type the words **Questions for Men**. Drag a **Submit** button into the next row of the table. Skip a row and click in the seventh row. Type the words **Questions for Women**. Drag a **Submit** button into the eighth row of the table. Your page should look like Figure 14.5.

6. Double-click the radio button for **Males**. In the dialog box, name the group **gender** and the value **Male**. Make sure that it is not selected and click **OK**. Repeat for the other radio button; the name should be **gender** and the value **Female**.

FIGURE 14.5 *Page Illustrating a Jump in a Survey as a Result of User Input*

7. Click just to the left of the *Q* in the text *Questions for men*. Insert a bookmark at this location named *male* by clicking **Insert > Bookmark.** Click just to the left of the *Q* in the text *Questions for women*. Insert a bookmark at this location named *women*. Save the page.

8. Our very simple survey needs to be connected to a database. Right-click inside the form and select **Form Properties** from the menu. Select the option to **Send to database . . . .** Click the **Options . . .** button and then click the **Create Database . . .** button. When successfully completed, click **OK** three times and save the page.

9. The action that you want is to go to the *Questions for men* when the gender option **male** is selected and go to the *Questions for women* when the gender option **female** is selected. We will do this with behaviors. Select the option button for the gender **male**. In the **behavior** task pane, click insert. From the **behavior** list, select **Go to URL**. In the Go to URL dialog box, click the **Browse** button and select the **Place in This Document** button on the left. Select the bookmark **male**. Click **OK** twice.

10. Repeat the same procedure for the **female** gender option, but substitute the bookmark for female.

11. View the page in **Design View**. Click inside the third row of the table. Right-click inside the row and select **cell properties**. Set the **Vertical alignment** to **Top** and check the **Specify height** check box. Type **2000** and select the **pixels** option in the **Height** area. Click **OK**.

12. Scroll down to the fifth row. It has the first **Submit** button in it. Click inside the row and make the same changes to the properties of this row. Repeat in the eighth row that has the second **Submit** button. Save the page and preview it in a browser.

13. Test both **Gender** radio buttons and **Submit** buttons. The browser should show the appropriate section of the page. The two **Submit** buttons should both save the data to the database.

WHEN THINGS GO WRONG

In the pages and scripts in the text, every effort has been made to make sure that they work as advertised. However, sometimes things go astray. What do you do then? First, take a deep breath. Finding errors in a page or script is at times very challenging. It requires patience and insight. Because there are many ways things can go astray, it is difficult to predict how your surveys might go wrong. Here are some ideas.

EXERCISE 14.4. Error Condition01: No Data or Incomplete Data in Database

1. In Expression, in the *chapter14* site, locate the page *survey_error01.asp*.

2. Right-click inside the survey form. Select **Form Properties**. Select **Send to Database . . .** then click the **Options** button. Click **Create Database**. When successfully completed, click **OK** three times and save the page.

3. Preview the page in a browser and enter some data.

4. Verify that everything is working by opening the database and ensuring that there are data in it.

5. Click in the second cell after the word **Gender**. Drag an **Input (Radio)** button into the cell and type the label **Male** after the button.

6. Click in the third cell. Drag another **Input (Radio)** button into that cell and type **Female** after it.

7. Double-click the first button. Enter **q3** for the group name and **male** as the value, make sure that **Not selected** is the **Initial State**. Click OK. Repeat for the other button, entering **q3** and **female** respectively. Save the page and preview it in a browser.

   This is a very simple survey that appears to work correctly. If you preview it in a browser, you'll see the form as shown in Figure 14.6A. After answering the three questions and clicking the **Submit** button, the confirmation page (see Figure 14.6B) shows the three variables **q1**, **q2**, and **q3** and the values that you gave in the survey. However, as you can see in Figure 14.6C, when you check the database, you see only data for the first two questions! This is a very common error. It has to do with the connection between the survey form and the database.

8. To diagnose this problem it is helpful to see exactly what is being saved in the database. Right-click inside the *survey_error1.asp* form. Select **Form properties**. Click the **Options** button and then the **Saved Fields** tab. This shows on the left side the fields that have been defined in the survey form. You can see that three have been defined: **q1**, **q2**, and **q3**. On the right side are the fields that have been defined in the database. As you can see in Figure 14.7, only **q1** and **q2** are present.

9. To fix this, click the **Database Results** tab. In the upper right of the dialog box, click the **Update Database** button. This remakes the connection between the form and the database, and it will include all of the variables on the form. The variables in the database may not be in the same order as on the form. The new variables will be added at the end of the database. This can sometimes be a challenge when trying to interpret the data.

FIGURE 14.6A *Error Condition 1: Data Not in Database*

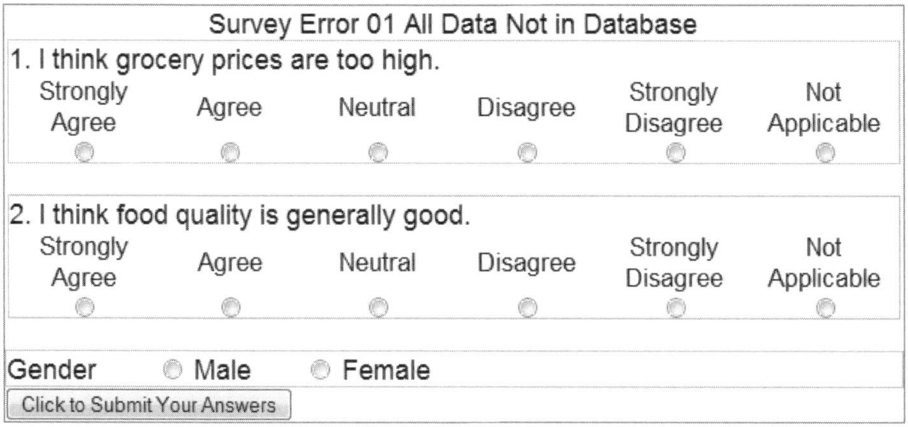

| Survey Error 01 All Data Not in Database |

1. I think grocery prices are too high.

Strongly Agree	Agree	Neutral	Disagree	Strongly Disagree	Not Applicable
⊚	⊚	⊚	⊚	⊚	⊚

2. I think food quality is generally good.

Strongly Agree	Agree	Neutral	Disagree	Strongly Disagree	Not Applicable
⊚	⊚	⊚	⊚	⊚	⊚

Gender ⊚ Male ⊚ Female

Click to Submit Your Answers

FIGURE 14.6B *Error Condition 1: Confirmation Form from Submission of Data Showing Three Questions*

Form Confirmation

Thank you for submitting the following information:

q1: 5
q2: 5
q3: Male
Submit1: Click to Submit Your Answers

Return to the form.

FIGURE 14.6C *Error Condition 1: Database View Showing Data from Only Two Questions*

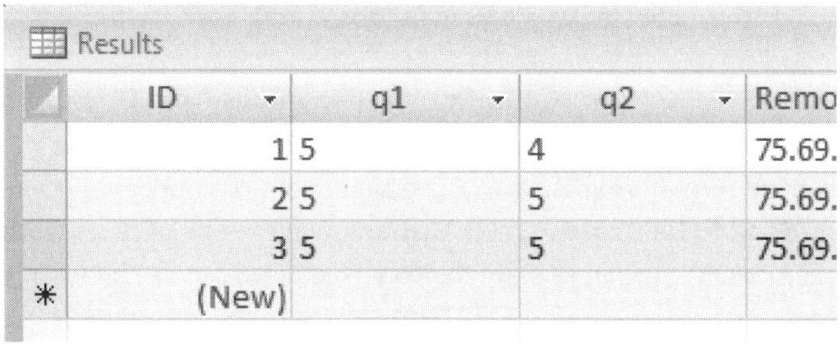

Results

ID	q1	q2	Remo
1	5	4	75.69.
2	5	5	75.69.
3	5	5	75.69.
* (New)			

FIGURE 14.7 *Database Connection Showing the Problem with Database and Survey Form*

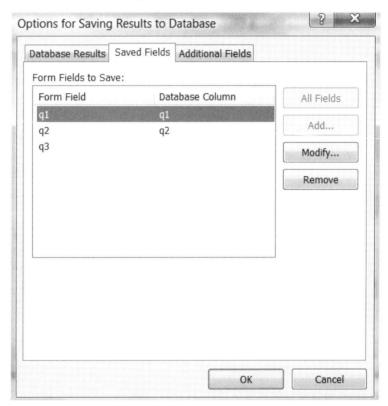

10. An alternative to the procedure in step 2 is to delete the database completely (make sure that you delete *survey_error01.mdb*). Open the *fpdb* folder and select the *survey_error01.mdb* file. Make sure before you do this that any data in the database is expendable. You cannot get it back once it is deleted.

11. Click the Delete key on the keyboard.

12. Right-click in the form and select **Form Properties > Options**. When you get an error about the connection, click **OK**. Now, click the **Create Database** button. Expression will create a new database that includes all of the variables from the form. Click **OK** three times and test the database. Data should be stored from all of the form fields.

 EXERCISE 14.5. **Error Condition 14–02: Values from One or More Possible Answers Are Not Stored in Database**

1. Open the page *survey_error02.asp* in Expression. Right-click inside the form, select Form Properties, **Send to Database . . .** click **Options**, and then click **Create Database**. When successful, click **OK** three times. Save the page and preview it in a browser.

FIGURE 14.8 *Database View Showing Incomplete and Incorrectly Coded Data*

ID	q1	q2	q3	q3a
1	a	5	male	
2	4	4		31
3	3	2		31
4	2	3	male	
5	1	sd		31
6	9	9		31
*	(New)			

2. Submit data that answers every possible answer for all questions. When done, open the database and inspect the data.

As you can see from Figure 14.8, there are many errors in the data. **Q1** has no answer value *5* and has both text answers and numbers. **Q2** has the same problems but with the 1 value. **Q3** has no value for *female* and there is an additional question labeled **q3a**. This error comes about frequently when an input control device (text box, option buttons, checkbox, and so on) is not coded properly. The solution is to double-click each input control and verify the variable names and values. When done. Save the page and then update the database using either of the techniques outlined in steps 2 or 3 of the previous exercise.

EXERCISE 14.6. **Error 14–03: Text on a Web Page Has Inconsistent Formatting**

1. Open the page *text_error.htm*. The text on the page is called *Greek text* and it is designed to look like English words, but they are not English or words. Designers use it to show where the text would be on a page. Notice that the text in the two paragraphs looks slightly different. The first is slightly bigger than the second paragraph. This comes about because the text was created in Word and the author used extensive formatting in Word.

   If you will recall, when we discussed style sheets it was stated that the styles should be applied in the Web page, not in the document. This is precisely why the text looks different. Switch to the **Code View**. Expression will highlight some of the formatting code in yellow. This is how Expression attempts to keep the look of the document in Word but create it on a Web page. The best thing is to get rid of the formatting and then apply styles from a style sheet.

2. Switch to the design view and select all of the Greek text on this page. From the menu, select **Format > Remove Formatting**. (Note that this will remove all of the formatting; you may need to center the table on the page again.) Now, create or attach an existing style sheet and apply the styles to the text.

SUMMARY

This chapter solved two problems. The first problem was how to carry data from one page to another. The first solution used query strings. The query strings were split off of the Web address and the value stored in the database. The second solution allowed users to input their IDs into a page and submit the page. The page created a query string with the submitted ID. The survey then stripped the ID and put it into a text box on the page so that it could be saved into the database. Either technique works and creates minimal hassle for the user.

The next problem involved programming a jump into a survey. When respondents answer a question one way, they are taken to another part of the survey where the questions are specific to only one group of respondents. If they answer the screening question another way, they would see a different set of questions. This was implemented using behaviors and bookmarks within the survey. Finally, three possible errors were discussed and solutions were illustrated. Unfortunately, there are far more possible errors, but these are three of the most common errors that students see, and now you know how to handle them.

KEY TERMS

query string	==
array	""
if() statement	alert message
else() statement	jump

DISCUSSION QUESTIONS

1. Look at an e-commerce Web site on the Internet. Click a link on the site's home page and notice the Web address. Does it use query strings to hold Web settings from page to page? Try to determine how what you checked caused a particular element in the query string.

2. Suppose that you are doing a longitudinal study of subjects over several years. You want them to complete a survey many times in the course of the study. Can you think of a way that you could pass an ID from one session to another that doesn't use the techniques that were outlined in this chapter? What might be the advantages and disadvantages of each technique for passing ID information?

CHAPTER

15

GENERAL TIPS ON DOWNLOADING AND ANALYZING YOUR DATA USING STATISTICS

LEARNING OBJECTIVES

■ To be able to download the data off the server and onto your computer

■ To be able to read data into statistical programs (SPSS and Minitab)

■ To be able to use descriptive statistics to examine your data

■ To be able to explain the importance of reliability when constructing scales

■ To be able to test a research hypothesis using inferential statistics: Understand the null hypothesis, Type I and Type II errors, statistical significant, effect size, and power

■ To be able to identify the difference between parametric and non-parametric statistics

DOWNLOADING DATA OUT OF THE WEB SURVEY

Let's assume your survey has been uploaded to the server and enough respondents have completed it so that you can begin to analyze the data. The first task is to get the data out of the Web server and onto your computer.

In prior exercises, we opened the database on the server to verify that everything worked. This was done by opening the survey in Microsoft Expression and double-clicking the *fpdb* folder and then double-clicking the Access database file therein. That file will have a name with the extension *.mdb*; the name was created when you created the database from the survey form. To get the data out of the Web server you must now export the data from Access on the server into another Access database located on your computer.

These procedures can be done at any time. However, you do not want someone taking the survey while you are working with the database; you might lose data. Once data collection is complete, the Web server administrator can turn off access to the survey, so that no one will be interacting with it except you, and you can extract the data at any time. If you would like to do an interim download, make sure that you do it at a time when the survey is quiet. Your system administrator can tell you when survey activity tends to be at a minimum.

Now you are ready to download the data into Access.

EXERCISE 15.1. Downloading Data from the Web Server into Access

1. Before opening the survey in Expression, launch Microsoft Access (see Figure 15.1) by clicking **Start > Programs** > **Microsoft Office** > **Microsoft Access**. The Access screen shots are from Access 2007; it may not look like older versions of Access, but it is functionally very similar.

2. Create a new database (**File** > **New**). In the task pane that now shows on the right side of the screen, select **Blank database . . . .** Next you will be prompted for a location for the new database. Be sure to put the data into a location where you can easily find it. In the **filename** box at the bottom of the screen, type the name of the new database. We suggest including the date in the filename as a way to avoid confusion about when the data was downloaded. See Figure 15.1.

3. Click **Create**.

4. That's it. You just created a shell for the data to be stored in. Close Access.

5. With Internet Explorer (IE) navigate to the Web site for Chapter Fifteen. Open the Web in Expression.

6. Now open *survey.asp* in Expression. Right-click inside the form and select **Form Properties**. Select **Send to Database** and then click **Options**. Click **Create Database**. When successful, click **OK** three times, save the page, and preview the survey in a browser.

7. If the first radio button is selected in the survey, double-click that button and click **Not Selected**. Do this for any buttons that are selected. They sometimes become checked when the survey is added to the server.

FIGURE 15.1 *Creating a New, Empty Access Database on the Desktop*

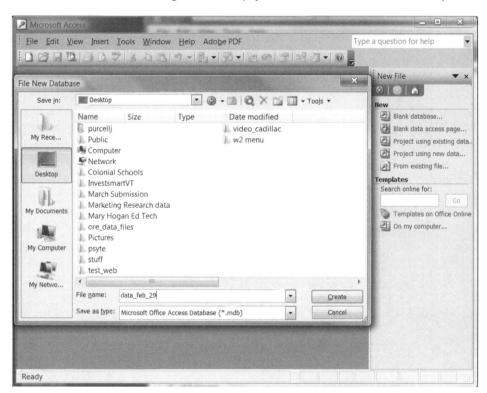

8. Preview the survey in a browser and enter data into the form to test each possible answer.

9. Double-click the *fpdb* folder and double-click the Access database that is linked to the survey. If asked about **Blocking Unsafe Expressions . . .** , answer **No**. Click **Open**. A copy of the database will open (refer to Figure 15.2).

10. In Access click **File** > **Export**, locate the shell database created above, select it, and click **Export** (see Figure 15.3).

11. In the next dialog box, there should be a name listed. This is the name for the table in Access that will receive the data. You can accept the name given or create your own name. Verify that **Definitions and Data** is selected in the **Export tables** section of the dialog box and finally, click **OK**.

12. The data are now located in the database on your computer. Close the Access database from the Web server and close Expression.

13. In Access 2007 the procedure is a bit different. When you open the database from the Web server it will open in Access 2007. Double-click the Results table. Click the **External Data** tab at the top of the window, then in the Export section click the down arrow for

FIGURE 15.2 *Access Dialog Showing Results Database Tables*

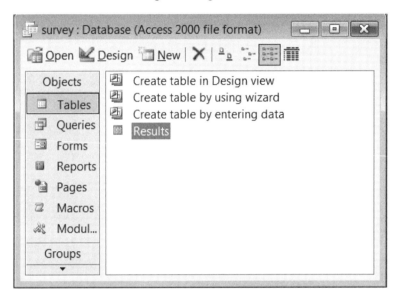

FIGURE 15.3 *Access Export Results Dialog Box*

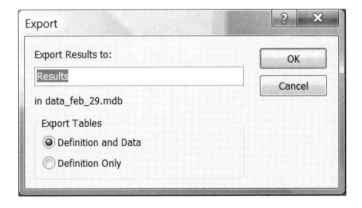

More. Select Access Database from the list, then navigate to where you created the shell in the above step. Select that file and click **OK**. Make sure you export the Definition and Data and click **OK**. Close the dialog box and close Access 2007.

EXERCISE 15.2. **Exporting Survey Data to Excel**

1. Exporting the data to Excel is even easier. Open the survey in Expression. Double-click the folder and double-click the database containing the survey data.

2. To export the data, click **File** > **Export**. In the dialog box, navigate to a location where you want to locate the data and, in the **filename** box, type a name for the spreadsheet. Remember, adding the date to the name will make it easier to keep files in order. Click the down arrow for **Save as type**, select **Excel 97–2003**. Click **Export**.

Which format should you export to? That depends on the data and what you will do with it. If you intend to analyze the data in statistical packages such as SPSS, SAS, or Minitab, it is best to download the data and export the file to Access. These statistical packages (and, we would venture to say, *all* other statistical packages, though we are only familiar with these three) will import an Access database directly. If you have one of the three statistical packages and are comfortable using it, Access is the best option. If you are going to do some rudimentary analyses in Excel, then export it into Excel and open that file directly.

Why use Access at all? Access has better data security. It is far more difficult to inadvertently delete data in Access than it is in Excel. An Access database is designed to protect data and will flag you when you are about to change or delete data. Excel will not. Therefore, it is safer to save the data in Access and then analyze with the statistical program.

The following exercise is based on SPSS version 16, the current version of the program. The keystrokes described are from that program. Previous versions will also import the data, but the keystrokes may be slightly different. For the remainder of this chapter, we will use a database that comes with the text. The data are from a fictitious survey of respondents' assessment of three types of breakfast cereals (Brands A, B, and C). Participants tasted a cereal and were asked to rate the cereal on sweetness and crunchiness. An answer of 5 indicates the respondent strongly believed the cereal was the right level of sweetness or crunchiness and 1 indicates the respondent felt strongly that it was not at the right level. The data for this exercise is in the Access database *cereal_data.mdb* found in the files for Chapter Fifteen.

If you have access to SPSS or Minitab then you may want to transfer your data into one of those statistical programs. However, if you do not have access to these databases, analyses can be conducted using Excel.

EXERCISE 15.3   Opening the Access Data in SPSS Version 16

1. In SPSS, select **File** > **Open Database** > **New Query**. The Database Wizard should open (see Figure 15.4). In the **ODBC Data Sources** list, select **MS Access Database**. Click **Next** (see Figure 15.5).

2. As shown in Figure 15.4 you will see the **OBDC Driver Login** dialog box, click **Browse** and locate the database file *cereal_data.mdb* in the files for Chapter Fifteen. Select the file and click **Open** and then **OK** (see Figure 15.6).

3. On the left side of the **Select Data** dialog box is a list of all the tables in the database. In this case, there is only one table listed. Select the table on the left and click the arrow

FIGURE 15.4 *SPSS Database Wizard Dialog for MS Access Databases*

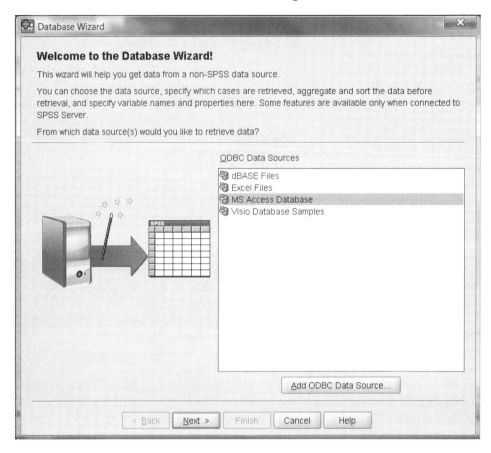

FIGURE 15.5 *SPSS Database Wizard Dialog to Select Database*

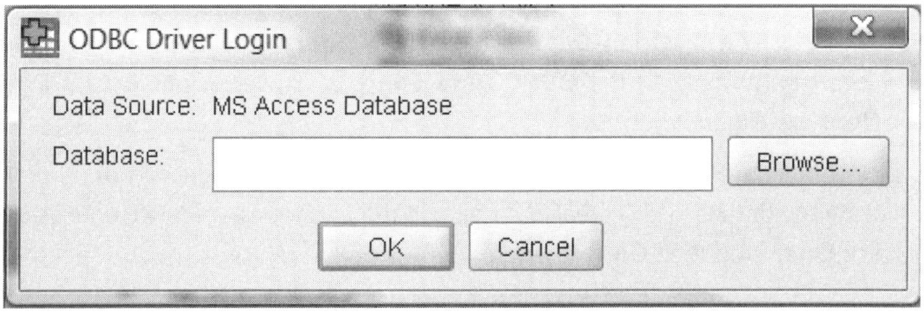

FIGURE 15.6 *SPSS Database Wizard Dialog to Select Data Fields to Import*

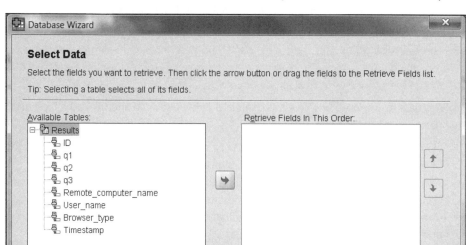

pointing to the right in the middle of the dialog box. This will bring all of the variables from the Access table into SPSS. You are done defining the data import. Click **Finish**.

4. The data are now in SPSS. Before going further, be sure to save the data in SPSS format by clicking **File** > **Save As**. Navigate to the location where you want to save the data. In the **filename** box, type the name you want for this data. Don't add any file extension; let the program add it (in this case *.sav*); and click **Save**. You are now ready to begin the analysis in SPSS.

EXERCISE 15.4. Opening the Data in Minitab 15

This exercise is based on Minitab version 15, the current version of the program. The keystrokes are from that program. Previous versions will also import the data, but the keystrokes may be slightly different. The data for this exercise is in the Access database *cereal_data.mdb* found in the files for Chapter Fifteen.

1. In Minitab click **File** > **Query Database (OBDC)**. (Refer to Figure 15.7.)

2. Click the tab marked **Machine Data Source**. Select the data source type **MS Access Database**. Click **OK**.

3. The next dialog box asks for a login name and password. You will only have to enter something if the data source is password-protected. Ours is not. Click the **Database** button on the left side of the dialog (see Figure 15.8 below).

4. Navigate to the location where the *chapter15* files are located and select the file *cereal_ data.mdb*. Click **OK** twice.

5. On the left side of the dialog box is a list of all of the objects in the database. At the top of the dialog box is a drop-down list of all available tables. Click the down arrow and select the table you created when you exported the data from the Web server. It is most likely called *Results*. When you select the *Results* table, the left side of the dialog box now shows all of the variables. Click the button that has the two greater-than symbols (>>) to bring all of the variables into Minitab. Then click **OK**. (See Figure 15.9.)

FIGURE 15.7 *Minitab Query Database Dialog*

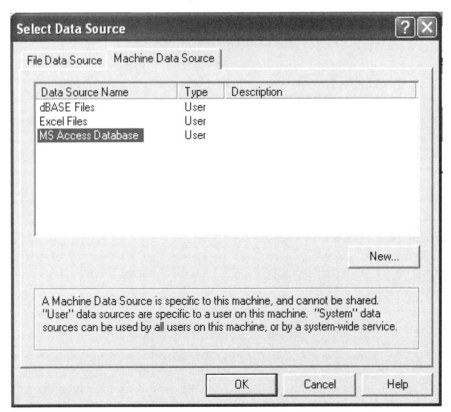

FIGURE 15.8 *Minitab Dialog to Select Database*

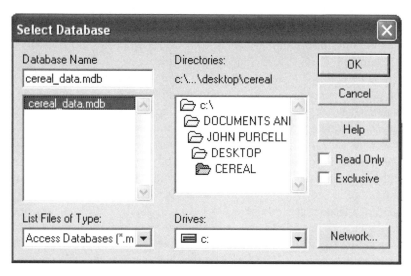

FIGURE 15.9 *Minitab Dialog to Bring Fields from Database into Minitab*

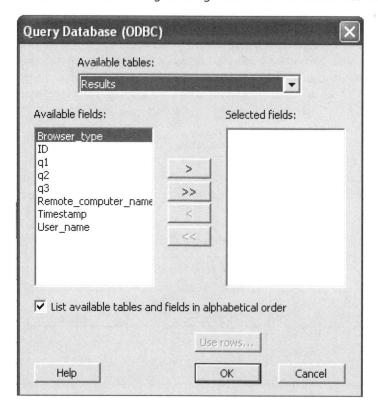

6. In Minitab, save the data in **Minitab** format (**File** > **Save Project**). You are now ready to begin analysis in Minitab.

Once the data are downloaded into Excel or a statistical program, researchers first conduct exploratory or preliminary analyses. Basic frequencies are computed to provide an examination of discrete categories. Frequency analyses should only be conducted using nominal (categorical data) or ordinal (ranked) data. During the data collection process, frequencies can be computed to assess the total number of participants (n) in the data set or the frequency (number and percentage) of males and females in the data set. Frequency distributions reveal the number and percentage of a discrete category. For instance, if it is important that your research sample represent 50 percent men and 50 percent women, you can evaluate your data set on an ongoing basis to examine the frequency of men and women during the collection process. Similarly, if a certain number of individuals are expected to participate in each condition of your experiment then frequencies can be checked to see which conditions may need additional participants. In Table 15.1, you can see there are almost twice as many females in the sample as there are males.

DESCRIPTIVE ANALYSES

Descriptive statistics can be used to organize and describe a data set. One of the most important initial analyses is to describe your participants. Just as you examined the number and percentage of men and women in our sample, you would do the same for all demographic information collected on your sample. The characteristics of your sample must be presented when communicating findings. How many men and women participated? What was the distribution of race? What were the range, mean, and standard deviation for age of your sample? What was the distribution of the education level of the sample?

For example, if you wanted to examine whether verdict decisions ("guilty of second degree murder," "guilty of manslaughter," "not guilty") differed by gender, you can use a statistic Chi Square. *Chi square analyses are non-parametric statistics used for categorical data. Chi square for Independence can be used to examine relationships*

TABLE 15.1. Frequency Table for Gender

What is your gender?

	Frequency	Percent
Female	83	62.9
Male	49	37.1
Total	132	100.0

TABLE 15.2. **Proportion of Men and Women and Verdict Decisions**

What is your verdict in this case * What is your gender Crosstabulation

			What is your gender		Total
			Female	Male	Female
What is your verdict in this case?	Second degree murder	Count	26	15	41
		% within What is your verdict in this case	63.4%	36.6%	100.0%
	manslaughter	Count	19	13	32
		% within What is your verdict in this case	59.4%	40.6%	100.0%
	not guilty	Count	38	21	59
		% within What is your verdict in this case	64.4%	35.6%	100.0%

between two categorical variables. **Crosstabs** *is a computer function that presents data in a table format. For example, Table 15.2 shows that almost twice as many women voted for second-degree murder (63.4 percent) as compared to men (36.6 percent).* Similarly, 64.4 percent of females voted "not guilty" compared to 35.6 percent of males voting "not guilty." Many researchers use graphs to examine their data. Bar graphs can be used to illustrate categorical data. Figure 15.10 provides an example of a bar graph.

Remember that a mean score represents the average score. Means can be affected by **outliers,** which are extreme scores within the distribution. Identifying exactly what constitutes an outlier is subjective and determined by the researcher. If your data set has extreme scores the median is more likely to represent the average in your sample. For example, let's assume you collected data on income and the income range was between $5,000 and $450,000. This range is extremely large, and you notice that only two individuals had incomes over $100,000. If you calculated a mean, the outliers (the

FIGURE 15.10 *Crosstabulation Results*

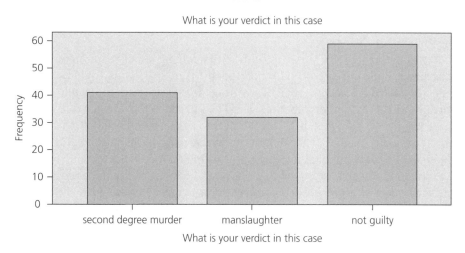

two highest incomes) might push the average to $80,000. However, if you calculated the median, the average would most likely be much lower and more representative of your sample. (For an in-depth review of measures of central tendency, see Salkind, 2000). A mode is not used as often yet provides important information for the researcher. As we have seen, the mode is the number that occurs most often in a data set. Figure 15.11 demonstrates that the mode value is "not guilty."

Variability refers to the extent to which scores vary (spread) around the mean. Variability reflects individual difference. We all differ, and participants will differ from one another. If everyone answered the question the same way, there would be no variability. So variability is expected, but should be considered because it represents the distribution of your sample.

Variance is a statistical term that represents the average squared distance from the mean. It provides researchers with an idea of the extent to which participants differ on one variable. ***Standard deviation*** is another statistical term that refers to the square root of the variance. For many, the standard deviation is easier to understand. The larger the standard deviation, the more spread out the scores are, and this will reflect the individual differences of your sample. ***Degrees of freedom*** refer to the number of scores that will vary to account for error variance. They are dictated by the sample size and change according to the statistical test used.

When we compute data analyses, one of the primary goals is to determine whether our hypothesis is supported or refuted. ***Parametric statistics*** are used to make inferences from a sample to a population. In this regard, they can be used for hypothesis testing. However, these statistics are based on the idea that the data are normally distributed. Therefore, it is extremely important to examine first whether your scores are normally distributed. In Chapter Six we showed that a normal distribution assumes data will be depicted as a bell-shaped curve that describes the mean, median, mode.

In Figure 15.11, you can see the distribution of scores of individuals' ratings of guilt for a defendant using a 7-point Likert scale. You can see that the mean in this distribution was 3.8 and the standard deviation was 1.65. This tells us the average score was 3.8 but scores could range an average of 1.65 or, if we round up, 2.0 points in either direction.

Researchers should be very careful when examining the distribution of their data. For instance, a mean score of 1.2 on a 7-point Likert scale would suggest that most people responded on the lower end of that scale. In this situation you would not have a normal distribution; your distribution would be skewed to the left side of the distribution. If you recall, a skewed distribution refers to a disproportionate number of scores that fall toward the upper or lower end of the distribution. Many statistical programs have an explore function that presents information on the thickness and skewness of the distribution. When scores tend to fall toward the lower end of the scale, this represents a basement effect. A ***basement effect*** refers to questions that have little variability and scores that tend to pile up on the lower end of the scale. Similarly, when scores tend to pile up around the upper end of the scale, this is called a ***ceiling effect***. Both basement and ceiling effects should be considered when examining data.

FIGURE 15.11 *Frequency Histogram*

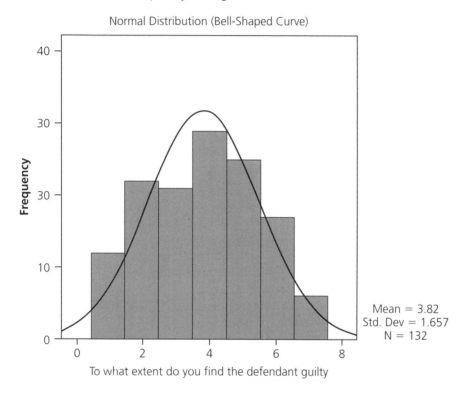

Normal Distribution (Bell-Shaped Curve)

Mean = 3.82
Std. Dev = 1.657
N = 132

To what extent do you find the defendant guilty

Considering Scale Construction and Issues of Reliability

There are two general types of reliability: (1) internal scale reliability and (2) interrater reliability. Most surveys measure man-made abstract constructs. For instance, if you were to measure heterosexuals' attitudes toward lesbians and gay men, you would either create your own survey to measure attitudes or use an existing survey with known validity and reliability. *Internal scale reliability* measures the consistency among scale items. Herek (1988) developed a survey designed to measure homophobic attitudes. The survey consists of twenty questions: ten designed to measure homophobic attitudes toward gay men; ten designed to measure homophobic attitudes toward lesbians. Before you can add up the total scale, some of the questions are reversed-scored; you must be careful when scoring these items. Once scoring is completed, you can examine the reliability of the scale. Most statistical packages examine scale reliability.

In Chapter Four we addressed one of the most commonly used measures of internal scale reliability, which is called Cronbach's alpha. As you recall, this is a measure of internal reliability and computes the consistency of the items in a construct. In other words, it examines the extent to which the items in the scale correlate with each other. When data are interval or ratio, Cronbach's measure of scale reliability can be used. Cronbach's alpha levels range from 0 to 1.0, and acceptable consistency is .70 or higher. Scale reliability is examined before constructing a total scale score. For instance, if you were to examine all twenty questions of Herek's survey, you would find your Cronbach's alpha was .69. However, you would find that two questions (your outliers) did not relate to any of the other items and ultimately reduced the reliability. If you were to eliminate those two items, your scale consistency would increase to .80. Therefore, when you construct your total scale, you leave out those two items. If items are eliminated in order to increase reliability, be sure to address this when discussing the methodology of the scale in your research report.

Another option for exploring the reliability of your scale is called split-half. When data are interval or ratio, *split-half reliability* compares one half of the scale construct with another half of the construct, revealing the correlation between the two halves. Another option to examine scale reliability is called the ***Guttman*** technique and is used for ordinal data. Once data are collected, the Guttman technique examines the strength of the order of the items. For instance if an individual agrees with a particular question, she will also agree with questions of a lower rank order (for example, I am willing to live two miles from a prison, I am willing to live fifty miles from a prison, I am willing to live a hundred miles from a prison).

Once you have examined the reliability of your scale, you can begin to construct the scale. To construct a scale that measures the general concept of "Attitudes Toward Lesbians and Gay Men (ATLG)," you would need to add up the scores on all twenty questions and then divide by the number of questions. This would provide you with a mean ATLG score for each participant. Many surveys are designed to measure multiple constructs. For example, this survey is designed to examine two separate constructs—attitudes toward gay men and attitudes toward lesbians. Thus you examine reliability of the ten questions designed to measure attitudes toward lesbians and then create the "attitudes toward lesbians" sub-scale. And you would do the same for "attitudes toward gay men."

Reliability is also necessary when two or more individuals are measuring behaviors. If you wanted to measure the content of Internet blogs or YouTube to examine aggression, you would ideally have individuals who are blind to the hypothesis do the data collection. When two or more people are collecting data you need to measure the consistency among raters (interrater reliability). For instance, if an individual goes to a psychiatrist and is diagnosed with paranoid schizophrenia and then goes to another psychiatrist and is diagnosed with a different disorder, the raters (psychiatrists) do not agree on a diagnosis and are therefore unreliable. It is extremely important to obtain reliability among raters. Table 15.3 demonstrates situations that dictate the appropriate reliability measure.

TABLE 15.3. **Measures of Interrater Reliability**

TYPE OF DATA	SITUATION	INTER-RATER RELIABILITY MEASURE
Nominal	Two raters that are classifying a set of subjects on a nominal variable (measuring how well raters agree)	Kappa
Ordinal	Can be used when the categories are ordered and raters come up with a weighting scale	Weighted Kappa
Ordinal	Have a set of participants rank order a set of stimuli. Measures the extent to which raters agree or participants agree in rank ordering	Kendall's Coefficient or Concordance W
Interval	Raters rate a set of subjects on an interval scale and you wish to see how consistent the ratings are across raters	Intra-class correlation coefficient (ICC)

TESTING YOUR RESEARCH HYPOTHESIS USING INFERENTIAL STATISTICS

So far, we have addressed descriptive analysis of data. Descriptive statistics summarize and describe the data and, as we have seen, inferential statistics are used to test hypotheses and assist researchers in interpreting their data. When researchers are interested in testing mean differences among groups, they conduct inferential statistical analyses to determine how significant the differences are significantly different. Let's say you want to examine gender differences in attitudes toward body image. One hundred males and one hundred females complete a survey on body image. You hypothesize that women will be more concerned with body image than men. The survey ranges in scores from 0 to 10. Male respondents have a mean score of 3.4 and females have a mean score of 4.6. You must examine whether the means differ significantly from each other. Now you can evaluate whether your hypothesis can be confirmed. In this situation, you are testing a hypothesis that examines mean differences among groups.

Statisticians use theories of probability and assume error variance to estimate whether differences among groups are significantly different. The ***null hypothesis*** assumes no differences between groups. ***Statistical significance (the p value)*** refers to outcomes that reject the null hypothesis as differences among groups are greater than chance. The *p* value examines the probability that the observed mean difference (or relationship) between variables in a sample occurred by chance. For example, in this example you are testing the population of the mean. The null and alternative hypotheses are

Ho: $\mu = \mu o$	OR	Ho: $\mu = \mu o$	OR	Ho: $\mu = \mu o$
Ha: $\mu \neq \mu o$		Ha: $\mu > \mu o$		Ha: $\mu < \mu o$

1. Where μo is some specified value of the population (sample) mean, either a nondirectional (hypothesize no direction but a difference between groups) or directional (includes a hypothesis of inequality) outcome has been predicted, and you can assume the sample is randomly selected and our observations are drawn from a normal distribution.

2. Set the level of significance (α, alpha) (accepted p value).

There are two ways of making an incorrect decision in hypothesis testing if the null is true, you might make the mistake of rejecting it (Type I error); or you might fail to reject a false null (Type II error).

There is always a probability of reaching a wrong conclusion when we test our hypotheses. A ***Type I error*** occurs when statistical hypothesis testing suggests no differences between groups, yet you say differences exist. ***Type II errors*** occur when the null hypothesis is false (suggesting there is a difference among groups), yet you claim there is no difference. Both errors are important to understand, but you must be very careful not to make Type II errors particularly when conducting applied research.

A Type II error can have great impact. For instance, suppose a new summer reading program has been instituted in the school system, and your job is to determine whether student reading improved significantly after participating in it. Your sample is fairly small (n = 35) and you conduct an experiment that compares a control group that did not participate in the program to students who completed it. Results found no significant difference between the control group and experimental group. Your results appear to suggest the summer reading program was not effective in improving reading skills. But before making this conclusion, you must consider that you may a have a false negative (Type II error). The results of the study could have great implications for individuals involved in the program as well as the community.

A Type I error suggests that researchers say there is a significant difference when the null hypothesis is actually true (false positive). Alpha level is one potential cause of Type I errors. For instance, if you conduct a research test and set your alpha level at .95, the results you obtain will be true. However, if we conduct a series of tests and make multiple comparisons, this increases the possibility of making a Type I error. The ***alpha level*** (α) generally accepted is .05. The alpha level provides the cutoff point that dictates how much error you are willing to accept. The smaller the alpha level (p value) the more stringent the test will be. If you set your "p" value to .05, then you are testing the hypothesis that, if you find a significant difference, you can be 95 percent sure that any significant differences found are not due to chance. If you set your alpha level at .05, the odds of finding a significant difference would be 5 in 100. In other words, for every one hundred analyses, five would be significant simply by chance. But if you conduct a series of all possible tests, the alpha level will increase. As seen in the box below, if you have two independent experiments with two groups each, by chance your alpha level has just increased to .0975.

You can avoid the problem of increasing an alpha level by using a technique called **Bonferonni,** which adjusts the alpha level to a more conservative level. To avoid a Type I error and alpha inflation, divide your alpha level (.05) by the number of comparisons you will make. For instance if you intend to make four comparisons, the calculation is .05/4 = .012.

$$P_{joint} = 1-(1-a)^k$$

Pj = joint probability

So, Pj = 1 (1−0.05)2 = 0.0975

Where p = probability, a = .05, and k = 2 groups

When researchers attempt to identify differences among groups, they need to consider the statistical power of a test. **Statistical power** refers to the sensitivity of an experiment's ability to identify whether the independent variable was truly effective in changing the dependent variable. Statistical power is dependent upon sample size. If your sample size is large (n > 100), power is usually not an issue. However, if your sample size is small (n < 30), be aware when interpreting results. Significance testing may suggest there are no differences among groups when the sample size is small, but this may not be true. The results (or lack of significant results) may be a product of low statistical power. (There are references available to explain how large your sample needs to be to achieve adequate power, and many statistical programs provide information on the power of your sample.) If your research shows no significant differences and you have a small sample, always check the power. If power is less than .80 (an 80 percent chance of identifying a difference among the groups), be careful how you interpret results. Power analyses provide an idea of how much confidence you can have in your results when you obtain nonsignificant results. Therefore, the higher the power, the more confident you can be that the results you found are true.

Power analyses assist you in identifying how many participants are necessary to obtain the effect size that your independent variable had on your dependent variable. Power will help reduce the chance of making a Type II error. The sensitivity of an experiment can also be seen by examining the effect size. If your research demonstrates significant differences among groups, examining the **effect size** of the results will reveal the strength of the association between the independent and dependent variables. If you have a large sample, you may find significant differences. However, always acknowledge the effect size. Often significant differences are found with small effect sizes. The effect size will determine the magnitude of the difference between the groups and describe how much error variance in the dependent variable can be accounted for by the independent variable.

There are different calculations to determine effect size. Some of the more common calculations for effect size are called *eta squared* (η^2), *Cohen's d and Cohen's f*. Eta squared provides values ranging from 0 to 1. The value obtained demonstrates the amount of variance the independent variable accounts for in the dependent variable (See Cohen, 1988; Graziano and Raulin, 2004; Green and Salkind, 2003; Pallant, 2001; or Shaughnessy et al., 2003, for more in-depth discussions and computations of power and effect size). According to Cohen (1988), the table below provides guidelines to interpret your effect size.

.01 = small effect size

.06 = moderate effect size

.14 = large effect size

Testing Your Research Hypothesis

Deciding how to test your research hypothesis is dependent upon your sample size, your hypothesis, and how your variables are measured. This is where understanding the scales of measurement will become extremely important, as this informs your decision on which statistical test you should use to test your hypothesis. We have addressed descriptive statistics, including measures of central tendency and variability. Parametric statistics that base assumptions on a normal distribution will be discussed next, followed by non-parametric statistical approaches.

Parametric Statistical Approaches If you recall, parametric statistics are based on the concept of normal distribution. Each parametric test has assumptions that must be considered before running a statistical test. There are three major assumptions: (1) the dependent variable must be measured on an interval or ratio scale, (2) random sampling is assumed, and (3) all observations should be independent of one another—that is, each measure should not be influenced by another variable (Pallant, 2001; Green & Salkind, 2003). Normal distributions are assumed, but many samples are not normally distributed. However, most statistical tests are robust enough to violate this assumption. Parametric tests should not be used with sample sizes less than 30 (n < 30). When your sample size is large, data may not have a normal distribution, but the sample means will most likely approximate normality, which will keep parametric tests valid. However, if sample sizes are small (< 30), parametric tests are no longer robust enough to violate the assumption of normality. This fact underscores the importance of conducting descriptive analyses of your data before conducting parametric tests.

When conducting experimental research, homogeneity of variance is an assumption that should be considered. ***Homogeneity of variance*** refers to equality of groups. It is assumed that the variance in one group should be equal to the variance in other groups. Statistical programs will produce a measurement of variance between groups. ***Levine's Test for Equality of Variance*** is designed to measure whether this assumption is violated. If the results of Levine's Test of Equality of Variance are significant, this suggests that the groups you are comparing do not have equal variances and that they differ from one another. If the groups differ, you cannot be sure the independent variable is the reason for the change in the dependent variable. Therefore, researchers want this test to be nonsignificant. If groups have an equal number of individuals and the sample sizes are large, this assumption can be overlooked, but it still should be mentioned as a limitation of the research study. Parametric statistics allow researchers to do one of two things—describe relationships or compare groups—to determine whether the observed relationship between variables or difference between means in a sample can be obtained by chance.

Parametric Statistic Options We will first address parametric research regarding relationships between variables. A correlation is a descriptive statistic that describes relationships between variables. ***Pearson product-moment correlations*** examine the magnitude and direction of relationships between two variables. As long as the variables are measured continuously (interval or ratio), a Pearson correlation can be used to assess potential relationships between variables. Correlations range from -1.00 to $+1.00$. A correlation of $+1.00$ indicates a perfect correlation in a positive direction. In a positive correlation, as one variable increases, the other variable increases. For example, the more we study, the higher our grade. A negative correlation would indicate that one variable increases while the other decreases. For example, the more we exercise, the less body weight we have. A correlation of 0 indicates no correlation between variables.

A ***partial correlation*** can also be used to examine the extent to which a third variable might be affecting the correlation results, and to control for these effects. The variable you control for must also be continuous (interval or ratio). For example, if you examine the correlation between student achievement and student-teacher ratio, you would expect that the higher the student-teacher ratio, the higher the student achievement. But there are other variables that can affect your results. Parent income or parent education can also covary with student achievement and student-teacher ratio. If you control for the effects of parent income, you may find that the actual relationship decreases because parent income most likely plays a significant role in student achievement.

Regression also examines relationships between variables, but the goal of regression is prediction. In order to use a regression, both the independent and dependent variables should be continuous (interval or ratio), and one variable is expected to predict another variable. For example, number of years of education should predict income level. Regressions are very similar to correlations as they work on a linear model.

Finally, standard Z scores should be mentioned as they can be very useful in research. A **Z score** is a standardized score that indicates how participants scored relative to other participants. A positive Z score indicates that the participant scored above the mean and a negative Z score suggests that the participant scored below the mean. The size of the Z score indicates how far from the mean the individual scored. The goal of Z scores is to combine all this information into a single value that specified a location within a distribution.

A Z score therefore specifies the precise location of any value (X) value within a distribution. The sign of the Z-score ($+$ or $-$) indicates whether the score is above the mean (positive) or below the X (negative). Z scores come in handy when researchers combine various measures to create a total score. If you wanted to examine the well-being of elderly adults, for example, you could examine the number of doctor appointments in the last six months, and use a survey that assesses depression (using a Likert-type scale from 1 to 7) and number of daily social contacts. All of these constructs are measured differently. However, they can be standardized using a Z score and combined to obtain a general measure of well-being.

$$Z = \frac{\bar{X} - \mu}{\frac{\sigma}{\sqrt{n}}} \text{ or } \frac{\bar{X} - x}{s}$$

Researchers also use parametric tests, statistical inferences, and hypothesis testing to determine whether mean differences exist between groups. To test mean differences among two independent groups, you could conduct a **t-test for independent groups**. Data for the independent variable will always be nominal with two independent groups, and the dependent variable should be continuous (interval or ratio). If you examine changes in mean differences from pre- to posttest and groups are dependent (related), a **paired t-test** should be used. To examine mean differences for more than two groups, an **analysis of variance (ANOVA)** is used.

In an ANOVA, the dependent variable is always measured on a continuous scale and the independent variables are nominal. An ANOVA (or *omnibus F-test*) examines mean differences among groups, wherein the null hypothesis assumes all group means are equal. If the *p* value reveals significance ($p < .05$ or lower) researchers then know that the group means differ.

The logic of ANOVA can be complicated but the underlying idea is fairly straightforward. ANOVA considers that there will always be variability between groups as well as within groups. ANOVA calculates both and, based on calculations, determines whether between-group variability is greater than chance. (See Graziano and Raulin, 2004; Pallant, 2001; Shaughnessy et al., 2003; or Turner and Thayer, 2001, for a more in-depth discussion of ANOVA.)

Multivariate Statistics. *Multivariate statistics* is a more advanced form of parametric research and refers to all statistical methods that simultaneously analyze multiple independent and dependent variables. Multivariate analyses typically examine more than two variables and, in that respect, help us to understand interrelationships that often mirror real life. The variables should be interrelated in such a way that you can only understand (or make theoretical sense of) them together, and that to analyze them separately would lead researchers to miss something. Often, in multivariate analyses, you are forming linear combinations of variables. These combinations are called linear functions or variates. A *function* is a variate and is such that the difference between groups is maximized for that variate. If we can interpret the essence of that variate or function, then we can better understand the underlying elements that separate the groups. These functions or variates help us understand and conceptualize what is going on in the data set.

One multivariate analysis is an extension of the ANOVA, called ***multivariate analysis of variance (MANOVA)***. This multivariate statistic allows researchers to examine multiple dependent variables. MANOVA assesses each group on two or more dependent variables. As mentioned, the null hypothesis tests the equality of variance between vectors of dependent variables. Another multivariate option is a multiple regression. ***Multiple regression*** is a statistical technique used to analyze relationships between multiple independent variables (predictors) and one single dependent variable.

Factor analysis is another multivariate option used when constructing a scale or survey in order to determine whether you are actually measuring what you intend to measure. Factor analyses are statistical procedures that are used to explain variability among variables so that the structure of the relationship among the variables can be detected and the number of variables can be reduced. In essence, factor analysis is a multivariate extension of scale reliability. The two main goals of factor analysis are data reduction and identification of underlying constructs. Data reduction is necessary when you take a large number of questions and want to reduce the number of questions without losing important information. This technique will tell you which questions are essential to the construct being measured and which questions could be eliminated. The second function of factor analysis is to help you identify the interrelationships among a large number of variables in terms of their common underlying dimensions (or factors). These factors should represent the constructs that your survey intends to measure. These are the most common parametric multivariate techniques used, but there are many other multivariate options available for more advanced statistical analysis. (For an in-depth discussion on multivariate statistics see Grimm and Yarnold, 2001.)

Non-Parametric Statistical Approaches. Non-parametric statistics do not directly test hypotheses involving population parameters as parametric tests do. Non-parametric tests are considered distribution-free techniques, where the validity of the test statistics is not a function of the distribution of the actual data. Non-parametric tests require less rigorous assumptions to maintain statistical validity. When some assumptions (such as normality of data) cannot be met and scales of measurement for your variables are typically nominal or ordinal, non-parametric techniques can be used. The key situations in which to use non-parametric tests include:

■ Distribution of data is known to be non-normal (small n)

- Sample sizes are small (n < 10–20 per group) or have highly unequal variances

- Variables are measured using an interval or ratio scale whose distributions are unknown, and the n's are small

- Data are nominal or ordinal

- There are no parametric options available

- You have interval or ratio data and there are extreme values or major outliers that will affect means

These six situations can be narrowed down to three basic situations where non-parametric techniques can be used. First, non-parametric techniques can be used when interval or ratio data do not meet parametric statistical assumptions. Let's say you want to test the hypothesis that home health care can reduce number of emergency room visits. You compare two groups of elderly individuals. One group has a home health nurse and the other group does not. The sample sizes are small (n = 15 in each group), and you are not sure whether your dependent variable (number of emergency room visits) is normally distributed among the groups. In this case, you might consider using a non-parametric technique (such as the Mann-Whitney-U or Wilcoxen Rank Sum test, analogous to a two-sample t-test).

The second context in which non-parametric techniques are commonly used is when data are nominal or ordinal. For example, you might ask respondents to rank-order the following people in terms of helpfulness:

Nurse	Relative	Clergy
Doctor	Neighbor	Volunteer

You could have thirty individuals rank-order these people in terms of helpfulness and then have them rank-order a list of hospital departments they found helpful. What you would want do is determine whether there is a correlation between these ranked items. A *Spearman rank order correlation* examines correlations between rank ordered items. A Chi Square (crosstabs) also allows researchers to examine relationships between categorical variables. Another non-parametric option is called *logistic regression*, which predicts the presence or absence of characteristics or determines an outcome based on values of a set of predictor variables. The dependent variable must be dichotomous (two categories) and independent variables can be any scale of measurement. For instance, if you want to predict whether something will or will not happen (such as graduation, business failure, heart disease, and so forth), you could use this technique to examine whether independent variable predictors can predict an event or non-event.

As you can see, most parametric statistics have non-parametric analogs. That is, if your data do not meet the assumptions for a parametric test, or your variables are not measured in such a way that accommodates a parametric test, there will most likely be a non-parametric analog that can be used to examine the data. Table 15.4 is intended to assist you in identifying which statistical technique is appropriate based on the purpose of your research and how your independent and dependent variables are measured.

Finally, there are miscellaneous techniques that have no parametric competitors (for example, factor analysis and multiple regression) and that often test the general properties of data rather than specific parameters. Let's say you examine the Dow Jones Industrial Index of U.S. stocks by the day to determine whether increases and decreases in the Dow Jones are a random process. In this situation, you are not testing the parameters of the populations; you are testing a general characteristic of the data.

Both parametric and non-parametric tests are subject to issues of validity. In both situations, data must match the analysis in terms of scales of measurement. Data in the population must meet certain distributional assumptions. If one or both of these are violated, the test is invalid. (Remember, "garbage in, garbage-out.") If a test is invalid, it no longer has the distribution you claim it to have. The distribution is typically unknown. If you do not know the distribution then the significance level is invalid because the p value is based on the distribution of the sample. If data violate these assumptions, you lose control of your alpha level (Type 1 Error) because the true degrees of freedom are unknown, and statistical power is lost. Statistical procedures assume variation between groups and within groups.

HELPFUL RESOURCES AND LINKS TO ANALYZE DATA

Explaining all aspects of data analysis and prospective statistical techniques is beyond the scope of this text. Therefore we have provided some resources to more in-depth tips on data analysis in the Appendix of this book. We have also provided a helpful table (Table 15.4) to help you decide which statistical analysis is appropriate for your research question and data set.

SUMMARY

This last chapter began with providing procedures to get the data you collected out of the Web and into a database where you can begin to examine the data. We demonstrated how to save the data file into a newly created Access file. Once in this newly created file, data could be exported to a database (such as Excel, SPSS, and so on) that will allow you to begin using statistics to analyze your data. Frequency analyses and measures of central tendency can be used to describe your data. Understanding measures of variability (such as variance, standard deviation) also helps you describe your data and the distribution of your data set.

Parametric statistics are based upon data that are normally distributed. When examining whether data are normally distributed, we look for skewed distributions and basement or ceiling effects. It is also

TABLE 15.4. Summary Table of Characteristics of Main Statistical Techniques

Purpose	Example of Question	Parametric Statistic	Non-parametric Alternative	Independent Variable Measurement	Dependent Variable Measurement	Essential Features
Exploring Relationships	What is the relationship between gender and dropout rates from therapy?	None	Chi-Square	One categorical variable (gender)	One categorical variable (drop-out): Complete therapy or not	The number of cases in each category is considered, not scores
	Is there a relationship between age and optimism scores?	Pearson Product Moment Correlation Coefficient	Spearman's Rank Order Correlation (Rho)	Two continuous variables: age, optimism scores	One sample with scores on two different measures, or same measure at Time 1 and Time 2	
	After controlling for the effects of socially desirable responding bias, is there still a relationship between optimism and life satisfaction?		Partial Correlation	None	Two continuous variables and one continuous variable you wish to control for (optimism, life satisfaction, scores on social desirability scale)	One sample with scores on two different measures, or same measure at Time 1 and Time 2
	How much of the variance in life satisfaction scores can be explained by self-esteem, perceived control and optimism? Which of these variables is the best predictor?	Multiple Regression	None	Set of two or more continuous independent variables (self-esteem, perceived control, optimism)	One continuous dependent variable (life satisfaction)	One sample with scores on all measures
	What is the underlying structure of the items that make up the positive and negative affect scale--how many factors are involved?	Factor analysis	None	Set of related continuous variables (items on the positive and negative affect scale)	One sample, multiple measures	
Comparing Groups	Are males more likely to drop out of therapy compared to females?	None	Chi Square	One categorical independent variable (gender)	One categorical dependent variable (dropout/complete therapy)	You are interested in the number of people in each category, not scores on a scale
	Are males more optimistic than females	Mann-Whitney samples t-test	One categorical U-Test	One continuous dependent independent variable (optimism scores)	Two groups: different people in each group	

Research question	Parametric statistic	Non-parametric alternative	Independent variable	Dependent variable	Sample
Is there a change in anxiety scores from Time 1 to Time 2?	Paired Samples t-test	Wilcoxon Signed Rank Test	One categorical independent variable (two levels: Time 1 and Time 2)	Continuous dependent variable: anxiety scores	Same people on two different occasions
Is there a difference in optimism scores for people who are under 35 years, 36–49, and 50+ years?	One-way between groups ANOVA	Kruskal-Wallis	One categorical independent variable (three or more levels) age group	One continuous dependent variable (optimism scores)	Three or more groups; different people in each group
Is there a change in anxiety scores from Time 1, Time 2, and Time 3?	One-way repeated measures ANOVA	Friedman test	One categorical independent variable (three or more levels) Time 1/ Time2/ Time 3	One continuous dependent variable (anxiety scores)	Three or more comparisons; same people sampled on three different occasions
Is there a difference in the optimism scores for males and females, who are under 35 yrs, 36–49, and 50+ years?	Two way between groups ANOVA	None	Two categorical independent variables (age group and gender)	One continuous dependent variable (optimism scores)	Two or more groups for each independent variable; different people in each group
Which intervention (math skills/confidence building) is more effective in reducing fear of statistics, measured across three time periods?	Mixed (between-within-subjects) ANOVA	None	One between-groups independent variable (two or more levels; type of intervention) and two or more levels of within groups (time periods)	One continuous dependent variable (Fear of statistics test scores)	Two or more groups with different people in each group, each measured on two occasions
Is there a difference between males and females, across three different age groups in terms of their scores on a variety of adjustment measures (anxiety, depression, and perceived stress)?	Multivariate ANOVA (MANOVA)	None	One or more categorical independent variables with two or more levels (age and gender)	Two or more related continuous dependent variables (anxiety, depression, and perceived stress scores)	
Is there a significant difference in the Fear of Statistics test scores for participants in the math skills group and the confidence building group, while controlling for their scores on this test at Time 1?	Analysis of Covariance (ANCOVA)	None	One or more categorical independent variables (two or more levels; type of intervention)	One continuous covariate variable (Fear of Statistics test scores at Time 1)	One continuous dependent variable (Fear of Statistics test scores at Time 2)

Reprint made possible by Pallant (2001)

important to examine scale and interrater reliability before testing hypotheses using inferential statistics. Inferential statistics test the null hypothesis and examine whether differences are statistically significant. Researchers should always be aware of Type I and Type II errors. Being cognizant of alpha inflation and using the Bonferroni technique may help alpha inflation. Statistical power will assist you in identifying whether you are making a Type II error, and effect size (eta squared, Cohen's *d* and *f*) will provide an index of the strength of the relationship between the independent and dependent variables.

Parametric statistics are based on the primary assumptions that the data are normally distributed, based on a random sample, and that each observation is independent of one another. Homogeneity of variance (Levine's test for homogeneity) will assist in determining the equality of groups. Statistical tests for parametric and non-parametric data were examined. Non-parametric statistics are considered distribution free techniques and should be considered when data are not normally distributed, if the N is less than 30, or the data are nominal or ordinal.

KEY TERMS

outliers
variability
variance
standard deviation
degrees of freedom
crosstabs
skewed distribution
basement effect
ceiling effect
internal scale reliability
parametric statistics
split-half reliability
Guttman technique
null hypothesis
statistical significance
Type I and Type II errors
alpha level
Bonferroni
statistical power
homogeneity of variance

Chi Square
Levine's test for homogeneity
Pearson product moment correlation
partial correlation
regression
Z score
t-test for independent groups
paired t-test
analysis of variance
effect size
multivariate statistics
function
multivariate analysis of variance
  (MANOVA)
multiple regression
factor analysis
non-parametric statistics
Spearman rank order correlation
logistic regression

DISCUSSION QUESTIONS

1. How would we examine the number of males and females in our sample that was exported into a statistical database?

2. Why is it necessary to examine the distribution of your sample? What are three things you would look for when examining the distribution of your sample?

3. What are the three assumptions associated with parametric statistics?

4. What are Type I and Type II errors? Which error would be worse for applied researchers? What are some ways we avoid these errors?

5. Name at least three conditions where parametric statistics would be appropriate and name at least three conditions were non-parametric statistics would be the preferred method to analyze data.

APPENDIX

USING PHOTOSHOP TO CREATE BUTTONS AND BANNERS

LEARNING OBJECTIVES

- To be able to use Photoshop to create simple buttons with text
- To be able to use Photoshop to create a simple banner for a survey page

Adobe Photoshop is a delightfully full-featured program for editing photos and creating graphics for Web sites. There are literally hundreds of commands and procedures that are part of the Photoshop program. This very brief tutorial is in no way a comprehensive treatment of such a rich program. We will demonstrate how to create simple buttons and banners and optimize them for use on the Web. If you need to do something more complicated, there are many people who can help. Any graphic designer, Web designer, or photographer can crop, focus, or retouch photos. I have found them to be very willing to help. Look for them in the phone book.

The figures in this section are from Photoshop CS3. This is the latest version of the software, but nothing that we will do could not be done with prior versions of Photoshop. The look of the workspace and screen shots might be slightly different, but the functions should be the same.

EXERCISE APPENDIX 1.1.   Creating Simple Buttons with Text

1. Open Photoshop by clicking the **Start** button, clicking the program list, and locating the **Launch** button from Photoshop.

2. Close any dialog boxes that might be open at the start.

3. Create a new document by clicking **File** > **New**. In the name box type **survey buttons**.

4. Set the width to be 120 pixels.

5. Set the height to be 60 pixels.

6. The resolution is always 72 pixels/inch for Web graphics.

7. The color mode is *RGB Color* in *8 bit.*

8. The **Background Contents** should be *White.* All the settings for this dialog are shown in Figure Appendix 1.1. Click **OK**.

9. The document is created. It is easier to work with graphics if you can measure their size. Click the menu choice **View** > **Rulers** to show rulers in the program.

10. In Figure Appendix 1.2 are two images of the Photoshop toolbar. On the image on the left the sixth button down on the right side is the **Gradient Tool**. We are not interested in this button, but in the button nested under it. Left-click this button and from the fly-out menu select the **Paint Bucket**. It is the sixth button on the right on the left toolbar. This tool is used to apply color to an object.

11. The next choice is what color to use. There is a palette that deals with color (see Figure Appendix 1.3). If it is not visible then select **Window** > **Color** to turn it on. The default is the color sliders. Click the **Swatches** tab at the top of the palette and select a light green color.

12. With the light green color selected, move the mouse over the graphic created above. When the mouse is over the graphic the cursor will turn into a paint bucket. Click inside the square and it will be colored light green.

FIGURE APPENDIX 1.1 *Background Contents Dialog Settings*

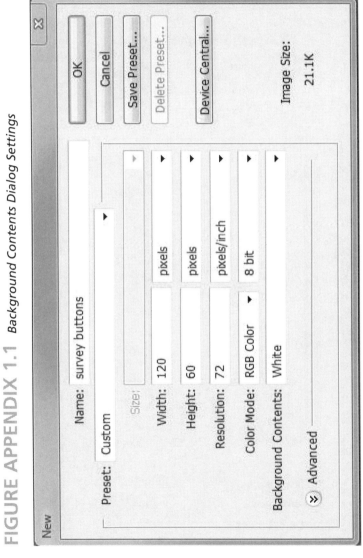

FIGURE APPENDIX 1.2 *The Photoshop Toolbar*

FIGURE APPENDIX 1.3 *The Color Palette*

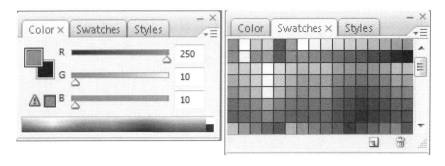

13. The eighth icon on the right side of the toolbar is the text tool and it is marked with the letter *T.* Click it.

14. Near the bottom of the toolbar is the foreground-background color indicator—two large overlapping squares with light green on top and black underneath. Above and to the left are two much smaller overlapping black and white squares. Click these to set the foreground color to black and the background color to white. The foreground color will be the type color on the button. Depending on which light green color you choose, you may want the type to be colored black or white. To switch the foreground color for the background color, click the double-headed arrow above and to the right of the foreground-background color button. Select the most appropriate color for your background.

15. Click the graphic approximately one-eighth inch from the left edge of the graphic. Type the words, **I Agree**. At the top of the Photoshop window is an option bar. On the far right edge are a circle with a slash through it and a check mark. Click the check mark to add the text to the graphic. If you do not want to add the text, click the circle and try again.

16. On the right side of the Photoshop window is the **Layer** palette. If you do not see it, click **Window** > **Layers**. There should be two layers in the palette: one titled **background** and a text layer titled **I Agree**. Each time text is added to a graphic, a new text layer is added as well. The text on my button is too small. To select the text on the button, double-click the rectangle with a *T* in it on the text layer. This will automatically select the text. If you need to, increase the size of this text to 18 points.

17. Now we'll make our first button. Select **File** > **Save for Web . . .**. On the right edge of the window, near the top of the settings, select the drop-down menu for **Presets**. From the list select **GIF 64 No Dither**. Then at the top of the setting click **Save**. Navigate to the exercise files and save the graphic with the filename *i_agree_2*. Do not type an extension; let Photoshop add it. Congratulations, your first button is done.

18. Making the **I Disagree** button is quite easy. In Photoshop, right click the **I Agree** layer. From the menu select **Duplicate**. A dialog will appear asking you for a new name for this layer. Type **I Disagree**.

FIGURE APPENDIX 1.4 *The Layer palette*

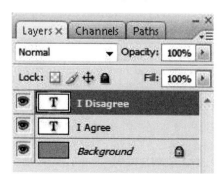

19. Click the eye to the left of the text icon of the **I Agree** layer. This turns the layer off and it can no longer be seen.

20. Double-click the text icon for the **I Disagree layer** and type **I Disagree**. Create the second button in the same manner as you did in step 17. Save the graphic with the name *i_disagree_2*.

21. When you have created all of the buttons that you need, save the *survey_buttons* file. Keep it handy as you will often have to make new buttons as the survey develops.

Using this procedure, the text on all of the buttons will be aligned the same way and be the same size. If more buttons are needed, repeat the process and then change the text as needed.

A banner is an identifier that usually is at the top of the page. As all of our text is inside a table, the banner could go in the first row of a table. In general, this is a good idea, as it reminds the respondent who is sponsoring the survey. However, it does take up room on the page. Use a banner or not as you wish.

EXERCISE APPENDIX 1.2.   Creating a Banner for Page Heads

1. Leave the previous file open and create a new one by clicking **File > New**.

2. The name is *survey_banner.*

3. The width is 600 pixels and the height is 120 pixels. The remainder of the settings are as in the previous example. Click **OK**.

4. We would like the background color of the banner to match the buttons. To make sure that the colors are the same, click the **eye dropper** tool from the tool box. It is two below the text tool.

5. Move the eye dropper into the background of the buttons. Click the background color. This will sample the color and set the foreground color to the green color.

6. In the tool box select the paint bucket. Click the new graphic to color it the same green.

7. As with the buttons, the text color in the banner needs to contrast with the green background. Select either black or white as appropriate.

8. Click the graphic about one-fourth inch from the left edge. Set the type size to be about 36 points. Type **Online Research Essentials** and then click the check mark on the options bar.

9. If the type needs to be repositioned on the graphic, make sure that the text layer is selected in the layer palette and then click the Move tool in the tool box. It is the first button on the right side. Left-click the text and it can be moved on the graphic.

10. Select the text tool again and click the graphic under the main heading. Make sure that the left edges of the two lines are lined up. Set the type size to 24 points and type **by John Purcell and Brenda Russell, PhD**. Click the check mark.

11. Adjust the position of the second line as needed. Save the file.

12. As before, save the file as a graphic with the filename *survey_banner.* Let Photoshop add the GIF extension.

The buttons and banner can be imported into the survey site as we did with the photo of my dog in Chapter Seven. This will keep the images in the correct location on the site.

SUMMARY

This appendix illustrated how to create simple buttons and graphics. The buttons are saved as GIFs to keep the graphics files small so that they can be easily transported over the Internet.

HELPFUL REFERENCES FOR STATISTICAL ANALYSES

Aron, A., & Aron, E. N. (1994). *Statistics for psychology.* Upper Saddle River, NJ: Prentice Hall.

Cohen, J. W. (1988). *Statistical power analysis for the behavioral sciences* (2nd ed.). Hillsdale, NJ: Erlbaum.

Cohen, J., & Cohen, P. (1983). *Applied multiple regression/correlation analysis for the behavioral sciences* (2nd ed.). New York: Erlbaum.

Daniel, W. (1990). *Applied nonparametric statistics* (2nd ed.). Boston: PWS-Kent.

Frankl, M. S., & Siang, S. (1999). Ethical and legal aspects of human subjects research on the Internet. American Association for the Advancement of Science, June, 10-11, Washington, D.C. http://www.aaas.org/spp/dspp/sfrl/projects/intres/main.htm

Gravetter, F. J., & Forzano, L. A. (2003). *Research methods for the behavioral sciences.* Belmont, CA: Thomson Wadsworth.

Graziano, A. M., & Raulin, M. L. (2004). *Research methods: A process of inquiry* (5th ed.). Boston: Pearson.

Green, S. B., & Salkind, N. J. (2005). *Using SPSS for windows and macintosh: Analyzing and understanding data* (4th ed.). Upper Saddle River, NJ: Pearson Prentice Hall.

Grimm, L. G., & Yarnold, P. R. (2001). *Reading and understanding multivariate statistics.* Washington, D. C.: American Psychological Association.

King, C. A. (1995). A prospective study of adolescent suicidal behavior following hospitalization. *Suicide and Life Threatening Behavior, 25(3),* 327–338.

Jackson, S. L. (2003). *Research methods and statistics: A critical thinking approach.* Belmont, CA: Thomson Wadsworth.

Kantowitz, B. H., Roediger, H. L., & Elmes, D. G. (1997). *Experimental psychology: Understanding psychological research* (6th ed.). Minneapolis/St. Paul: West Publishing Group.

Lomax, R. G. (2001). Statistical concepts: *A second course for education and the behavioral sciences* (2nd ed.). Hillsdale, NJ: Erlbaum.

Pallant, J. (2001). *SPSS survival manual: A step by step guide to data analysis using SPSS.* Philadelphia: Open University Press.

Ray, W. J. (2003). *Methods toward a science of behavior and experience* (7th ed.). Belmont, CA: Thomson Wadsworth.

Shaughnessy, J. J., Zechmeister, E. B., & Zechmeister, J. S. (2003). *Research methods in psychology* (6th ed.). Boston: McGraw Hill.

Tabachnick, B. G., & Fidell, L. S. (1996). *Using multivariate statistics* (3rd ed.). New York: Harper Collins.

Turner, J. R., & Thayer, J. F. (2001). *Introduction to analysis of variance.* Thousand Oaks, CA: Sage.

U.S. Department of Health and Human Services. (1996). Mental Health: A Report of the Surgeon General. Rockville, MD: U.S. Department of Health and Human Services.

USEFUL LINKS FOR STATISTICAL ANALYSIS

http://math.about.com/od/statistics/Statistics_Tutorials_and_Resources.htm

Statistics tutorial and resource.

www.psych.utoronto.ca/courses/c1/Welcome.htm

Interesting website for psychology statistics, but overall informative Web site.

http://davidmlane.com/hyperstat/

Hyperstats online statistics. Answers all your statistical questions.

http://talkstats.com/

Discussion forum for statistics.

www.socialresearchmethods.net/selstat/ssstart.htm

A helpful guide to help researchers determine the appropriate statistical technique to use.

www.uwsp.edu/psych/stat/14/nonparm.htm#I1

Helpful guidelines for categorical data (Chi Square) and non-parametric statistics.

www.uwsp.edu/psych/stat/2/prelim.htm#III

Scales of measurement and basic statistical concepts.

www.uwsp.edu/psych/stat/indexTests.htm

Summary of statistical tests.

www.uwsp.edu/psych/stat/1/expdes.htm#III5

Example of experimental method.

www.uwsp.edu/psych/stat/index.htm

Great guide to statistics.

www.mathworks.com/access/helpdesk/help/toolbox/stats/

Statistics Toolbox, from descriptive statistics to experimental designs.

http://faculty.vassar.edu/lowry/webtext.html

Concepts of inferential statistics.

www.businessbookmall.com/Taxonomy%202.pdf

Flowchart of parametric statistics.

http://abacus.bates.edu/~ganderso/biology/resources/statistics.html#parametric

Bates College Painless Guide to Statistics.

http://sunzi1.lib.hku.hk/hkjo/view/7/700231.pdf

The Process of Social Research: A Conceptual Codification with a Flow Chart.

GLOSSARY

Symbols

"". This represents the null or empty value in script code.

**
**. The HTML code for a line break. It creates a new line on the page.

<h1> and </h1>. The beginning and ending HTML style tags. These cause the text between the two codes to display in large size and bold on the screen.

<HTML> and </HTML>. The opening and closing tags for the HTML code that creates a Web page.

<p> or <p> and </p>. These HTML tags create a paragraph on a page.

<script> and </script>. These HTML tags begin and end a script block in a Web page.

==. The comparison operator. This compares two values and is evaluated to "true" if they are equal and false if they are not.

A

ABAB reversal design. A single-case experimental design that measures baseline stages (A). Treatment is then introduced (B) and withdrawn (A) again. This design attempts to incorporate experimenter control by introducing treatment and taking it away two or more times to determine treatment effect.

ABBA counterbalancing. A counterbalancing technique to control for practice and testing effects where one order (AB) is followed by the next order (BA).

Abstract. A summary of the research the authors conducted.

Accidental sample. See convenience sample.

Accuracy. Measures used must be accurate and precise.

Active server page (ASP). A technology for processing interactive Web pages (such as surveys) on a Web server.

Age ranges. Using categories of ages in a survey rather than the exact age.

Alert message. A message that appears on the screen when some action has happened.

All Caps. Converts the text into all capital letters.

Alpha level (α). Generally accepted is .05. The alpha level provides the cut off point that dictates how much error you are willing to accept; the probability at which a null hypothesis is rejected. The smaller the alpha level the more stringent the test will be.

Analysis of variance (ANOVA). A common parametric statistical test designed to examine the difference between two or more means. A one-way ANOVA tests the differences in means in one independent variable. A factorial ANOVA measures mean differences among two or more independent variables.

Applied research. Research concerned with the practical application of research findings.

Apply Styles window. Part of the task pane the deals with applying styles.

Archival data (archives). Any existing records or archives that are public record. These might include media, community, state, government documents, or other running records. Archival data are used most often in conjunction with multiple methods of assessment.

Arial, Helvetica, sans-serif. A commonly used type family that tells the browser to display the text in any generic sans-serif type face.

Array. A data structure similar to a table that consists of a group of values.

Aspect ratio. The ratio of a picture's width to its height.

Attach Style Sheet. Linking a style sheet to a page so that the styles on the sheet become available to format objects on the page.

B

Back-end tasks. Refers to the tasks that are done on the server when a survey is submitted; most often refers to saving the data in a database.

Base 10. A system of representing numbers with 10 figures. The numerals 0–9 are used to represent numbers in base 10. A computer works in base 2.

Baseline. Behavior before intervention is presented.

Basement effect. The lowest limit of performance that can be assessed or measured by an instrument or process. Individuals who perform near to or below this limit are said to have reached the basement, and the assessment may not be providing a valid estimate of their performance levels.

Basic research. Research conducted to address essential questions about human behavior. Questions might relate to thinking, learning, memory, biology, personality, and social behavior.

Behavioral measures. Response to stimuli that can be measured through direct observation.

Beneficence. An ethical standard that suggests that researchers "do no harm," be it physical or psychological, and treat participants with respect.

Between-subjects design. An experimental design that randomly assigns participants to one group who are tested only once.

Blind. Participants or researchers are unaware of the experimenters' hypothesis.

Block randomization. A technique used to balance participant characteristics and potential confounds by randomly assigning participants to groups in such a way that the groups are equal in size.

Blocking unsafe expressions. An error message that frequently appears when a database is opened in Access.

Bonferroni. A multiple-comparison correction used when several dependent or independent statistical tests are being performed simultaneously.

Bookmarks. Links on a Web page that, when clicked, take the user to a different location on the same Web page.

C

Cascading Style Sheet (CSS). A collection of styles that are created by the survey author to control the look of objects on a Web page.

Ceiling effect. The highest limit of performance that can be assessed or measured by an instrument or process. Individuals who perform near to or above this upper limit are said to have reached the ceiling, and the assessment may not be providing a valid estimate of their performance levels.

Cell padding. The amount of space between the edge of each cell and the text inside the cell. In most surveys this should be set to zero pixels.

Cell spacing. The amount of space between the cells of the table. This also is set to zero pixels.

Checklists. Checklists can be used as a data collection method. Participants or researchers can check off the presence or absence of an event or behavior.

Chi square. A non-parametric statistical technique for categorical variables.

Chronbach's alpha. A common measure of internal scale reliability (consistency).

Chunking. Divides the information presented on a page into sections. Each section should contain about 4–5 questions, enough to fit on one screen; this is an amount that a person can reasonably complete in a short time.

Citations. References that include the author's name, date of publication, where it was published, and page number.

Class="style1." Code in a HTML tag that assigns a style, "style1," to that tag.

Clear Styles. Command that removes the HTML style from an object.

Close-ended questions. Questions whose response formats are made up by the researcher. Closed-ended questions are analogous to multiple choice questions on a test in that participants are provided with responses to choose from.

Cluster sampling. Used when there is no sampling frame available for the group of participants you want to study.

Code view. A view of a Web page that shows just the code that defines the page.

Coding the input controls. Assigning variables and setting the properties of input controls that have been added to a survey.

Cohen's effect size. A calculation for effect size where values range from 0 to 1 and the value obtained demonstrates the amount of variance the independent variable accounts for in the dependent variable.

Common toolbar. A toolbar consisting of frequently used tools. This toolbar consists of formatting tools (such as type face, size, and alignment); list commands (bullet list and numbered list); commands to save and create new pages; and commands to create hyperlinks, and so on.

Comparison operator. The operator "==" compares two values and is evaluated to "true" if they are equal and false if they are not.

Concatenation. The joining of two text items together.

Conditions (or treatments). The values assigned to the independent variable. Participants are randomly assigned to only one of various possible experimental conditions so that each person is assigned to only one group (or condition).

Confidence interval. A term used by researchers when making determinations as to how similar the sample mean is to the population mean. Population scores fall within a range of values as dictated by a specified confidence level.

Confirmation bias. A social psychological term that refers to potential bias an experimenter brings to a study.

Confirmation page. A page that shows when a survey has been successfully submitted to the server. It indicates to respondents that they have completed the survey and the results have been processed.

Confounds. Variables that are not controlled or experimental.

Consent form or page. Information pertaining to the basic procedures that will take place in the study, research, or survey. This should include how long (expected duration) it will take participants to complete the act as well as the basic procedures that will take place. Lays out the purpose of the survey, the uses of the data, how the respondent's privacy will be protected, and any technical considerations (such as browser compatibility, settings, and so forth) that are required to successfully complete the survey.

Construct validity. The extent to which the measure truly captures the theoretical construct it is designed to measure.

Content analysis. A procedure that researchers use primarily with archival data to objectively examine existing information and make inferences pertaining to the research question.

Continuous scale. Rating scales (i.e., Likert-type) used where participants choose numeric values that underlie a continuum of a construct (such as age, attitudes, etc). Interval and ratio data would be considered continuous data.

Control group. In an experiment, the group of subjects that do not receive the treatment (independent variable).

Convergent validity. When two variables (or scales) are similar and correlated to one another, they exhibit convergent validity.

Convenience sample. A non-probability sampling technique where samples are obtained from individuals willing and able to respond to your study.

Cookies. Text that is placed on the computer when a page is visited. Only the site that created the cookie can read it and write to it. It can be used to prevent rapid resubmissions of surveys.

Correlation. Exists when two variables vary together. When scores on one variable correlate with another variable, we say the variables are correlated (or related).

Correlational designs. Designs that do not manipulate variables but rather seek to describe behaviors or events as they occur naturally and to identify relationships between variables.

Counterbalancing. Systematically varying the presentation of conditions.

Cross-sectional survey research designs. One or more samples is obtained from different populations all at once.

Cross-tabs. Two categorical variables are provided in a contingency table that allow researchers to examine frequency analyses of scores or percentages.

D

Database. Software that stores a collection of data. The easiest way to think of a database is as a table. A table consists of rows and columns. In a database, each row is a single respondent's responses to the survey. Each column in the table is a variable that will store the input from a specific question in the survey.

Debriefing statements. Statements that fully disclose to the participants of research the true nature and purpose of a research project after its completion.

Deception. Researchers sometimes intentionally withhold information or deceive participants regarding the true nature of the research.

default.htm or **index.htm.** The name of the first page that will be displayed in a Web site.

Degrees of freedom. Any of the unrestricted, independent random variables that constitute a statistic.

Dependent variable. A measure of the effect or outcome of a treatment or independent variable.

Descriptive methods. Study designs that allow researchers to examine characteristics of variables.

Descriptive statistics. Describe the nature of your sample and can be computed to describe what is typical of groups or the characteristics of your sample.

Descriptors. Each database uses specific key words (descriptors) that can be found in the thesaurus. These descriptors can be used to identify key topics of the research.

Design view. View of a Web page where the text and graphics are displayed in a manner roughly equivalent to how it will show in a browser. The design view allows the page creator to add text and graphics to a page and see how it will look.

Diffusion of treatment. This can occur when participants who are placed into an experimental condition change their behavior because of real or perceived information that they have obtained about the other research conditions.

Discrete categories. A categorical way of obtaining information, for example, when offering a participant categorical options such as "yes," "no," or "other."

Distribute columns evenly. When working with tables this command forces the columns to be of equal width on the page.

Divergent validity. Measures (surveys) are compared to determine whether they are correlated or differ from each other. The amount that the measures differ is the amount they exhibit divergent validity.

Document window. An area of the Expression program interface where surveys and other pages will be created. The document window has a white background and resembles a piece of paper. Text, graphics, forms, and the like can be added to the page.

document.write(). A command that writes information to the screen in a script. What it writes to the screen is placed inside the parentheses and enclosed in double quotation marks.

Domain names. Unique names that are associated with the numerical address (or IP address) of a Web page.

Double-barreled questions. Those questions that are actually addressing two or more issues.

Double-blind procedure. Experimenters and participants are blind to the treatment conditions; this procedure limits experimenter effects and reactivity.

Drop-down box. A form control that has a list of responses that appear when the user clicks a down arrow.

Duration. The amount of time it takes to complete a response once the user has begun. This can be the time it takes to solve problem, answer a question, or finish a response.

E

Effect size. 1: Measures the strength of the relationship between the independent and dependent variables regardless of the size of the sample. 2: Comparing results across studies allows one to calculate the magnitude of a relationship between an intervention and an outcome.

else() statement. See *If, Then, Else statements*

Empirical. We base our knowledge simply on observations.

Event. Some action in the browser window. Examples include onload (when to page loads into memory), onclick (when an object is clicked), ondoubleclick (when an object is double-clicked), and so on.

Experiment. A study in which an experimenter observes the manipulation effects of changes in an independent variable over a dependent variable. Only experiments can corroborate the existence of cause-and-effect relations among variables.

Experimental control. A necessary element of the scientific method that uses manipulation, holding conditions constant, and balancing to isolate effects of variables.

Experimental designs. Experimental designs use random assignment and experimental control to determine whether the independent variable affected the dependent variable. Experiments have three unique characteristics, and conditions include treatment and control conditions. An independent variable is manipulated (treatment group) by the experimenter; the experimenter utilizes methods to control for possible error; and a control group is used to compare the effectiveness of a treatment.

Experimental group (treatment group). In an experiment, the group of subjects that receives the treatment (independent variable).

Experimenter effects. Any potential biases that the experimenter brings into the study.

Experimental pilot. Piloting or pre-testing the strength of an experimental manipulation that helps researchers identify problems before they put their study online.

External validity. This occurs when findings are replicated across different populations. This also means that research can be generalized across several other groups, individuals, situations, and so forth.

Extraneous variable. Any potential variable that can confound your results and affect the outcome of your study. Researchers can control for some extraneous variables by thinking about them during the planning stage, measuring, and statistically controlling for variables that can confound your study.

F

Fabrication. When a researcher makes up conclusions and results and either records or reports them.

Factor. Another term for independent variable, particularly when using experimental designs.

Factor analysis. A statistical technique used when constructing a scale or survey to determine how data expressed as values or measurements are transformed into linear combinations called factors. A multivariate extension of scale reliability with primary goals of data reduction and identifying underlying constructs.

Factorial designs (or complex designs). Experimental designs that examine two or more independent variables (factors) and allow researchers to explore potential interactions between variables.

Filter questions. Those questions used in a survey to determine whether additional questions will be asked.

Firefox, Opera, and Safari. Browsers that can be used to access the Internet.

Firewalls. A system of software and hardware designed to prevent unauthorized access to a network.

Focus group. A method to obtain data. Focus groups are typically used when you are not sure what the important questions or issues may be.

Font color button. A button on the common toolbar of Expression that controls the color of text.

Forced choice. Surveys that offer forced options for participants to answer (yes-no) or questions similar to multiple choice formats.

Form. An area on a Web page that contains the controls that a user uses to input opinions and data. All data that are to be submitted in the survey should be in a form and there should be only one form per Web page.

Form control(s). Any of a variety of devices that, when placed on a Web page within a form, allow the user to input information into a survey. Examples include text boxes, option buttons, check boxes, text areas, and submit buttons.

Form properties. Settings for a form that designate how the information in the form will be processed, what will happen in the browser window after the form is processed, what type of database the form will send its data to, and so on.

fpdb folder. The folder that is created by Expression to hold the Access database that will contain information that is uploaded to the server.

Frequency. How often a behavior occurs, how long a behavior lasts, or the latency of a response.

Function. 1: A script (or block of code) that is designed to do a specific task on a Web page. A function is written in the code of the page and is triggered by an event. 2: A set of ordered pairs in which none of the first elements of the pairs appears twice. 3: A variate produced from a linear combinaton of variables where the difference between groups is maximized for that variate.

Funnel ordering. A natural flow of questions leading from general to more specific information.

G

GIF. A graphic format that greatly reduces the size of a file. It is useful for buttons and banners.

Global variable. A variable that is created outside of any function. It retains its value when any specific function ends.

global.asa. A special file created by Expression to hold the settings that the form needs to connect to the database.

Greater than minimal risk. Participants are assumed to be greater than minimal risk if they are a protected population or there is the possibility for them to be hurt physically or psychologically in a research study.

Guttman technique. A measure for scale reliability for ordinal data.

H

Head section. Part of the code that defines a Web page. The head section loads into the computer's memory first.

Hexadecimals. Numbers expressed in base sixteen.

Heterogeneous populations. Those populations which are diverse or dissimilar.

Hidden field. A field in a survey form that is not seen by the user of the form. It often has a fixed value.

Historical events. Shared events that occur outside of the study.

Holding conditions constant. All variables—such as setting of the experiment, experimental stimuli (except for manipulation), participant instructions, room, or interviewers—are all the same.

Homogeneity of variance. Equality of groups. The assumption that the variance of two sets of numbers are equal.

Homogeneous populations. Those populations that share similar characteristics.

HTML. A coding language that defines a Web page, HyperText Markup Language tells the browser software how to display the information on the page and what happens when a user clicks different elements on the page.

HTML tags. HTML code that defines how an element will look and what happens when the object is clicked.

Human subjects review boards (HSRB). See *Institutional review boards (IRB)*.

Hyperlink. An element on a Web page. It consists of two parts: the link you are to click, and the destination page you will be brought to in response to that click.

Hypothesis. A tentative explanation (a question that is waiting for evidence that refutes or supports the hypothesis) that can be tested.

I

I, Then, Else statements. JavaScript code that sets up a branching action as a result of some value. The Else statement is optional. The If statement is a test that evaluates to true or false. An example would be If(A == 10).

If A has the value of 10, the statement is true. Whatever is specified next will then be executed (this is the Then part of the statement). If A is not equal to 10, the statement is false. If there is no Else statement, then nothing else happens in the function. If there is an Else statement, then that is executed.

Incidence. The number of new cases of a disorder reported during a specific time period.

Independent variable. The variable of interest that is considered to be the cause of the results. In an experiment, researchers control or manipulate this variable.

Inferential statistics. Used to test hypotheses and assist researchers in interpreting their data.

Informed consents. Forms provided to potential participants as a vehicle to make an decisions on whether or not to participate in the study.

Input (Checkbox Box). An input control that a user can check. A checkbox can be checked or not. If there is more than one checkbox, they function independently.

Input (Radio). An input control that a user can check. An option button comes on a page in groups. The group of option buttons can have one checked at a time. If another button in the same group is checked, then the first is unchecked.

Input (Submit). The submit button initiates the processing of the survey.

Input (Text). An input control that allows a user to type text into a survey.

Institutional review boards (IRB). Most institutions have an ethics review board that assesses the ethicality of the research plan before it is executed.

Instrumentation effects. Instruments can become dated or inaccurate and should be assessed to determine whether threats to validity are due to problems associated with instrumentation.

Integrity. Individuals conducting research should be "honest, fair, and respectful of others" (APA, 1992) while understanding how their own values or biases can affect the research.

Interactions. What occurs when one level of one independent variable differs across another level of another independent variable.

Internal hyperlinks. See *Bookmarks*.

Internal scale reliability. Measuring the consistency (or relationship) among scale items.

Internal validity. The extent to which experimenters can be confident that the change in the dependent variable is due to the effects of the independent variable and not some other explanation. Internal validity takes into consideration the subject, testing, and environment in which the data collection took place.

Interrater reliability. The extent to which two raters agree upon what they are rating.

Interval scale. A scale of any measurement possessing equal magnitudes and equal intervals, but not at an absolute zero.

IP address. The unique number assigned to every computer connected to the Internet. Computers send information on the Internet to these numbers.

J

JavaScript. A scripting language that is used to give Web pages advanced capabilities.

JPEG or jpg. A graphic format that was designed to give photographs excellent quality when viewed on the Internet.

Jump. Moving to another part of a survey based on a user's response to a question. An example might be a set of questions when the subject reports being male and a different set of questions for female subjects.

Justice. All participants should be treated equally and afforded equal opportunities.

L

Latency. The amount of time between the time the stimulus is presented and the time taken to respond.

Levine's test for homogeneity. A test to determine if variances are equal.

Levine's Test for Equality of Variance. A statistic designed to measure equality of groups.

Likert scale. A scale in which respondents indicate their level of agreement with statements that express a favorable or unfavorable attitude toward a concept being measured.

Likert-type. See *Continuous scale.*

Linux. An operating system that is frequently used for Web servers. It is available to anyone at no cost (though the technical assistance and documentation may have a cost).

Loaded questions. Questions using words that can be emotionally laden, such as "radical," "homophobic," or "racist."

Local Web site. A Web site that is developed on your computer without using a server.

Logistic regression. A non-parametric statistical technique used to predict the presence or absence of characteristics or determine an outcome based on values of a set of predictor variables. The dependent variable must be dichotomous (two categories) and independent variables can be any scale of measurement.

Longitudinal designs. Survey designs that follow the same people over time.

M

Manage Styles. A tab in the Apply Styles task pane that allows the developer to manipulate styles, create new styles, and duplicate styles.

Manipulation checks. Assessments of the extent to which experimenter manipulation was successful.

Margin of error. See *Sampling error.*

Matched pair designs. Matches participants on important dependent variable characteristics to create groups than can compared.

Math.random(), Math.round(), Math.ceil(), and Math.floor(). Methods that perform mathematical operations on a value. Math.random() generates a random number between 0 and 1. Math.round() rounds the number off to a specified number of decimal places. Math.ceil() rounds a number up to the next higher value. Math.floor() rounds a value down to the next lower value.

Maturation. A threat to internal validity that can be a significant problem to researchers when studying individuals over a period of time during which physical and mental maturation can take place.

mdb file extension. The three-letter extension given to Access databases.

Mean. A measure that represents the average score.

Measures of central tendency. Measures used to summarize data (i.e., mean, median, mode).

Median. An average score representing the midpoint (or 50th percentile) of a score.

Method. A routine that performs some function on a value. For examples see Math.random().

Microsoft Access. A relational database management system from Microsoft. Expression will create Access databases to hold the data from a survey automatically.

Microsoft Expression. A Web development tool that is used to create, edit, and manipulate Web sites and pages.

Minimal risk. Any risk that a participant would normally encounter in everyday life.

Mixed designs. Experiments that include both between-subjects variables and within-subjects variables.

Mode. The number that occurs most often in a data set.

Mortality. Rate of participants that drop out of your study for some reason or another.

Mozilla Firefox. A free Web browser available at www.mozilla.com.

Multi-group design. Experiment that includes one or more independent variables with more than two groups (levels).

Multiple baselines across individuals or situations. Single-case designs are conducted that examine individuals or situations to determine whether changes occur from baseline as a result of intervention.

Multiple regression. A statistical technique used to analyze relationships between multiple independent variables (predictors) and a single continuous dependent variable.

Multivariate analysis of variance (MANOVA). An extension of ANOVA that has categorical independent variables and multiple dependent variables. MANOVA is a statistical test that measures varying group effects on many dependent variables.

Multivariate statistics. A set of statistical tools to analyze data matrices using regression or pattern recognition techniques.

Mutually exclusive. If a participant is in one category, he or she cannot be included in another category.

N

New Style dialog. A dialog box that allows you to define any of the attributes of text or an object.

No thank you page. Shown after a user declines to participate in a survey, this page thanks participants for their time and consideration and provides alternate means for the respondent to contact the survey sponsor (e-mail, surface mail, phone number, and so forth).

Nominal variable. A scale of measurement that is categorical in nature.

Non-equivalent control group. Designs that use already existing groups and compare them. Therefore, the control group does not have the same characteristics as the experimental group.

Non-malfeasance. An ethical motto all researchers should abide: "Do no harm."

Non-parametric statistics. Statistics that do not directly test hypotheses using population parameters. Non-parametric tests are considered distribution-free techniques, where the validity of the test statistics is not a function of the distribution of the actual data.

Non-probability sampling. All members of the sample do not have an equal opportunity to be included in the sample. This includes convenience and purposive sampling procedures.

Normal distribution. A theoretical frequency distribution represented by a normal curve.

not equal to (≠). An operator used within the script of an HTML code.

Null hypothesis. Assumes no differences (equality) between groups.

O

Object. Text, graphics, a table, and so on. Styles can control almost every aspect of the object, including type face, type style, alignment, color, background color, and border color.

Observer bias. When researchers are aware of the hypothesis, this may bias their interpretation of the data.

One shot. See *Cross-sectional survey research designs*.

Onload event. When a page is loaded into a browser.

Onclick event. When an object, such as a button, is clicked by the user.

Open-ended question. Similar to an essay question, this type of question format allows respondents to write their answers freely.

Opera browser. An alternative free browser to Internet Explorer or Firefox. The browser can be downloaded at www.opera.com.

Operational definitions. Researchers must be careful to define the variables to be measured.

Order effects (sequence effects). The possibility that the order of the stimuli can affect an individual's response.

Ordinal. Measures of these variables are considered to be ranked on a continuum underlying some classification system. The values can be categorized from first to last, from long to short, or from top to bottom.

Outlier. A value far from most others in a set of data.

P

Page title. An element of a Web page that is found in the head section. The page title shows at the top of a browser window.

Paired t-test. A parametric statistic used to examine two related groups (pre-post test) or two matched groups to determine whether differences exist or whether an intervention brought about a change in some characteristic of the respondent.

Parametric statistics. Inferential statistics based on hypothesis testing and the assumption that data is normally distributed.

Partial correlation. Typically used to examine the extent to which a third variable might be affecting the correlation results. Partial correlations allow researchers to control for effects of a third variable.

Participant privacy. All participants have the right to privacy. It is the researchers' responsibility to maintain anonymity and confidentiality of data by keeping all data in a secure area not accessible to others; nor should any data have identifying information anywhere in the surveys.

Pearson product-moment correlation. Examining the magnitude and direction of relationships between two variables. As long as the variables are measured continuously (interval or ratio) then a Pearson Correlation can be used to assess potential relationships between variables.

Physical measures. Those elements that we can physically examine and have an accepted standard for how things are measured (such as height, weight, time, and so forth).

Physiological measures. Measurements of physiological responses such as heart rate, perspiration, breathing, and so on.

Pictures and graphics. Images of all kinds used in Web pages. In general, a picture is taken with a camera and a graphic is created with a drawing program.

Pictures toolbar. A toolbar that contains all of the tools available in Expression for working with images.

Pilot. Testing your study before it is implemented to a larger sample. Testing can help identify problems and provide feedback to researchers. Piloting is also necessary in an experiment to examine the strength of the experimental manipulation.

Placebo. An inert substance that looks like the drug being tested but has no therapeutic effects.

Plagiarism. Stealing another person's ideas or work and passes it off as your own.

Population. All possible participants of interest in your study.

Predictions. Statements referring to the future.

Pretest/posttest. A common research technique that measures individuals before and after an intervention or treatment.

Prevalence. The frequency of a disorder in a particular population.

Primary and secondary resource. The resource that publishes the original research study. Research in primary resources will provide detailed information according to the authors.

Probability sampling. Every person has an equal chance to be included in your study. There are three probability sampling approaches (simple random sampling, stratified random sampling, and cluster sampling).

Production server. The ultimate place where a Web survey will reside once it is completed. Web developers will usually work on a development server, where the security settings are somewhat looser. When the site is done it will then be moved to a production server.

Progress indicators. Graphics or text that indicate to users how far along they are in completing the survey.

Psychological harm or stress. Researchers must evaluate the extent to which their research may cause psychological harm or stress to participants. Precautions should be taken to eliminate or reduce the potential for psychological harm or stress.

Psychological measures. Agreed-on or accepted standard ways to assess more abstract concepts such as personality, beauty, or intelligence. Psychological measures do not assess physical attributes, but rather constructs that have been agreed on by observers that in some way provide a measure of the concept.

Pt or **points.** A measurement system for the size of type. A point is 1/72 of an inch.

Public domain. Existing data that is considered public (i.e., media sources) that can be used for research.

Publishing the site. In Expression this is the command to move a site to another location on the Internet. It may be from a development to a production server.

Purposive sampling. A technique for choosing the people you want to be included in your study based on particular characteristics they may have.

Q

Quasi-experimental design. A type of experiment conducted in the real world and not a laboratory which therefore lacks experimental control.

Query string. A URL encoded with a list of variables that the Web server receives.

Questionnaire. See *Survey.*

Quick Select Area. The area above the document area in Expression where the HTML tags used in the document are displayed. Clicking the tag allows the user to select the object on the page.

R

Random block design. A common research technique created before your research is presented to participants to obtain random assignment and control for order effects.

Random block schedule. The result of a random block design that provides a group of random blocks that include one trial of each condition in the experiment.

Random groups design. Once participants have been randomly selected to participate in your study, they are randomly assigned to either treatment or experimental group. Everyone in the experiment has an equal chance of being assigned to either treatment or control group.

Random number. The number generated in the fourth line used in surveys.

Random sample. In a random sample, each person has an equal chance of participating in the research study.

Ratio scales. Scales that have an absolute zero point and are separated by equal intervals. Scales measuring physical attributes of objects, weight, and width are just few examples of ratio scales.

Reactivity (demand characteristics). Another threat to external validity that suggests individuals react to the presence of the experimenter.

Regression. The relationship between the mean value of a random variable and the corresponding values of one or more independent variables.

Regression to the mean. A threat to the internal validity that can occur when subjects are selected based on extreme scores.

Reliability. The degree to which a test is consistent.

Reliable. Consistency across time and populations.

Remote Web site. The location where you publish a Web site.

Repeated-measures design (or dependent groups design). Participants are assigned to all conditions of the experiment, and are measured after receiving all levels of the experiment.

Representative sample. A sample that is truly represents the characteristics of the greater population or individuals you are studying.

Resample. A process that reduces the size of the file for the Web.

Resolution. The amount of information that can be displayed on the screen and is measured by the number of pixels that can be displayed in the horizontal dimension (such as 800) by the number of pixels in the vertical dimension (such as 600).

Respect. This principle states that researchers must value a person's autonomy. Participants must be treated as autonomous individuals capable of making their own conscious decisions whether to participate in research.

Response set. If all questions have the same anchor there is a potential for participants to go down the survey clicking the same response without paying attention to the questions.

Risk-benefit analysis. Researchers should always weigh the risks and benefits to participants and to society before conducting any research. Benefits should always outweigh risks to participants.

S

Safari browser. A free alternative browser from Apple Corporation. It can be downloaded at www.apple.com.

Sample. A subset of individuals from a population.

Sampling error. Lets you know how well your sample matches the population. In essence, the difference between sample and population estimates. A small margin of error suggests there is little difference between your sample and the population.

Sampling frame. The actual population of people (or clusters of people) from which your sample will be drawn; for example, the registrar's list of students attending a college.

Sans-serif typeface. A typeface that does not have embellishments at the ends of letters. It is a very clean and easy-to-read look.

Scale reliability (or **Cronbach's alpha reliability).** Examines the relationships between items on a scale of a self-report measure.

Secondary resource. A source that mentions or cites original research conducted by someone else, or simply describes the findings of another research study.

Self-report measures. Those measures to which individuals respond on their own. Participants provide all necessary information by self-reporting attitudes and behaviors.

Semantic differential scale. A 7-point scale that includes a list of adjectives where one side of the scale is one adjective and the other side of the scale is the extreme opposite.

Semi-structured interview. An interview technique that guides participants along in the question-answer period. Interviewers ask questions in a specified manner, ensuring each question is answered to the best of the respondent's ability.

Sensitivity of an experiment. The strength of the independent variable on the dependent variable when experimental error is reduced, and variables are held constant.

Simple random sampling. The most basic sampling technique. With this technique every person has an equal chance of being included in your sample. If there are ten thousand people in your proposed sample, then you coordinate a randomized system so that each person can be included.

Single-case design. Sometimes known as *applied behavioral analysis,* this design introduces an independent variable (or treatment) to one person (n = 1) and measures that person repeatedly.

Skewed distribution. A disproportionate number of scores fall toward the upper or lower end of the distribution. The shape of the distribution of scores is not normal; the curve is asymmetrical; the mean, median, and mode will not be at the same point.

Soft return. Forces the text onto two lines but doesn't add the extra space between paragraphs associated with a normal return. A soft return is created by holding down the Shift key while you hit Enter.

Spam blocker. A program used to detect any unsolicited or unwanted e-mail in your mail program's inbox. This prevents spam messages from getting into your inbox. A spam blocker will filter through messages based on certain criteria.

Spearman rank order correlation. A non-parametric statistical test for correlation between two rank-ordered scales. It yields a statement of the degree of interdependence of the scores of the two scales.

Split cells. A command that allows you to divide an existing table cell into additional rows or columns.

Split-half reliability. A measure of consistency where a test is split in two and the scores for each half of the test are compared with one another.

Split view. A view of the page in design view beside a view of the underlying code.

Standard deviation. A measure of dispersion in a frequency distribution, equal to the square root of the mean of the squares of the deviations from the arithmetic mean of the distribution.

Statistical power. The sensitivity of an experiment's ability to identify whether the independent variable was truly effective in changing the dependent variable. Statistical power is dependent upon sample size.

Statistical significance (the *p* value). Outcomes that reject the null hypothesis as differences among groups are greater than chance. The *p* value examines the probability that the observed mean difference (or relationship) between variables in a sample occurred by chance.

Stratified random sampling. In this procedure your population is divided up into sub-populations called strata, and random samples are then drawn from each of these strata. The larger the standard deviation, the more spread out the scores are, reflecting individual differences.

Structural tags. HTML codes that give style to text on a page. The tags <**H1**>**example**</**H1**> would make the word *example* show on the screen in bold and large type.

Style sheet. A collection of styles that can govern how objects on a Web page will look. See *Cascading Style Sheet*.

Style tags. Built-in formats that can be used to change the way text looks in a browser.

Styles. A collection of settings for objects on a page.

Subweb. A sub-part of an existing Web. The domain name is *xyz.edu*. A subweb could be *surveys.xyz.edu*—surveys would be the subweb on the domain name *xyz* and the extension *edu* indicates that it is an educational institution.

Submit button. This will trigger the processing of the information to the Web server. After clicking the Submit button, the user is brought to a confirmation page.

Successive independent samples design. Independent samples of a cross section of the population are given the same survey. Also see *cross-sectional design*.

Survey (or questionnaire). An instrument that assesses individuals' self-reports of behaviors, thoughts, attitudes, opinions, and feelings.

Survey plan. Shows all of the elements of the survey and should take into consideration all of the respondents' possible answers at each point in the survey. It should also show the sequence of pages that the respondent will see based on what they answer.

Systematic sampling. A random sampling procedure where participants are selected based on numeric intervals.

T

Tag. HTML code that tells the browser how to display the content of the page.

Task panes. Areas in Expression at the sides of the document window. Various task panes are available. The task pane gives specific information about the site, a page, or items on the page.

Temporal precedence. The first of three scientific method elements; the cause must precede the event, or the cause must come before the event or outcome.

Testing effects. Taking one test can affect subsequent tests and can be a threat to internal validity.

Testing the survey. Taking the survey repeatedly to ensure that all of the control elements are coded correctly and working as expected.

Test-retest reliability. If respondents are tested once, the scores on one test should be similar to subsequent tests.

Text area box. An input device that allows the user to type information into a survey. They are often used instead of a text box, because they allow the user to input a great deal more information.

Theory. An explanation for research findings.

Time sampling. When observers systematically or randomly choose times to make observations.

Time-series design. Data collected on a single variable over a period of time. Time-series designs should include non-equivalent control groups to improve validity and comparing treatment to a non-equivalent group.

Treatment group. See *Experimental group.*

T-test for independent groups. A statistical test designed to measure differences between two independent groups. T-test for Independence is a statistical test designed to measure mean differences between two independent groups.

Type I error. The possibility of rejecting the null hypothesis when the null hypothesis is true.

Type II error. The possibility of accepting the null hypothesis when the null hypothesis is false.

V

Valid. Measuring what is supposed to be measured; measuring the "truthfulness" of a construct.

Valign. The vertical alignment of the selected cell.

Var. Command in JavaScript that creates a variable.

Variability. The extent to which scores vary (spread) around the mean.

Variable. Something that changes or varies.

Variable scope. See *Global variable.*

Variance. A statistical term that represents the average squared distance from the mean; square of the standard deviation.

Visio 2007. Diagramming software for Microsoft Windows.

W

Web servers. Computers connected to the Internet that hold and send out pages to browsers.

Wildcard. A symbol used in a library database that uses the root word to bring up all forms of that word.

Window properties or modifiers. When a new window is created the properties of the window can be modified or specified by the script code.

Windows Server. An operating system created by Microsoft for use on Web and other servers. Windows-based servers have the advantage of working very closely and seamlessly with Microsoft Expression and making complicated tasks much easier.

Z

Z score. A measure that quantifies the distance between a data point and the mean of a data set; a standardized score that indicates how participants scored, relative to other participants. A positive Z score indicates the participant scored above the mean and a negative score suggests the participant scored below the mean. The size of the Z score indicates how far from the mean the individual scored.

REFERENCES

Advogato.org. (2008, January). *Digital divide.* Retrieved January 8, 2008, from www.advogato.org/article/411.html.

Allard, G., Butler, J., Shea, M. T., & Faust, D. (2002). Errors in hand scoring objective personality tests: The case of the Personality Diagnostic Questionnaire-Revised (PDQ-R). *Professional Psychology: Research and Practice, 26,* 304–308.

American Psychological Association. (2002). Ethical principles of psychologists and code of conduct. *American Psychologist, 57,* 1060–1073.

Anderson, T., & Kanuka, H. (2003). *E-research: Methods, strategies, and issues.* Boston: Pearson.

Appleby, G. (2001). Framework for practice with working-class gay and bisexual men. *Journal of Gay & Lesbian Social Services: Issues in Practice, Policy & Research, 12*(3–4), 5–46.

Aron, A., & Aron, E. N. (1994). *Statistics for psychology.* Upper Saddle River, NJ: Prentice Hall.

Ballard, C., & Prine, R. (2002). Citizen perceptions of community policing: Comparing Internet and mail survey responses. *Social Science Computer Review, 20,* 485–493.

Bassett, E. H., & O'Riordan, K. (2002). Ethics of Internet research: Contesting the human subjects model. *Journal of Ethics and Information Technology, 4,* 233–247.

Beck, A. T., & Steer, R. A. (1987). *Manual for the Beck Depression Inventory.* San Antonio, TX: The Psychological Corporation.

Beede, K. E., & Kass, S. J. (2006). Engrossed in conversation: The impact of cell phones on simulated driving performance. *Accident Analysis & Prevention, 38*(2), 415–421.

Bem, S. L. (1985). Androgyny and gender schema theory: A conceptual and empirical investigation. *Nebraska symposium on gender: Psychology of gender,* pp. 179–226.

Birnbaum, M. H. (2004) Human research and data collection via the Internet. *Annual Review of Psychology, 55,* 803–832.

Bosnjak, M., & Tuten, T. L. (2003). Prepaid and promised incentives in Web surveys: An experiment. *Social Science Computer Review, 21*(2), 208–217.

Bouchard, T. J., Jr., Lykken, D. T., McGue, M., Segal, N. L., & Tellegen, A. (1990). Sources of human psychological differences: The Minnesota study of twins reared apart. *Science, 250,* 223–228.

Brown, T. (2003). Internet research: Self-monitoring and judgments of attractiveness. *Behavior Research Methods, Instruments, and Computers, 32,* 521–527.

Brown v. Board of Education et al., 347 U.S. 483 (1954).

Buchanan, T. (2002). Online assessment: Desirable or dangerous? *Professional Psychology: Research and Practice, 33,* 148–154.

Buros Institute of Mental Measurements. (2007). *The seventeenth mental measurements yearbook.* K. F. Geisinger, R. A. Spies, J. F. Carlson, & B. S. Plake (Eds.). Lincoln: University of Nebraska Press.

Butcher, J. N. (2003). Computerized psychological assessment. In J. R Graham & J. A. Naglieri (Eds.), *Handbook of psychology: Assessment psychology* (pp. 141–163). New York: Wiley.

Butcher, J. N., Perry, J. N., & Atlis, M. M. (2000). Validity and utility of computer-based test interpretation. *Psychological Assessment, 12,* 6–18.

Cho, C. H., & Khang, H. (2006). The state of Internet-related research in communications, marketing, and advertising: 1994–2003. *Journal of Advertising, 35*(3), 143–163.

Cohen, J. W. (1988). *Statistical power analysis for the behavioral sciences* (2nd ed.). Hillsdale, NJ: Erlbaum.

Cohen, J., & Cohen, P. (1983). *Applied multiple regression/correlation analysis for the behavioral sciences* (2nd ed.). Hillsdale, NJ: Erlbaum.

Cozby, P. C. (2001). *Methods in behavioral research* (7th ed.). Mountain View, CA: Mayfield.

Cozby, P. C. (2004). *Methods in behavioral research* (8th ed.). New York: McGraw-Hill.

Cronbach, L. J. (1951). Coefficient alpha and the internal structure of tests. *Psychometrika, 16*(3), 297–334.

Daniel, W. (1990). *Applied nonparametric statistics* (2nd ed.). Boston: PWS-Kent.

Davis, S. F., & Smith, R. (2005). *An introduction to statistics and research methods: Becoming a psychological detective.* Upper Saddle River, NJ: Pearson Prentice Hall.

Department of Health and Human Services. (1996). *Protection of human subjects* (Code of Federal Regulations 45 CFR 46). Washington, D.C.: DHHS.

Dillman, D. (2007). *Mail and Internet surveys: The tailored design method* (2nd ed.). New York: Wiley.

Dodd, D., Russell, B., & Jenkins, C. (1999). Smiling in school yearbook photographs: Gender differences from kindergarten to adulthood. *Psychological Record, 49*(4), 543–554.

Ecommerce Guide (2008). *Retail sales expected.* Retrieved January 8, 2008, from www.escalate.ca/news-003/online-retail-sales-expected-at-us-65-billion-dollars-in-2004.html.

Epstein, J., Klinkenberg, W. D., Wiley, D., & McKinley, L. (2001). Insuring sample equivalence across Internet and paper-and-pencil assessments. *Computer in Human Behavior, 17,* 339–346.

Ess, C., & Assocation of Internet Researchers. (2002). *Ethical decision-making and Internet research; Recommendations from the AoIR Ethics Working Committee.* Available from www.aoir.org/reports/ethics.pdf.

Festinger, L., Riecken, H., & Schachter, S. (1956). *When prophecy fails.* Minneapolis: University of Minnesota Press.

Finger, M. S., & Ones, D. S. (1999). Psychometric equivalence of the computer and booklet forms of the MMPI: A meta-analysis. *Psychological Assessment, 11,* 58–66.

Fowler, F. J., Jr. (1984). *Survey research methods.* Newbury Park, CA: Sage.

Fraley, R. C. (2004). *How to conduct behavioral research over the Internet.* New York: Guilford Press.

Gosling, S. D., Vazire, S., Srivastava, S., & John, O. (2004). Should we trust Web-based studies: A comparative analysis of six preconceptions about Internet questionnaires. *American Psychologist, 59*(2), 93–104.

Gravetter, F. J., & Forzano, L. A. (2003). *Research methods for the behavioral sciences.* Belmont, CA: Thomson Wadsworth.

Gray, R. J. (1999). New plans to investigate research misconduct and improve research integrity. *Professional Ethics Report, Fall 1999.* URL retrieved March 18, 2007 from www.aaas.org/spp/sfrl/per/per19.htm.

Graziano, A. M., & Raulin, M. L. (2004). *Research methods: A process of inquiry.* Boston: Pearson Education Group.

Green, S. B., & Salkind, N. J. (2003). *Using SPSS for Windows and Macintosh: Analyzing and understanding data.* Upper Saddle River, NJ: Prentice Hall.

Grimm, L. G., & Yarnold, P. R. (2001). *Reading and understanding multivariate statistics.* Washington, D. C.: American Psychological Association.

Hall, J. A. (1984). *Nonverbal sex differences: Accuracy of communication and expressive style.* Baltimore, MD: Johns Hopkins University Press.

Haney, C., Banks, W. C., & Zimbardo, P. G. (1973). Interpersonal dynamics in a simulated prison. *International Journal of Criminology and Penology, 1,* 69–97.

Heerwegh, D. (2004). Using progress indicators in Web surveys. *Annual Meeting of the American Association for Public Opinion Research.* Phoenix, Arizona.

Herek, G. M. (1988). Heterosexuals' attitudes toward lesbians and gay men: Correlates and gender differences. *The Journal of Sex Research, 25*(4), 451–471.

Jacklin, C., & Reynolds, C. (1993). Gender and childhood socialization. In A. E. Beall & R. J. Sternberg (Eds.), *The psychology of gender.* New York: Guilford Press.

Jackson, S. L. (2008). *Research methods: A modular approach.* Belmont, CA: Thomson.

James, J. M., & Bolstein, R. (1990). The effect of monetary incentives and follow-up mailings on the response rate and response quality in mail surveys. *Public Opinion Quarterly, 54*(3), 346–361.

Johnson, W., McGue, M., & Iacano, W. G. (2007). Socioeconomic status and school grades: Placing their association in broader context in a sample of biological and adoptive families. *Intelligence, 35*(6), 526–541.

JupiterOnlineMedia. (2007). *Resolution stats.* Retrieved August 9, 2007, from www.thecounter.com/stats/2007/August/res.php.

Kantowitz, B. H., Roediger, H. L., & Elmes, D. G. (1997). *Experimental psychology: Understanding psychological research* (6th ed.). Minneapolis/St. Paul: West Publishing Group.

Keith-Spiegel, P., & Koocher, G. P. (1985). *Ethics in psychology: Professional standards and cases.* New York: Crown Publishing Group/Random House.

Knapp, H., & Kirk, S. A. (2003). Using pencil and paper, Internet and touch-tones phones for self-administered surveys: Does methodology matter? *Computers in Human Behavior, 19*(1), 117–134.

Krantz, J. H., Ballard, J., & Scher, J. (1997). Comparing results of laboratory and world-wide samples of the determinants of female attractiveness. *Behavior Research Methods Instrument Computing, 29,* 264–69.

Kraus, R., Olson, J., Banaji, M., Bruckman, A., Cohen, J., & Couper, M. (2004). Psychological research online: report of board of scientific affairs' advisory group on conduct of research on the Internet. *American Psychologist, 59*(2), 105–117.

Landis, J. R., & Koch, G. G. (1977). The measure of observer agreement for categorical data. *Biometrics, 33,* 159–174.

Latane, B., & Darley, J. M. (1970). *The unresponsive bystander: Why doesn't he help?* (pp. 446–455). New York: Appleton-Century-Crofts.

Leedy, P. D., & Ormrod, J. E. (2005). *Practical research: Planning and design* (8th ed.). Upper Saddle River, NJ: Pearson Education.

Leider, S. (1999). Sexual minorities of community college campuses. ERIC Digest # ED447841. Eric Clearinghouse for Community Colleges, University of California at Los Angeles. Los Angeles, CA.

Loftus, E. F. (1979). *Eyewitness testimony.* Cambridge, MA: Harvard University Press.

Lomax, R. G. (2001). *Statistical concepts: A second course for education and the behavioral sciences* (2nd ed.). Hillsdale, NJ: Erlbaum.

Lott, B., & Maluso, D. (1993). The social learning of gender. In A. E. Beall & R. J. Sternberg (Eds.), *The psychology of gender.* New York: Guilford Press.

Microsoft Computer Dictionary. (2002). (5th ed.). Redmond, WA: Microsoft Press.

Milgram, S. (1963). Behavioral study of obedience. *The Journal of Abnormal Social Psychology, 67*(4), 371–378.

Myers, D. G. (2008). *Social psychology* (9th ed.). New York: McGraw Hill.

National Commission for the Protection of Human Subjects of Biomedical and Behavioral Research. (1979, April 18). *Belmont report: Ethical principles and guidelines for the protection of human subjects of research.* Retrieved, August 18, 2007, from http://ohsr.od.nih.gov/mpa/belmont.php3.

Naglieri, J. A., Drasgow, F., Schmit, M., Handler, L., Prifitera, A., Margolis, A., & Velasquez, R. (2004). Psychological testing on the Internet: New problems, old issues. *American Psychologist, 59*(3), 150–162.

Niederst, J. (2001). *Web design in a nutshell.* Sebastopol, CA: O'Reilly.

Nielsen/NetRatings. (2006). *Two-thirds of active U.S. Web population using broadband, up 28 percent year-over-year to an all time high, according to Nielsen/NetRatings.* Retrieved April 30, 2006 from the World Wide Web: www.nielsen-netratings.com.

Nunnally, J., & Bernstein, I., (Eds.). (1994). *Psychometric theory.* New York: McGraw-Hill.

Osgood, C. E., Suci, G. J., & Tannenbaum, P. H. (1957). *The measurement of meaning.* Urbana: University of Illinois Press.

Oswald, D., & Russell, B. (2006). Perceptions of sexual coercion in heterosexual dating relationships: The role of aggressor gender and tactics. *Journal of Sex Research, 43*(1), 87–95.

Pallant, J. (2001). *SPSS Survival manual: A step by step guide to data analysis using SPSS for windows (Version 10).* Philadelphia: Open University Press

Parsons, H. M. (1974). What happened at Hawthorne? *Science, 183,* 922–932.

Potosky, D., & Bobko, P. (2004). Selection testing via the Internet: Practical considerations and exploratory empirical findings. *Personnel Psychology, 57*(4), 1003–1034.

Pryor, J. B., Reeder, G. D., Patel, A. M., & Monroe, A. E. *The infection of bad company: Stigma-by-association as a function of implicit anti-stigma attitudes.* Manuscript submitted for publication.

Ray, W. J. (2003). *Methods toward a science of behavior and experience* (7th ed.). Belmont, CA: Thomson Wadsworth.

Refsnes. (2007, August). *Refsnes data.* Retrieved August 9 2007, from www.w3schools.com/browsers/browsers_display.asp.

Riva, G. (2001). The mind over the Web: The quest for the definition of a method for Internet research. *Cyber Psychology and Behavior, 4*(1), 7–16.

Riva, G., Teruzzi, T., & Anolli, L. (2003). The use of Internet in psychological research: Comparison of online and offline questionnaires. *CyberPsychology and Behavior, 1,* 73–80.

Robinson, L. M., Sclar, D. A., Skaer, T. L., & Galin, R. S. (1999). National trends in prevalence of attention deficit/hyperactivity disorder and the prescribing of methylphenidate among school aged children: 1990–1995. *Clinical Pediatrics, 38*(4), 209–217.

Roethlisberger, F. J. (1977). *The elusive phenomena: An autobiographical account of my work in the field of organized behavior at the Harvard Business School.* Cambridge, MA: Division of Research, Graduate School of Business Administration (distributed by Harvard University Press).

Rosnow, R. L., & Rosenthal, R. (2008). *Beginning behavioral research: A conceptual primer.* Upper Saddle River, NJ: Pearson Prentice Hall.

Russell, B., Perkins, J., & Grinnell, H. (2008). Interviewees' overuse of the word "Like" and hesitations: Effects in simulated hiring decisions. Psychological Reports, *102,* 111–118.

Salkind, N. J. (1990). *Child development.* Fort Worth, TX: Holt, Rinehart & Winston.

Salkind, N. J. (2000). *Statistics for people who (think they) hate statistics.* Thousand Oaks, CA: Sage.

Sandler, J. (2007). Computer equivalency of the psychopathic personality inventory-revised: In a non-incarcerated population. *Criminal Justice and Behavior, 34*(3), 399–410.

Scheck, B., & Neufeld, P. (1992). *The innocence project.* Retrieved February 1, 2007, from World Wide Web: http://innocenceproject.org.

Schonlau, M., Fricker, R. D., Jr., Elliott, M. N. (2002). *Conducting research surveys via e-mail and the Web.* Santa Monica, CA: RAND.

Shaughnessy, J., Zechmeister, E., & Zechmeister, J. (2003). *Research methods in psychology* (6th ed.). New York: McGraw-Hill.

Shaughnessy, J., Zechmeister, E., & Zechmeister, J. (2005). *Research methods in psychology* (7th ed.). New York: McGraw-Hill.

Siang, S. (1999). Researching ethically with human subjects in cyberspace. *Professional Ethics Reports,* Fall 1999. Retrieved March 18, 2007, from www.aaas.org/spp/sfrl/per/per19.htm.

Sidman, M. (1960). *Tactics of scientific research.* New York: Basic Books.

Siegel, S., & Castellan, N., Jr. (1988). *Nonparametric statistics for the behavioral sciences.* New York: McGraw-Hill.

Stern, S. R. (2003). Encountering distressing information in online research: a consideration of legal and ethical responsibilities. *New Media and Society, 5,* 249–266.

Studebaker, C. A., Robbennolt, J. K., Penrod, S. D., Pathak-Sharma, M. K., Groscup, J. L., & Devenport, J. L. (2002). Studying pretrial publicity effects: New methods for improving ecological validity and testing external validity. *Law and Human Behavior, 26*(1), 19–41.

StudyResponse Project (2004). *The StudyResponse project: An online social science research resource.* Retrieved February 1, 2007, from http://istprojects.syr.edu/~studyresponse/studyresponse/index/htm.

Tabachnick, B. G., & Fidell, L. S. (1996). *Using multivariate statistics* (3rd ed.). New York: Harper Collins.

Tamingthebeast.com. (2008, January). Retrieved January 8, 2008, from www.tamingthebeast.net/blog/ecommerce/2007-online-sales-0507.htm.

Thomas, S. J. (2004). *Using Web and paper questionnaires for data-based decision making.* Thousand Oaks, CA: Sage.

Turner, J. R., & Thayer, J. F. (2001). *Introduction to analysis of variance.* Thousand Oaks, CA: Sage.

U.S. Department of Commerce (2005). *Computer and Internet use in the United States: 2003.* U.S. Department of Commerce Publication, P23–208. Washington, D.C.: U.S. Department of Commerce.

Wechsler, D. (1997). *WMS-III manual.* New York: The Psychological Corporation.

Winer, B. J., Brown, D. R., & Michels, K. M. (1991). *Statistical principles in experimental design* (3rd ed.). New York: McGraw-Hill.

INDEX

333